Five-a-Day
Fruit & Vegetable
Cookbook

Five-a-Day Fruit & Vegetable Cookbook

**Over 200 recipes to ensure you achieve the
health experts' recommended five-portion
daily minimum for you and your family**

KATE WHITEMAN • MAGGIE MAYHEW • CHRISTINE INGRAM

LORENZ BOOKS

This edition is published by Lorenz Books

Lorenz Books is an imprint of Anness Publishing Ltd
Hermes House, 88–89 Blackfriars Road, London SE1 8HA
tel. 020 7401 2077; fax 020 7633 9499
www.lorenzbooks.com; info@anness.com

UK agent: The Manning Partnership Ltd, 6 The Old Dairy,
Melcombe Road, Bath BA2 3LR; tel. 01225 478444;
fax 01225 478440; sales@manning-partnership.co.uk

UK distributor: Grantham Book Services Ltd,
Isaac Newton Way, Alma Park Industrial Estate, Grantham,
Lincs NG31 9SD; tel. 01476 541080; fax 01476 541061;
orders@gbs.tbs-ltd.co.uk

North American agent/distributor: National Book Network,
4501 Forbes Boulevard, Suite 200, Lanham, MD 20706;
tel. 301 459 3366; fax 301 429 5746; www.nbnbooks.com

Australian agent/distributor: Pan Macmillan Australia,
Level 18, St Martins Tower, 31 Market St, Sydney,
NSW 2000; tel. 1300 135 113; fax 1300 135 103;
customer.service@macmillan.com.au

New Zealand agent/distributor: David Bateman Ltd,
30 Tarndale Grove, Off Bush Road, Albany, Auckland;
tel. (09) 415 7664; fax (09) 415 8892

Publisher: Joanna Lorenz
Project Editor: Linda Fraser
Designers: Nigel Partridge and Patrick McLeavey
Photography and styling: William Lingwood (fruit recipes),
Don Last (fruit reference) and Patrick McLeavey (vegetable
reference and recipes)
Food for photography: Bridget Sargeson (fruit recipes),
Christine France (fruits) and Jane Stevenson (vegetables)
Indexer: Hiliary Bird
Production Controller: Ben Worley

Previously published in two separate volumes,
The World Encyclopedia of Vegetables and
The World Encyclopedia of Fruit

10 9 8 7 6 5 4 3 2 1

NOTES

For all recipes, quantities are given in both metric and
imperial measures and, where appropriate, measures are also
given in standard cups and spoons. Follow one set, but not a
mixture, because they are not interchangeable.

Standard spoon and cup measures are level.
1 tsp = 5ml, 1 tbsp = 15ml, 1 cup = 250ml/8fl oz

Australian standard tablespoons are 20ml. Australian readers
should use 3 tsp in place of 1 tbsp for measuring small
quantities of gelatine, flour, salt, etc.

Medium (US large) eggs are used unless otherwise stated.

The diets and information in this book are not intended to
replace advice from a qualified medical practitioner, doctor
or dietician. Always consult your health practitioner before
adopting any of the suggestions in this book. Neither the
author nor the publishers can accept any liability for failure
to follow this advice.

CONTENTS

MAKE IT FIVE   6

FRUIT

DISCOVERING FRUIT   10
EQUIPMENT   12
PURCHASING, PREPARING AND COOKING   14
APPLES, PEARS, QUINCES AND MEDLARS   18
APPLE, PEAR AND QUINCE RECIPES   38
STONE FRUITS   58
STONE FRUIT RECIPES   72
BERRIES AND CURRANTS   92
BERRY AND CURRANT RECIPES   112
CITRUS FRUITS   134
CITRUS FRUIT RECIPES   148
EXOTIC FRUITS   170
EXOTIC FRUIT RECIPES   198
MELONS, GRAPES, FIGS AND RHUBARB   226
MELON, GRAPE, FIG AND RHUBARB RECIPES   240

VEGETABLES

DISCOVERING VEGETABLES   254
EQUIPMENT   256
PURCHASING, PREPARING AND COOKING   258
ONIONS AND LEEKS   262
ONION AND LEEK RECIPES   274
SHOOTS AND STEMS   286
SHOOT AND STEM RECIPES   298
ROOTS   312
ROOTS RECIPES   332
GREENS   348
GREENS RECIPES   366
BEANS, PEAS AND SEEDS   382
BEAN, PEA AND SEED RECIPES   394
SQUASHES   406
SQUASH RECIPES   418
VEGETABLE FRUITS   430
VEGETABLE FRUIT RECIPES   446
SALAD VEGETABLES   460
SALAD VEGETABLE RECIPES   472
MUSHROOMS   484
MUSHROOM RECIPES   492
INDEX   504

MAKE IT FIVE

Research has shown that eating a balanced diet with at least five portions of fruit and vegetables a day can significantly reduce the risk of many chronic diseases such as heart disease, cancer and stroke as well as offering many other health benefits. Eating more of them can also help you to increase fibre intake, reduce fat intake and maintain a healthy weight.

Frozen fruit and vegetables are just as good as fresh, and are sometimes even better because they are frozen so soon after picking. Canned fruit and vegetables make a good substitute, but try to buy ones canned in water or fruit juice rather than brine or sugar syrup.

Balance and Variety

Eating a healthy diet doesn't have to mean giving up all your favourite foods. It's all about balance and making sure you eat the right proportions of the right foods. Balance, moderation and variety are the key words.

There are five main food groups: starchy foods such as potatoes, pasta and bread; fruit and vegetables; dairy foods such as milk, yogurt and cheese; protein foods such as meat, chicken, fish and tofu; and foods high in fat and sugar such as cakes and cookies.

Starchy foods and fruit and vegetables should make up the largest part of each meal. Protein foods and dairy products are important, but should be eaten in moderation. Fatty and sugary foods should be enjoyed only as an occasional treat.

As with all foods, different types of fruit and vegetables contain different combinations of fibre and nutrients. To ensure you obtain the maximum benefit, make sure you eat a variety.

How Big is a Portion?

The size of a portion, and how many times you can count it in a single day, varies depending on the type of fruit or vegetable. Use the table below to check whether you're eating enough.

ONE PORTION	HOW MUCH IS THAT?	HOW DOES IT COUNT?
Fruit (fresh, frozen or canned)	• 1 medium-size piece of fruit such as an apple or banana • 2 smaller pieces of fruit such as satsumas or figs • a handful of small fruits such as grapes or strawberries • 3 heaped tablespoons of fruit salad • half a larger piece of fruit such as a grapefruit • 5cm/2in slice of very large fruit such as melon	Every portion of fruit you eat counts towards your daily five.
Dried fruit	• 3 small fruits such as apricots • 15ml/1 tbsp very small dried fruits such as raisins	Dried fruit counts as only one portion a day, no matter how much of it you eat.
100% pure fruit or vegetable juice	• one glass	Juices count as only one portion a day, no matter how many glasses of juice you drink.
Vegetables	• 3 heaped tablespoons cooked vegetables such as carrots or peas	Every portion of vegetables you eat counts towards your daily five. **But remember** – potatoes are counted as a starchy food, not a vegetable, so they can't be included in your daily five portions.
Salad	• 1 cereal bowl	Every portion of salad you eat counts towards your daily five.
Beans and lentils	• 45ml/3 tbsp cooked beans or lentils such as kidney beans or chickpeas	Beans and lentils count as only one portion a day, no matter how many portions you eat.

Easy Ways to Five

If you don't usually eat five portions of fruit and vegetables a day, achieving this target can sometimes seem like an unmanageable task. The good news is that it doesn't need to be a struggle. There are so many delicious ways to prepare fruit and vegetables, and clever ways to "sneak" them into your diet that you'll find it a pure pleasure achieving your daily target. Listed below are some simple ways to work more fruits and vegetables into your diet.

• Enjoy a fresh fruit smoothie at any time of day. Simply blend soft fruits such as raspberries or mangoes with milk to make a rich, creamy drink that is packed with nutrients. Unlike fruit juices, smoothies still contain all the fibre of the original fruit.
• Add a chopped banana, or a handful of strawberries or raisins to a bowl of cereal in the morning. It will taste like a special breakfast but it's actually helping you on your way to five-a-day.
• When you feel like a sweet treat, eat a few dried apricots or figs instead of reaching for the cookie tin. They taste just as sweet, but they're healthier and can count as one of your portions.

Above: Snacking on raw vegetables is an easy way to eat more fruit and veg. They taste great and are low in fat too.

Above: Drink your way to five portions a day with a delicious, healthy blend of ripe strawberries, yogurt and milk.

• Instead of spreading jam on toast, use a mashed banana instead. It tastes great and is so much healthier than a sugar-packed spread.
• Desserts and cakes don't need to be all bad. Although they are high in fat and sugar so should be eaten in moderation, choosing a slice of cake packed with dried fruit, or a dessert containing lots of fruit will contribute to your five daily portions – rather than just offering empty calories.
• When making sandwiches, add plenty of extra salad. They will look more appealing and taste much nicer.
• Chopped raw vegetables such as carrots, cucumber and peppers make a great snack at any time of day and are so much healthier than a packet of potato chips or a cookie.
• Add a few extra chopped vegetables to non-vegetable dishes such as meat stews, or stir baby spinach into mashed potatoes just before serving.

About this Book

The recipes in this book have been specially designed to make the most of the delicious fruits and vegetables that are available in the supermarket, helping you to enjoy a tastier, healthier diet. There is a huge choice of recipes for every occasion – from healthy salads and low-fat desserts, to rich and creamy risottos, spicy curries, golden pies and pizzas and indulgent cakes. No matter what your mood, you are sure to find the perfect recipe to help you on your way to five-a-day.

Left: Eating a variety of different fruits and vegetables every day is essential to good health.

FRUIT

DISCOVERING FRUIT

FRUITS ARE NATURE'S most bountiful and versatile creation. No other foods offer such a variety of colours, textures, scents and flavours. Almost all fruits are pleasing to the senses of sight, smell and taste. Just think of the crispness of an apple, the velvety skin of a peach, the jewel-like colours of redcurrants, the juicy tartness of citrus fruits. There is nothing like the sight of a glorious display of fruit in a market to lift the spirits and whet the appetite. Without colourful, health-giving fruits, our diet would be infinitely more dull.

Fruit is not only good for the soul; it is a supremely healthy food, bursting with natural energy-giving sugars, minerals and vitamins. When energy levels are low, a few grapes, a banana or an apple will revitalize us in moments. Fruit provides the perfect guilt-free snack, since most varieties are completely fat free and contain very few calories. Nearly all fruits have a high proportion of water – between 75 and 90 per cent – which makes them wonderfully thirst quenching in hot weather. Picture the pleasure of eating a large wedge of chilled watermelon or a

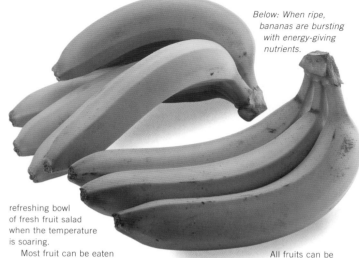

Below: When ripe, bananas are bursting with energy-giving nutrients.

refreshing bowl of fresh fruit salad when the temperature is soaring.

Most fruit can be eaten raw, just as it is (be sure to wash it first), although some varieties may need peeling. Nothing beats a simple dessert of perfectly ripe juicy fruit, perhaps served with a scoop or two of vanilla ice cream or a dollop of cream, or with some good cheese – try crisp apples with a wedge of farmhouse Cheddar or Lancashire cheese, juicy, ripe pears with either blue Stilton or Gorgonzola, or raspberries and sliced peaches with mascarpone cheese.

All fruits can be served on their own, or used to create sweet and savoury dishes of infinite variety, from pies to puddings, cakes, muffins, ice creams, mousses, soufflés and featherlight fruit-topped pavlovas.

You could easily base an entire meal on fresh fruit without repeating any colours, textures or flavours. The meal might begin with the classic combination of melon with Parma ham, or a refreshing fruit soup, followed by Normandy pheasant with apples and cider, then a platter of cheese, fresh and dried fruit and nuts and finally a tropical fruit salad, a bowl of bright red berries or a lemon tart.

Fruit is enormously rewarding to cook with and is very versatile. Almost all fruits complement each other, so you can create all manner of interesting combinations. Although the recipes in this book concentrate on the use of fruits in sweet dishes, they have an important role to play in savouries too. Tart fruits like gooseberries, rhubarb and cranberries cut the richness of fatty fish like mackerel, and can also enhance the sometimes insipid flavour of poultry. Dried fruits are used extensively in North African and Middle Eastern cooking – the combination of meat and sweet, sticky dates, prunes or

Below: The vibrant seeds from ripe pomegranates can be eaten raw as they are or added to both sweet and savoury dishes.

dried apricots is superb. Most fruits also marry well with exotic spices, such as cinnamon, ginger and vanilla, and even those fruits that are relatively bland can be lifted by the addition of a squeeze of lemon or lime juice.

The hundreds of different kinds of fruit can be divided into four main categories: soft fruits, such as raspberries, strawberries, blueberries and red-, black- and whitecurrants; stone fruits, including peaches, apricots, cherries and plums; "pome" fruits of the apple and pear families; and citrus fruits. In addition there are the "one-offs" that do not fit into any other category. These include figs, grapes, melons and rhubarb (which is actually a vegetable, but is always treated as an honorary fruit).

Fruits are no longer the seasonal produce they once were. Nowadays, thanks to sophisticated transportation methods, all types of fruit from every country are available almost all year round. Travellers who have enjoyed exotic produce abroad now find it

Above: Orleans Reinette apples – one of the "pome" fruits.

Left: Watermelons, like other melon varieties, are in a category of their own.

gracing the shelves of their local greengrocer or supermarket, giving less fortunate stay-at-homes a taste of the Tropics. The disadvantage of this is that we no longer wait with eager anticipation for a particular fruit to come into season; somewhere in the world it will be grown year-round. So strawberries, raspberries and peaches have ceased to be exclusively summer treats, but can be bought in almost any season, although they will never taste as good as when freshly picked, and are still always at their best and cheapest in the summer.

There are many other ways of savouring fruits throughout the year. They can be frozen, bottled or preserved in other ways – as juices or liqueurs or macerated in alcohol; canned, dried or candied; or made into jams, jellies, curds, chutneys and relishes. There is no time of year when fruit is not readily available in one form or another, so you need never go without nature's most precious bounty.

EQUIPMENT

Although most fruits can be prepared with the aid of a good sharp knife, a wide variety of special implements is available to make the task easier, safer and more efficient. The following items are very useful – provided you have space for them in your kitchen.

Peeling and Coring

Paring knife The most useful item in any kitchen. Choose a really sharp knife with a short blade and a handle that is comfortable to hold. Always use a stainless steel knife for preparing fruit, as the acids may damage other metals.

Apple corer This utensil removes apple and pear cores in one easy movement. Place over the core at the stem end and push down firmly right through the fruit, then twist slightly and pull out the core and pips.

Apple segmenter Use this handy device to core and slice an apple into twelve even-size segments in one simple operation.

Apple processor Perfect for people with a huge glut of home-grown apples, this hand-cranked implement peels, cores and neatly slices the fruit into rings in seconds. The processor is expensive to buy, but worth it if you have apple trees that bear fruit in abundance.

Above right: Apple corer
Below left: Paring knife
Below right: Apple segmenter

Above: Fixed- and swivel-blade vegetable peelers

Pineapple easy slicer Cores and slices a pineapple in one easy corkscrew-like action. This simple-to-operate utensil is useful for keeping the pineapple shell intact for use as a serving container, but only works with smaller pineapples.

Swivel-blade vegetable peeler Use this tool to pare off the thinnest possible layer of peel or skin so that no nutrients are lost.

Fixed-blade vegetable peeler This type of peeler takes a thicker strip of peel or skin than the swivel-blade version.

Grating and Zesting

Box grater Choose a stainless steel grater with four different grating

Right: Box grater
Below: Canelle knife and citrus zester

Left: Pineapple easy slicer

surfaces and make sure it will stand firmly on a chopping board or in a bowl. Most include a flat blade suitable for slicing lemons or limes.

Citrus zester The row of holes at the top of the zester shaves off thin shreds of zest, leaving behind the bitter pith.

Canelle knife This tool has a tooth-like blade that pares off the zest in ribbons or julienne strips. Combined zesters/canelle knives are available.

Juicing

Lemon squeezer Hand-operated squeezers catch the juice in the base. Basic models can also be used for limes and small oranges. Some have interchangeable heads to accommodate citrus fruits of various sizes.

Left: Citrus press
Below: Reamer

Citrus press

These hand-operated chrome juicers have a geared mechanism to enable as much juice as possible to be extracted. When the handle is pulled forward, the juice is squeezed into a container.

Electric juice extractor These machines will extract juice from other fruits besides citrus. They take up a lot of space, but are invaluable for lovers of fresh fruit juice.

Stoning and Preparing

Cherry stoner The bowl of this implement has a hole through which the cherry stone is ejected when the fruit is pressed. Useful for large quantities.

Grapefruit knife A curved knife serrated on both sides. Run it between the membranes and flesh to release the segments.

Grapefruit segmenter This curved implement has a V-shaped blade. Position with the point against the inside of the rind and push down, round and inwards to cut out the segments.

Melon baller Insert this small round scoop into the melon flesh and twist to remove neat balls of fruit. It comes in various sizes and can also be used for other fruits. Tiny ones sometimes double as a cherry stoner.

Preserving

Funnel Essential for pouring hot jams and jellies into jars. Stainless steel funnels will withstand heat better than plastic ones.

Jelly bag A heavy muslin filter bag for straining jellies and juices. Suspend it from the legs of a chair placed upside down or, far better, buy one on a stand.

Preserving pan Especially designed for preserving, this is a thick-bottomed double-handled pan. The heavy base prevents the fruit preserve from burning and sticking.

Sugar thermometer Use this for checking the temperature of a syrup or to determine whether the setting point of a jam and jelly has been reached.

Reamer This wooden device enables you to squeeze the fruit directly into a bowl or pan. Insert into the cut fruit and twist.

Lemon tap A simple gadget that turns citrus fruit into a "juice jug". If only a small amount of juice is required, leave the tap inserted in the fruit to keep the juice fresh between squeezings.

Below: Lemon squeezer

Left: Cherry stoner

Below: Grapefruit knife

Above: Sugar thermometer
Below: Funnel with strainer

Above: Melon baller

PURCHASING, PREPARING AND COOKING

BUYING FRUIT

Obviously, the best time to buy fruit is when it is fully ripe and at its peak. The exceptions are fruits, such as bananas and pears, that ripen quickly and should therefore be bought at different stages of maturity so that they are not all ready at the same time. You are most likely to find top quality fruits in markets and shops that have a quick turnover of fresh produce, preferably with a daily delivery. Although most fruits are now available almost year round, they are best and cheapest when in season in the country of origin. Only buy as much fruit as you need at one time so that it remains fresh and appetizing.

PREPARING FRUIT

For some fruits, the only preparation needed is washing or wiping with a damp cloth; others must be peeled or skinned, cored, stoned or seeded. Wash fruit only just before using. If necessary, cut away any bruised or damaged parts.

Firm Fruit

Peeling

Some firm fruits, such as eating apples and pears, can be eaten raw without peeling. For cooking, peeling is often necessary. Pare off the skin as thinly as possible to avoid losing the valuable nutrients under the skin.

1 Wash the fruit and pat dry using kitchen paper. Use a small, sharp paring knife or a vegetable peeler to pare off the skin in long, thin vertical strips. Pears are best peeled by this method.

2 Alternatively, for apples, thinly peel all round the fruit in a spiral.

Coring

1 To core whole apples and pears, place the sharp edge of a corer over the stem end of the fruit.

2 Press down firmly, then twist slightly; the core, complete with pips, will come away in the centre of the corer. Pull out the core from the handle end.

Storing
Storage methods depend on the type of fruit, but there are some basic guidelines:
• Do not wash fruit before storing, but only when ready to use.
• Store fruit at the bottom of the fridge or in the salad crisper.
• Do not refrigerate unripe fruit; keep it at room temperature or in a cool, dark place, depending on the variety (see individual fruits).
• Fragile fruits, such as berries, are easily squashed, so spread them out in a single layer on a tray lined with kitchen paper.

Segmenting

1 Halve the fruit lengthways, then cut into quarters or segments.

2 Cut out the central core and pips with a small sharp knife.

Preventing discoloration
Some fruits, such as apples, pears and bananas, quickly oxidize and turn brown when exposed to the air. To prevent discoloration, brush cut fruits with lemon juice. Alternatively, acidulate a bowl of cold water by stirring in the juice of half a lemon. Drop the cut fruits into the bowl immediately after preparing.

Citrus Fruit

Peeling

It is very important to remove all of the bitter white pith that lies just beneath the rind of citrus fruits.

1 To peel firm-skinned fruits, hold the fruit over a bowl to catch the juice and use a sharp knife to cut off the rind.

2 For loose-skinned fruit, such as tangerines, pierce the skin with your thumb at the stalk end and peel off the rind. Finally, pull off all the white shreds adhering to the fruit.

Segmenting

Use a small serrated knife to cut down between the membranes enclosing the segments; carefully ease out the flesh.

Grating

Citrus zest adds a wonderful flavour to many dishes. If it is to be eaten raw, grate it finely, using the fine face of a grater. Remove only the coloured zest, if you grate too deeply into the peel, you will be in danger of including the bitter white pith. For cooking, pare off long, thin strips of zest using a zester.

Garnishing and decorating

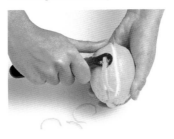

To make thick julienne strips of zest, cut lengthways, using a canelle knife.

To make twists, slice the fruits thinly, cut to the centre, then twist the ends in opposite directions to make an S-shape.

Soft Fruit

Peeling

Fruits such as peaches, nectarines and apricots can be peeled with a sharp paring knife, but this may waste some of the delicious flesh. It is better to loosen the skins by dipping them *briefly* in boiling water.

1 Make a tiny nick in the skin.

2 Cover with boiling water and leave for 15–30 seconds, depending on the ripeness of the fruit. Remove the fruit with a slotted spoon and peel off the skin, which should come away easily.

Removing stones and pips

To stone peaches, apricots etc, cut all around the fruit through the seam. Twist the halves in opposite directions, then lever out the stone with a knife.

To stone cherries, put the fruit in a cherry stoner and push the bar into the fruit. The stone will be ejected.

To remove grape pips, cut the grapes in half, then pick out the pips with the tip of a small sharp knife.

COOKING FRUIT

Most fruits can be cooked and in a great variety of ways.

Poaching

Apples and pears, stone fruits, figs, rhubarb and even grapes can be poached, either whole, halved or in segments. The classic poaching liquid is syrup and usually consists of 1 part sugar boiled with 2 parts water for about 2 minutes or until clear. The syrup can be flavoured with lemon, orange or spices, such as cinnamon or vanilla. Red or white wine can also be used for poaching, usually with added sugar. Alternatively, use fruit juice.

Bring the poaching liquid to the boil. Lower the heat and add the fruit. Simmer gently until the fruit is just tender.

Stewing

This method is suitable for all fruits that can be poached.

Cut up the fruit. Put in a saucepan with just enough water, wine or fruit juice to cover. Add sugar to taste. Simmer gently until tender. Only stir if you want the fruit to become a pulp.

Grilling

Any firm fruits can be grilled, with or without sugar. Tropical fruits, such as pineapple and bananas, are particularly good for grilling. For desserts, they can be cut into 2.5cm/1in wedges or chunks and threaded on to skewers to make kebabs. Brush the fruit with clear honey before grilling.

For savoury dishes, halve the fruit or cut into pieces, removing the core if necessary. Brush with melted butter and grill under a medium heat, turning occasionally until tender and browned on all sides.

Baking

Apples and pears; stone fruits, such as peaches, nectarines, apricots and plums; figs and rhubarb can be baked whole or in halves, wedges or slices according to type.

1 Put the fruit in a shallow ovenproof dish, add a little water, and sprinkle with sugar to taste.

2 Top the fruit with small pieces of butter. Bake in a preheated oven at 180°C/350°F/Gas 4 until tender.

Microwave Cooking

All fruits which can be conventionally cooked can be microwaved, with excellent results, although the skins on some fruits, such as plums, may not soften sufficiently in the short cooking time. Whole fruits, such as apples, should be scored, or they may burst. Place the fruit in a suitable dish, cover and cook on High for the time recommended, or until tender.

Sautéeing

Slice or dice the fruit (peel it or not, as you wish) and toss quickly in hot butter until lightly browned all over. Add sugar and flavourings to taste.

Deep Frying

For fruit fritters, such as pineapple, apple or banana, peel the fruit and cut into chunks.

Heat oil for deep frying to 185°C/360°F or until a cube of dried bread sizzles when it is added to the pan. Coat the pieces of fruit in batter and deep fry until the fritters rise to the surface of the hot oil and are golden brown. Drain the fritters on kitchen paper and sprinkle with sugar.

Puréeing

Fruit can be puréed for sauces, fools, ice creams and sorbets. Some types must be cooked first; others, like berries, can be puréed raw.

For berries, wash briefly and push through a fine nylon sieve, using the back of a large spoon or ladle. If you prefer, purée the berries in a food processor, then sieve the purée to remove any pips.

For cooked, peeled fruit, mash with a potato masher for a coarse purée. For a finer purée, whizz cooked, peeled fruit in a food processor or push through a food mill.

Caramelizing

Fruits look pretty when caramelized. Small fruits like cherries can be used whole; larger fruits should be cubed.

1 Combine 200g/7oz/scant 1 cup granulated sugar and 60ml/4 tbsp water in a small heavy-based saucepan. Stir over a low heat until the sugar has dissolved. When the mixture boils, add 5ml/1 tsp lemon juice and boil until the syrup turns a deep golden brown.

2 Carefully add 15ml/1 tbsp hot water (protecting your hand with an oven glove as the mixture will "spit") and shake the pan to mix.
3 Spear a piece of fruit on a fork and dip it into the caramel to coat. Leave on an oiled baking sheet until the caramel cools and hardens.

Candying

Also known as crystallized or glacé fruits, candied fruits make a delicious end to a meal. Suitable fruits include citrus (slices and peel), cherries and other stone fruits, physalis and pineapple. For professional results, the candying process is a lengthy one, but this simplified method works well for candied citrus zest or for fruit that is to be eaten within a few days.

1 Cut the fruit into slices or chunks. Make a syrup, using 225g/8oz/1 cup granulated sugar and 150ml/¼ pint/²/₃ cup water; follow the instructions under Caramelizing. Immerse the pieces of fruit in the syrup. Leave in a cool, dry place to soak for 2 weeks. Drain.

2 Place the fruit on a rack over a baking sheet. Dry for 3–6 hours in a very low oven (maximum of 50°C/122°F/Gas low). Cool, then store in an airtight container.

Frosting

Try this technique with grapes, red– and blackcurrants and cranberries. Eat on the day they are prepared.

Leave the fruit on the stalk. Dip in lightly beaten egg white, then roll in caster sugar until frosted all over. Leave to dry before serving.

Drying

Suitable fruits include apples, pears, stone fruits, figs, grapes and bananas. Commercial dehydrators are available, but you can dry the fruit in a low oven.

Prepare the fruit: peel, core and slice apples; peel, core and halve pears; halve and stone peaches or similar fruits. Leave smaller fruits whole. Lay the fruit on clean wooden slatted trays, cut-side up. Dry in an oven preheated to the lowest possible temperature. Cool completely before storing.

Preserving in Alcohol

All fruits can be preserved in alcohol. In the eighteenth century, seafarers discovered that their cargoes of exotic fruits could be preserved in barrels of rum. Dark rum is still the classic preserving spirit, but brandy and other spirits can also be used.

The ideal container is a purpose-made *rumtopf*, but a wide-mouthed preserving jar will do. Start with summer fruits, then add other fruits as they come into season.

1 Wash and dry the fruit. Place in a bowl and cover with an equal weight of sugar. Leave for 1 hour.

2 Tip the fruit mixture into a *rumtopf* or preserving jar. Pour in just enough rum to cover the fruit completely. Cover the jar with clear film and store in a cool, dark place.
3 Continue to fill the jar with fruits as they come into season, using only half as much sugar by weight as fruit; cover the fruit with rum each time. When the jar is full, leave for at least two months before using the fruit.

APPLES, PEARS, QUINCES AND MEDLARS

A bowlful of apples, polished to shiny perfection, is one of life's pleasures — beautiful to behold, delicious and healthy to eat. Pears are almost as popular, with juicy flesh whose scent is almost as tempting as their taste. Quinces are even more aromatic, while medlars are intriguing — not least because they can only be eaten when they are on the verge of rotting. They are all "pome" fruits, with an indentation in the stalk end, the coarse brown remains of a flower at the other and a tough central core containing a number of brown pips.

APPLES

Ever since Adam bit into the fruit of the Tree of Knowledge, apples have been the stuff of myth and legend. The Ancient Greeks and Romans believed them to be aphrodisiacs, and for the Celts crab apples were a symbol of fertility. In the Middle Ages, the cult of the apple continued in such customs as apple-bobbing at Hallowe'en and wassailing at Christmas.

The most popular of all fruits, apples are also convenient, perfect for eating raw as a nutritious snack and ideal for making into a multitude of hot and cold puddings and desserts. There are thousands of named varieties worldwide, but the choice of those available to buy is, sadly, decreasing year by year. However, because apples are now grown in every temperate country in the world, some varieties can be found in the shops all year round. Delicious as they may be, no shop-bought apples can ever beat the flavour and crisp texture of home-grown apples that have been freshly picked.

Apples come in many shapes and sizes, from tiny cherry-size crab apples to huge cooking varieties like Howgate Wonder, Reverend W. Wilkes and the unbelievably warty Knobby Russet, which looks remarkably like a huge toad. They can be round, oval, or "cornered", with four distinct corners around the calyx, like the Catshead, which is shaped like the face of a Siamese cat.

Left: Granny Smith apples – first cultivated in Australia in the nineteenth century.

Colours range from bright, shiny red through vivid greens, yellows and pale creamy-white to golden russet, while the skins may be ultra-thin or unpalatably thick. As for taste and texture, there is an almost infinite variety – something to suit every palate, from crisp and sour to soft and sweet.

History

Apples have been eaten since prehistoric times, when only wild crab apples existed. The Romans adored apples and were the first people to cultivate the fruit; by the first century AD they were growing at least a dozen varieties throughout the Roman Empire.

The most famous of all apple-growers was the nineteenth-century English nurseryman, Thomas Laxton. With his sons, he hybridized hundreds of varieties of apples, many of which still exist today and bear his name.

The Pilgrim Fathers introduced apples to the New World, planting pips that they had taken with them from England. They proved so popular that in the eighteenth century John Chapman (popularly known as "Johnny Appleseed") planted apple orchards across about 10,000 square miles of North America, using discarded apple pips from cider-making plants. A century later, apple-growing in Australia took off when Mrs Maria Smith cultivated the first Granny Smith apple in her garden in Sydney.

Above: Laxton's Fortune

Below: Braeburn – crisp, juicy apples, which make excellent eating.

Varieties

With over 7,000 named varieties of apples it would be impossible to list more than a tiny fraction. In any case, only about a dozen varieties are readily available in the shops, although nurseries can supply many more to people who wish to grow apples in their gardens.

Growing your own apples will allow you to enjoy exotically flavoured fruit, like the pineapple-flavoured Pine Golden Pippin or Ananas Reinette, or the Winter Banana, which develops a creamy texture and a banana flavour when laid down. D'Arcy Spice is a small golden apple with the flavours of cinnamon and allspice, while Anisa is one of several aniseed-flavoured apples. Other apples are redolent of melon,

Below: Beauty of Bath

strawberries, raspberries, peaches, lemons and even fennel.

Uniquely in Britain, apples are categorized as eating (or dessert) fruit or cooking apples. Other countries regard all apples as suitable for both eating and cooking. Of course, there are cider apples as well; many are disagreeably sour, but some are very pleasant to eat.

EATING APPLES

Ashmead's Kernel These late variety apples were first cultivated in Gloucestershire in the seventeenth century. Their flesh has a good acid/sugar balance and develops a strong, spicy, aniseed flavour in some seasons.

Beauty of Bath A beautiful small flattish green apple extensively flushed with red, with sharp, sweet, juicy flesh. Beauty of Bath apples should be eaten straight from the tree, as they rot almost as soon as they are picked. Consequently, you are unlikely to find this apple in the shops.

Blenheim Orange This apple was discovered growing out of a wall in Blenheim Palace in England in the nineteenth century and was named by permission of the Duke of Marlborough, but it also has 67 synonyms!
It is a dual-purpose apple, good for both cooking and eating, with a pleasantly nutty flavour. It is suitable for cooking in dishes, such as apple charlotte and apple crumble, and for serving as a dessert fruit.

Braeburn This crisp, juicy apple with a smooth pale green skin, heavily flushed with red, makes excellent eating. Braeburn apples are grown only in the southern hemisphere, as they need plenty of daylight.

Above: Empire

Above left: Egremont Russet – this sweet crisp apple is delicious served at the end of a meal with a wedge of strong-tasting cheese, such as farmhouse Cheddar or Lancashire.

Cox's Orange Pippin A greenish-yellow apple of medium size, with some orange-red russetting. The firm, crisp, juicy flesh of this sweet fruit, with its overtones of acidity, make it one of the world's best and most popular apples. Cox's Orange Pippins are excellent for cooking as well as eating raw.

Crispin Large, pale yellowish-green apples with firm and juicy creamy-white flesh and a pleasant mild flavour.

Discovery Bred from the Worcester Pearmain, Discovery was the first apple to be commercially grown in Britain. It is particularly attractive for its highly coloured bright red skin and contrasting hard, crisp white flesh. It is best eaten straight from the tree.

Egremont Russet Russet apples have rough, porous skins which allow the water to evaporate out, giving a denser flesh and intensifying the nutty flavour. Egremont Russet is the most readily available. It is golden russet in colour, sometimes with a bright orange flush, and has a crisp texture and very sweet taste. It can be used for eating or cooking and goes superbly with cheese.

Elstar This sweet, crisp and juicy apple is a cross between Ingrid Marie and Golden Delicious. Originally bred in Holland, it is now grown extensively throughout Europe. Picked in mid-autumn, Elstar apples will keep for 3–4 months.

Empire A dark red American apple with a shiny skin, best for eating raw, but suitable for cooking. It has crisp green, juicy flesh and a slightly tart flavour.

Above: Cox's Orange Pippin

Left: Jonagold – these dual-purpose apples have a superb flavour.

Fuji This sweet apple has greenish-yellow skin with a rosy blush and crisp, juicy white flesh. It is also suitable for cooking.

Gala This colourful eating apple from New Zealand has a yellow ground colour flushed with bright orange and red. The yellow flesh is very sweet, juicy and crisp. It is at its best when absolutely fresh. Good for either cooking or eating. **Royal Gala** is similar, but red all over.

Golden Delicious Originally grown from a chance seedling in the USA, this conical, freckled, golden apple has become ubiquitous. At its peak, the cream flesh is juicy and crisp with a mild flavour; unfortunately most commercially grown Golden Delicious are sold when they are under- or over-ripe and are consequently tasteless and mealy in texture. Golden Delicious are suitable for cooking or eating.

Granny Smith First grown in Australia by the eponymous "Granny" Smith, this largish

Right: Golden Delicious

all-purpose apple is bright green, becoming yellow as it ripens. Usually sold under-ripe, it has firm, crunchy flesh and a tart flavour.

Greensleeves This James Grieve/Golden Delicious cross has more flavour than a James Grieve and better acidity. It is an early fruiting variety, which should be eaten immediately after picking.

Ida Red By far the favourite North American apple for making apple sauce. American-grown fruits have a good acid flavour, which is often lacking in the European-grown apples.

James Grieve A Scottish apple raised in Edinburgh in the late nineteenth century, with tart, juicy flesh that bruises easily when handled. James Grieve is good for cooking and eating, but, like most early varieties, it does not store well and should be kept for no more than 2–3 weeks after picking.

Jonagold A hybrid of Jonathan and Golden Delicious, this large round green-tinged yellow apple has creamy

Above: Gala are best eaten very fresh, when the flesh is crisp and juicy.

Left: Katy

Right: Orleans Reinette

white flesh and a superb flavour. It can be used for cooking or eating.

Jonathan This smallish, round, orange-red North American apple has white, juicy flesh and a fragrant, slightly acidic flavour. It can be used for cooking.

Katy A highly coloured early apple bred in Sweden from the Worcester Pearmain. Their flesh is crisp, sweet and juicy and they are best eaten immediately after picking.

Kidd's Orange Red A New Zealand apple bred from Cox's Orange Pippin. This deliciously crisp apple is highly aromatic, but needs many hours of sunshine to develop its full flavour and colour, so it cannot be successfully grown in Northern Europe.

Laxton's Fortune A cross between Cox's Orange Pippin and Wealthy, these apples have yellowish skin heavily tinged with red, and sweet, juicy, lightly aromatic flesh. You are most likely to find them in farm shops.

Laxton's Superb Greenish-yellow and partially covered with red, this all-purpose apple has crisp, very juicy flesh. It is sweet with some acidity.

McIntosh A Canadian apple that is popular throughout North America. It is wonderfully decorative, with deep red waxy skin, which can be polished to a superb sheen, but the skin is quite tough. The pale flesh is melting (and sometimes mushy) with a hint of fresh strawberry flavour.

Orleans Reinette One of the best apples of all, this large orange-flecked russet has a rough skin, but juicy, sweet, aromatic flesh. Orleans Reinette is ideal for cooking and eating.

Pink Lady A pretty Australian cross between Golden Delicious and Lady Williams, this large all-purpose apple has a mild flavour, and is becoming increasing available in supermarkets and greengrocers.

Pomme d'Api Also known as Lady apple, this very attractive fruit has a yellow skin suffused with a bright red blush. Pomme d'Api is a late apple with good keeping qualities.

Red Delicious This North American apple was first grown in the nineteenth century. It has an exceptionally sweet flavour,

Above:
Pink Lady

Above: Spartan – a Canadian apple with a tough skin, but delicious, floral-scented flesh.

Left: Grown mostly in the United States, colourful Red Delicious is another apple with a tough skin that hides juicy, sweet flesh.

but tough skin. Red Delicious apples can be grown in Europe, but not always successfully.

Spartan Another Canadian apple raised in 1926 from McIntosh and Newton's Pippin. It inherits a tough skin from McIntosh, but tastes highly aromatic with a floral perfume.

Worcester Pearmain A conical yellow apple flushed with bright red. The juicy white flesh has a hint of strawberry flavour. Worcester Pearmain are best eaten straight from the tree, but can also be used for cooking.

Above: Worcester Pearmain

Above: Greensleeves

Below left: With their shiny, bright red skin and crisp cream flesh, Washington Red apples are worth looking out for at farmer's markets.

Above: Lord Lambourne

Above: Originally bred in Holland, Elstar apples are now grown throughout Europe.

Other eating varieties of note
Less well-known apple varieties worth looking out for include Lord Derby, Lord Lambourne, Red Pippin, Rome Beauty, Starking, Sturmer Pippin, Tydeman's Late Orange, Washington Red, Winesap and Winston.

Below left: Royal Gala – sweet, juicy and crisp, this apple is good for either cooking or eating.

Below right: Red Pippin – a tasty Cox's Orange Pippin cross.

Above: Bramley's Seedling

Below: Howgate Wonder

COOKING APPLES

Bramley's Seedling The *nonpareil* of cookers, this large, flattish green apple (sometimes faintly flushed with red) has coarse, white, juicy, acid flesh, which cooks into a frothy purée. Bramleys are perfect for baking or as the basis of apple sauce.

Grenadier An irregularly shaped conical apple with yellow skin. The acid flesh is faintly green, firm and juicy. It breaks down during cooking. Grenadiers do not keep well.

Howgate Wonder This apple can grow to an enormous size – in 1997, the world record was achieved with a specimen weighing 1.6kg/3lb 14oz! The juicy white flesh breaks up during cooking and has an uninspiring flavour, so this variety is grown mainly for exhibition.

Reverend W. Wilkes Very large conical apple with pale greenish-white skin. The fine, very white flesh is crisp, juicy and acidic. The apple can be eaten raw, but it is best as a cooker. It keeps well.

Nutrition

Apples were once believed to be the most nutritious of fruits, giving rise to the saying that "an apple a day keeps the doctor away". In fact, they have fewer vitamins than many other fruits (although they contain some vitamins C and A), but are high in pectin and are a good source of dietary fibre. They provide 52 kilocalories per 100g/3¾oz.

Buying and Storing

Choose apples with undamaged skins and never buy bruised fruits. If possible, smell the fruits to determine their fragrance (not easy when they are pre-bagged) and squeeze gently to ensure they are firm. Do not be too seduced by the skin colour of an apple; those gorgeous-looking specimens with thick, vivid red, waxy skins often have woolly, tasteless flesh.

Apples continue to ripen after they have been picked, so their colour and texture may change during storage. For short-term storage, they can be kept in a ventilated polythene bag in the fridge. To store pick-your-own apples, wrap each one in newspaper and place folded-side down in a single layer in wooden or fibre trays. Keep in a cool, dry, dark place and check occasionally to make sure none has gone rotten. A bad fruit will taint all the others, so remove it immediately.

Dried Apples These have a sweet, concentrated flavour and are an extremely useful storecupboard ingredient. Eat them straight from the

Below: Dried apple rings

Drying apples at home

1 Peel the apples, remove the cores and slice the fruit into rings. Soak in salted water for a few minutes to prevent discoloration.

2 Thread the apple rings on to string. Hang them from the ceiling or suspend across the room until they are completely dry.

3 Alternatively, arrange the rings in a single layer on a wire rack on a baking sheet, making sure that they are not touching. Place in an oven set to 70°C/150°F/Gas Low for several hours until dried.

packet as a nutritious snack, add them to home-made muesli or soak them in water, then cook them in sweet and savoury dishes like fruit compotes, apple sauce or casseroles. Dried apples are available commercially, but it is easy to dry your own when there is a glut, and you can choose your favourite varieties. Russets are particularly delicious when dried.

Preparing

Most apples can be eaten with the skin on. To peel, use a vegetable peeler or small, sharp knife, either in a spiral following the circumference of the apple, or peeling downwards in strips from stem to calyx. Peeled apples go brown very quickly; brush them with lemon juice or drop them into water acidulated with lemon juice or cider vinegar immediately.

Cooking

Some apples are only suitable for eating raw, but most can be cooked in such classic sweet dishes as apple pies, crumbles and tarts, baked apples and strudel. Sweet apples combine well with other fruits, like blackberries, quinces and lemon, and dried fruits like raisins or cranberries. Aromatic spices like cinnamon, nutmeg and cloves highlight their flavour. Their high pectin content will help other fruit jellies and jams to set, or they can be made into crab apple jelly, apple cheese and chutney.

Tart apples make excellent accompaniments for game birds, black pudding and sausages, and rich meats like pork, duck and goose. They go well with red cabbage and are a vital ingredient in Waldorf salad.

To bake apples, core them with an apple corer and score around the circumference to prevent the skin from bursting. Stuff with dried fruit, nuts, butter and sugar and bake in a preheated oven at 180°C/350°F/Gas 4 until soft.

To cook sliced apples and rings, sauté in butter and sugar to help them keep their shape. To stew, cook in the minimum amount of water, or with butter and seasonings.

Making apple purée

1 Peel, core and thickly slice the apples, immediately dropping the pieces into a bowl of cold water acidulated with lemon juice or cider vinegar.

2 Barely cover the base of a saucepan with cold water. Add the apple pieces and cook to a purée, adding sugar to taste towards the end.

3 If you are using firmer eating apples, which will not disintegrate to a purée, cook until very tender, then rub through a coarse sieve.

CRAB APPLES AND CIDER APPLES

Crab apples have grown wild in hedgerows for thousands of years and were eaten in prehistoric times. The fruits are smaller and often more colourful than cultivated varieties. Nowadays crab apples are often grown for their ornamental qualities. The fruits can be vivid yellow, green, orange or bright red.

Crab apples are seldom worth eating raw (and may be completely inedible), although some are perfectly palatable for those without too sweet a tooth. You may find larger self-seeded crab apples, which have grown from the pips of cultivated apples that have become wild; these can be eaten.

Thanks to their high pectin content, all crab apples make wonderful jellies, either on their own or mixed with other wild fruits, such as haw berries.

Cider apples are closer to eating apples than crab apples, but usually have a bitter or sour flavour due to their

Below: Crab apples are almost always too sour to eat raw.

high tannin content. There are hundreds of different varieties with wonderful names like Strawberry Norma and Foxwhelp, and each local grower will insist that his is the best. Some, like Tom Putt, are sweet enough to eat; these are used to make sweet cider.

Apple Drinks

Apple juice, cider and apple brandies, such as Calvados, are the main drinks made from apples. Apple juice is made by crushing eating apples; the best is pressed from a single variety, such as Cox's Orange Pippin or Russet, but most commercial apple juices are made from a mixture of varieties or, worse, from concentrate. Apple juice may be fizzy or still.

Cider may have been brought to Britain by the Phoenicians or the Celts; it has certainly been around for thousands of years. It is a fermented drink made from the juice of cider apples and, depending on the variety of fruit and

Left: Cider – the best is still made by artisan producers.

Right and far right: Calvados and applejack are both types of apple brandy.

pressing technique, can range from sweet and gassy to cloudy and flat. The best ciders are still made by small producers using artisan methods; some of these ciders can be lethally strong. The strongest and crudest cider is scrumpy. It is made from the apples of the poorest quality, but can certainly pack a punch!

Apple brandy is made from fermented and distilled apple juice. The best of all is Calvados, the famous apple brandy from Normandy, which is double distilled and aged in oak. Calvados may only be produced within a defined area; other apple brandies must be labelled *eau-de-vie de cidre* or simply "apple brandy" ("applejack" in North America).

Fermented apple juice can also be made into cider vinegar, which has a strong apple taste and is excellent for making fruit chutneys or adding extra flavour to casseroles containing apples.

PEARS

There are almost as many varieties of pears as there are apples, but only a dozen or so are available in the shops. Pears are related to apples, but are more fragile and are more often eaten raw than cooked. They have fine white granular flesh and a central core containing the pips. Most pears have the familiar shape, wider at the bottom than the top, but some are apple-shaped, while "calabash" pears have an elongated neck, like a gourd. Pears are less vividly coloured than apples, generally varying from bronze to gold, green or yellow, but there are some beautiful red varieties, too.

Right: Anjou pears are sweet, juicy and aromatic.

History

Wild pears are native to Europe and Asia, where they have grown since prehistoric times. They were cultivated by the ancient Phoenicians and the Romans, and they became a royal delicacy for the ancient Persian kings. Their popularity spread so fast that in medieval Italy over 200 varieties of

Below: Beurré Bosc

pear were cultivated. By the seventeenth century, the French were growing 300 different varieties, inspired by Louis XIV's passion for the fruit. There are now said to be more than 5,000 named varieties growing throughout the world.

Varieties

Cooking pears (which cannot be eaten raw) do exist, but almost all the pears available in the shops are eating fruit, which can also be cooked. Pears are seasonal, so only a few varieties are available at any one time.

Anjou These large pears have greenish-yellow skin with brown speckles or russetting. The flesh is juicy and sweet. Suitable for eating and cooking.

Beth This modern pear variety resembles Williams Bon Chrétien in flavour and texture, but has the added advantage of being longer keeping.

Beurré Bosc and **Beurré Hardi** These elongated pears have an uneven green-gold skin, which becomes yellow and completely russetted as the fruit ripens. The creamy white flesh is firm and juicy with a buttery texture (hence the name, which means "buttered"), and the flavour is deliciously sweet and aromatic with some acidity. Both varieties are excellent for eating and cooking.

Beurré Superfin These medium-to-large pears are round and conical in shape. Their uneven, almost knobbly skin is pale greenish-yellow, which changes to yellow with bronze russetting as they ripen. The creamy white flesh is firm, buttery and extremely juicy, with a sweet flavour having a hint of acidity. A truly delicious pear.

Conference First cultivated in Berkshire in 1770, these long, conical pears have remained a favourite in Britain, largely because they keep so well. The yellowish-green skin with extensive russetting turns yellower when the pears are mature. The granular flesh is tender, sweet and juicy. Excellent for eating and cooking.

Doyenné du Comice (also known as **Comice**) This large, roundish pear is one of the finest of all, with creamy white, melting, very juicy flesh and a sweet, aromatic flavour. The thick, yellowish-green skin is covered with speckles and patches of russetting. Doyenné du Comice are best eaten raw, and are delicious with Brie or Camembert.

Forelle A beautiful golden pear with a dark red flush on one side. The grainy flesh is crisp, with a fresh flavour that goes well with cheese, but is at its best when cooked.

Josephine de Malines A French pear, first raised in 1830. The medium-size fruits are round conical in shape, with

Below: Conference are one of the best-loved English pears.

yellowish-green skin flushed with red and some russetting, The tender flesh can be white or pinkish and is very juicy, with an aromatic flavour. It keeps well.

Merton Pride An exceptionally sweet and juicy pear with a superb flavour. The conical fruits have yellow skin wih brown freckles.

Onward A cross between Laxton's Superb and Doyenné du Comice, these roundish pears are best peeled before eating as they have ribbed skin. The yellowish-green skin is flushed with red and mottled with pale russetting. The creamy white flesh is exceptionally good – soft, melting, juicy and very sweet.

Packham's Triumph The first successful Australian pear was produced by Charles Packham in 1896 and remains a favourite. A largish eating pear, it has a smooth green, lightly russetted skin, which changes to yellow as it ripens. The soft white flesh is succulent and sweet, with a touch of acidity.

Passacrena Very plump, roundish pears with russetted greenish-yellow skin. The flesh can sometimes be rather gritty, but is very juicy and sweet.

Above: Doyenné du Comice, also known simply as Comice, are very juicy and aromatic.

Right: Forelle are ideal pears to use for cooking.

Red Williams These pears have shiny, speckled skins, at first green with a red blush, turning to yellow flushed with red. The flesh is sweet and juicy.

Rocha A Portuguese pear with greenish-yellow skin with russet spotting and brown markings at the stem end. The firm white flesh has a sugary flavour and, unlike many other pears which pass their prime almost as soon as they reach it, the fruit remains in excellent condition for several days.

Williams Bon Chrétien Known as "Barlett" in the United States, these irregularly shaped pears are generally swollen on one side of the stalk. The speckled skin is golden yellow with russet patches and sometimes a red tinge. The delicious tender flesh is creamy white and very juicy, and the flavour is sweet and slightly musky. Unfortunately, these superb pears do not keep well. Williams Bon Chrétien are suitable for cooking and eating.

Winter Nelis This roundish medium-size pear has thick but tender greenish-yellow skin with cinnamon brown russetting and sometimes a pink flush. The creamy white flesh is soft and very juicy, and the flavour is sweet. These pears can be cooked or eaten raw.

Left: Packham's Triumph

Nutrition

Pears contain a small amount of vitamins A and C and some potassium and riboflavin. They provide around 60 kilocalories per 100g/3¾oz.

Pears should always be bought when they are in perfect condition, as they deteriorate quickly. Once past their best, they become woolly or squashy and unpleasant. Test for ripeness by pressing the stem end between your forefinger and thumb; it should give a little, but the pear should still be quite firm. Once ripe, pears should be eaten within a couple of days, or they will "go over". Keep ripe fruit in the bottom of the fridge.

Above: Suitable for both eating and cooking, Williams Bon Chrétien have delicious creamy white flesh. They don't keep very well, so use them as soon as they have ripened

Above: The firm-fleshed Rocha will remain in good condition for several days in your fruit bowl.

Below: Juicy, with a red blush, Red Williams make excellent eating.

Dried pears Although dried pears are most often used in winter fruit compotes and savoury casseroles, they have a delicate flavour and are delicious eaten raw. They are readily available in the shops, but it is easy to prepare your own.

Canned pears Pears are among the most successful of all canned fruit and may be used to make almost any dessert that calls for cooked pears. They are often canned in heavy syrup, but are now available in the healthier alternative of apple juice. Purée drained canned pears, flavour them with pear liqueur, lemon or preserved ginger syrup and freeze for a quick and easy sorbet.

Preparing and Cooking

Most pears are eaten raw, by themselves or with a robust cheese, such as Gorgonzola, Parmesan, Stilton or Roquefort. They also make a good addition to winter salads. Whether or not to peel pears before eating raw is a matter of preference, but they should always be peeled before cooking. Pears discolour quickly once they are peeled, so rub the cut surface with a little lemon juice immediately or place them a bowl of acidulated water. For whole poached pears, simply peel,

Right: Dried pears

leaving on the stalk. Use an apple corer to core the pears if you want to stuff them with nuts or dried fruit. Poach in port or red wine spiced with cinnamon, cloves and thinly pared lemon rind, or in a vanilla-flavoured syrup. For sautéed or grilled pears, peel and quarter or halve the fruit and scoop out the cores with a melon baller.

Eating or cooking pears can also be cooked in compotes, tarts, terrines, trifles and the famous Poires Belle Hélène (poached pears with vanilla ice cream and hot chocolate sauce). They make marvellous fritters and go very well with ingredients such as nuts and spices, port and marsala. Cooked pears are also excellent in savoury dishes; for example they can either be made into chutney, or casseroled with game birds or venison. They can be preserved with sugar and vinegar, or pickled with mustard seeds and horseradish. If you are cooking eating pears, use them while they are still slightly underripe.

Pears may also be dried, canned, crystallized and distilled into spirits like *eau-de-vie de poires* and Poire William. The bottle in which this liqueur is sold sometimes contains a whole pear, an apparent illusion as the neck is too narrow to allow the pear to pass. The effect is achieved by placing the bottle necks over the infant fruits on the tree so that each pear grows inside a bottle. When it has ripened, the bottle is topped up with the pear-flavoured liqueur.

Left: Canned pears

Drying pears

1 Peel the pears and cut them in half lengthways.

2 Scoop out the cores with a small melon baller, removing all the fibrous part of the fruit.

3 Brush them with lemon juice to prevent discoloration. Spread out in a single layer on a rack over a baking sheet and dry in an oven set to 70°C/150°F/Gas Low for several hours until dried.

ASIAN OR NASHI PEARS

There are many varieties of Asian pear, but their characteristics are very similar. Round rather than pear-shaped, the fruits have a golden-brown russet skin and very crisp, white, juicy flesh. The crunchy texture resembles that of an apple but is more granular. It would be a shame to spoil the crisp texture by cooking. Asian pears are best eaten straight from the fridge, to be enjoyed as a "drink on a stalk". They also make excellent additions to fruit salads or savoury winter salads.

HOSUI PEARS

These pears have much the same crunch and juiciness of Tientsin pears, but look more like apples, with greeny-brown mottled flesh, which tastes like a cross between an apple and an unripe pear.

PERRY PEARS

With the demise of the most famous of the sparkling alcoholic pear drinks, perry pears have largely fallen into disfavour. A few small producers still press perry pears into juice, wine or "champagne" perry, but although there are still about 300 known varieties, you will never find these fruit in the shops. Perry pears are smaller than their eating pear counterparts. Although they look delicious, they contain large quantities of tannin and taste bitter and astringent, whether they are eaten raw or cooked.

Left: Tientsin pears are best eaten chilled.

TIENTSIN PEARS

These pears from China and Korea are very similar to Asian or Nashi pears in taste and texture. They are available when Asian or Nashipears are out of season. They look rather like elongated apples, tapering gently at both ends. The skin is pale yellow, slightly speckled with light brown. The pure white flesh is exceptionally juicy and crunchy – perfect for a hot day. Tientsin pears are best eaten chilled to appreciate their refreshing quality, and make the perfect healthy alternative to ice lollies.

Left: Asian pears are round rather than pear-shaped and their crunchy texture resembles that of apples, too.

QUINCES

These highly aromatic fruits are known as "apple" or "pear" quinces, according to their shape. Unripe fruits have a downy skin, while ripe quinces have the smooth texture of a pear. Raw quinces are inedible, but they make excellent natural air fresheners – a quince kept in the glove compartment will shrivel but not rot, and will fill your car with the most delicious aroma for up to six months.

History

Quinces originate from Turkestan and Persia, but are grown all over Europe. It is said that they were the mythical golden apples of the Hesperides and that the golden apple Paris gave to Aphrodite, the goddess of Love, was in

Above: Quinces may have been the mythical golden apples of Hesperides.

fact a quince. To the Ancient Greeks and Romans, quinces were a symbol of happiness, love and fruitfulness. The fruits were widely grown in Britain from the sixteenth to the eighteenth century, but their popularity has declined. In Spain, however, they are still highly prized and are used to make a thick fruit paste called *membrillo*.

Choosing and Storing

Quinces are not readily available in the shops, but you may find them growing in gardens. The skin of ripe quinces should be uniformly golden yellow; unripe fruit may still have patches of down, which can be rubbed off. Quinces keep well – the best way to store them is in a bowl in your kitchen or living room. They will fill the room with their delicious scent.

Preparing and Cooking

Quinces are always cooked. They are prepared in much the same way as pears. For jellies and fruit pastes, the skin is left on as it contributes valuable pectin, as do the pips (the word "marmalade" comes from the Portuguese word for quince, *marmelo*). Quince jelly can be spread on bread or served with pork and game. Quinces can be baked whole like apples or pears, stuffed with a rich mixture of butter, sugar and cream. One or two quinces also make a good addition to an apple pie. Peel and slice the quinces

---

Quince jelly
Makes about 2kg/4¹⁄₂lb

1 Roughly chop 1kg/2¹⁄₄lb quinces. Put in a large, heavy-based pan with 2 litres/3¹⁄₂ pints/8 cups water.

2 Bring to the boil, then simmer until the quinces are very tender.

3 Pour into a jelly bag set over a bowl; let the juice run through, but do not squeeze the bag or the finished jelly will be cloudy.

4 Measure the strained juice and pour into a large, heavy-based pan. Add 500g/1¹⁄₄lb/2¹⁄₂ cups preserving sugar for each 600ml/1 pint/ 2¹⁄₂ cups of the juice. Bring to the boil, stirring until the sugar has dissolved completely. Boil rapidly until setting point is reached.

5 Skim the jelly and pour into sterilized jars. Cover the jars while the jelly is still hot, then label once the jars are cool enough to handle.

(this will be easier to achieve if you parboil them for 10 minutes), then toss them with the apple slices, sugar and cinnamon before layering them in the pie.

In Spain, quince pulp is boiled with sugar to make the fruit paste, *membrillo*, which is then cooled, cut into squares and served with soft cheeses or as a sweet. The French equivalent is known as *cotignac*, while quince cheese is similar, but softer and more spreadable.

Quinces marry well with almost all meats, from poultry to beef and game, and also make a wonderful scented addition to spirits such as vodka, grappa or *eau-de-vie*.

Japonica Quince
As the name suggests, this cultivated quince came originally from Japan. The hard yellowish fruits are virtually inedible raw, but can be cooked and used like quinces. Their perfume is less intense, but they are still sufficiently aromatic to make an excellent addition to pies and tarts. They can also be made into both quince jelly and quince cheese.

Above: Japonica quinces are not edible raw, but they make a wonderful jelly.

MEDLARS

Medlar trees resemble pear trees, but the fruits are quite different. They look rather like large golden brown rosehips with a russetted skin and a distinctive open five-point calyx end, for which the French have an indelicate term (*cul de chien*). They are eaten when overripe, almost rotten. The process is known as "bletting" and is traditionally achieved by spreading out unripe fruit on straw and leaving it to decay for several weeks, by which time the flesh can be spooned out. To speed up the bletting process, whole unripe medlars can be frozen to break up the cell structure, then left to decay at room temperature. The flesh has a dry, sticky texture. It tastes a little like the flesh of dried dates, but is more tart. Medlars are not to everyone's taste; the nineteenth-century horticulturalist George Bunyard described several different varieties of medlar as "all of equal unpleasantness".

Above: Medlars are nowadays seldom sold in shops, nor eaten much either.

History

Medlars were first discovered in the Transcaucasus, but are found growing wild in Asia Minor and southern Europe. They were cultivated by the Assyrians, who then introduced them to Ancient Greece. In Victorian times in England, they were often enjoyed at the end of a meal with the port, but they are seldom eaten nowadays.

Choosing and Storing

Medlars are seldom sold in shops, but are sometimes cultivated or found growing wild. They are extremely hard and, if left on the tree, are unlikely to ripen sufficiently to be eaten. They are therefore picked in their unripe state and left to "blet". A bletted medlar will be soft and yielding to the touch.

Preparing and Cooking

To eat bletted medlars raw, peel back the skin from the five points of the calyx and suck out the flesh, leaving the five pips behind, or scrape it out with a spoon. Unripe medlars can be used with bletted fruits to make medlar jelly, or baked to make a thick sauce that goes well with rich meats. Medlar jelly is made in the same way as quince jelly.

APPLE, PEAR AND QUINCE RECIPES

*Apples, pears and quinces are wonderfully versatile.
Dutch Apple Cake and Chocolate, Pear and Pecan Pie
are just two of the tempting tea-time treats in store,
while Hot Quince Soufflés and Iced Pear Terrine
with Calvados and Chocolate Sauce make
memorable desserts.*

ICED PEAR TERRINE WITH CALVADOS AND CHOCOLATE SAUCE

THIS TERRINE, BASED ON A CLASSIC FRENCH DESSERT, MAKES A REFRESHING AND IMPRESSIVE END TO ANY MEAL. FOR FLAVOUR, BE SURE THE PEARS ARE RIPE AND JUICY.

SERVES EIGHT

INGREDIENTS
1.5kg/3–3½lb ripe Williams pears
juice of 1 lemon
115g/4oz/½ cup caster sugar
10 whole cloves
90ml/6 tbsp water
julienne strips of orange rind,
  to decorate
For the sauce
200g/7oz plain chocolate
60ml/4 tbsp hot strong black coffee
200ml/7fl oz/1 cup double cream
30ml/2 tbsp Calvados or brandy

1 Peel, core and slice the pears. Place them in a saucepan with the lemon juice, sugar, cloves and water. Cover and simmer for 10 minutes. Remove the cloves. Allow the pears to cool.

2 Process the pears with their juice, in a food processor or blender until smooth. Pour the purée into a freezerproof bowl, cover and freeze until firm.

3 Meanwhile, line a 900g/2lb loaf tin with clear film. Allow the film to overhang the sides of the tin. Remove the frozen pear purée from the freezer and spoon it into a food processor or blender. Process until smooth. Pour into the prepared tin, cover and freeze until firm.

4 Make the sauce. Break the chocolate into a large heatproof bowl. Place the bowl over a saucepan of hot water. When the chocolate has melted, stir in the coffee until smooth. Gradually stir in the cream and then the Calvados or brandy. Set the sauce aside.

5 About 20 minutes before serving, remove the loaf tin from the freezer. Invert the terrine on to a plate, lift off the clear film and place the terrine in the fridge to soften slightly. Warm the sauce over a pan of hot water. Place a slice of terrine on each dessert plate and spoon over some of the sauce. Decorate with julienne strips of orange rind and serve at once.

QUINCE AND GINGER MOUSSE WITH ALMOND BISCUITS

QUINCES AND GINGER ARE PERFECTLY MATCHED FLAVOUR PARTNERS. AS WITH ANY QUINCE RECIPE,
YOU CAN SUBSTITUTE PEARS OR APPLES WITH EQUALLY DELICIOUS RESULTS.

SERVES FOUR

INGREDIENTS
  450g/1lb quinces
  75g/3oz/⅓ cup caster sugar
  grated rind of ½ lemon
  90ml/6 tbsp water
  2 pieces stem ginger in syrup, finely
    chopped, plus 15ml/1 tbsp syrup
    from the jar
  15ml/1 tbsp powdered gelatine
  150ml/¼ pint/⅔ cup double cream
  2 egg whites
  mint leaves and blackberries dusted
    with caster sugar, to decorate
For the biscuits
  50g/2oz/¼ cup butter
  30ml/2 tbsp caster sugar
  50g/2oz/½ cup plain flour
  50g/2oz/½ cup ground almonds
  a few drops of almond essence

1 Grease four ramekins and line the bases with non-stick baking paper. Peel the quinces, core and put in a saucepan with the sugar, lemon rind and 60ml/4 tbsp of the water. Bring to the boil, lower the heat, cover and simmer for 10 minutes or until softened. Remove the lid; continue cooking until the liquid has almost evaporated.

2 Cool the quince mixture slightly, then purée in a food processor or blender. Press the purée through a sieve into a large bowl, then stir in the ginger and ginger syrup and set aside.

3 Pour the remaining 30ml/2 tbsp water into a small heatproof bowl and sprinkle the gelatine on top. Leave to soak for 5 minutes. Stand the bowl in a pan of hot water until the gelatine has dissolved, stirring occasionally.

4 Lightly whip the cream. Stir the gelatine into the quince purée, then fold in the whipped cream. In a grease-free bowl, whisk the egg whites to stiff peaks; fold into the quince mixture. Divide among the prepared ramekins, level the tops and chill until firm. Preheat the oven to 190°C/375°F/Gas 5.

5 Make the biscuits. Line a baking sheet with non-stick baking paper. Cream the butter and sugar until smooth. Add the flour, almonds and almond essence and mix to a dough with a knife. Roll out thinly on a lightly floured surface; cut into rounds with a 7.5cm/3in cutter. Transfer to the baking sheet. Chill for 10 minutes, then bake for 10–12 minutes.

6 Cool slightly on the paper, then lift on to a wire rack to cool. Run a knife around each mousse; turn out on to dessert plates. Discard the paper. Decorate and serve with the biscuits.

SPICED APPLE CRUMBLE

ANY FRUIT CAN BE USED IN THIS POPULAR DESSERT, BUT YOU CAN'T BEAT THE FAVOURITES OF
BLACKBERRY AND APPLE. HAZELNUTS AND CARDAMOM SEEDS GIVE THE TOPPING EXTRA FLAVOUR.

SERVES FOUR TO SIX

INGREDIENTS
    butter, for greasing
    450g/1lb Bramley apples
    115g/4oz/1 cup blackberries
    grated rind and juice of 1 orange
    50g/2oz/⅓ cup light muscovado sugar
    custard, to serve
For the topping
    175g/6oz/1½ cups plain flour
    75g/3oz/⅓ cup butter
    75g/3oz/⅓ cup caster sugar
    25g/1oz/¼ cup chopped hazelnuts
    2.5ml/½ tsp crushed cardamom seeds

VARIATIONS
This wonderfully good-natured pudding
can be made with all sorts of fruit. Try
plums, apricots, peaches or pears, alone
or in combination with apples. Rhubarb
makes a delectable crumble, especially
when partnered with bananas.

1 Preheat the oven to 200°C/400°F/
Gas 6. Generously butter a 1.2 litre/
2 pint/5 cup baking dish. Peel and
core the apples, then slice them into
the prepared baking dish. Level the
surface, then scatter the blackberries
over. Sprinkle the orange rind and light
muscovado sugar evenly over the top,
then pour over the orange juice. Set the
fruit mixture aside while you make the
crumble topping.

2 Make the topping. Sift the flour into a
bowl and rub in the butter until the
mixture resembles coarse breadcrumbs.
Stir in the caster sugar, hazelnuts and
cardamom seeds. Scatter the topping
over the top of the fruit.

3 Press the topping around the edges
of the dish to seal in the juices. Bake
for 30–35 minutes or until the crumble
is golden. Serve hot, with custard.

BAKED STUFFED APPLES

THIS TRADITIONAL APPLE DESSERT IS EXCEPTIONALLY SIMPLE AND SPEEDY. BAKE THE APPLES IN THE
OVEN ON THE SHELF UNDER THE SUNDAY ROAST FOR A DELICIOUS END TO THE MEAL.

SERVES FOUR

INGREDIENTS
    4 large Bramley apples
    75g/3oz/½ cup light muscovado sugar
    75g/3oz/⅓ cup butter, softened
    grated rind and juice of ½ orange
    1.5ml/¼ tsp ground cinnamon
    30ml/2 tbsp crushed ratafia biscuits
    50g/2oz/½ cup pecan nuts, chopped
    50g/2oz/½ cup luxury mixed glacé
      fruit, chopped

COOK'S TIP
Use a little butter or oil to grease the
baking dish, if you like, or pour a small
amount of water around the stuffed
apples to stop them from sticking to the
dish during baking.

1 Preheat the oven to 180°C/350°F/
Gas 4. Wash and dry the apples.
Remove the cores with an apple corer,
then carefully enlarge each core cavity
to twice its size, by shaving off more
flesh with the corer. Score each apple
around its equator, using a sharp knife.
Stand the apples in a baking dish.

2 Mix the sugar, butter, orange rind
and juice, cinnamon and ratafia crumbs.
Beat well, then stir in the nuts and
glacé fruit. Divide the filling among the
apples, piling it high. Shield the filling in
each apple with a small piece of foil.
Bake for 45–60 minutes until all the
apples are tender.

APPLE CRÊPES WITH BUTTERSCOTCH SAUCE

THESE WONDERFUL DESSERT CRÊPES ARE FLAVOURED WITH SWEET CIDER, FILLED WITH CARAMELIZED APPLES AND DRIZZLED WITH A RICH, SMOOTH BUTTERSCOTCH SAUCE.

3 Make the filling. Core the apples and cut them into thick slices. Heat 15g/ ½ oz/1 tbsp of the butter in a large frying pan. Add the apples to the pan. Cook until golden on both sides, then transfer the slices to a bowl with a slotted spoon and set them aside.

4 Add the rest of the butter to the pan. As soon as it has melted, add the muscovado sugar. When the sugar has dissolved and the mixture is bubbling, stir in the cream. Continue cooking until it forms a smooth sauce.

5 Fold each pancake in half, then fold in half again to form a cone; fill each with some of the fried apples. Place two filled pancakes on each dessert plate, drizzle over some of the butterscotch sauce and serve at once.

SERVES FOUR

INGREDIENTS
  115g/4oz/1 cup plain flour
  a pinch of salt
  2 eggs
  175ml/6fl oz/¾ cup creamy milk
  120ml/4fl oz/½ cup sweet cider
  butter, for frying
For the filling and sauce
  4 Braeburn apples
  90g/3½ oz/scant ½ cup butter
  225g/8oz/1⅓ cups light
    muscovado sugar
  150ml/¼ pint/⅔ cup double cream

1 Make the crêpe batter. Sift the flour and salt into a large bowl. Add the eggs and milk and beat until smooth. Stir in the cider; set aside for 30 minutes.

2 Heat a small heavy-based non-stick frying pan. Add a knob of butter and ladle in enough batter to coat the pan thinly. Cook until the crêpe is golden underneath, then flip it over and cook the other side until golden. Slide the crêpe on to a plate. Repeat with the remaining mixture to make seven more.

VARIATIONS
You could just as easily use plums, pears, strawberries or bananas to fill the crêpes. If you like, add a touch of Grand Marnier to the apples towards the end of cooking.

PEAR AND CINNAMON FRITTERS

IF YOU DON'T LIKE DEEP FRYING AS A RULE, DO MAKE AN EXCEPTION FOR THIS DISH. FRITTERS ARE IRRESISTIBLE, AND A WONDERFUL WAY OF PERSUADING CHILDREN TO EAT MORE FRUIT.

SERVES FOUR

INGREDIENTS
   3 ripe, firm pears
   30ml/2 tbsp caster sugar
   30ml/2 tbsp Kirsch
   groundnut oil, for frying
   50g/2oz/1 cup amaretti biscuits,
      finely crushed
For the batter
   75g/3oz/¾ cup plain flour
   1.5ml/¼ tsp salt
   1.5ml/¼ tsp ground cinnamon
   60ml/4 tbsp milk
   2 eggs, separated
   45ml/3 tbsp water
To serve
   30ml/2 tbsp caster sugar
   1.5ml/¼ tsp ground cinnamon
   clotted cream

1 Peel the pears, cut them in quarters and remove the cores. Toss the wedges in the caster sugar and Kirsch. Set aside for 15 minutes.

2 Make the batter. Sift the flour, salt and cinnamon into a large bowl. Beat in the milk, egg yolks and water until smooth. Set aside for 10 minutes.

3 Whisk the egg whites in a grease-free bowl until they form stiff peaks; lightly fold them into the batter. Preheat the oven to 150ºC/300ºF/Gas 2.

4 Pour oil into a deep heavy-based saucepan to a depth of 7.5cm/3in. Heat to 185ºC/360ºF or until a bread cube, added to the oil, browns in 45 seconds.

5 Toss a pear wedge in the amaretti crumbs, then spear it on a fork and dip it into the batter until evenly coated. Lower it gently into the hot oil and use a knife to push it off the fork. Add more wedges in the same way but do not overcrowd the pan. Cook the fritters for 3–4 minutes or until golden. Drain on kitchen paper. Keep hot in the oven while cooking successive batches.

6 Mix the sugar and cinnamon and sprinkle some over the fritters. Sprinkle a little cinnamon sugar over the clotted cream; serve with the hot fritters.

VARIATIONS
Also try apples, apricots and bananas.

POACHED PEARS IN PORT SYRUP

THE PERFECT CHOICE FOR AUTUMN ENTERTAINING, THIS SIMPLE DESSERT HAS A BEAUTIFUL RICH COLOUR AND FANTASTIC FLAVOUR THANKS TO THE TASTES OF PORT AND LEMON.

SERVES FOUR

INGREDIENTS
    2 ripe, firm pears, such as Williams
        or Comice
    pared rind of 1 lemon
    175ml/6fl oz/¾ cup ruby port
    50g/2oz/¼ cup caster sugar
    1 cinnamon stick
    60ml/4 tbsp cold water
    fresh cream, to serve
To decorate
    30ml/2 tbsp sliced hazelnuts, toasted
    fresh mint, pear or rose leaves

COOK'S TIP
Choose pears of similar size, with the stalks intact, for the most attractive effect when fanned on the plate.

1 Peel the pears, cut them in half and remove the cores. Place the lemon rind, port, sugar, cinnamon stick and water in a shallow pan. Bring to the boil over a low heat. Add the pears, lower the heat, cover and poach for 5 minutes. Let the pears cool in the syrup.

2 When the pears are cold, transfer them to a bowl with a slotted spoon. Return the syrup to the heat. Boil rapidly until it has reduced to form a syrup that will coat the back of a spoon lightly. Remove the cinnamon stick and lemon rind and leave the syrup to cool.

3 To serve, place each pear in turn on a board, cut side down. Keeping it intact at the stalk end, slice it lengthways, then using a palette knife, carefully lift it off and place on a dessert plate. Press gently so that the pear fans out. When all the pears have been fanned, spoon over the port syrup. Top each portion with a few hazelnuts and decorate with fresh mint, pear or rose leaves. Serve with cream.

APPLE CHARLOTTES

THESE TEMPTING LITTLE FRUIT CHARLOTTES ARE A WONDERFUL WAY TO USE WINDFALLS.

SERVES FOUR

INGREDIENTS

175g/6oz/¾ cup butter
450g/1lb Bramley apples
225g/8oz Braeburn apples
60ml/4 tbsp water
130g/4½oz/scant ⅔ cup caster sugar
2 egg yolks
a pinch of grated nutmeg
9 thin slices white bread,
  crusts removed
extra-thick double cream or custard,
  to serve

COOK'S TIP

A mixture of cooking and eating apples gives the best flavour, but there's no reason why you can't use only cooking apples; just sweeten the pulp to taste.

1 Preheat the oven to 190°C/375°F/ Gas 5. Put a knob of the butter in a saucepan. Peel and core the apples, dice them finely and put them in the pan with the water. Cover and cook for 10 minutes or until the cooking apples have pulped down. Stir in 115g/4oz/ ½ cup of the caster sugar. Then boil, uncovered, until any liquid has evaporated and what remains is a thick pulp. Remove from the heat, beat in the egg yolks and nutmeg and set aside.

2 Melt the remaining butter in a separate saucepan over a low heat until the white curds start to separate from the clear yellow liquid. Remove from the heat. Leave to stand for a few minutes, then strain the clear clarified butter through a muslin-lined sieve.

3 Brush four 150ml/¼ pint/⅔ cup individual charlotte moulds or pudding tins with a little of the clarified butter; sprinkle with the remaining caster sugar. Cut the bread slices into 2.5cm/1in strips. Dip the strips into the remaining clarified butter; use to line the moulds or tins. Overlap the strips on the base to give the effect of a swirl and let the excess bread overhang the tops of the moulds or tins.

4 Fill each bread case with apple pulp. Fold the excess bread over the top of each mould or tin to make a lid; press down lightly. Bake for 45–50 minutes or until golden. Run a knife between each charlotte and its mould or tin, then turn out on to dessert plates. Serve with extra-thick double cream or custard.

HOT QUINCE SOUFFLÉS

THESE DELICIOUS FRUITS ARE MORE OFTEN PICKED THAN PURCHASED AS THEY ARE SELDOM FOUND IN SHOPS OR MARKETS. YOU CAN USE PEARS INSTEAD, BUT THE FLAVOUR WILL NOT BE AS INTENSE.

SERVES SIX

INGREDIENTS
    2 quinces, peeled and cored
    60ml/4 tbsp water
    115g/4oz/½ cup caster sugar,
        plus extra for sprinkling
    5 egg whites
    melted butter, for greasing
    icing sugar, for dusting
For the pastry cream
    250ml/8fl oz/1 cup milk
    1 vanilla pod
    3 egg yolks
    75g/3oz/⅓ cup caster sugar
    25g/1oz/¼ cup plain flour
    15ml/1 tbsp Poire William liqueur

3 Make the pastry cream. Pour the milk into a small saucepan. Add the vanilla pod and bring to the boil over a low heat. Meanwhile, beat the egg yolks, caster sugar and flour in a bowl until smooth.

7 Preheat the oven to 220°C/425°F/ Gas 7. Place a baking sheet in the oven to heat up. Butter six 150ml/¼ pint/ ⅔ cup ramekins and sprinkle the inside of each with caster sugar. In a grease-free bowl, whisk the egg whites to stiff peaks. Gradually whisk in the remaining caster sugar, then fold the egg whites into the pastry cream.

1 Cut the quinces into cubes. Place in a saucepan with the water. Stir in half the sugar. Bring to the boil, lower the heat, cover and simmer for 10 minutes or until tender. Remove the lid; boil until most of the liquid has evaporated.

4 Gradually strain the hot milk on to the yolks, whisking frequently until the mixture is smooth.

5 Discard the vanilla pod. Return the mixture to the clean pan and heat gently, stirring until thickened. Cook for a further 2 minutes, whisking constantly, to ensure that the sauce is smooth and the flour is cooked.

8 Divide the mixture among the prepared ramekins and level the surface of each. Carefully run a sharp knife between the side of each ramekin and the mixture, then place the ramekins on the hot baking sheet and bake for 8–10 minutes until the tops of the soufflés are well risen and golden. Generously dust the tops with icing sugar and serve the soufflés at once.

6 Remove the pan from the heat and stir in the quince purée and liqueur. Cover the surface of the pastry cream with clear film to prevent it from forming a skin. Allow to cool slightly, while you prepare the ramekins.

COOK'S TIP
Poire William is a clear, colourless pear eau-de-vie, which sometimes is sold with a ripe pear in the bottle. Kirsch, made from cherries, also works well in this recipe to complement the flavour of the quinces.

2 Cool slightly, then purée the fruit in a blender or food processor. Press through a sieve into a bowl; set aside.

TARTE TATIN

IF YOU USE READY-ROLLED PUFF PASTRY, THIS TASTY TART CAN BE MADE VERY EASILY.

SERVES SIX TO EIGHT

INGREDIENTS

3 Braeburn or Cox's Orange
   Pippin apples
juice of ½ lemon
50g/2oz/¼ cup butter, softened
75g/3oz/⅓ cup caster sugar
250g/9oz ready-rolled puff pastry
cream, to serve

1 Preheat the oven to 220°C/425°F/
Gas 7. Cut the apples in quarters and
remove the cores. Toss the apple
quarters in the lemon juice to prevent
them discolouring.

2 Spread the butter over the base of a
20cm/8in heavy-based omelette pan
that can safely be used in the oven.
Sprinkle the caster sugar over the base
of the pan and add the apple wedges,
rounded side down.

3 Cook over a medium heat for
15–20 minutes or until the sugar and
butter have melted and the apples are
golden. Cut the pastry into a 25cm/10in
round and place on top of the apples;
tuck the edges in with a knife. Place the
pan in the oven and bake for 15–20
minutes or until the pastry is golden.
Carefully invert the tart on to a plate.
Cool slightly before serving with cream.

COOK'S TIP
To turn out the Tarte Tatin, place the
serving plate upside down on top of it,
then, protecting your arms with oven
gloves, hold both pan and plate firmly
together and deftly turn them over. Lift
off the pan.

FILO-TOPPED APPLE PIE

WITH ITS SCRUNCHY FILO TOPPING AND MINIMAL BUTTER, THIS PIE MAKES A REALLY LIGHT DESSERT. IT'S A GOOD CHOICE FOR THE APPLE PIE ADDICT WATCHING HIS OR HER FAT INTAKE.

SERVES SIX

INGREDIENTS
900g/2lb Bramley apples
75g/3oz/⅓ cup caster sugar
grated rind of 1 lemon
15ml/1 tbsp lemon juice
75g/3oz/½ cup sultanas
2.5ml/½ tsp ground cinnamon
4 large sheets filo pastry, thawed
    if frozen
25g/1oz/2 tbsp butter, melted
icing sugar, for dusting

VARIATION
To make filo crackers, cut the buttered filo into 20cm/8in wide strips. Spoon a little of the filling along one end of each strip, leaving the sides clear. Roll up and twist the ends to make a cracker. Brush with more butter; bake for 20 minutes.

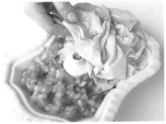

1 Peel, core and dice the apples. Place them in a saucepan with the caster sugar and lemon rind. Drizzle the lemon juice over. Bring to the boil, stir well, then cook for 5 minutes or until the apples have softened. Stir in the sultanas and cinnamon. Spoon the mixture into a 1.2 litre/2 pint/5 cup pie dish and level the top. Allow to cool.

2 Preheat the oven to 180°C/350°F/ Gas 4. Place a pie funnel in the centre of the fruit. Brush each sheet of filo with melted butter. Scrunch up loosely and place on the fruit to cover it completely.

3 Bake for 20–30 minutes until the filo is golden. Dust the pie with icing sugar before serving with custard or cream.

CHOCOLATE, PEAR AND PECAN PIE

THE RICHNESS OF DEEP, DARK CHOCOLATE COUPLED WITH JUICY PEARS GIVES A CLASSIC PECAN PIE AN OUT-OF-THE-ORDINARY TWIST. THE RESULT IS UTTERLY DELICIOUS — AND UTTERLY IRRESISTIBLE.

SERVES EIGHT TO TEN

INGREDIENTS

300g/11oz shortcrust pastry, thawed
   if frozen
3 small pears
165g/5½oz/scant ¾ cup caster sugar
150ml/¼ pint/⅔ cup water
pared rind of 1 lemon
50g/2oz good quality plain chocolate
50g/2oz/¼ cup unsalted butter, diced
225g/8oz/¾ cup golden syrup
3 eggs, beaten
5ml/1 tsp pure vanilla essence
150g/5oz/1¼ cups pecan
   nuts, chopped
15ml/1 tbsp maple syrup (optional)
ice cream, to serve

1 Preheat the oven to 200°C/400°F/ Gas 6. Roll out the pastry on a lightly floured surface and line a deep 23cm/ 9in fluted flan tin. Chill the pastry case for 20 minutes, then line it with non-stick baking paper and baking beans. Bake for 10 minutes. Lift out the paper and beans and return the pastry case to the oven for 5 minutes. Allow to cool.

2 Peel the pears, cut them in half and remove the cores with a small spoon. Place 50g/2oz/¼ cup of the sugar in a pan with the water. Add the lemon rind and bring to the boil. Add the pears. Cover, lower the heat and simmer for 10 minutes. Remove the pears from the pan with a slotted spoon and set aside to cool. Discard the cooking liquid.

3 Break the chocolate into a large heatproof bowl. Melt over a pan of barely simmering water. Beat in the butter until combined. Set aside. In a saucepan, heat the remaining sugar and golden syrup together over a low heat until most of the sugar has dissolved. Bring to the boil, lower the heat and simmer for 2 minutes.

4 Whisk the eggs into the chocolate mixture until combined, then whisk in the syrup mixture. Stir in the vanilla essence and pecan nuts.

5 Place the pear halves flat side down on a board. Using a fine sharp knife, make lengthways cuts all along each pear, taking care not to cut all the way through. Using a palette knife, lift the pear halves and arrange in the pastry case. Pour the pecan mixture over the top, so that the pears are visible through the mixture.

6 Bake for 25–30 minutes or until the filling is set, then allow to cool on a wire rack. If you like, glaze the surface of the pie with maple syrup before serving with ice cream.

FRENCH APPLE TART

THIS GLORIOUS TART MAKES A TRULY INDULGENT DESSERT. FOR AN EARLY MORNING TREAT, TRY A SLICE FOR BREAKFAST WITH A CUP OF STRONG BLACK COFFEE.

SERVES EIGHT

INGREDIENTS
    350g/12oz sweet shortcrust pastry,
       thawed if frozen
    whipped cream, to serve
For the filling
    115g/4oz/½ cup butter, softened
    115g/4oz/½ cup caster sugar
    2 large eggs, beaten
    115g/4oz/1 cup ground almonds
    25g/1oz/¼ cup plain flour
For the topping
    3 Braeburn apples
    60ml/4 tbsp apricot jam
    15ml/1 tbsp water

1 Preheat the oven to 190°C/375°F/ Gas 5. Place a baking sheet in the oven to heat up. Roll out the shortcrust pastry on a lightly floured surface and line a 23cm/9in fluted flan tin.

2 Beat all the ingredients for the filling together until light and fluffy. Spoon into the pastry case and level the surface.

3 Make the topping. Peel the apples, remove the cores, and cut them in half. Place each half, cut side down, on a board. Using a sharp, fine knife, slice the apples thinly, keeping the shape, then press down lightly to fan each apple half in a row.

VARIATION
A redcurrant glaze would also look good on this tart. Warm redcurrant jelly with a little lemon juice and brush it over the apples. Sieving is not necessary.

4 Using a palette knife, carefully transfer each row of apple slices to the tart, arranging them on the filling so that they resemble the spokes of a wheel. You may need to overlap the slices in the middle slightly to fit. Press the slices down well into the filling. Warm the apricot jam with the water, then press the mixture through a sieve into a small bowl.

5 Using a pastry brush, brush half the jam glaze over the apples. Place the tin on the hot baking sheet and bake the tart for 45 minutes or until the pastry is golden and the apples have started to singe slightly.

6 Warm the remaining jam glaze and brush it over the apples. Let the tart cool slightly before serving with cream.

DUTCH APPLE CAKE

THE APPLE TOPPING MAKES THIS CAKE REALLY MOIST. IT IS EQUALLY AS GOOD HOT OR COLD.

MAKES EIGHT TO TEN SLICES

INGREDIENTS
    250g/9oz/2¼ cups self-raising flour
    10ml/2 tsp baking powder
    5ml/1 tsp ground cinnamon
    130g/4½oz/generous ½ cup
      caster sugar
    50g/2oz/¼ cup butter, melted
    2 eggs, beaten
    150ml/¼ pint/⅔ cup milk
For the topping
    2 Cox's Orange Pippin apples
    15g/½oz/1 tbsp butter, melted
    60ml/4 tbsp demerara sugar
    1.5ml/¼ tsp ground cinnamon

VARIATION
Add a few sultanas or raisins to the
apples if you like.

1 Preheat the oven to 200°C/400°F/
Gas 6. Grease and line a 20cm/8in
round cake tin. Sift the flour, baking
powder and cinnamon into a large
mixing bowl. Stir in the caster sugar.
In a separate bowl, whisk the melted
butter, eggs and milk together, then stir
the mixture into the dry ingredients.

2 Pour the cake mixture into the
prepared tin, smooth the surface, then
make a shallow hollow in a ring around
the edge of the mixture.

3 Make the topping. Peel and core the
apples, slice them into wedges and slice
the wedges thinly. Arrange the slices
around the hollow of the cake mixture.
Brush with the melted butter, then
scatter the demerara sugar and ground
cinnamon over the top.

4 Bake for 45–50 minutes or until the
cake has risen well, is golden and a
skewer inserted into the centre comes
out clean. Serve immediately as a
dessert with cream, or remove from the
tin, peel off the lining paper and cool on
a wire rack before slicing.

PEAR AND POLENTA CAKE

*POLENTA GIVES THE LIGHT SPONGE THAT TOPS SLICED PEARS A NUTTY CORN FLAVOUR THAT
COMPLEMENTS THE FRUIT PERFECTLY. SERVE AS A DESSERT WITH CUSTARD OR CREAM.*

MAKES TEN SLICES

INGREDIENTS
    175g/6oz/¾ cup golden caster sugar
    4 ripe pears
    juice of ½ lemon
    30ml/2 tbsp clear honey
    3 eggs
    seeds from 1 vanilla pod
    120ml/4fl oz/½ cup sunflower oil
    115g/4oz/1 cup self-raising flour
    50g/2oz/⅓ cup instant polenta

1 Preheat the oven to 180°C/350°F/
Gas 4. Generously grease and line a
21cm/8½in round cake tin. Scatter
30ml/2 tbsp of the golden caster sugar
over the base of the prepared tin.

COOK'S TIP
Use the tip of a small, sharp knife to
scrape out the vanilla pod seeds. If you
do not have a vanilla pod, use 5ml/1 tsp
pure vanilla essence instead.

2 Peel and core the pears. Cut them
into chunky slices and toss in the lemon
juice. Arrange them on the base of the
prepared cake tin. Drizzle the honey
over the pears and set aside.

3 Mix together the eggs, seeds from
the vanilla pod and the remaining
golden caster sugar in a bowl.

4 Beat the egg mixture until thick and
creamy, then gradually beat in the oil.
Sift together the flour and polenta and
fold into the egg mixture.

5 Pour the mixture carefully into the tin
over the pears. Bake the cake for about
50 minutes or until a skewer inserted
into the centre comes out clean. Cool in
the tin for 10 minutes, then turn the
cake out on to a plate, peel off the
lining paper, invert and slice.

APPLE AND CIDER SAUCE

THIS SAUCE COULDN'T BE SIMPLER TO MAKE. IT TASTES GREAT WITH ROAST PORK, DUCK OR GOOSE.

MAKES 450G/1LB

INGREDIENTS
450g/1lb Bramley apples
150ml/¼ pint/⅔ cup sweet cider
2.5ml/½ tsp cider vinegar
25g/1oz/2 tbsp butter
2 whole cloves
a few sprigs of fresh thyme
15ml/1 tbsp clear honey
10ml/2 tsp Dijon mustard

1 Peel, core and slice the apples. Place them in a saucepan with the cider, cider vinegar, butter, cloves and thyme. Simmer over a low heat for 10 minutes or until the apples are soft and pulpy, stirring occasionally, then raise the heat and cook until most of the liquid has evaporated.

2 Remove the cloves and thyme sprigs and beat in the honey and mustard. Taste and add more honey if necessary, but the sauce is best when slightly tart.

COOK'S TIP
Press the sauce through a sieve if you prefer it to be perfectly smooth.

APPLE AND RED ONION MARMALADE

THIS MARMALADE CHUTNEY IS GOOD ENOUGH TO EAT ON ITS OWN. SERVE IT WITH PORK SAUSAGES FOR THOROUGHLY MODERN HOT DOGS OR IN A HAM SANDWICH INSTEAD OF MUSTARD.

MAKES 450G/1LB

INGREDIENTS
60ml/4 tbsp extra virgin olive oil
900g/2lb red onions, thinly sliced
75g/3oz/½ cup demerara sugar
2 Cox's Orange Pippin apples
90ml/6 tbsp cider vinegar

1 Heat the oil in a large, heavy-based saucepan and add the onions.

2 Stir in the sugar and cook, uncovered, over a medium heat for about 40 minutes, stirring occasionally, or until the onions have softened and become a rich golden colour.

3 Peel, core and grate the apples. Add them to the pan with the vinegar and continue to cook for 20 minutes until the chutney is thick and sticky. Spoon into a sterilized jar and cover.

4 When cool, label and store in the fridge for up to 1 month.

STONE FRUITS

One of life's greatest joys is to bite into a perfectly ripe, juicy stone
fruit and savour the wonderful sweetness of the sticky juices.
Stone fruits herald summer – the season starts with cherries,
continues with sun-drenched peaches and apricots, and ends with
plums, from gorgeous greengages to fat, juicy Victorias. Although
stone fruits (or "drupes") may seem very different, they are all
members of the Prunus family and share the characteristics of soft,
juicy flesh and a single stone. Stone fruits are often grown in
greenhouses, but nothing beats the taste of a sun-ripened fruit,
so it is worth waiting until they are in season.

PEACHES

Sometimes known as the "queen of fruits", peaches are certainly among the most beautiful. Their downy, velvety skin is yellow, flushed with red, and they are voluptuously curvaceous – the French call one variety *tétons de Venus* (Venus' breasts).

The most familiar peaches are round or "beaked", with a pointed end, but they can also be flat and disc-shaped. The delicate fine-textured flesh, which can be yellow, white or tinged with red, encloses a heavily ridged stone. In some peaches, the flesh clings firmly to the stone; these are known as "clingstone". In "freestone" fruit, the flesh comes away easily and cleanly from the stone.

Peaches and nectarines originated from the same species and are very similar, except that peaches have fuzzy skin, while nectarines are smooth. So alike are they that peach trees sometimes spontaneously produce nectarines and vice versa.

History

Peaches have been grown in China since the fifth century BC and are regarded as a symbol of longevity and immortality. Even today, some Chinese families place peach trees or branches outside their front doors to ward off evil spirits. Peaches were taken along the old silk routes to Persia where they were discovered by Alexander the Great, who introduced them to the Greeks and Romans; the word "peach" comes from

Above: Mireille, a white-fleshed peach.

the Latin *Persicum malum* (Persian apple). Immensely popular in Europe, peaches were introduced to America by Christopher Columbus and spread so profusely that they were once thought to be indigenous. Nowadays, so many are grown in Georgia that it is known as the "peach state".

Varieties

Peaches are seldom sold by variety, but by the colour of their flesh – yellow or white. Which you choose is a matter of preference; some people believe that white peaches have the finer flavour.

Yellow varieties include Elegant Lady, Royal George and Bellegarde. Mireille is a popular white peach. The finest peaches of all are the *pêches de vigne*, small red-fleshed fruits that are grown in vineyards. They do not look particularly attractive, being covered in greyish down, but the flavour is superb. You are unlikely to find them outside markets in France.

Nutrition

Peaches are a source of vitamins A, B and C and provide about 60 kilocalories per 100g/3¾oz.

Buying and Storing

Peaches do not ripen successfully after picking, so always buy ripe fruit. The fruits should be handled carefully. Press gently to ensure that they are firm, with some "give". Never buy greenish peaches, except for chutney-making, and avoid fruit with bruised skin. Peaches do not keep well. Firm fruit can be kept at room temperature for a day or two to soften; ripe peaches can be kept in the fridge for not more than two days.

Left: Elegant Lady – a popular yellow variety of peach.

Dried peaches These are not as widely available as dried apricots, but are becoming increasingly popular. Use them in compotes and cakes, or eat them on their own. Peaches are also crystallized or glacéed as a sweetmeat.

Canned peaches Available in syrup or apple juice, canned peaches are fine for cooking, but lack the delicate texture and flavour of the fresh fruit.

Above: Dried peaches

Stoning a peach or nectarine

1 Slice through the seam line all around the peach.

2 Twist the two halves in opposite directions to separate them.

3 Lever out the stone with a knife.

Glacé peaches The fruits are coated in a thick syrup, which hardens to a shiny glaze. Glacé peaches are often included in boxes of assorted glacé fruits. They are very sweet, with a melting texture.

Preparing and Serving

A really ripe peach is delicious eaten on its own or in a fruit salad. Peaches combine well with most other fruits and nuts, particularly raspberries, a marriage that inspired Escoffier to create his famous dessert, Peach Melba, in honour of the great singer

Above: Glacé peaches are coated in a thick sugar syrup and are very sweet.

Left: Canned peaches, available in halves or slices, are fine for cooking but lack the flavour of the fresh fruit.

Dame Nellie Melba. Fresh peaches feature in ice cream sundaes and can be used to make luxurious drinks like Bellini (Champagne, peach liqueur and crushed peach pulp) or Champagne cocktails. They are also made into liqueurs and peach wine and brandy.

The fuzzy skin of a peach is not particularly pleasant to eat, so the fruit is best peeled. Nick the fruit, place it in a heatproof bowl and pour over boiling water. Leave for 15–30 seconds, depending on how ripe the fruits are, then drain and refresh in cold water. The skins will peel off easily.

Cooking and Serving

Peaches can be cooked in a multitude of ways – poached whole in vanilla-flavoured syrup or wine; macerated in alcohol; in compotes, soufflés, pies,

tarts, pancakes, ice creams and sorbets. They make very good jams and jellies, while spiced peaches are delicious with cured or cold meats. Underripe green-tinged peaches can be made into excellent relishes and chutneys.

Peaches are also good, raw or cooked, in salads and are natural partners for gammon and duck. They can be substituted for mangoes in South-east Asian dishes and are particularly good with crab and lobster.

To poach peaches in syrup, put 1 litre/1¾ pints/ 4 cups water in a pan. Add 500g/1¼lb/2 cups granulated sugar, 2 strips of pared lemon rind, a piece of cinnamon and half a split

vanilla pod. Bring to the boil, stirring to dissolve the sugar. Boil for about 5 minutes, then add six to eight peeled peaches (whole or halved) and poach gently until tender, turning occasionally. Leave the fruit to cool in the syrup.

Peaches make a delicious sweet after-dinner liqueur, Crème de Peche, which can be drunk on its own, or combined with Champagne or sparking white wine to make an unusual cocktail. To make a classic Bellini, put some fresh peach pulp in a Champagne glass, add a teaspoon of peach liqueur and top up with Champagne.

Left: Peach liqueur

NECTARINES

The botanical name for nectarines is *Prunus persican*, meaning "Persian plum", although these smooth-skinned fruits are a variant of peaches and natives of China. They taste very similar to peaches, with a touch more acidity. The flesh can be yellow, white or pinkish and is delicate and sweet. Unlike peaches, they

do not require peeling, so some people prefer them as a dessert fruit. They can be prepared and cooked in exactly the same way as peaches. Nectarines are sometimes crossed with peaches, but the fuzzy peach skin is generally dominant, so the hybrids are often actually peaches.

Left: Smooth-skinned white nectarines

Nutrition

Nectarines have a lower calorie count than peaches (containing only about 45 kilocalories per 100g/3¾oz). They are a good source of potassium and phosphorus, dietary fibre and vitamins A and C.

Buying and Storing

Like peaches, nectarines do not continue to mature after picking, so choose ripe fruit. The skins should be bright and smooth, with no blemishes or wrinkles. Nectarines can be kept at room temperature or in the fridge for two or three days.

Left: Yellow nectarines

APRICOTS

These round, yellow-orange fruit have velvety skins flushed with pink. The flesh is firm, sweet and fragrant, and contains little juice. The kernel of the stone is edible and is used to flavour jams, biscuits and Amaretto liqueur.

Left: Ripe apricots are deliciously fragrant.

History

Apricots grew wild in China thousands of years ago and were introduced to Persia and Armenia, from where they got their Latin name *Prunus armeniaca*. Alexander the Great brought apricots to Southern Europe; they were prized by the Romans and Greeks, who called them "golden eggs of the sun". They were first successfully cultivated in Northern Europe in the sixteenth century.

Nutrition

Apricots contain the antioxidant beta-carotene, and are a rich source of minerals and vitamin A. An average 65g/2½oz apricot provides only 20 kilocalories.

Above: Turkish sun-dried apricots

Below: Semi-dried apricots

Buying and Storing

Apricots do not travel well, nor do they continue to ripen after picking, so those that you buy may be disappointing. Look for plump fruit with a rich colour and smooth skin. Do not buy dull-looking or greenish fruit, as their flesh will be woolly. Keep apricots at room temperature for a couple of days, or store in a polythene bag in the fridge for up to five days.

Dried and canned apricots Because apricots are so delicate, they are often preserved by drying or canning. The best dried apricots come from Turkey; they are burnished orange and have a rich flavour. Dried apricots can be substituted for fresh apricots and make excellent jams. Use them just as they are in slow-cooked dishes that contain plenty of liquid, like stews and casseroles, but, unless they are semi-dried, soak them in warm water for a couple of hours before using them in sweet dishes.

Preparing and Cooking

Ripe apricots are delicious raw and can be used in fruit salads and platters. Because

Right: Canned apricots

the flesh is dry, they will not disintegrate during cooking, which makes them ideal for tarts, flans and Danish pastries. Apricots can be poached in syrup or sweet white wine and served with yogurt or spice-flavoured ice cream; they are also very tasty when halved, stuffed with crushed amaretti biscuits and baked, or caramelized and served over *pain perdu*. Apricots make wonderful jams and conserves.

Both fresh and dried apricots make frequent appearances in Middle Eastern and North African recipes, where they go particularly well with lamb, poultry and rice dishes.

PLUMS

There are thousands of varieties of plum, all differing in size, shape, colour and flavour. These members of the rose family originate from three main types – European, Japanese and Western Asian. The skins can vary from blue-black to purple, red, green and yellow. They have a long season, and one variety or another is available almost all year round. All plums have smooth skins with a bloom and juicy flesh with plenty of acidity.

Dessert plums can be eaten on their own; they are usually larger than cooking plums (up to 10cm/4in long) and are sweet and very juicy. Cooking plums are drier, with tart flesh that is ideal for pies, flans and cakes.

Right: Victorias are the most prolific dessert plum.

History

Wild plums originated in Asia at least 2,000 years ago. They were first cultivated by the Assyrians, then adopted by the Romans, who hybridized them with great enthusiasm; the historian Pliny wrote of the huge numbers of plum cross-breeds available. The Crusaders brought plums to Europe, where they became highly prized. Nowadays they are grown in almost all temperate countries.

Varieties

There are over 2,000 varieties of plum, ripening at different times throughout summer and autumn, although only a dozen or so are available in the shops. Japanese varieties are large, round and juicy; they can be purplish-red with orange flesh, or orangey-yellow

with yellow flesh. On the whole, dark-coloured plums have bitter skins, while the red and yellow varieties tend to be sweeter. Most dessert plums can be cooked as well as eaten raw.

DESSERT PLUMS

Denniston's Superb An early variety of plum, with medium-size green fruits flushed with red. These plums have an excellent sweet flavour.
Gaviota These large round plums have yellow skins deeply tinged with scarlet, and sweet, juicy red flesh. They are best eaten raw.
Marjorie's Seedling These small purple plums with a green flush have bitter skins and sweet, green, almost translucent flesh. They are good for eating raw and for cooking.
Santa Rosa and **Burbank** Large and round, with bright red skins, these two North American varieties of plum are mainly grown in California. They have juicy, deep yellow flesh and a pleasantly tart flavour, which makes them good for both cooking and eating raw.

Above: Mirabelles – the golden-skinned variety of these small wild plums, which grow on long stalks like cherries, are best when cooked.

Victoria The most prolific of all dessert plums, Victorias were first cultivated in 1840 from a stray seedling found in Sussex, England. Since then, these large oval fruits with yellow skins flushed with scarlet, and sweet, juicy flesh have become ubiquitous. They are good for bottling and canning, stewing or eating raw.

Left: Marjorie's Seedling have sweet, almost transluscent green flesh and are good for cooking and eating raw.

COOKING PLUMS

Beach plums These small plums grow wild along the Atlantic coast of North America, especially near Cape Cod. They have dark purplish-black skins and tart flesh which makes them unsuitable for eating raw, but they make excellent jams and jellies.

Cherry plums or **Mirabelles** These very small wild plums are round and grow on long stalks like cherries. They have black, red or yellow skins, which can taste rather bitter, but all have sweet, juicy flesh. These plums can be eaten raw, but are best stewed or baked, or made into jams, sauces and jellies. Golden mirabelles are delicious in tarts and soufflés, and are also made into a plum *eau-de-vie*, called Mirabelle.

Czar Large, rather acidic dark blue-black plums with golden flesh, these can be eaten raw, but are more usually used for cooking. They are best eaten straight from the tree.

Nutrition

Plums contain more antioxidant than any other fruit. They provide about 40 kilocalories per 100g/3¾oz.

Buying and Storing

Plums are delicate, so make sure that the ones you buy are unblemished. They should be plump and firm, with some "give" (but never squashy), and they should be fully coloured for their variety. Plums should always have a pleasant aroma.

These fruit ripen rapidly and quickly become overripe, so store them in the fridge for only a day or two. For cooking at a

Above: Angelino – the skin colour varies from red to almost black, but the flesh of these plums is always yellow.

Left: Sweet-tasting Avalon plums

Below: Red-fleshed Spanish Autumn Rose plums

Quetsch Also known as *Svetsch* or *Zwetschen*, these small purplish-black plums have a beautiful bloom. Although their flesh is sweet, they are seldom eaten raw, but are used in Eastern Europe to make plum breads and *pflaumenkuchen*, yeast dough topped with purple plums. Quetsch plums are also used for making Slivovitz and other plum brandies.

Other varieties of note Angelino, Autumn Rose, Avalon, Circiela Queen Rose, Reeves Seedling, Stanley and Sungold

later date, plums can be frozen: halve
the fruit and remove the stones. Place
on trays and open freeze, then pack the
fruit into polythene bags and seal.

Preparing and Cooking

Dessert plums are delicious eaten on
their own. Dual varieties (suitable for
eating and cooking) and cooking
plums make excellent pies and tarts,
compotes, crumbles, dumplings,
sauces, mousses and soufflés. They can
be poached, baked or stewed, either
whole or in halves or slices. It is not
recommended that plums with tough
skins are cooked in the microwave, as
they will not soften in the short cooking
time. Cook plums until just tender; do
not let them disintegrate. Plums
make tasty ice cream, and the
poached fruit goes very well
with ice creams flavoured
with spices like cardamom,
nutmeg and cinnamon.

Plums go extremely well in
savoury dishes. The Chinese make
them into a thick sweet-sour sauce to
serve with Peking duck, lamb or pork.
Spiced stewed plums are good with
gammon, cured meats, terrines and
poultry. Plums add a special flavour to
beef or lamb casseroles.

Plums also make superb jams
and jellies. They can be
preserved in many different

Above: Circiela Queen Rose

Below: Reeves Seedling

Below: Stanley

ways; dried (as prunes), crystallized and
candied, bottled or made into wine,
liqueurs and plum brandy.

Preserved plums There are many ways
of preserving plums, the best-known
being by drying them as prunes. In
Spain, Elvas plums are partially dried,
then rolled in granulated sugar. The
Portuguese candy sweet greengages,
while Carlsbad plums (named after
the spa town, now Karlovy Vary)
are a speciality of the Czech
Republic. These plums
(usually Quetsch) are
candied in hot syrup
until shrivelled, then
halved and stuffed into
dried damsons. The
process gives them a very
intense flavour. Carlsbad plums are
considered a great delicacy and are
packed into attractive wooden boxes.

Soaking prunes

Sometimes prunes need to be soaked for at least 4 hours before using. Place in a bowl and cover with cold water or tepid weak tea for added flavour. Leave overnight if possible to plump up. For compotes and purées it is not necessary to soak the prunes; cook them directly in wine, water or fruit juice until very tender.

Prunes These wrinkled dried purple or red plums can be prepared in various ways. The plums can be left to dry naturally on the tree, but are more often sun-dried. They can also be desiccated in a low oven. The finest variety of "pruning" plum is the Agen, which is grown in France and California. These prunes are sold complete with stones and must be soaked overnight before being cooked.

Left: Chinese plum sauce has a wonderful sweet-sour flavour and is classically served with Peking duck.

Nowadays, stoned no-soak prunes are also widely available, but they tend to be flabbier than the traditional variety. Apart from their famed laxative qualities, prunes have other healthful properites. They are said to be an excellent cure for hangovers, give a great energy boost, and are purported to be an aphrodisiac.

Culinary Uses

Cooked prunes are traditionally served with custard, but they are equally good with thick cream. They make excellent ice cream, especially when combined with Armagnac. Prunes are often used in savoury dishes, particularly in Middle Eastern cooking, and they go extremely well with pork and chicken. They are an essential ingredient in Scottish cock-a-leekie soup. They go well with citrus flavours and can be made into a compote with red wine and orange or lemon zest.

Below: Californian prunes

Left: Slivovitz – black Madjarka plums are crushed with their stones and slowly fermented to make this eau-de-vie from Croatia.

Puréed prunes can be sweetened, then spiced up with a little ground cinnamon or nutmeg and served as a sauce with vanilla ice cream.

Below: French Agen prunes

GREENGAGES

These small members of the plum family have green skins, sometimes tinged with yellow or rose pink, which turn golden as the fruit ripens. There are many varieties of greengage; all have firm flesh and a delicious honeyed flavour. "Transparent" gages have fine, translucent flesh; if you hold the fruit up to the light, you can clearly see the shadow of the stone. These golden gages have a particularly sweet flavour.

History

Wild greengages from Asia Minor were probably introduced to Britain by the Romans, but disappeared from cultivation until Sir Thomas Gage brought them from France in the eighteenth century (and gave them his name). In France, they are known as *Reine-Claude* after the wife of François I, who adored their sweet flavour.

Preparing and Cooking

The deliciously sweet flavour of greengages makes them ideal for eating raw. They can also be gently poached in syrup, puréed for mousses and fools or made into excellent compotes and jam.

Below: Greengages, named after Sir Thomas Gage, have firm flesh with a deliciously sweet flavour.

DAMSONS

These small plum-like fruits take their name from Damascus, which is probably where they originated. They have deep blue-black skins with an attractive bloom. The flavour is very strong and tart, which makes them more suitable for cooking than eating raw. Damsons grow wild in hedgerows, but are also commercially available.

Preparing and Cooking

Damsons can be stewed and used in pies, tarts, ice creams and fools, but they are most commonly used for bottling or for jams and jellies. Once cooked with sugar, they develop a pleasantly spicy flavour. A traditional old English sweetmeat is damson cheese, very thick fruit pulp boiled with sugar to make a solid jam similar to quince cheese, which can be eaten with bread and butter or biscuits.

The tart flavour of damsons makes them particularly suitable for savoury dishes, such as pork or lamb casseroles. The fruit can also be made into wine or damson gin.

Above: Once cooked, damsons have a pleasantly spicy flavour.

Damson cheese

Damson cheese is a traditional English country dish with a very distinctive flavour, which is an acquired taste. The "cheese" is potted and aged for several months before being eaten. To make 2.5kg/5½lb damson cheese, put 1.5kg/3½lb damsons in a saucepan, barely cover with water and simmer until the flesh is so tender that it falls off the stones. Sieve the pulp, weigh it and return it to the pan with three-quarters of its weight in soft light brown sugar. Boil until the jam is clear, skimming the surface frequently. Pot the jam in oiled straight-sided containers, seal and leave in a cool dark place for at least two months. Serve with bread and butter, and eat with a knife and fork.

BULLACES

The small round plums known as "black bullaces" have bluish-purple skins and mouth-puckeringly acid flesh. So-called "white" bullaces are pale greenish-yellow. They can be found throughout Europe in late autumn growing in thorny hedgerows long after the other wild fruits like sloes and blackberries have finished. Although very bitter and virtually inedible when raw, bullaces can be cooked with sugar to make pies and tarts. They are also good for jams and other preserves.

Right: The pale greenish-yellow fruits, known as "white" bullaces are almost inedible raw, but can be cooked with sugar to make delicious jams and jellies or a filling for pies.

SLOES

Sloes are the fruit of the blackthorn, a thorny shrub, which grows wild throughout Europe (hence its botanical name, *prunus spinosa,* which means spiny plum). These small wild fruits resemble tiny plums. The blue-black skins have a slight bloom. The flesh is highly astringent and cannot be eaten raw. Sloes ripen late and can be picked from the hedgerows in autumn, but they only become edible after the first frosts. They can be made into jams, jellies, sloe wine and liqueurs, but their chief claim to fame is that they are the principal ingredient of the irresistible sloe gin.

Make sloe gin as soon as the fruit is ripe, and with any luck you'll have a bottle ready in time for Christmas. For each 750ml/1¼ pint bottle of gin, you will need 250g/9oz/2 cups sloes and 130g/4½oz/generous ½ cup caster sugar. Wash the sloes and prick them all over with a darning needle. Pack them loosely into a perfectly clean flagon or bottle, add the sugar and top up with gin. If you like, add two or three drops of almond essence and shake well. Seal and leave for at least three months before drinking, shaking the bottles three times a week. If pricking the sloes seems too much trouble, freeze them for several hours to crack the skin. Purists however allege that this compromises the flavour of the gin.

Left: Sloes are small wild fruits, which grow in hedgerows throughout Europe. They are best picked in late autumn, after the first frosts.

CHERRIES

Cherry trees in blossom are one of the great delights of spring, followed in summer by clusters of bright shiny fruit hanging in pairs from long, elegant stalks. The skin of these small round stone fruits can vary in colour from pale creamy-yellow to deepest red or almost black. The firm juicy flesh can be sweet or sour, depending on the variety, of which there are hundreds. Cherries are categorized into three main groups: sweet (for eating), sour (for cooking) and hybrids such as the nobly named Dukes and Royals, which are suitable for eating raw or cooking.

History

The original wild sweet cherries, known as Mazzards, were found in Asia Minor and were cultivated by the Chinese 3,000 years ago. Mazzards were known to the Ancient Egyptians, Greeks and Romans, and still exist today. Sour cherries were brought to Rome from Greece and all modern varieties derive from these early specimens.

Varieties

Sweet cherries fall into two main groups: **Bigarreaus,** with firm, crisp flesh, and **Geans** or **Guines,** with a softer texture. Today, there are also many hybrids. Sour cherries range from almost sweet to bitter and tart; they are full of flavour and are mainly used for preserving or in the manufacture of liqueurs.

SWEET CHERRIES

BIGARREAUS The best-known of these are the **Napoleons,** large pale yellow cherries tinged with light red. Their crisp fragrant flesh is slightly tart. **Bing** cherries are large, heart-shaped deep red fruit with a superb flavour. They are widely grown in North America. **GEANS/GUINES** These fruits have soft, juicy flesh and come in many colours. **Black Tartarian** are deep purplish-black from the skin right through to the stone. **Early Rivers** have dark purple skins and flesh, and very small stones. They are fragrant, sweet and juicy. **Ranier** has golden skin with a pink blush. The famous Swiss black cherry jam is made from intensely dark guines.

Above: Bright red Colney cherries

Left: Napoleons are one of the sweet cherry varieties, with slightly crisp, tart, fragrant flesh.

Left: Widely grown in North America, sweet Bing cherries have a superb flavour.

SOUR CHERRIES

Most sour cherries are too tart to eat, but are ideal for cooking. The two main types are **Morello** and **Amarelle**. Morellos have dark juice, and amarelles have light, almost colourless juice. The small, dark red morello cherries (known in France as *griottes*) are inedible raw, but are delicious preserved in either brandy or syrup.

Montmorency These are bright red cherries with a sweet-sour flavour. They have given their name to a range of dishes which include the fruit, from duck to gâteaux and ice creams.

English cherries are small, bright orange-red fruit with soft translucent flesh. They are mainly used for preserving in brandy.

Above: Dried sour Montmorency and Bing cherries

Left and below: Maraschino cherries may be bottled with their stalks.

Right: Morello cherries, which are often preserved in brandy.

Maraschino cherries
These small wild fruit from Dalmatia are *Damasca* or *Amaresca* cherries. They are distilled into a colourless sweet, sticky Italian liqueur called Maraschino. The familiar bottled Maraschino cherries beloved of barmen were originally Damasca cherries preserved in Maraschino liqueur; nowadays, the vibrant red fruits sold as "maraschino" tend to be ordinary cherries tinted with artificial colouring and steeped in syrup flavoured with bitter almonds. Check the label before buying.

Nutrition

Cherries contain vitamins A and C and some dietary fibre. Their calorie content varies with the type; sweet cherries provide about 77 kilocalories per 100g/3¾oz, while the same quantity of sour fruit provides about 56 kilocalories.

Buying and Storing

Choose plump cherries with shiny, unblemished skins. It is best to buy them still on the stalk. As a rule of thumb, pale cherries are very sweet, while dark cherries tend to be more acidic; if possible, taste before you buy.

Unwashed cherries will keep for a few days in the fridge; wash them just before using. They can also be removed from their stalks and frozen.

Preparing and Cooking

Sweet cherries often need no preparation other than washing and are best eaten on their own or in fruit salads. They make unusual sweets when left on the stalk and dipped into melted dark chocolate. Stoned fresh cherries make a delicious filling for sponge cakes and pavlovas, or an attractive decoration for gâteaux and desserts. There is no reason not to cook with sweet cherries, but they may not have much flavour, due to their low acidity. Although fresh cherries can be served as they are, for cooking they should be stoned.

Cherries can be preserved by drying in the sun or in a low oven, or by placing in sugar or brandy. Candied – or glacé – cherries are a popular ingredient in baking.

Dual-purpose and sour cherries can be cooked in tarts, pies, compotes and sauces. They go well with sweet spices, citrus flavours and chocolate; the classic combination of cherries and chocolate is found in Black Forest Gâteau. In Eastern Europe, they are made into a sweet-sour soup or pickled in spiced vinegar as an accompaniment for rich meats. Cherries go well with all game and are classically served with duck. Amarelle and Morello cherries are used for making jam and preserves, or for crystallizing as glacé cherries.

Below: Brightly coloured, sweet and sticky glacé cherries are a popular baking ingredient.

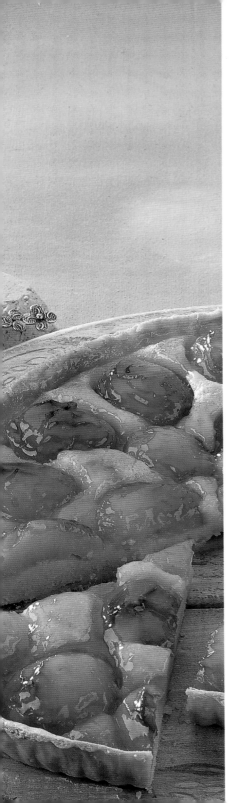

STONE FRUIT RECIPES

Juicy and full of flavour, peaches, plums, apricots, cherries and nectarines make perfect partners for crisp pastry. Try the irresistible Baked Lattice Peaches or Plum and Marzipan Pastries. For simpler, but equally delicious desserts, plump for Peach Melba Syllabub or Plum and Custard Creams.

PLUM AND CUSTARD CREAMS

IF YOU WERE RELUCTANTLY RAISED ON STEWED PLUMS AND CUSTARD, THIS SOPHISTICATED VERSION, PRETTILY LAYERED IN A GLASS, WILL BRING A SMILE TO YOUR LIPS.

SERVES SIX

INGREDIENTS
    675g/1½lb red plums, stoned
      and sliced
    grated rind and juice of 1 orange
    50g/2oz/¼ cup caster sugar
    400g/14oz carton ready-made
      custard
    300ml/½ pint/1¼ cups double cream
    30ml/2 tbsp water
    15ml/1 tbsp powdered gelatine
    1 egg white
    plum slices and fresh mint sprigs,
      to decorate

COOK'S TIP
Use a long metal skewer or thin metal spoon handle to marble the custard and plum purée mixtures together.

1 Put the plums in a saucepan with the orange rind and juice. Add the caster sugar and heat, stirring constantly, until the sugar has dissolved. Cook the plums for 5 minutes until tender. Cool slightly, then purée in a food processor until smooth. Press through a sieve into a bowl and set aside to cool.

2 Put the custard in a saucepan, add half the cream and heat until boiling. Meanwhile, pour the water into a heatproof bowl and sprinkle the gelatine on top; set aside for 5 minutes until sponged. Whisk the soaked gelatine into the hot custard until it has dissolved. Allow the mixture to cool.

3 Whip the remaining cream to soft peaks, then fold it into the custard mixture. In a grease-free bowl, whisk the egg white to soft peaks; fold it into the custard too. Set aside, stirring occasionally, until just starting to set.

4 Quickly spoon alternate spoonfuls of the custard and plum purée into six tall dessert glasses. Marble the mixtures together. Chill for 2–3 hours or until the custard has set. Decorate each dessert with plum slices and fresh mint sprigs just before serving.

SPICED FRUITS JUBILEE

BASED ON THE CLASSIC CHERRIES JUBILEE, THIS IS A GREAT WAY TO USE A GLUT OF ANY STONE FRUIT. THE SPICED SYRUP IS A DELICIOUS BONUS. SERVE WITH THE BEST DAIRY VANILLA ICE CREAM.

SERVES SIX

INGREDIENTS
115g/4oz/½ cup caster sugar
thinly pared rind of 1 unwaxed lemon
1 cinnamon stick
4 whole cloves
300ml/½ pint/1¼ cups water
225g/8oz tart red plums, stoned
and sliced
225g/8oz nectarines, stoned
and chopped
225g/8oz/1½ cups cherries, stoned
5ml/1 tsp arrowroot
75ml/5 tbsp brandy
vanilla ice cream, to serve

1 Put the sugar, lemon rind, cinnamon stick, cloves and water in a pan. Bring to the boil, stirring. Lower the heat and simmer for 5 minutes, then lift out the spices with a slotted spoon and discard.

2 Add the fruit, cover the pan and simmer for 5 minutes. Drain the fruit and set it aside; return the syrup to the pan. Boil it, uncovered, for 2 minutes or until thick and syrupy.

3 Put the arrowroot in a small bowl and stir in 30ml/2 tbsp of the brandy. Stir the mixture into the syrup. Continue cooking and stirring, until the sauce thickens. Return the fruit to the pan.

4 Place scoops of ice cream in serving bowls and spoon the hot fruit over. Warm the remaining brandy in a small pan, then set it alight. Ladle it over the fruit at the table for maximum effect.

PEACH MELBA SYLLABUB

IF YOU ARE MAKING THESE SOPHISTICATED TEMPTATIONS FOR A DINNER PARTY, COOK THE PEACHES AND RASPBERRIES THE DAY BEFORE TO ALLOW THE FRUIT TO CHILL. WHIP UP THE SYLLABUB AT THE VERY LAST MINUTE TO MAKE A DELICIOUS, LIGHT-AS-A-CLOUD TOPPING.

SERVES SIX

INGREDIENTS
    4 peaches, peeled, stoned and sliced
    300ml/½ pint/1¼ cups blush or red
      grape juice
    115g/4oz/⅔ cup raspberries
    raspberry or mint leaves, to decorate
    ratafias or other dessert biscuits,
      to serve
For the syllabub
    60ml/4 tbsp peach schnapps
    30ml/2 tbsp blush or red grape juice
    300ml/½ pint/1¼ cups double cream

VARIATIONS
Use dessert pears and sliced kiwi fruit
instead of peaches and raspberries.
Instead of the syllabub, top the fruit with
whipped cream flavoured with Advocaat
and finely chopped stem ginger.

1 Place the peach slices in a large saucepan. Add the grape juice. Bring to the boil, then cover, lower the heat and simmer for 5–7 minutes or until tender.

2 Add the raspberries and remove from the heat. Set aside in the fridge until cold. Divide the peach and raspberry mixture among six dessert glasses.

3 For the syllabub, place the peach schnapps and grape juice in a large bowl and whisk in the cream until it forms soft peaks.

4 Spoon the syllabub on top of the fruit and decorate each portion with a fresh raspberry or mint leaf. Serve with ratafias or other dessert biscuits.

NECTARINE AND HAZELNUT MERINGUES

IF IT'S INDULGENCE YOU'RE SEEKING, LOOK NO FURTHER. SWEET NECTARINES AND CREAM SYLLABUB PAIRED WITH CRISP HAZELNUT MERINGUES MAKE A SUPERB SWEET.

SERVES FIVE

INGREDIENTS
    3 egg whites
    175g/6oz/¾ cup caster sugar
    50g/2oz/½ cup chopped
      hazelnuts, toasted
    300ml/½ pint/1¼ cups double cream
    60ml/4 tbsp sweet dessert wine
    2 nectarines, stoned and sliced
    fresh mint sprigs, to decorate

VARIATIONS
Use apricots instead of nectarines if you
prefer, or try this with a raspberry filling.

1 Preheat the oven to 140°C/275°F/ Gas 1. Line two large baking sheets with non-stick baking paper. Whisk or beat the egg whites in a grease-free bowl until they form stiff peaks when the whisk or beaters are lifted. Gradually whisk in the caster sugar a spoonful at a time until the mixture forms a stiff, glossy meringue.

2 Fold in two-thirds of the chopped toasted hazelnuts, then spoon five large ovals on to each lined baking sheet. Scatter the remaining hazelnuts over five of the meringue ovals. Flatten the tops of the remaining five ovals.

3 Bake the meringues for 1–1¼ hours until crisp and dry, then carefully lift them off the baking paper and cool completely on a wire rack.

4 Whip the cream with the dessert wine until the mixture forms soft peaks. Spoon some of the cream syllabub on to each of the plain meringues. Arrange a few nectarine slices on each. Put each meringue on a dessert plate with a hazelnut-topped meringue. Decorate each portion with mint sprigs and serve the meringues immediately.

BLACK CHERRY CLAFOUTIS

THIS FAVOURITE RECIPE HAS BEEN REPRODUCED WITH ALL MANNER OF FRUIT, BUT YOU SIMPLY CAN'T BEAT THE CLASSIC VERSION USING SLIGHTLY TART BLACK CHERRIES.

SERVES SIX

INGREDIENTS
25g/1oz/2 tbsp butter, for greasing
450g/1lb/2 cups black
   cherries, stoned
25g/1oz/¼ cup plain flour
50g/2oz/½ cup icing sugar, plus extra
   for dusting
4 eggs, beaten
250ml/8fl oz/1 cup creamy milk
30ml/2 tbsp Kirsch

1 Preheat the oven to 180°C/350°F/ Gas 4. Use the butter to thickly grease a 1.2 litre/2 pint/5 cup gratin dish. Scatter the cherries over the base.

2 Sift the flour and icing sugar together into a large mixing bowl and gradually whisk in the eggs until the mixture is smooth. Whisk in the milk until blended, then stir in the Kirsch.

3 Pour the batter carefully over the cherries, then bake for 35–45 minutes or until just set and lightly golden.

4 Allow the pudding to cool for about 15 minutes. Dust liberally with icing sugar just before serving.

VARIATIONS
Try other liqueurs in this dessert. Almond-flavoured liqueur is delicious teamed with cherries. Hazelnut, raspberry or orange liqueur would also work nicely.

ICED GIN AND DAMSON SOUFFLÉS

FOR AN UNFORGETTABLE TASTE SENSATION, USE SLOE GIN FOR THESE DELICIOUS INDIVIDUAL FROZEN SOUFFLÉS. THEY ARE PERFECT FOR A PARTY AND CAN BE MADE AHEAD.

MAKES SIX

INGREDIENTS
    500g/1¼lb damsons
    250ml/8fl oz/1 cup water
    275g/10oz/1¼ cups caster sugar
    30ml/2 tbsp gin or sloe gin
    4 large egg whites
    300ml/½ pint/1¼ cups double
      cream, whipped
    fresh mint leaves, to decorate

1 You will need six 150ml/¼ pint/⅔ cup ramekins. Give each a collar of greased non-stick baking paper that extends about 5cm/2in above the rim.

2 Slice two damsons and set aside for the decoration. Put the rest of the damsons in a pan with half the water and 50g/2oz/¼ cup of the caster sugar. Cover and simmer the mixture for about 7 minutes, or until the damsons are tender. Press the pulp through a sieve placed over a bowl to remove all the stones and skin, then stir in the gin or sloe gin and set aside.

3 Combine the remaining sugar and water in the clean pan and heat gently until the sugar has dissolved. Bring to the boil and cook the syrup until it registers 119°C/238°F on a sugar thermometer, or until a small amount of the mixture dropped into a cup of cold water can be moulded to a soft ball.

4 Meanwhile, whisk the egg whites in a grease-free bowl until they form stiff peaks. Still whisking, slowly pour in the hot syrup until the meringue mixture is stiff and glossy. Fold in the whipped cream and fruit purée until combined.

5 Spoon into the dishes to come 2.5cm/1in above the rim of each. Freeze until firm. Remove from the freezer 10 minutes before serving. Remove the collars, then decorate each with damson slices and mint leaves.

CARAMELIZED APRICOTS WITH PAIN PERDU

PAIN PERDU IS A FRENCH INVENTION THAT LITERALLY TRANSLATES AS "LOST BREAD". AMERICANS CALL IT FRENCH TOAST, WHILE A BRITISH VERSION IS KNOWN AS POOR KNIGHTS OF WINDSOR.

SERVES FOUR

INGREDIENTS

75g/3oz/6 tbsp unsalted
    butter, clarified
450g/1lb apricots, stoned and
    thickly sliced
115g/4oz/½ cup caster sugar
150ml/¼ pint/⅔ cup double cream
30ml/2 tbsp apricot brandy or brandy
For the pain perdu
600ml/1 pint/2½ cups milk
1 vanilla pod
50g/2oz/¼ cup caster sugar
4 large eggs, beaten
115g/4oz/½ cup unsalted
    butter, clarified
6 brioche slices, diagonally halved
2.5ml/½ tsp ground cinnamon

1 Heat a heavy-based frying pan, then melt a quarter of the butter. Add the apricot slices and cook for 2–3 minutes until golden. Using a slotted spoon, transfer them to a bowl. Add the rest of the butter to the pan with the sugar and heat gently, stirring, until golden.

2 Pour in the cream and apricot or brandy and cook gently until the mixture forms a smooth sauce. Boil for 2–3 minutes until thickened, pour the sauce over the apricots and set aside.

3 To make the pain perdu, pour the milk into a saucepan and add the vanilla pod and half the sugar. Heat gently until almost boiling, then set aside to cool.

4 Remove the vanilla pod and pour the flavoured milk into a shallow dish. Whisk in the eggs. Heat a sixth of the butter in the clean frying pan. Dip each slice of brioche in turn into the milk mixture, add it to the pan and fry until golden brown on both sides. Add the remaining butter as needed. As the pain perdu is cooked, remove the slices; keep hot.

5 Warm the apricot sauce and spoon it on to the pain perdu. Mix the remaining sugar with the cinnamon and sprinkle a little of the mixture over each portion.

COOK'S TIP
To clarify the butter, melt it in a small saucepan, then leave it to stand for a few minutes. Carefully pour the clear butter (the clarified butter) on the surface into a small bowl, leaving the milky solids behind in the pan.

FRESH CHERRY AND HAZELNUT STRUDEL

SERVE THIS WONDERFUL OLD-WORLD TREAT AS A WARM DESSERT WITH CUSTARD, OR ALLOW IT TO COOL AND OFFER IT AS A SCRUMPTIOUS CAKE WITH AFTERNOON TEA OR COFFEE.

SERVES SIX TO EIGHT

INGREDIENTS
75g/3oz/6 tbsp butter
90ml/6 tbsp light muscovado sugar
3 egg yolks
grated rind of 1 lemon
1.5ml/¼ tsp grated nutmeg
250g/9oz/generous 1 cup ricotta
  cheese
8 large sheets filo pastry, thawed
  if frozen
75g/3oz ratafias, crushed
450g/1lb/2½ cups cherries, stoned
30ml/2 tbsp chopped hazelnuts
icing sugar, for dusting
crème fraîche, to serve

1 Preheat the oven to 190°C/375°F/ Gas 5. Soften 15g/½oz/1 tbsp of the butter. Place it in a bowl and beat in the sugar and egg yolks until light and fluffy. Beat in the lemon rind, nutmeg and ricotta, then set aside.

2 Melt the remaining butter in a small pan. Working quickly, place a sheet of filo on a clean tea towel and brush it generously with melted butter. Place a second sheet on top and repeat the process. Continue until all the filo has been layered and buttered, reserving some of the melted butter.

3 Scatter the crushed ratafias over the top, leaving a 5cm/2in border around the outside. Spoon the ricotta mixture over the biscuits, spread it lightly to cover, then scatter over the cherries.

4 Fold in the filo pastry border and use the dish towel to carefully roll up the strudel, Swiss-roll style, beginning from one of the long sides of the pastry. Grease a baking sheet with the remaining melted butter.

5 Place the strudel on the baking sheet and scatter the hazelnuts over the surface. Bake for 35–40 minutes or until the strudel is golden and crisp. Dust with icing sugar and serve with a dollop of crème fraîche.

BAKED LATTICE PEACHES

IF YOU WOULD RATHER USE NECTARINES FOR THE RECIPE, THERE'S NO NEED TO PEEL THEM FIRST.

MAKES SIX

INGREDIENTS

3 peaches
juice of ½ lemon
75g/3oz/scant ½ cup white marzipan
375g/13oz ready-rolled puff pastry,
  thawed if frozen
a large pinch of ground cinnamon
beaten egg, to glaze
caster sugar, for sprinkling
For the caramel sauce
  50g/2oz/¼ cup caster sugar
  30ml/2 tbsp cold water
  150ml/¼ pint/⅔ cup double cream

1 Preheat the oven to 190°C/375°F/
Gas 5. Place the peaches in a large
bowl and pour over boiling water to
cover. Leave for 60 seconds, then drain
the peaches and peel off the skins. Toss
the skinned fruit in the lemon juice to
stop them going brown.

2 Divide the marzipan into six pieces
and shape each to form a small round.
Cut the peaches in half and remove
their stones. Fill the stone cavity in each
with a marzipan round.

3 Unroll the puff pastry and cut it in
half. Set one half aside, then cut out six
rounds from the rest, making each
round slightly larger than a peach half.
Sprinkle a little cinnamon on each
pastry round, then place a peach half,
marzipan side down, on the pastry.

4 Cut the remaining pastry into lattice
pastry, using a special cutter if you have
one. If not, simply cut small slits in rows
all over the pastry, starting each row
slightly lower than the last. Cut the
lattice pastry into six equal squares.

5 Dampen the edges of the pastry
rounds with a little water, then drape a
lattice pastry square over each peach
half. Press around the edge to seal,
then trim off the excess pastry and
decorate with small peach leaves made
from the trimmings. Transfer the peach
pastries to a baking sheet. Brush with
the beaten egg and sprinkle with the
caster sugar. Bake for 20 minutes or
until the pastries are golden.

6 Meanwhile, make the caramel sauce.
Heat the sugar with the water in a small
pan until it dissolves. Bring to the boil
and continue to boil until the syrup
turns a dark golden brown. Stand back
and add the cream. Heat gently, stirring
until smooth. Serve the peach pastries
with the sauce.

COOK'S TIP
Take care when adding the cream to the
hot caramel as the mixture is liable to
spit. Pour it from a jug, protecting your
hand with an oven glove, and use a long-
handled wooden spoon for stirring.

PEACH AND REDCURRANT TARTLETS

TART REDCURRANTS AND SWEET PEACHES MAKE A WINNING COMBINATION IN THESE SIMPLE TARTLETS.

MAKES FOUR

INGREDIENTS
   25g/1oz/2 tbsp butter, melted
   16 × 15cm/6in squares of filo pastry,
     thawed if frozen
   redcurrant sprigs, to decorate
   icing sugar, for dusting
For the filling
   150ml/¼ pint/⅔ cup double cream
   125g/4¼oz carton peach and mango
     fromage frais
   a few drops of pure vanilla essence
   15ml/1 tbsp icing sugar, sifted
For the topping
   2 peaches
   50g/2oz/½ cup redcurrants

COOK'S TIP
To strip redcurrants from their stalks,
pull the stalks through the tines of a fork.

1 Preheat the oven to 190°C/375°F/
Gas 5. Use a little of the butter to grease
four large bun tins or individual tartlet
tins. Brush the pastry squares with
butter, stack them in fours, then place in
the tins to make four pastry cases.

2 Bake for 12–15 minutes until golden.
Cool the filo cases on a wire rack.

3 Make the filling. Whip the cream to
soft peaks, then lightly fold in the
fromage frais, vanilla essence and icing
sugar. Divide among the pastry cases.

4 Slice the peaches and fan them out
on top of the filling, interspersing with
a few redcurrants. Decorate with redcurrant sprigs and dust with icing sugar.

PLUM AND MARZIPAN PASTRIES

THESE DANISH PASTRIES CAN BE MADE WITH ANY STONED FRUIT. TRY APRICOTS, CHERRIES, DAMSONS
OR GREENGAGES, ADDING A GLAZE MADE FROM CLEAR HONEY OR A COMPLEMENTARY JAM.

MAKES SIX

INGREDIENTS
   375g/13oz ready-rolled puff pastry
   90ml/6 tbsp plum jam
   115g/4oz/½ cup white
     marzipan, coarsely grated
   3 red plums, halved and stoned
   1 egg, beaten
   50g/2oz/½ cup flaked almonds
For the glaze
   30ml/2 tbsp plum jam
   15ml/1 tbsp water

1 Preheat the oven to 220°C/425°F/
Gas 7. Unroll the pastry, cut it into six
equal squares and place on one or two
dampened baking sheets.

2 Spoon 15ml/1 tbsp jam into the
centre of each pastry square. Divide the
marzipan among them. Place half a
plum, hollow-side down, on top of each
marzipan mound.

3 Brush the edges of the pastry with
beaten egg. Bring up the corners and
press them together lightly, then open
out the pastry corners at the top. Glaze
the pastries with a little beaten egg,
then press a sixth of the flaked almonds
on to each.

4 Bake the pastries for 20–25 minutes
or until they are lightly golden.

5 Meanwhile, make the glaze by
heating the jam and water in a small
pan, stirring until smooth. Press the
mixture through a sieve into a small
bowl, then brush it over the tops of the
pastries while they are still warm. Leave
to cool on a wire rack.

YELLOW PLUM TART

IN THIS TART, GLAZED YELLOW PLUMS SIT ATOP A DELECTABLE ALMOND FILLING IN A CRISP PASTRY SHELL. WHEN THEY ARE IN SEASON, GREENGAGES MAKE AN EXCELLENT ALTERNATIVE TO THE PLUMS.

SERVES EIGHT

INGREDIENTS
   175g/6oz/1½ cups plain flour
   a pinch of salt
   75g/3oz/scant ½ cup butter, chilled
   30ml/2 tbsp caster sugar
   a few drops of pure vanilla essence
   45ml/3 tbsp iced water
   cream or custard, to serve
For the filling
   75g/3oz/⅓ cup caster sugar
   75g/3oz/scant ½ cup butter, softened
   75g/3oz/¾ cup ground almonds
   1 egg, beaten
   30ml/2 tbsp plain flour
   450g/1lb yellow plums or greengages,
      halved and stoned
For the glaze
   45ml/3 tbsp apricot jam, sieved
   15ml/1 tbsp water

1 Sift the flour and salt into a bowl, then rub in the chilled butter until the mixture resembles fine breadcrumbs. Stir in the caster sugar, vanilla essence and enough of the iced water to make a soft dough.

COOK'S TIP
Ceramic baking beans are ideal for baking blind, but any dried beans will do. You can use them over and over again, but make sure you keep them in a special jar, separate from the rest of your dried beans, as you cannot use them for conventional cooking.

2 Knead the dough gently on a lightly floured surface until smooth, then wrap in clear film and chill for 10 minutes.

3 Preheat the oven to 200°C/400°F/ Gas 6. Roll out the pastry and line a 23cm/9in fluted flan tin, allowing excess pastry to overhang the top. Prick the base with a fork and line with non-stick baking paper and baking beans.

4 Bake blind for 10 minutes, remove the paper and beans, then return the pastry case to the oven for 10 minutes. Remove and allow to cool. Trim off any excess pastry with a sharp knife.

5 To make the filling, whisk or beat together all the ingredients except the plums or greengages. Spread on the base of the pastry case. Arrange the plums or greengages on top, cut side down. Make a glaze by heating the jam with the water. Strain through a sieve into a small bowl then brush a little of the jam glaze over the top of the fruit.

6 Bake the tart for 50–60 minutes, until the almond filling is cooked and the plums or greengages are tender. Warm any remaining jam glaze and brush it over the top. Cut into slices and serve with cream or custard.

APRICOT PARCELS

THESE LITTLE FILO PARCELS CONTAIN A SPECIAL APRICOT AND MINCEMEAT FILLING. A GOOD WAY TO USE UP ANY MINCEMEAT AND MARZIPAN THAT HAVE BEEN IN YOUR CUPBOARD SINCE CHRISTMAS!

MAKES EIGHT

INGREDIENTS

350g/12oz filo pastry, thawed
   if frozen
50g/2oz/¼ cup butter, melted
8 apricots, halved and stoned
60ml/4 tbsp luxury mincemeat
12 ratafias, crushed
30ml/2 tbsp grated marzipan
icing sugar, for dusting

COOK'S TIP

Filo pastry dries out quickly, so keep any squares not currently being used covered under a clean damp dish towel. Also, work as quickly as possible. If the filo should turn dry and brittle, simply brush it with melted butter to moisten.

1 Preheat the oven to 200°C/400°F/ Gas 6. Cut the filo pastry into 32 × 18cm/7in squares. Brush four of the squares with a little melted butter and stack them, giving each layer a quarter turn so that the stack acquires a star shape. Repeat to make eight stars.

2 Place an apricot half, hollow up, in the centre of each pastry star. Mix together the mincemeat, crushed ratafias and marzipan and spoon a little of the mixture into the hollow in each apricot.

3 Top with another apricot half, then bring the corners of each pastry together and squeeze to make a gathered purse.

4 Place the purses on a baking sheet and brush each with a little melted butter. Bake for 15–20 minutes or until the pastry is golden and crisp. Lightly dust with icing sugar to serve. Whipped cream, flavoured with a little brandy, makes an ideal accompaniment.

CRUNCHY-TOPPED FRESH APRICOT CAKE

ALMONDS ARE PERFECT PARTNERS FOR FRESH APRICOTS, AND THIS IS A GREAT WAY TO USE UP FIRM FRUITS. SERVE COLD AS A CAKE OR WARM WITH CUSTARD FOR A DESSERT.

MAKES EIGHT SLICES

INGREDIENTS
175g/6oz/1½ cups self-raising flour
175g/6oz/¾ cup butter, softened
175g/6oz/¾ cup caster sugar
115g/4oz/1 cup ground almonds
3 eggs
5ml/1 tsp almond essence
2.5ml/½ tsp baking powder
8 firm apricots, stoned and chopped
For the topping
30ml/2 tbsp demerara sugar
50g/2oz/½ cup flaked almonds

1 Preheat the oven to 160°C/325°F/ Gas 3. Grease an 18cm/7in round cake tin and line with non-stick baking paper. Put all the cake ingredients, except the apricots, in a large mixing bowl and whisk until creamy.

2 Fold the apricots into the cake mixture, then spoon into the prepared cake tin. Make a hollow in the centre with the back of a large spoon, then scatter 15ml/1 tbsp of the demerara sugar over for the topping, with the flaked almonds.

3 Bake for 1½ hours or until a skewer inserted into the centre comes out clean. Scatter the remaining demerara sugar over the top of the cake and leave to cool for 10 minutes in the tin. Remove from the tin, peel off the paper and finish cooling on a wire rack.

PICKLED PEACH AND CHILLI CHUTNEY

THIS IS A REALLY SPICY, RICH CHUTNEY THAT IS GREAT SERVED WITH COLD ROAST MEATS SUCH AS HAM, PORK OR TURKEY. IT IS ALSO GOOD WITH A STRONG FARMHOUSE Cheddar CHEESE.

MAKES 450G/1LB

INGREDIENTS
    475ml/16fl oz/2 cups cider vinegar
    275g/10oz/1⅔ cups light
      muscovado sugar
    225g/8oz/1 cup dried dates, stoned
      and finely chopped
    5ml/1 tsp ground allspice
    5ml/1 tsp ground mace
    450g/1lb ripe peaches, stoned and
      cut into small chunks
    3 onions, thinly sliced
    4 fresh red chillies, seeded and
      finely chopped
    4 garlic cloves, crushed
    5cm/2in piece of fresh root ginger,
      finely grated
    5ml/1 tsp salt

1 Place the vinegar, sugar, dates and spices in a large saucepan and bring to the boil, stirring occasionally.

2 Add all the remaining ingredients and return to the boil. Lower the heat and simmer for 40–50 minutes or until thick. Stir often to prevent the mixture from burning on the base of the pan.

3 Spoon into sterilized jars and seal. When cold, store the jars in the fridge and use within 2 months.

COOK'S TIP
To test the consistency of the finished chutney before bottling, spoon a little of the mixture on to a plate: the chutney is ready once it holds its shape.

NECTARINE RELISH

THIS SWEET AND TANGY FRUIT RELISH GOES VERY WELL WITH HOT ROAST MEATS, ESPECIALLY PORK AND GAME BIRDS SUCH AS GUINEA FOWL AND PHEASANT. MAKE WHILE NECTARINES ARE PLENTIFUL AND KEEP TIGHTLY COVERED IN THE FRIDGE TO SERVE AT Christmas FOR A REALLY SPECIAL TREAT.

MAKES 450G/1LB

INGREDIENTS
    45ml/3 tbsp olive oil
    2 Spanish onions, thinly sliced
    1 fresh green chilli, seeded and
      finely chopped
    5ml/1 tsp finely chopped
      fresh rosemary
    2 bay leaves
    450g/1lb nectarines, stoned and cut
      into chunks
    150g/5oz/1 cup raisins
    10ml/2 tsp crushed coriander seeds
    350g/12oz/2 cups demerara sugar
    200ml/7fl oz/scant 1 cup red
      wine vinegar

1 Heat the oil in a large pan. Add the onions, chilli, rosemary and bay leaves. Cook, stirring often, for 15–20 minutes or until the onions are soft.

COOK'S TIP
Jars of this relish make a welcome gift. Add a colourful tag reminding the recipient to keep it in the fridge.

2 Add all the remaining ingredients and bring to the boil slowly, stirring often. Lower the heat and simmer for 1 hour or until the relish is thick and sticky, stirring occasionally.

3 Spoon into sterilized jars and seal. Cool, then chill. The relish will keep in the fridge for up to 5 months.

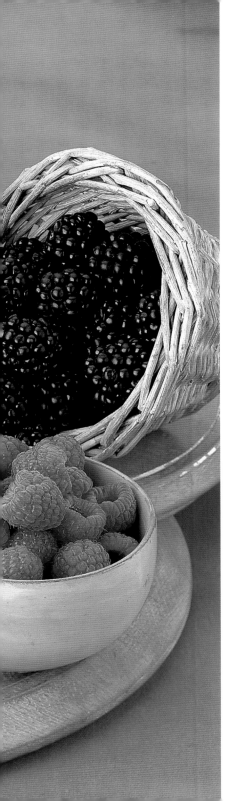

BERRIES AND CURRANTS

Small wonders — that sums up the splendour of berries.
The glowing colours and delectable flavours of strawberries and
raspberries, gooseberries, currants, loganberries and blackberries
(to name but a few of the many varieties) give us immense
pleasure. Whether you brave the brambles or pick up a punnet
at your local supermarket, these wonderful treats
are there for the taking.

STRAWBERRIES

For centuries, strawberries have been the most highly prized soft fruit. A sixteenth-century enthusiast, on tasting his first strawberry, summed up their eternal appeal: "Doubtless God could have made a better berry, but doubtless He never did". Nowadays, greenhouse-grown strawberries are available all year round, but these fruits are at their seductive best when grown outdoors.

History

Cultivated strawberries derive from the small wild fraises des bois, tiny fragrant woodland fruits that grow in all temperate countries and which were transplanted into kitchen gardens as early as Roman times. By the fourteenth century, the French had become strawberry enthusiasts, but it was another hundred years before the first bowls of strawberries and cream were served in England, at a banquet given by Cardinal Wolsey in 1509.

The cultivated strawberries we enjoy so much today were developed in the nineteenth century from small scarlet wild strawberries from Virginia. These were crossed with the larger yellow Chilean pine strawberries, which the aptly named French Captain Frézier (the French word for strawberry is *fraise*) had brought to Brittany in 1712. Once the perfect balance of flavour and size had been achieved, enthusiasm for cultivated strawberries blossomed and they remain one of the world's favourite fruits.

Varieties

Strawberries come in many different sizes, colours and shapes, ranging from conical to globular to oval or heart-shaped. New varieties are constantly being developed.

Left: Fraise de Bois liqueur is a wild strawberry version of crème de fraise.

Above: These tiny wild woodland fruits, fraises des bois, have a lovely perfumed flavour.

Below: Cultivated strawberries like these are now one of the world's favourite fruits.

Below: Fragrantly scented and vanilla-flavoured white fraises des bois.

Above: Gorella – conical-shaped and deep red when ripe.

Left: Cambridge Favourite – medium-size strawberries that are popular with both commercial growers and gardeners.

Below: Elsanta have a great flavour.

FRAISES DES BOIS

The smallest wild strawberries are the **Hautbois** varieties, whose tiny red fruits taste wonderfully fragrant. **Alpine** strawberries are generally a little larger and less juicy, with a highly perfumed flavour. Yellow and white varieties look less appealing, but have a delicious flavour of vanilla.

SUMMER STRAWBERRIES

Cambridge Favourite Medium-size berries with an attractive colour and flavour, this variety is indeed a favourite with strawberry-growers large and small.
Elsanta Largish, firm berries with attractive glossy flesh and an excellent sweet flavour.
Elvira These Dutch strawberries were developed in the 1970s. The oval berries are a deep glossy red.
Gorella A deep red conical berry with paler red flesh. This is an extremely consistent variety.
Perpetual and remontant strawberries As their name implies, these late-season strawberries go on to fruit continuously throughout the autumn. Although they are juicier than summer berries, they are not as sweet, so are better for cooking than other varieties. They can be picked while they are still green and made into jams, sauces and compotes.

Preparing strawberries

1 Wipe the strawberries with a piece of damp kitchen paper.

2 Hold the strawberry between your thumb and forefinger and twist off the green frill and stalk. Try to remove the central hull in the same movement.

Below: Chocolate-dipped strawberries make a delectable after-dinner treat, or a delightful decoration for chocolate cakes and desserts.

Nutrition

Strawberries are rich in vitamins B and C and contain considerable amounts of potassium, iron and fibre. 100g/3¾oz strawberries provide less than 30 kilocalories.

Buying and Storing

Size and colour are not necessarily indications of quality. Some smaller, greenish varieties taste succulent and delicious. Try always to buy locally grown fruits and check those at the bottom of the punnet, making sure they are not squashed or mouldy.

Strawberries should ideally be eaten the day they are bought. If this is not possible, keep the berries in the fridge for a day or two, covering them with clear film to prevent them from drying out and from permeating other foods with their scent. Remove from the fridge at least an hour before you serve them.

Frozen strawberries are never as good as fresh, as the texture collapses after freezing, but they are fine for sauces and ice cream. To freeze whole strawberries, sprinkle with a little sugar and pack in a single layer in a plastic box, or open freeze on a tray, then pack in a rigid container. Puréed strawberries can be frozen with or without added sugar.

Preparing and Serving

It is best not to wash strawberries, as they easily become waterlogged. If they are very dirty, wipe them gently.

Really ripe strawberries need no other accompaniment than cream or crème fraîche and perhaps a little sugar. Improbable though this may sound, a grinding of black pepper or sprinkling of balsamic vinegar will bring out the flavour of the fruit. Strawberries are seldom improved by cooking, although they make delicious jam. They are best used in their raw state in such desserts as strawberry tartlets, shortcake and pavlovas. They have an affinity with chocolate and make a fine decoration for chocolate terrines and mousses, or they can be dipped into melted chocolate and served as petits fours.

To "dress up" strawberries, macerate them in red wine, Champagne or orange juice. The classic dish, Strawberries Romanov, simply consists of fresh strawberries macerated in orange juice and orange liqueur. Puréed strawberries can be served as a coulis or made into ice creams and sorbets.

Arbutus (tree strawberry)

The arbutus is a tall shrub, whose bright red fruits look like strawberries, but have a different taste. The sweet spiky berries have a soft, slightly mushy texture and a faint flavour of vanilla. You will not find arbutus berries in shops, but the shrubs can be found growing in Europe, as far north as western Ireland (where they are known as Killarney strawberries), and in the United States and China. The berries are unexciting to eat raw, but are used to make jellies and liqueurs.

RASPBERRIES

Perhaps surprisingly, raspberries are a member of the rose family, as you might guess if you have ever been pricked by a raspberry thorn. Native to hilly areas of Europe and Asia, they grow best in a cool, damp climate and can be found even in Alaska. The deep red (or sometimes yellow) jewel-like fruits have a sweet, intense flavour, and indeed many people prefer them to strawberries.

History

Wild raspberries have been eaten since prehistoric times, but, perhaps because they were so plentiful in the wild, the fruits were not cultivated until the Middle Ages. Nowadays, in colder climates, raspberries are cultivated from native European raspberry varieties, while in North America, they derive from an indigenous species better suited to the drier, hotter conditions that prevail there.

Varieties

Although there are many different varieties of raspberry, and new ones are constantly being developed, those sold in shops and markets are not identified specifically. Gardeners have their own favourites:
Heritage is a late-fruiting variety with outstanding flavour.
Malling Jewel fruits in mid-season, and is a heavy cropper.
Wild raspberries You will often find these tiny, fragrant fruits growing in

Above: Raspberries – deep red fruits, with a wonderfully intense flavour.

Above: Arctic raspberries, grown in the chilly climes of Alaska.

Below: Yellow or golden raspberries are worth seeking out, since they have a delectable flavour.

cool, damp areas of woodland. They are full of pips, but their exquisite flavour makes up for this deficiency.
Yellow and golden raspberries Clear golden berries, not widely available, but worth seeking out for their fine flavour.

Nutrition

Raspberries are a valuable source of vitamin C, potassium, niacin and riboflavin, and dietary fibre. They contain 25 kilocalories per 100g/3¾oz. Raspberry juice is said to be good for the heart, while the leaves have long been renowned for their beneficial effects during childbirth; raspberry leaf tea is said to prevent miscarriages, ease labour and help the uterus to contract after the birth.

Buying and Storing

Raspberries are ripe when they are brightly and evenly coloured. They are always sold hulled, but if you are picking your own, they should slide easily off the hulls. When buying raspberries in a punnet, check the bottom to make sure it is not stained red or leaking – a sure sign that the fruit is soft and past its best.

If possible, always eat raspberries the day they are bought or picked; if necessary, they can be stored for up to two days in the bottom of the fridge, but bring them out at least an hour before serving.

Raspberries freeze very well; whole berries emerge almost as good as before. Open freeze the fruit in a single

Left: Raspberry vinegar makes a sharp, yet refreshingly fruity addition to home-made salad dressing.

layer on a baking sheet, then pack into rigid cartons. Less than perfect raspberries can be puréed and sieved, then sweetened with a little caster sugar or icing sugar before being frozen.

Preparing and Serving

Do not wash raspberries unless this is unavoidable; they are seldom very dirty, and washing will ruin the texture and flavour. All you need do is gently pick off any bits of leaf or stalk.

Good raspberries have such a wonderful flavour that they are best eaten on their own, with a little sugar and cream. They go well with other fruits, like oranges, apples, pears, figs and melon. In the classic dish, Peach Melba, raspberries are used as a coulis to coat a lightly poached peach. They also make delicious fillings for pastries, pavlovas and tartlets, and, because they look so attractive, they are ideal for decoration.

Raspberries can be crushed with a little icing sugar, then pushed through a nylon or stainless steel sieve to make sauces, coulis or bases for ice creams and sorbets. They can be cooked in pies; apple and raspberry is a classic combination. They are rich in pectin, so make excellent jams and jellies. Raspberry vinegar is delicious and makes delectable dressings and sauces.

Preparing a raspberry coulis
1 Put the raspberries in a bowl and crush to a purée with a fork.

2 Tip the purée into a sieve set over a clean bowl. Rub through, using the back of a large spoon.

3 Sweeten to taste with icing or caster sugar and stir well.

CLOUDBERRIES

These deep golden relatives of the raspberry grow on boggy land in the cold northern climates of Scandinavia, Siberia, Canada and even the Arctic Circle. Because they lack warmth, the berries ripen slowly, allowing the flavour

Left: Popular in Scandinavia, cloudberry jam makes a colourful topping for chocolate mousse or soufflé.

to develop to an extraordinary intensity and sweetness, almost like honeyed apples (Canadians call cloudberries "baked apple berries"). These unusual berries are particularly highly prized in Scandinavian countries, where they are made into excellent jams and desserts, and also into wonderful fruit soups.

Cloudberries are also distilled into a nectar-like liqueur, which tastes delicious with bitter chocolate. The berries have a particular affinity with chocolate; try topping a chocolate mousse or soufflé with a spoonful of cloudberry jam.

Above: Brightly coloured cloudberries have an amazingly intense flavour.

BLACKBERRIES ᴬᴺᴰ DEWBERRIES

These two relations of the raspberry and the rose are virtually indistinguishable, the main difference being that blackberries are larger and grow on thorny upright bushes or brambles, while dewberries trail. The shiny purplish-black berries are made up of a number of segments (drupelets), each containing a hard seed. They grow wild almost everywhere in the world, but are also cultivated to give a larger, juicier berry with better keeping properties. Buying cultivated blackberries, however, is not nearly as much fun as picking your own from the hedgerows.

Below: Large, cultivated blackberries

History

Archeological excavations show that man has eaten blackberries since Neolithic times. The Ancient Greeks prized them as much for the medicinal properties of their leaves as for the fruit, and they have remained popular throughout the centuries. Not everyone appreciates the qualities of wild brambles, though; after they had been introduced to Australia by the early settlers, they were declared a noxious weed in some areas!

Nutrition

Blackberries are rich in dietary fibre and vitamin C and are often used to make health drinks. They also contain some calcium, phosphorus and potassium. Blackberries typically contain about 30 kilocalories per 100g/3¾oz.

Choosing and Storing

Whether you pick or buy blackberries, they should be plump and tender, but not wet or mushy. Look for large, shiny fruit, and if you are buying a punnet check that the underside is not stained. Legend has it that blackberries should not be picked after September, or the Devil will be in them and they will taste impossibly sour.

Blackberries do not keep well. If you cannot eat them immediately, store them for no more than one day in the bottom of the fridge.

Preparing and Cooking

If you must wash blackberries, do so just before serving and drain them well on kitchen paper.

Freezing blackberries

Blackberries freeze well. Open freeze perfect specimens in a single layer on a baking sheet, then pack into rigid containers. Damaged berries can be puréed and sieved, then sweetened with sugar or honey.

Above: Wild blackberries – also known as brambles.

Left: Dewberries – a smaller, but very similar fruit to blackberries, which grow on long trailing branches.

Right: Crème de mûre – this richly flavoured blackberry liqueur is seldom drunk on its own. It is more often used as a colourful flavouring for cocktails.

Blackberry Kir Royale

For a delicious variation on the classic Kir Royale, which is usually made with crème de cassis (blackcurrant liqueur), pour a little crème de mûre into a champagne flute and top up with Champagne or sparkling white wine. Alternatively, to make an exceptionally luxurious cocktail, put some blackberries in a champagne flute, add a dash of orange liqueur, such as Cointreau, and top up with Champagne or sparkling white wine.

Ripe, juicy blackberries are best eaten just as they are, with sugar and cream. They make a tasty addition to breakfast cereal or a fruit salad. Blackberries can be puréed and sieved to make coulis, ice cream, sorbets and fools. They make delicious jam or bramble jelly and are the classic partner for apples in a pie or crumble. There is no need to cook them before using them in a pie filling or a pudding.

Left: English Bramble liqueur

Above: Dewberry flowers, which appear before the fruits develop.

Blackberries go well with many other fruits besides apples, and can be used in savoury game dishes. Use them to flavour spirits, such as vodka or *eau-de-vie*, or make a cordial to combat a cold. Commercially produced *crème de mûre* (blackberry liqueur) enhances the flavour of any dessert that incorporates fresh uncooked blackberries.

HYBRID BERRIES

There is a wide variety of raspberry/blackberry crossbreeds. Some of these occurred naturally, like the loganberry; others have been cultivated to produce a more robust or better-flavoured fruit. All these hybrids can be cooked and frozen in the same way as raspberries or blackberries.

Loganberries The first loganberry appeared in 1881 at Santa Cruz in California in the garden of Judge J.H. Logan. It was a natural hybrid, probably derived from a cross between a native dewberry and a raspberry. Since then, loganberries have been

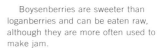

Right: Tayberries were bred in Scotland.

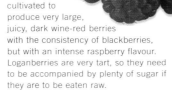

cultivated to produce very large, juicy, dark wine-red berries with the consistency of blackberries, but with an intense raspberry flavour. Loganberries are very tart, so they need to be accompanied by plenty of sugar if they are to be eaten raw.

Youngberries These are a dewberry-loganberry hybrid and resemble a dark red, elongated blackberry, but taste rather like a sweeter loganberry.

Boysenberries An even more elaborate hybrid – a cross between a youngberry and a raspberry, but resembling a large reddish-purple blackberry.

Left: Large, sweet boysenberries are mostly used to make jam.

Boysenberries are sweeter than loganberries and can be eaten raw, although they are more often used to make jam.

Tayberries Tayberries are arguably the finest hybrid of all. Bred in Scotland, they are a cross between the American blackberry Aurora and a tetraploid raspberry. They grow on long, spiny canes. The bright red, elongated berries have a slightly tart, aromatic flavour and although they can be eaten raw, they are better cooked.

Tummelberries are similar to tayberries, but fruit later in the season. Other, similar crossbreeds include **sunberries** and **wineberries.**

Above: Loganberries, which look more like reddish blackberries, have an intense raspberry flavour.

Left: Dark red youngberries are a hybrid of the dewberry and loganberry, but taste rather like a sweeter version of loganberry.

MULBERRIES

Mulberries grow on magnificent dome-headed trees, which can often be very ancient and grow up to 10m/30ft across, so they are rarely found in small modern gardens! Silkworms feed on the leaves, but the berries are left to drop to the ground as they ripen and have a delicious, slightly musky flavour. Luscious black mulberries taste very good but beware – they stain everything with which they come into contact. Legend has it that rubbing a stain created by a ripe mulberry with an unripe mulberry (if you can reach one) will remove it.

Right: Mulberries taste very good, but the juice stains terribly.

dark wine-red berries resemble loganberries.

History

Black mulberries are native to Western Asia. They were known to the Ancient Greeks, but it was the Roman emperor Justinian who deliberately encouraged their propagation as part of an enterprise in silk production.

In the sixteenth century, it was discovered that silkworms preferred to feed on the white mulberry leaves, and many of these trees were planted in Europe in the vain hope of stimulating a silk trade. Some of these white mulberry trees still survive today.

Varieties

White mulberries are actually pinkish or pale red. There is also an American red mulberry, whose leaves turn beautifully yellow in autumn.
Black mulberries are considered finer than the white variety. The elongated,

Preparing and Serving

Ripe mulberries can be eaten just as they are, with or without the addition of cream and are usually sweet enough not to need sugar. They also make a good addition to summer pudding.

Over-ripe fruit is best used for jams, jellies and sauces. Mulberries make excellent ice creams, fools and sorbets. Mulberry sauce goes well with richly flavoured roast meats, such as game, duck and lamb.

HUCKLEBERRIES

These berries, which gave their name to Mark Twain's famous character Huckleberry Finn, are quite similar to blueberries, but have a tougher skin and hard internal seeds. They have a sharper flavour than blueberries, but can be eaten and cooked in exactly the same way.

Another variety of huckleberry is the **tangleberry**, which grows on the coast of North America. These purplish-blue berries are sweeter than huckleberries and have a subtle tang of the sea.

Right: Huckleberries, which are similar to blueberries, have fairly tough skins and a sharp flavour.

BLUEBERRIES AND BILBERRIES

Blueberries and bilberries (also known as blaeberries, whortleberries or whinberries) are both small, round blue-black berries with a silvery bloom. They grow on shrubs on inhospitable, peaty moors and uplands. The flavour is mild and sweet and the texture firm.

American blueberries are generally larger and sweeter than bilberries. Nowadays, they are often cultivated, resulting in large, perfect berries that sometimes lack the distinctive flavour of the wild fruit.

Right: Blueberries – mild and sweet flavoured.

Nutrition

Blueberries and bilberries are a source of vitamin C, iron and dietary fibre. They provide about 60 kilocalories per 100g/3¾oz.

Buying and Storing

The best blueberries and bilberries are those you pick yourself. If you buy them, look for plump berries of uniform size. Reject shrivelled specimens, or those without the characteristic bloom. Unwashed berries will keep for up to a week in the bottom of the fridge.

Blueberries and bilberries can be frozen just as they are, provided they are in a sealed bag. Alternatively, poach them in a little lemon-flavoured syrup and then freeze.

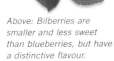

Above: Bilberries are smaller and less sweet than blueberries, but have a distinctive flavour.

Above: Dried blueberries are available in specialist food shops and greengrocers. They make a tasty addition to home-made fruit cakes and muesli, and are delicious scattered into fresh fruit salads or over breakfast cereal.

Preparing and Cooking

Blueberries and bilberries have soft seeds, so they can be eaten raw. Simply rinse and drain them first. However, they are more usually baked in pies or muffins, or used as a jam-like topping for cheesecake. To cook, make a light sugar syrup and flavour it with lemon, orange and cinnamon or allspice, and poach the berries until tender.

Blueberry Pie is a classic dessert, as is Blueberry Grunt, which consists of blueberries stewed with lemon and spice, baked with a dumpling-like topping. Blueberries can also be made into a sauce to serve with game.

ELDERBERRIES

Although you can seldom buy elderberries, you will find them growing all over the countryside throughout the summer. First come the creamy-white flowerheads, whose flavour goes very well with gooseberries. These are followed by flat, wide clusters of small, almost black berries with a sweet, slightly sickly taste.

History

Elderberries have grown in Europe and Asia since prehistoric times. The bushes themselves were little loved, perhaps because of their unattractive smell, but the berries provided sustenance for the poor. People often used elderberries as a fabric dye and to make wine; later the berries were used to add colour and extra flavour to thin, cheap wines.

Nutrition

Elderberries are an excellent source of vitamin C.

Choosing and Storing

Never pick elderberries growing close to a road, as they will be contaminated by dust and pollution. Good elderberries should be shiny and black. For elderflower syrup, choose creamy flowerheads that are fully open, but whose petals have not begun to drop. Use both flowers and berries as soon as possible after picking.

Below: Elderberries can be cooked with other fruits in pies, tarts and fools or used to make jellies and sauces.

Preparing and Cooking

Use a fork to strip the berries off the stalks. Elderberries can be cooked in the same way as redcurrants or other berries. Flowers should be shaken to dislodge any insects or loose petals and briefly rinsed in cold water.

Sprigs of elderflowers can be dipped in batter to make fritters, or made into a flavoured syrup. The berries can be made into jellies, or used to bulk out other berries in pies

tarts and fools. Elderberries can be made into a savoury sauce for pork and game. They are often used to make vinegar, and are excellent for making wine. Elderflowers can be made into a refreshing summer drink. To make eight 750ml/1¼ pint bottles, you will need about 12 large elderflower heads. Choose blossoms that are fully open, but not shedding their petals, and wash thoroughly. Place in a large pan and pour over 7 litres/12 pints boiling water. Add 250g/9oz caster sugar, 2 thinly sliced lemons and 120ml/4fl oz/½ cup white wine or cider vinegar. Stir and leave to macerate in a cool place for three days, stirring twice a day. Strain the liquid and pour into sterilized wine bottles. Cork very firmly and leave for at least a week before drinking.

Left: Elderflowers can be made into fritters and intensely flavoured drinks.

Stripping elderberries

Hold the stalk in one hand and run a fork through the berries.

ROWANBERRIES

These bright orangey-red berries are the fruit of the mountain ash. They grow in large clusters and are a great favourite with wild birds. Rowanberries are not available commercially.

Nutrition

Rowanberries are very rich in vitamin C and pectin.

Preparing and Cooking

The best known use for rowanberries is in a glorious deep orange jewel-like jelly with a bittersweet flavour, which goes

particularly well with rich meats and game. Rowanberries are also used to add colour to sweet apple dishes, such as pies and crumbles, or they can be made into compotes and sauces. Cook them in the same way as other berries. They cannot be eaten raw.

Right: Make Rowanberries into a vibrant jelly.

ROSE HIPS

These are the seed pods of roses, and appear after the plants have finished flowering. They vary in colour from orange to deep red and make a beautiful sight in autumn in gardens and hedgerows. Hips contain extremely hairy seeds, which must be removed before they can be eaten.

Nutrition

Rose hips are so rich in vitamin C that in wartime Britain they were picked by both children and adult volunteers and used in vast quantities to make bright pink rose hip syrup for pregnant women and babies. A single rose hip typically contains twenty times more vitamin C than an orange.

Right: Rose hips are enormously rich in vitamin C.

Preparing and Cooking

Very ripe rose hips can be eaten raw, but they do not taste particularly pleasant. Plump rose hips can be made into a bittersweet jelly to serve with poultry or game, or sweetened with sugar or honey and boiled to a syrup. Rose hips can also be used to flavour vinegar, and make an attractive garnish for salads.

Before cooking rose hips, top and tail them, cut them in half and scoop out every trace of the seeds and prickly hairs. If making jelly or syrup, strain the liquid twice through a double layer of muslin.

HAWS

The fruit of the hawthorn or May tree, these small wine-red berries follow the white spring blossom. They have a bitter, pungent taste.

Preparing and Cooking

Haws cannot be eaten raw, but make a delicious jelly when combined with crab apples. Elderberries can be added to the mixture to make a hedgerow jelly. Haws also make a good sauce for rich meats and game.

Right: Wine-red haws are pretty to look at, but have a bitter, pungent taste.

GOOSEBERRIES

The gooseberry, a botanical cousin of the blackcurrant, is native to Europe and North America. The fruits, which grow on dauntingly spiny bushes, come in many varieties – hard and sour, succulently soft and sweet, smooth and hairy – and in a range of colours, from vivid green to luscious purple.

History

Gooseberries were popular all over Britain well before Tudor times, when they grew wild in many kitchen gardens. The Tudors served them in savoury sauces and in all manner of sweet dishes. They were first cultivated in the sixteenth century and became so popular that in the nineteenth century competitors formed gooseberry clubs to see who could grow the biggest berry (some are reputed to have been grown to the size of a bantam's egg).

For some reason, their popularity did not spread abroad; even today the French use them only in a sauce to cut the richness of oily fish. There is no specific French word for gooseberry; it shares its name with the redcurrant and is known as *groseille de maquereau* ("redcurrant for mackerel").

Varieties

Gooseberries have a very long season. Early gooseberries are usually bright green and rather hard. They cannot be eaten raw, but taste wonderful cooked. These are followed by the softer, mid-season fruits, which are not generally identified by variety when sold in supermarkets and greengrocers, but which you may find in gardens and farm shops.

Early Sulphur A very early variety with golden, almost transparent berries and a lovely sweet flavour.

Goldendrop As attractive as its name, this small round yellow gooseberry has a fine rich flavour, which makes it ideal for eating

raw as a dessert fruit. Ready to pick in mid-summer.

Langley's Industry A large red hairy berry with a lovely sweet flavour. Ideal for the less green-fingered gardener, it will grow vigorously anywhere and can be picked early for cooking, or left to ripen fully on the bush to eat raw like grapes.

Above: Huge, deep-red London berries are sweet enough to eat raw.

Leveller A mid-season, yellowish-green berry with a sweet flavour.

London This huge mid-season berry is deep red or purple. For thirty-seven years, between 1829 and 1867, it was the unbeaten British champion in major gooseberry competitions! These dessert gooseberries can be eaten raw, just as they are.

Left: Green gooseberries – these early-cropping fruits cannot be eaten raw, but are delicious cooked.

Right: Fully ripe red gooseberries are quite sweet enough to be eaten just as they are.

Nutrition

Gooseberries are high in vitamin C and also contain vitamins A and D, potassium, calcium, phosphorus and niacin. They are rich in dietary fibre and provide only 17 kilocalories per 100g/3¾oz.

Buying and Storing

For cooking, choose slightly unripe green gooseberries. Check that they are not rock hard. Dessert varieties should be yielding and juicy (if possible, taste before you buy). Gooseberries will keep in the fridge for up to a week.

To freeze whole gooseberries, top and tail them and open freeze on baking sheets. Pack the frozen berries into polythene bags. Alternatively, purée and sieve them, sweeten and freeze in rigid containers.

Below: You may find Leveller berries, which have a lovely sweet flavour, in garden centres, pick-your-own farms and farm shops.

Preparing

For recipes using whole gooseberries, wash, then top and tail them (this is not necessary if you are making jam or jelly, or are going to sieve the cooked fruit).

Cooking

Gooseberries are rich in pectin, particularly when they are slightly unripe, which makes them ideal for jams and jellies. Their tartness makes an excellent foil for oily fish and rich poultry or meat.

Cook gooseberries very gently with a little water and sugar to taste until all the fruit has collapsed. If you like, flavour them with cinnamon, lemon or herbs. A few fennel or dill seeds will enhance a gooseberry sauce for fish.

In England, the first gooseberries of the season were traditionally used to make a Whitsun pie. They also make a good filling for suet pudding or crumble.

Worcestershire berries

A North American species of gooseberry that grows on a bush with evil spines. The small purplish-red berries are not much bigger than blackberries, but have the distinctive veining of gooseberries and a gooseberry flavour. Worcestershire berries can be eaten raw or cooked.

Topping and tailing gooseberries

1 Hold the gooseberry between your forefinger and thumb.
2 Snip off the stem and flower end with sharp scissors or trim with a knife.

Puréed, sieved and mixed with whipped cream, they make the perfect fruit fool. Gooseberries have an extraordinary affinity for elderflowers, which come into season at the same time as the early fruit and add a delicious muscat flavour to the berries.

Below: Sweet-tasting Early Sulphur are golden and almost translucent.

CRANBERRIES

These tart, bright red berries grow wild on evergreen shrubs in peaty marshland all over northern Europe and North America. They are closely related to blueberries and bilberries, but are much more sour and are always served cooked. **Cowberries** and **lingonberries** are very similar, but smaller.

Cranberries are sometimes known as "bounceberries", since they were traditionally tested for firmness by being bounced seven times. Any which failed the bounce test were too squashy and were therefore discarded. Because of their waxy skins, cranberries keep for much longer than other berries, which helps to explain their popularity.

History

For centuries before the first settlers arrived in America, the native Americans prized wild cranberries for their nutritional and medicinal value, and used them to make a dye for fabric and for decorative feathers. Although cranberries were already known in Britain, the Pilgrim Fathers found that the American berries were larger and more succulent.

Right: Bright red cranberries can be used in sweet and savoury dishes.

Below: Dried cranberries

Cranberry sauce

1 Thinly pare an orange with a swivel-bladed vegetable peeler, taking care to remove only the zest. Squeeze the juice and put it in a saucepan with the zest.

2 Add 350g/12oz/3 cups cranberries and cook gently for a few minutes until the cranberry skins pop.

3 Stir in caster sugar to taste and simmer for 5 minutes. Stir in 30ml/2 tbsp port (optional). Pour the cranberry sauce into a bowl, then cool and chill before serving.

They called them "craneberries" because the pink blossoms resembled a crane's head, or possibly because the cranes, which lived in the marshlands, were partial to the berries.

Cranberries featured in the first ever Thanksgiving feast in 1620 and have been a traditional part of the celebrations ever since. Commercial cultivation began in the nineteenth century, and nowadays cranberries are available frozen, canned, dried, as juice and in jellies and relishes.

Nutrition

Cranberries contain vitamins C and D, potassium and iron. They were considered to be a good protection against scurvy. They are naturally very low in kilocalories (but need sweetening to make them palatable).

Buying and Storing

Look for plump, firm, bright red berries and make sure that those at the bottom of the pack are neither squashed nor shrivelled. Fresh cranberries will keep in the fridge for four weeks, or they can be frozen in polythene bags and used without being thawed first.

Preparing and Cooking

Cranberries can be used in sweet or savoury dishes. Their most famous incarnation is as cranberry sauce, which is served with turkey or red meat and game. Their distinctive tartness even adds zest to firm-fleshed fish. The berries are high in pectin, so they make excellent jams and jellies. They combine well with orange and apple, and can be mixed with blackberries and raspberries to make an autumnal variation on summer pudding.

Cranberries should be stewed slowly with sugar to taste and a little water or orange juice until the skins pop. Dried cranberries can be used in the same way as raisins. Cranberry juice can be mixed with soda water and white wine or grape juice to make a refreshing drink. It is also good with orange juice and vodka.

Cranberry and chestnut stuffing

The traditional Christmas accompaniments of cranberries and chestnuts can be combined to make the perfect stuffing for turkey or other poultry. To make about 450g/1lb (enough to stuff a 4.5–5.5kg/10–12lb bird), soften 115g/4oz finely chopped onion in 25g/1oz butter in a saucepan. Stir in 175g/6oz unsweetened chestnut purée and 30ml/2 tbsp cooked cranberries or chunky cranberry sauce. Season to taste with salt and pepper and mix thoroughly. Take the pan off the heat and stir in 225g/8oz fresh white breadcrumbs. Coarsely crumble or chop 115g/4oz cooked chestnuts (canned chestnuts are fine) and fold into the stuffing mixture. Leave to cool completely before stuffing the bird.

Below: Cranberry juice and soda makes a refreshing drink.

BLACKCURRANTS, REDCURRANTS AND WHITECURRANTS

These native European berries, with their glowing colours, make a beautiful sight in summer, hanging like tiny bunches of grapes on the bush. Each berry contains a mass of small seeds. Currants can be eaten whole, but because they are highly acidic, this is seldom the preferred option.

Right: Blackcurrants grow wild all over Europe. The fruits have a tart flavour and are usually cooked.

History

Currants grow wild all over Europe and even as far north as Siberia. For some inexplicable reason, they were not cultivated by the Romans, but became popular only in the sixteenth century, when they were prized for their health-giving properties.

Nutrition

All currants, particularly blackcurrants, are very rich in vitamin C. Blackcurrants are used in cordials, throat sweets and other remedies designed to ward off colds; in the past, they were used as a cure for quinsy (an inflammation of the throat). They are high in pectin.

Buying and Storing

Choose plump, firm currants with shiny skins. They will keep in the fridge for several days. They can be frozen very successfully: strip the currants from the

Below: Buffalo currants are a type of blackcurrant with larger berries.

stalks, then rinse and drain them. Freeze in rigid containers. Sweetened or unsweetened blackcurrant purée also freezes well.

Preparing

Strip the currants from the stalks, if this has not already been done. If you wish, you can pick off the calyx tops before cooking the currants by pinching them between the nails of your forefinger and thumb. However, this is a tedious process, and is seldom necessary.

BLACKCURRANTS

Although they are often combined with other currants in cooking (as in summer pudding), blackcurrants are different from other types. They have tougher skins and, unlike other currants, which grow on old wood, they fruit on new wood. Both the bushes and the currants themselves are highly aromatic and the fruits have a luscious tart flavour.

Cooking

Blackcurrants can be added raw to fruit salads if they are not too tart, but are usually cooked in a little water, with sugar to taste. Simmer until just tender – do not overcook them or they will lose their fresh flavour. Blackcurrants make wonderful jams and jellies and combine well with soft cheeses, rich meats and game. To serve blackcurrants with meat, sauté them lightly in butter, adding a

Stripping currants off the stalk

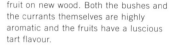

Hold the bunch of currants by the stem and strip off the berries with the tines of a fork.

Right: Whitecurrants are less tart than other currants and can be eaten raw.

pinch of sugar. They adapt well to other flavourings, such as mint and lemon, and are used to make the liqueur crème de cassis, which is the basis for Kir Royale and similar drinks.

1 Put the redcurrants (as many as you have) in a preserving pan with just enough water to cover. Simmer for 8–10 minutes or until the currants are very soft.

REDCURRANTS

Redcurrants can be eaten raw. Small bunches look very decorative if frosted with egg white and caster sugar. They are an essential ingredient for summer pudding and make a good addition to creamy desserts, such as crème brûlée. For a refreshing summer drink, purée 450g/1lb/4 cups redcurrants with 500ml/18 fl oz/2 cups water and sugar to taste, then press the purée gently through a sieve placed over a jug. Serve with sparkling water or soda water, or add a dash of vodka or gin.

The most familiar use of redcurrants, however, is in the jewel-like redcurrant jelly that goes so well with lamb and venison. Cumberland sauce (for game, ham and rich meats) is made by heating redcurrant jelly with lemon zest, port and sometimes mustard.

2 Strain through a jelly bag, then measure the liquid. Pour it back into the pan and add 350g/12oz/ 1½ cups granulated sugar for every 600ml/1 pint/2½ cups liquid. Stir over a medium heat until the sugar has dissolved.

WHITECURRANTS

These beautiful, translucent, silvery-golden currants are an albino strain of redcurrants. They are less tart than other types and can be eaten raw. They look wonderfully decorative frosted with egg white and sugar. **Pink currants** are an even more attractive variety, with a beautiful pink flush.

Above: Redcurrant jelly

Left: Redcurrants are an essential ingredient for summer pudding.

3 Boil briskly for 10 minutes or until setting point is reached, skimming off any scum as it rises to the surface. Pour the jelly into sterilized jars, seal and label.

BERRY AND CURRANT RECIPES

For sheer beauty, berries take a lot of beating. Make the most of their tantalizing colours and flavours by serving them simply, as a topping for shortcakes or in a summer pudding. Fresh Blueberry Muffins, Berry Brûlée Tarts, Bramble Jelly — these present the berries at their best.

SUMMER PUDDING

NO FRUIT BOOK WOULD BE COMPLETE WITHOUT THIS WELL-LOVED CLASSIC RECIPE. DON'T RESERVE IT SOLELY FOR SUMMER: IT FREEZES WELL AND PROVIDES A DELICIOUS DESSERT FOR CHRISTMAS DAY, AS A LIGHT AND REFRESHING ALTERNATIVE TO THE TRADITIONAL PUDDING.

SERVES FOUR TO SIX

INGREDIENTS

7-8 × 1cm/½in thick slices of day-old white bread, crusts removed
800g/1¾lb/6–7 cups mixed berry fruit, such as strawberries, raspberries, blackcurrants, redcurrants and blueberries
50g/2oz/¼ cup golden caster sugar
lightly whipped double cream or crème fraîche, to serve

3 Fold over the excess bread, then cover the fruit with the remaining bread, trimming to fit snugly. Place a small plate or saucer directly on top of the pudding, that fits inside the basin. Weight it with a 900g/2lb weight if you have one, or use a couple of full cans.

4 Leave the pudding in the fridge for at least 8 hours or overnight. To serve, run a knife between the pudding and the basin and turn it out on to a plate. Spoon any reserved juices over the top and serve with whipped cream or crème fraîche.

1 Trim a slice of bread to fit in the base of a 1.2 litre/2 pint/5 cup pudding basin, then trim another 5–6 slices to line the sides of the basin.

2 Place all the fruit in a saucepan with the sugar. Cook gently for 4–5 minutes until the juices begin to run – it will not be necessary to add any water. Allow the mixture to cool slightly before spooning the berries and enough of their juices to moisten the bread lining the pudding basin. Save any leftover juice to serve with the pudding.

HOT BLACKBERRY AND APPLE SOUFFLÉS

AS THE BLACKBERRY SEASON IS SO SHORT AND THE APPLE SEASON SO LONG, IT'S ALWAYS WORTH FREEZING A BAG OF BLACKBERRIES TO HAVE ON HAND FOR TREATS LIKE THIS ONE.

2 Cook the blackberries and diced apple with the orange rind and juice in a pan for 10 minutes or until the apple has pulped down well. Press through a sieve into a bowl. Stir in 50g/2oz/¼ cup of the caster sugar. Set aside to cool.

3 Put a spoonful of the fruit purée into each prepared dish and smooth the surface. Set the dishes aside.

4 Whisk the egg whites in a large grease-free bowl until they form stiff peaks. Very gradually whisk in the remaining caster sugar to make a stiff, glossy meringue mixture.

5 Fold in the remaining fruit purée and spoon the flavoured meringue into the prepared dishes. Level the tops with a palette knife, and run a table knife around the edge of each dish.

6 Place the dishes on the hot baking sheet and bake for 10–15 minutes until the soufflés have risen well and are lightly browned. Dust the tops with icing sugar and serve immediately.

MAKES SIX

INGREDIENTS
    butter, for greasing
    150g/5oz/⅔ cup caster sugar, plus
        extra for dusting
    350g/12oz/3 cups blackberries
    1 large cooking apple, peeled, cored
        and finely diced
    grated rind and juice of 1 orange
    3 egg whites
    icing sugar, for dusting

COOK'S TIP
Running a table knife around the edge of the soufflés before baking helps them to rise evenly without any part sticking to the rim of the dishes.

1 Preheat the oven to 200°C/400°F/ Gas 6. Generously grease six 150ml/ ¼ pint/⅔ cup individual soufflé dishes with butter and dust with caster sugar, shaking out the excess sugar. Put a baking sheet in the oven to heat.

SUMMER BERRY CRÊPES

THE DELICATE FLAVOUR OF THESE FLUFFY CRÊPES CONTRASTS BEAUTIFULLY WITH TANGY BERRY FRUITS.

SERVES FOUR

INGREDIENTS
    115g/4oz/1 cup self-raising flour
    1 large egg
    300ml/½ pint/1¼ cups milk
    a few drops of pure vanilla essence
    15g/½oz/1 tbsp butter
    15ml/1 tbsp sunflower oil
    icing sugar, for dusting
For the fruit
    25g/1oz/2 tbsp butter
    50g/2oz/¼ cup caster sugar
    thinly pared rind of ½ orange
    juice of 2 oranges
    350g/12oz/3 cups mixed summer
        berries, such as sliced strawberries,
        yellow raspberries, blueberries
        and redcurrants
    45ml/3 tbsp Grand Marnier or other
        orange liqueur

1 Preheat the oven to 150°C/300°F/
Gas 2. To make the crêpes, sift the flour
into a large bowl and make a well in the
centre. Break in the egg and gradually
whisk in the milk to make a smooth
batter. Stir in the vanilla essence. Set
the batter aside in a cool place for up to
half an hour.

2 Heat the butter and oil together in an
18cm/7in non-stick frying pan. Swirl to
grease the pan, then pour off the
excess fat into a small bowl.

3 If the batter has been allowed to
stand, whisk it thoroughly until smooth.
Pour a little of the batter into the
hot pan, swirling to cover the base of
the pan evenly. Cook until the mixture
comes away from the sides and the
crêpe is golden underneath.

4 Flip the crêpe over with a large
palette knife and cook the other side
briefly until golden.

5 Slide the crêpe on to a heatproof
plate. Make seven more crêpes in the
same way, greasing the pan with more
butter and oil mixture as needed. Cover
the crêpes with foil or another plate and
keep them hot in the oven.

COOK'S TIP
For safety, when igniting a mixture for
flambéing, use a long taper or long
wooden match. Stand back as you set
the mixture alight.

6 To prepare the fruit, melt the butter
in a heavy-based frying pan, stir in the
sugar and cook gently until the mixture
is golden brown. Add the orange rind
and juice and cook until syrupy.

7 Add the fruits and warm through,
then add the liqueur and set it alight.
Shake the pan to incorporate the
liqueur until the flame dies down.

8 Fold the pancakes into quarters and
arrange two on each plate. Spoon over
some of the fruit mixture and dust
liberally with the icing sugar. Serve any
remaining fruit mixture separately.

FRESH BERRY PAVLOVA

PAVLOVA IS THE SIMPLEST OF DESSERTS, BUT IT CAN ALSO BE THE MOST STUNNING. FILL WITH A MIX OF BERRY FRUITS IF YOU LIKE — RASPBERRIES AND BLUEBERRIES MAKE A MARVELLOUS COMBINATION.

SERVES SIX TO EIGHT

INGREDIENTS

4 egg whites, at room temperature
225g/8oz/1 cup caster sugar
5ml/1 tsp cornflour
5ml/1 tsp cider vinegar
2.5ml/½ tsp pure vanilla essence
300ml/½ pint/1¼ cups double cream
150ml/¼ pint/⅔ cup crème fraîche
175g/6oz/1 cup raspberries
175g/6oz/1½ cups blueberries
fresh mint sprigs, to decorate
icing sugar, for dusting

COOK'S TIP
To begin, invert a plate on the baking paper and draw round it with a pencil. Turn the paper over and use the circle as a guide for the meringue.

1 Preheat the oven to 140°C/275°F/ Gas 1. Line a baking sheet with non-stick baking paper. Whisk the egg whites in a large grease-free bowl until they form stiff peaks. Gradually whisk in the sugar to make a stiff, glossy meringue. Sift the cornflour over and fold it in with the vinegar and vanilla.

2 Spoon the meringue mixture on to the paper-lined sheet, using the circle drawn on the paper as a guide (see Cook's Tip). Spread into a round, swirling the top, and bake for 1¼ hours or until the meringue is crisp and very lightly golden. Switch off the oven, keeping the door closed, and allow the meringue to cool for 1–2 hours.

3 Carefully peel the paper from the meringue and transfer it to a serving plate. Whip the cream in a large mixing bowl until it forms soft peaks, fold in the crème fraîche, then spoon the mixture into the centre of the meringue case. Top with the raspberries and blueberries and decorate with the fresh mint sprigs. Sift icing sugar over the top and serve at once.

GOOSEBERRY AND ELDERFLOWER FOOL

GOOSEBERRIES AND ELDERFLOWERS ARE A MATCH MADE IN HEAVEN, EACH BRINGING OUT THE FLAVOUR
OF THE OTHER. SERVE WITH AMARETTI OR OTHER DESSERT BISCUITS FOR DIPPING.

SERVES SIX

INGREDIENTS
   450g/1lb/4 cups gooseberries, topped
     and tailed
   30ml/2 tbsp water
   50–75g/2–3oz/¼–⅓ cup caster sugar
   30ml/2 tbsp elderflower cordial
   400g/14oz carton ready-made
     custard
   green food colouring (optional)
   300ml/½ pint/1¼ cups double cream
   crushed amaretti biscuits, to decorate
   amaretti biscuits, to serve

1 Put the gooseberries and water in
a pan. Cover and cook for 5–6 minutes
or until the berries pop open.

2 Add the sugar and elderflower cordial
to the gooseberries, then stir vigorously
or mash until the fruit forms a pulp.
Remove the pan from the heat, spoon
the gooseberry pulp into a bowl and set
aside to cool.

3 Stir the custard into the fruit. Add a
few drops of food colouring, if using.
Whip the cream to soft peaks, then fold
it into the mixture and chill. Serve in
dessert glasses, decorated with crushed
amaretti, and accompanied by amaretti.

FRUITS OF THE FOREST WITH WHITE CHOCOLATE CREAMS

COLOURFUL FRUITS MACERATED IN A MIXTURE OF WHITE COCONUT RUM AND SUGAR MAKE A FANTASTIC ACCOMPANIMENT TO A DELIGHTFULLY CREAMY WHITE CHOCOLATE MOUSSE.

SERVES FOUR

INGREDIENTS
  75g/3oz white cooking chocolate,
    in squares
  150ml/¼ pint/⅔ cup double cream
  30ml/2 tbsp crème fraîche
  1 egg, separated
  5ml/1 tsp powdered gelatine
  30ml/2 tbsp cold water
  a few drops of pure vanilla essence
  115g/4oz/1 cup small
    strawberries, sliced
  75g/3oz/½ cup raspberries
  75g/3oz/¾ cup blueberries
  45ml/3 tbsp caster sugar
  75ml/5 tbsp white coconut rum
  strawberry leaves, to decorate
    (optional)

1 Melt the chocolate in a heatproof bowl set over a pan of hot water. Heat the cream in a separate pan until almost boiling, then stir into the chocolate with the crème fraîche. Cool slightly, then beat in the egg yolk.

2 Sprinkle the gelatine over the cold water in another heatproof bowl and set aside for a few minutes to swell.

COOK'S TIP
For a dramatic effect, decorate each white chocolate cream with dark chocolate leaves, made by coating the veined side of unsprayed rose leaves with melted chocolate. Let it dry before gently pulling off the leaves.

3 Set the bowl in a pan of hot water until the gelatine has dissolved completely. Stir the dissolved gelatine into the chocolate mixture and add the vanilla essence. Set aside until starting to thicken and set.

4 Brush four dariole moulds or individual soufflé dishes with oil; line the base of each with non-stick baking paper.

5 In a grease-free bowl, whisk the egg white to soft peaks, then fold into the chocolate mixture.

6 Spoon the mixture into the prepared dariole moulds or soufflé dishes, then level the surface of each and chill for 2–3 hours or until firm.

7 Meanwhile, place the fruits in a bowl. Add the caster sugar and coconut rum and stir gently to mix. Cover and chill until required.

8 Ease the chocolate cream away from the rims of the moulds or dishes and turn out on to dessert plates. Spoon the fruits around the outside. Decorate with the strawberry leaves, if using, then serve at once.

FRESH STRAWBERRY ICE CREAM

YOU CAN MAKE THE ICE CREAM BY HAND IF YOU FREEZE IT OVER A PERIOD OF SEVERAL HOURS, WHISKING IT EVERY HOUR OR SO, BUT THE TEXTURE WON'T BE AS GOOD.

SERVES SIX

INGREDIENTS

300ml/½ pint/1¼ cups creamy milk
1 vanilla pod
3 large egg yolks
225g/8oz/1½–2 cups strawberries
juice of ½ lemon
75g/3oz/¾ cup icing sugar
300ml/½ pint/1¼ cups double cream
sliced strawberries, to serve

1 Put the milk into a pan, add the vanilla pod and bring to the boil over a low heat. Remove from the heat. Leave for 20 minutes, then remove the vanilla pod. Strain the warm milk into a bowl containing the egg yolks; whisk well.

2 Return the mixture to the clean pan and heat, stirring, until the custard just coats the back of the spoon. Pour the custard into a bowl, cover the surface with clear film and set aside to cool.

COOK'S TIP
Use free-range eggs if possible, bought from a reputable supplier.

3 Meanwhile, purée the strawberries with the lemon juice in a food processor or blender. Press the strawberry purée through a sieve into a bowl. Stir in the icing sugar and set aside.

4 Whip the cream to soft peaks, then gently but thoroughly fold it into the custard with the strawberry purée. Pour the mixture into an ice cream maker. Churn for 20–30 minutes or until the mixture holds its shape. Transfer the ice cream to a freezerproof container, cover and freeze until firm. Soften briefly before serving with the strawberries.

BLACKCURRANT SORBET

THIS LUSCIOUS SORBET IS EASILY MADE BY HAND, BUT IT IS IMPORTANT TO ALTERNATELY FREEZE AND BLEND OR PROCESS THE MIXTURE FIVE OR SIX TIMES TO GET THE BEST RESULT. IF YOU MAKE LOTS OF ICE CREAM AND SORBETS, IT IS WORTH INVESTING IN AN ICE-CREAM MAKER.

SERVES SIX

INGREDIENTS

300ml/½ pint/1¼ cups water, plus
   30ml/2 tbsp
115g/4oz/½ cup caster sugar
225g/8oz/2 cups blackcurrants
30ml/2 tbsp crème de cassis or other
   blackcurrant liqueur
5ml/1 tsp lemon juice
2 egg whites

3 Pour the chilled blackcurrant syrup into a freezerproof bowl; freeze until slushy, whisking occasionally. Whisk the egg whites in a grease-free bowl until they form soft peaks, then fold into the semi-frozen blackcurrant mixture.

4 Freeze the mixture again until firm, then spoon into a food processor or blender and process. Alternately freeze and process or blend until completely smooth. Serve the sorbet straight from the freezer.

1 Pour 300ml/½ pint/1¼ cups of the water into a saucepan and add the sugar. Place over a low heat until the sugar has dissolved. Bring to the boil and boil rapidly for 10 minutes, then set the syrup aside to cool.

2 Meanwhile, cook the blackcurrants with the remaining 30ml/2 tbsp water over a low heat for 5–7 minutes. Press the blackcurrants and juice through a sieve placed over a jug, then stir the blackcurrant purée into the syrup with the liqueur and lemon juice. Allow to cool completely, then chill for 1 hour.

RASPBERRY AND ROSE PETAL SHORTCAKES

ROSEWATER-SCENTED CREAM AND FRESH RASPBERRIES FORM THE FILLING FOR THIS DELECTABLE DESSERT. THOUGH THEY LOOK IMPRESSIVE, THESE SHORTCAKES ARE EASY TO MAKE.

MAKES SIX

INGREDIENTS
    115g/4oz/½ cup unsalted
      butter, softened
    50g/2oz/¼ cup caster sugar
    ½ vanilla pod, split, seeds reserved
    115g/4oz/1 cup plain flour, plus
      extra for dusting
    50g/2oz/⅓ cup semolina
    icing sugar, for dusting
For the filling
    300ml/½ pint/1¼ cups double cream
    15ml/1 tbsp icing sugar
    2.5ml/½ tsp rosewater
    450g/1lb/4 cups raspberries
For the decoration
    12 miniature roses, unsprayed
    6 mint sprigs
    1 egg white, beaten
    icing sugar, for dusting

1 Cream the butter, caster sugar and vanilla seeds in a bowl until pale and fluffy. Sift the flour and semolina together, then gradually work the dry ingredients into the creamed mixture to make a biscuit dough.

VARIATIONS
Other soft red summer berries, such as mulberries, loganberries and tayberries, would be equally good in this dessert.

COOK'S TIP
For best results, serve the shortcakes as soon as possible after assembling them. Otherwise, they are likely to turn soggy from the berries' liquid.

2 Gently knead the dough on a lightly floured surface until smooth. Roll out quite thinly and prick all over with a fork. Using a 7.5cm/3in fluted cutter, cut out 12 rounds. Place these on a baking sheet and chill for 30 minutes.

3 Meanwhile, make the filling. Whisk the cream with the icing sugar until soft peaks form. Fold in the rosewater and chill until required.

4 Preheat the oven to 180°C/350°F/ Gas 4. To make the decoration, paint the roses and leaves with the egg white. Dust with sugar; dry on a wire rack.

5 Bake the shortcakes for 15 minutes or until lightly golden. Lift them off the baking sheet with a metal fish slice and cool on a wire rack.

6 To assemble the shortcakes, spoon the rosewater cream on to half the biscuits. Add a layer of raspberries, then top with a second shortcake. Dust with icing sugar. Decorate with the frosted roses and mint sprigs.

FRESH CURRANT BREAD–
AND–BUTTER PUDDING

FRESH MIXED CURRANTS ADD A TART TOUCH TO THIS SCRUMPTIOUS HOT PUDDING.

SERVES SIX

INGREDIENTS
  8 medium-thick slices day-old bread,
    crusts removed
  50g/2oz/¼ cup butter, softened
  115g/4oz/1 cup redcurrants
  115g/4oz/1 cup blackcurrants
  4 eggs, beaten
  75g/3oz/6 tbsp caster sugar
  475ml/16fl oz/2 cups creamy milk
  5ml/1 tsp pure vanilla essence
  a large pinch of grated nutmeg
  30ml/2 tbsp demerara sugar
  single cream, to serve

1 Preheat the oven to 160°C/325°F/
Gas 3. Generously butter a 1.2 litre/
2 pint/5 cup oval baking dish.

VARIATION
A mixture of blueberries and raspberries
would work just as well as the currants.

2 Spread the slices of bread generously
with the butter, then cut them in half
diagonally. Layer the slices in the dish,
buttered side up, scattering the currants
between the layers.

3 Beat the eggs and caster sugar
lightly together in a large mixing bowl,
then gradually whisk in the milk, vanilla
essence and a large pinch of freshly
grated nutmeg.

4 Pour the milk mixture over the bread,
pushing the slices down. Scatter the
demerara sugar and a little nutmeg over
the top. Place the dish in a baking tin
and fill with hot water to come halfway
up the sides of the dish. Bake for
40 minutes, then increase the oven
temperature to 180°C/350°F/Gas 4 and
bake for 20–25 minutes more or until
the top is golden. Cool slightly, then
serve with single cream.

CRANBERRY AND BLUEBERRY STREUSEL CAKE

CRANBERRIES ARE SELDOM USED IN SWEET DISHES BUT ONCE THEY ARE SWEETENED, THEY HAVE A GREAT FLAVOUR AND ARE PERFECT WHEN PARTNERED WITH BLUEBERRIES.

MAKES TEN SLICES

INGREDIENTS
  175g/6oz/¾ cup butter, softened
  115g/4oz/½ cup caster sugar
  350g/12oz/3 cups plain flour
  2 large eggs, beaten
  5ml/1 tsp baking powder
  5ml/1 tsp pure vanilla essence
  115g/4oz/1 cup cranberries
  115g/4oz/1 cup blueberries
  50g/2oz/⅓ cup light muscovado sugar
  2.5ml/½ tsp crushed cardamom seeds
  icing sugar, for dusting

1 Preheat the oven to 190°C/375°F/ Gas 5. Grease and base-line a 21cm/ 8½in round springform cake tin.

2 Cream the butter and caster sugar together until smooth, then blend in the flour with your fingers until the mixture resembles fine breadcrumbs. Take out 200g/7oz/generous 1 cup of the mixture and set this aside.

3 Beat the eggs, baking powder and vanilla essence into the remaining mixture until soft and creamy. Spoon on to the base of the prepared tin and spread evenly. Arrange the cranberries and blueberries on top, then sprinkle the muscovado sugar over.

4 Stir the cardamom seeds into the reserved flour mixture, then scatter evenly over the top of the fruit. Bake for 50–60 minutes or until the topping is golden. Cool the cake in the tin for 10 minutes, then remove the sides of the tin. Slide it on to a wire rack, lifting it off its base at the same time. Cool the cake completely, then dust with icing sugar and serve with whipped cream.

FRESH BLUEBERRY MUFFINS

MAKE THESE POPULAR AMERICAN TREATS IN PAPER CASES FOR MOISTER MUFFINS — IF YOU CAN'T FIND THEM, JUST GREASE THE TIN WELL BEFORE FILLING. THESE ARE BEST SERVED SLIGHTLY WARM.

MAKES TWELVE

INGREDIENTS
275g/10oz/2½ cups plain flour
15ml/1 tbsp baking powder
75g/3oz/6 tbsp caster sugar
250ml/8fl oz/1 cup milk
3 eggs, beaten
115g/4oz/½ cup butter, melted
a few drops of pure vanilla essence
225g/8oz/2 cups blueberries
For the topping
50g/2oz/½ cup pecan nuts,
    coarsely chopped
30ml/2 tbsp demerara sugar

COOK'S TIP

Don't be tempted to beat the muffin mixture; it should be fairly wet and needs to be quite lumpy. Overmixing will create tough muffins.

1 Preheat the oven to 200°C/400°F/ Gas 6. Stand 12 paper muffin cases in a muffin tin, or simply grease the tin thoroughly. Sift the flour and baking powder into a large bowl. Stir in the caster sugar. Mix the milk, eggs, melted butter and vanilla essence in a jug and whisk lightly. Add to the flour mixture and fold together lightly.

2 Fold in the blueberries, then divide the mixture among the muffin cases. Scatter a few nuts and a little demerara sugar over the top of each. Bake for 20–25 minutes, or until the muffins are well risen and golden.

3 Remove the hot muffins from the tin; cool slightly on a wire rack.

BLUEBERRY PIE

AMERICAN BLUEBERRIES OR EUROPEAN BILBERRIES CAN BE USED FOR THIS PIE. YOU MAY NEED TO ADD A LITTLE MORE SUGAR IF YOU ARE LUCKY ENOUGH TO FIND NATIVE BILBERRIES.

SERVES SIX

INGREDIENTS

2 × 225g/8oz ready-rolled shortcrust
   pastry sheets, thawed if frozen
800g/1¾lb/7 cups blueberries
75g/3oz/6 tbsp caster sugar, plus
   extra for sprinkling
45ml/3 tbsp cornflour
grated rind and juice of ½ orange
grated rind of ½ lemon
2.5ml/½ tsp ground cinnamon
15g/½oz/1 tbsp unsalted
   butter, diced
beaten egg, to glaze
whipped cream, to serve

1 Preheat the oven to 200°C/400°F/
Gas 6. Use one sheet of pastry to line a
23cm/9in pie tin, leaving the excess
pastry hanging over the edges.

2 Mix the blueberries, caster sugar,
cornflour, orange rind and juice, lemon
rind and cinnamon in a large bowl.
Spoon into the pastry case and dot with
the butter. Dampen the rim of the pastry
case with a little water and top with the
remaining pastry sheet.

VARIATION
Substitute a crumble topping for the
pastry lid. The contrast with the juicy
blueberry filling is sensational.

3 Cut the pastry edge at 2.5cm/1in
intervals, then fold each section over
on itself to form a triangle and create
a sunflower edge. Trim off the excess
pastry and cut out decorations from the
trimmings. Secure them to the pastry lid
with a little of the beaten egg.

4 Glaze the pastry with the egg and
sprinkle with caster sugar. Bake for
30–35 minutes or until golden. Serve
warm or cold with whipped cream.

BERRY BRÛLÉE TARTS

THIS QUANTITY OF PASTRY IS ENOUGH FOR EIGHT TARTLETS, SO FREEZE HALF FOR ANOTHER DAY.
THE BRÛLÉE TOPPING IS BEST ADDED NO MORE THAN TWO HOURS BEFORE SERVING THE TARTS.

MAKES FOUR

INGREDIENTS
   250g/9oz/2¼ cups plain flour
   a pinch of salt
   25g/1oz/¼ cup ground almonds
   15ml/1 tbsp icing sugar
   150g/5oz/⅔ cup unsalted butter,
     chilled and diced
   1 egg yolk
   about 45ml/3 tbsp cold water
For the filling
   4 egg yolks
   15ml/1 tbsp cornflour
   50g/2oz/¼ cup caster sugar
   a few drops of pure vanilla essence
   300ml/½ pint/1¼ cups creamy milk
   225g/8oz/2 cups mixed berry fruits,
     such as small strawberries,
     raspberries, blackcurrants
     and redcurrants
   50g/2oz/½ cup icing sugar

1 Mix the flour, salt, ground almonds and icing sugar in a bowl. Rub in the butter by hand or in a food processor until the mixture resembles fine breadcrumbs. Add the egg yolk and enough cold water to form a dough. Knead the dough gently, then cut it in half and freeze half for use later.

2 Cut the remaining pastry into four equal pieces and roll out thinly.

COOK'S TIP
If you possess a culinary blowtorch – and are confident about operating it safely – it will easily melt and caramelize the brûlée topping.

3 Use the pastry rounds to line four individual tartlet tins, letting the excess pastry hang over the edges. Chill for 30 minutes.

4 Preheat the oven to 200°C/400°F/ Gas 6. Line the pastry with non-stick baking paper and baking beans. Bake blind for 10 minutes. Remove the paper and beans and return the tartlet cases to the oven for 5 minutes until golden. Allow the pastry to cool, then carefully trim off the excess pastry.

5 Beat the egg yolks, cornflour, caster sugar and vanilla essence in a bowl.

6 Warm the milk in a heavy-based pan, pour it on to the egg yolks, whisking constantly, then return the mixture to the clean pan.

7 Heat, stirring, until the custard thickens, but do not let it boil. Remove from the heat, press a piece of clear film directly on the surface of the custard and allow to cool.

8 Scatter the berries in the tartlet cases and spoon over the custard. Chill the tarts for 2 hours.

9 To serve, sift icing sugar generously over the tops of the tartlets. Preheat the grill to the highest setting. Place the tartlets under the hot grill until the sugar melts and caramelizes. Allow the topping to cool and harden for about 10 minutes before serving the tarts.

BRAMBLE JELLY

THIS JELLY IS ONE OF THE BEST. IT HAS TO BE MADE WITH HAND-PICKED WILD BLACKBERRIES FOR THE BEST FLAVOUR. MAKE SURE YOU INCLUDE A FEW RED UNRIPE BERRIES FOR A GOOD SET.

MAKES 900G/2LB

INGREDIENTS
    900g/2lb/8 cups blackberries
    300ml/½ pint/1¼ cups water
    juice of 1 lemon
    about 900g/2lb/4 cups caster sugar
    hot buttered toast or English muffins,
        to serve

VARIATION
Redcurrant jelly is made in the same way, but with less sugar. Reduce the quantity to 350g/12oz/1½ cups for every 600ml/1 pint/2½ cups juice.

1 Put the fruit, water and lemon juice into a large saucepan. Cover the pan and cook for 15–30 minutes or until the blackberries are very soft.

2 Ladle into a jelly bag or a large sieve lined with muslin and set over a large bowl. Leave to drip overnight to obtain the maximum amount of juice.

3 Discard the fruit pulp. Measure the exuded juice and allow 450g/1lb/2 cups sugar to every 600ml/1 pint/2½ cups juice. Place both in a large heavy-based pan and bring the mixture slowly to the boil, stirring all the time until the sugar has dissolved.

4 Boil rapidly until the jelly registers 105°C/220°F on a sugar thermometer or test for setting by spooning a small amount on to a chilled saucer. Chill for 3 minutes, then push the mixture with your finger; if wrinkles form on the surface, it is ready. Cool for 10 minutes.

5 Skim off any scum and pour the jelly into warm sterilized jars. Cover and seal while the jelly is still hot and label when the jars are cool. Serve the jelly with hot buttered toast or English muffins.

STRAWBERRY JAM

CAPTURE THE VERY ESSENCE OF SUMMER IN A JAR OF DELICIOUS HOME-MADE STRAWBERRY JAM.

MAKES ABOUT 1.4KG/3LB

INGREDIENTS
    1kg/2¼lb/8 cups small strawberries
    900g/2lb/4 cups granulated sugar
    juice of 2 lemons
    scones and clotted cream, to serve

1 Layer the strawberries and sugar in a large bowl. Cover and leave overnight.

2 The next day, scrape the strawberries and their juice into a large heavy-based pan. Add the lemon juice. Gradually bring to the boil over a low heat, stirring until the sugar has dissolved.

COOK'S TIPS
For best results when making jam, don't wash the strawberries unless absolutely necessary. Instead, brush off any dirt, or wipe the strawberries with a damp cloth. If you have to wash any, pat them dry and then spread them out on a clean dish towel to dry further.

    To sterilize jam jars, wash in hot soapy water, then rinse thoroughly and drain. Place the jars on a baking sheet and dry in a warm oven for 15–20 minutes.

3 Boil steadily for 10–15 minutes or until the jam registers 105°C/220°F on a sugar thermometer. Alternatively, test for setting by spooning a small amount on to a chilled saucer. Chill for 3 minutes, then push the jam with your finger; if wrinkles form on the surface, it is ready. Cool for 10 minutes.

4 Pour the strawberry jam into warm sterilized jars, filling them right to the top. Cover and seal while the jam is still hot and label when the jars are cool. Serve the jam with scones and clotted cream. This strawberry jam can be stored in a cool dark place and should keep for up to one year.

CITRUS
FRUITS

No family of fruits seems to store up sunshine more successfully

than citrus fruits. Golden oranges and tangerines, yellow

lemons, deep green limes — their glowing colours light up a

room, and the delicious scent of their essential oils tempts the

tastebuds. Wonderfully versatile, they can be juiced, enjoyed just

as they are or used in both sweet and savoury dishes. All citrus

fruits have tough, bitter peel that is highly scented and contains

aromatic essential oils. Inside, the fruit is segmented and

encloses juicy flesh, with a more or less acid flavour.

The fruits ripen on the tree and do not continue to develop after

picking, so they have excellent keeping qualities.

GRAPEFRUIT

One of the largest citrus fruits, grapefruit can vary in diameter from 10–18cm/4–7in. Most have deep yellow skins, but the flesh can range from very pale yellow (confusingly called "white"), through rosy pink to deep pink (known as "ruby"). Generally speaking, the pinker the flesh, the sweeter the grapefruit will be.

Above: Sweetie is a very sweet variety of grapefruit that needs no sugar.

History

Grapefruit are descended from the original West Indian **pomelo** or **shaddock**, a large sour fruit (the pomelos sold today are a cross between a grapefruit and a shaddock). These fruits were brought to Europe from the West Indies in the seventeenth century and are now grown in every sub-tropical country of the world.

Varieties

The main varieties of grapefruit are white, pink or ruby, but you may also find the green-skinned **Sweetie,** whose flesh, as the name implies, is so sweet that it needs no sugar.

Nutrition

One of the most filling fruits, yet very low in calories (about 43 kilocalories per 100g/3¾oz), grapefruit are an excellent source of dietary fibre and vitamin C; one fruit provides one-and-a-half times the adult daily requirement.

Buying and Storing

Choose fruits that feel heavy for their size; they will be juicy. The skin can be thin or thick, depending on the variety, but it should be plump and firm; if it is puffy and coarse, the flesh will be dry. Avoid grapefruit with bruised or damaged skin. You cannot ripen grapefruit once they have been picked, but they can be kept in a cool place or in the fridge for a week or more.

Preparing and Serving

Grapefruit are best eaten raw and chilled, although in the 1960s it was fashionable to sprinkle them with brown sugar or brush with melted butter and caramelize them under the grill. They constitute the perfect breakfast food; perhaps the easiest way to enjoy them is freshly squeezed into a glass, but half a grapefruit on its own or with a little sugar is more satisfying. The fruits can also be used to make delicious marmalade to round off your breakfast. Grapefruit can be used to start or finish a main meal. The tart flavour goes well with

Above: White grapefruit have pale yellow flesh.

Segmenting grapefruit

1 Cut the grapefruit in half and remove the pips.

2 Using a curved, serrated grapefruit knife, cut between the skin and flesh.

3 Using a small, sharp paring knife, cut carefully between the membrane that separates the segments. Start at the centre, work out to the skin, then around the segment and back to the centre again.

4 Finally, cut out the central core of the grapefruit with a sharp knife and remove the membrane.

seafood; grapefruit segments mixed with prawns and avocado make a refreshing starter. They combine well with smoked fish and poultry, and segments are sometimes served as a garnish to cut the richness of liver or sweetbreads. The segments can also be used in fruit salads, mousses and sorbets. Grapefruit juice makes an unusual addition to salad dressings, and the peel, without the pith, can be candied to be used in cakes or coated with chocolate.

Left: The flesh of pink grapefruit can range from rosy pink to deep pink. As a rule of thumb, the pinker the colour, the sweeter the grapefruit.

Below: Chocolate-coated grapefruit peel – a delectable sweet treat.

POMELOS

Although they resemble grapefruit, true pomelos are not a hybrid of the grapefruit, but a species in their own right. They are sometimes known as "shaddocks" after the sea captain who brought them from Polynesia to the West Indies. They are much larger than grapefruit, with thick yellow dimpled skin, pinkish-yellow flesh and a sharp, refreshing flavour, which often needs a little sugar to make it palatable.

Below: Pomelos sold today are a smaller, rounder and smoother-skinned cross between the original pomelo or shaddock and grapefruit.

UGLI FRUIT

Despite its large size, baggy shape and mottled green skin, the Ugli is a hybrid of the grapefruit, orange and tangerine. It may not be the beauty of the citrus family, but the flavour is sweet and delicious – a cross between grapefruit and tangerine. The peel can be candied like grapefruit.

LEMONS

Arguably the most useful of all fruit, the distinctively shaped lemon can be very large or quite small, with thick or thin, smooth or knobbly skin. The skin contains aromatic essential oils, and a good lemon will perfume the air with its fragrance. The juicy, pale yellow, acid flesh enhances almost any other food and never fails to awaken and refresh the tastebuds.

History

Originally from India or Malaysia, lemons were introduced into Assyria where they were discovered by the soldiers serving Alexander the Great. They took them back to Greece, where the lemons were used as a condiment and for medicinal and cosmetic purposes. The Crusaders brought lemons to Europe from Palestine, and their cultivation became widespread. Like limes, lemons became invaluable as a protection against scurvy and were carried by sailors on every sea voyage.

Nutrition

Rich in vitamin C and very low in calories, lemons only provide about 22 kilocalories per 100g/3¾oz.

Buying and Storing

Choose lemons that are firm and heavy for their size. Smooth-skinned lemons are best for juicing and cooking, while

Left: Smooth-skinned lemons are best for juicing and cooking.

the knobbly skinned varieties are easier to grate. Lemons become paler as they ripen and lose some juiciness and acidity, so avoid light yellow fruit; look instead for deep yellow specimens with glossy unblemished skins. Do not buy lemons with patches of mould, or those with hard, shrivelled skins.

Lemons have often been treated with diphenyl, an ethylene gas that keeps the skins yellow and fresh-looking. If you are going to use the lemon rind, buy untreated or "unwaxed" fruit.

Lemons do not ripen once picked. They can be kept in a cool room or the fridge for at least a week.

Preparing and Cooking

Although few people would choose to eat a lemon raw, these citrus fruits are infinitely versatile. Their high ascorbic acid (vitamin C) content prevents oxidization, so lemon juice is often brushed over cut fruit or white vegetables, such as potatoes, celeriac or artichokes, to stop them from turning brown. Lemons can be distilled into alcoholic drinks, such as *limoncello*, a sweet *digestivo*, which is served straight from the freezer.

Every part of the lemon can be used in sweet and savoury cooking, from the juice to the zest. Lemon wedges are traditionally served as an accompaniment to fish dishes, particularly fried fish; their acidity counteracts the fattiness of all fried

Zesting or grating a lemon
1 Choose an unwaxed lemon. Hold it firmly in one hand.

2 Scrape a zester down the length of the lemon to pare off fine slivers of zest.

3 Chop the pared zest finely with a sharp knife if desired.

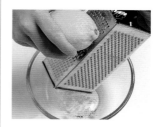

4 For grating, choose a knobbly skinned lemon if possible. Grate it on the fine side of a grater, taking care to remove only the yellow zest. Work over a bowl, or, if you prefer, work over a piece of foil – this makes it easy to transfer the grated rind to a bowl or pan with the aid of a pastry brush.

foods. Lemon slices are a popular addition to tea and cold drinks, or can be used to garnish any number of sweet or savoury dishes. Whole lemons can be preserved in salt and are widely used in North African dishes, such as Moroccan *tagines*.

Lemons give a wonderful flavour to sweet dishes. They can be used for jellies, jams and lemon curd or lemon cheese and make refreshing mousses, sorbets and ice creams.

Lemon juice Lemon juice can be drunk on its own, with added sugar, or as a refreshing long drink, such as lemonade. It enhances the flavour of most other foods and can be used as a healthy substitute for salt. Use it in dressings, sauces and marinades; marinating fish for a long time in lemon juice will even "cook" the fish without heat, as in the South American dish

Above: Knobbly-skinned lemons are easier to grate.

ceviche. Lemon juice will also tenderize meat. A few drops added to the cooking water helps poached eggs to coagulate, and a couple of spoonfuls will turn fresh cream into soured cream.

Lemon juice has non-culinary uses, too. It acts as a bleach and can be used as a household cleaner or cosmetically, to whiten the skin or lighten blonde hair.

Lemons yield more juice if they are warmed before squeezing; roll them between the palms of your hands for a minute or two, cover with boiling water or microwave on High for 30 seconds before squeezing. Do not squeeze lemons too hard, or the juice will become bitter.

Lemon zest and peel
The essential oils in lemon zest have an aromatic flavour that enhances many dishes. The zest can be obtained by grating or peeling into strips with a zester or canelle knife. Use it as a flavouring for butter, sauces, custards, mousses, cakes, biscuits and tarts. For a milder lemon flavour, rub a lump of sugar over the surface of a lemon so that it absorbs the oils, then add the sugar cube to a sauce or pudding.

Lemon peel (including the white pith) contains pectin, which helps to set jams and jellies. Strips of peel (minus pith) can be added to casseroles, or candied to serve with coffee or to add to cakes and puddings.

Below: Lemon juice enhances the flavour of most other fruits.

CITRON

A lemon or pear-shaped citrus fruit originally from China, citrons are large fruit, sometimes up to 20cm/8in long, with thick, knobbly, greenish skin. They give very little juice, but this can be used like lemon juice. Citron flesh is very bitter and unpalatable, but the attractive green peel can be candied and used like candied lemon peel; it develops a lovely translucency. The peel can also be used for marmalade and jams. In Corsica, citrons are used to make a liqueur called *Cédratine*.

Right: Citrons are large fruit with bitter, unpalatable flesh.

LIMES

Limes are the smallest members of the true citrus family. They have thin, fairly smooth, green skins and a highly aromatic, acid flavour. Unlike lemons, limes will grow in tropical regions and are an essential ingredient of South-east Asian, Mexican, Latin American and Caribbean cooking.

History

Limes originated in India. Attempts were made to grow them in Mediterranean countries, but they proved insufficiently hardy. They do very well in Egypt, however, where they are more plentiful than lemons. They are widely grown in the West Indies, and it was from these islands that supplies came for the British Navy, to supplement the sailors' rations and help to prevent scurvy. Limehouse, in London's docklands, takes its name from the warehouses where the fruit was stored.

Varieties

There are basically three types of lime:
Tahitian Large limes, with pale fine-grained pulp and a very acidic flavour.
Mexican Smaller fruit with bright green skin and a very aromatic flavour.
Key Lime Pale yellowish-green fruit, very juicy with a strong, sharp flavour. Not surprisingly, these are the main ingredient of Florida key lime pie.

Nutrition

High in vitamin C, limes contain some potassium, calcium and phosphorus, and provide about 20 kilocalories per 100g/3¾oz.

Right: Limes have a sharper flavour than lemons.

Buying and Storing

Limes are the most perishable of all citrus fruit and quickly dry out developing brown patches on their skins. Choose unblemished fruits that feel heavy for their size and avoid those with yellowish skins, as they may have lost some of their tanginess. Store limes in the fridge for up to a week.

Preparing and Serving

Limes can be used in the same way as lemons, but will add a sharper flavour, so use fewer of them. Classic *ceviche* is made by marinating chunks of white fish in lime juice until they turn opaque. Freshly squeezed juice is used in rum punches, margaritas and daiquiris, or commercially made into a cordial.

Strips of lime zest can be buried in caster sugar to add a delicious fragrance. A few drops of lime juice squeezed over tropical fruit, such as papayas, melons and prickly pears will do wonders for the flavour. In Caribbean and Latin American cooking, limes are cooked with fish, poultry and meat, while in South-east Asia they are made into pickles and chutneys to serve with curries. Limes can be made into jams and jellies and add a special zing to marmalade. One of the world's great desserts is Florida key lime pie, which is similar to a lemon meringue pie. Lime blossoms are dried and made into infusions or used to flavour ice creams and mousses.

Paring and cutting julienne strips of citrus rind
1 Wash and dry the lime, lemon or orange. Using a swivel-blade vegetable peeler, peel downwards to remove long strips of rind. Do not include the bitter white pith.
2 With a small sharp knife, square off the strips.
3 Cut them lengthways into fine julienne strips.

KAFFIR LIMES

These are not true limes, but belong to a sub-species of the citrus family. Pale green and gnarled, the fruits have a haunting, scented citrus bouquet, but unfortunately the flesh is inedible. In Thailand and Indonesia, the finely grated rind is sometimes used in cooking, but it is the leaves that are most useful in culinary terms. When torn or shredded, they impart a distinctive flavour to soups, fish and chicken dishes, and curries.

Right: Kaffir limes are not eaten, but the finely grated rind is used in South-east Asian cooking.

KUMQUATS

Kumquats are not true citrus fruits, but belong to a similar species, *Fortunella*. Their name comes from the Cantonese *kam kwat*, meaning "golden orange". The small, elongated fruits are about the size and shape of a large olive, with thin, edible, orange-coloured rind. The rind is sweeter than the sour pulp and the two eaten together provide a delicious sour-sweet sensation.

Nutrition

Kumquats are a source of vitamins C and A and have some calcium, phosphorus and riboflavin. They provide about 65 kilocalories per 100g/3¾oz.

Buying and Storing

Look for unblemished fruit with taut orange-coloured rind. They can be kept in the fridge for up to a week.

Preparing and Cooking

Kumquats can be eaten whole, just as they are, or sliced into miniature rings and used in winter salads and fruit salads. They taste superb poached in syrup, and can also be bottled with sugar and alcohol and served whole or chopped with ice cream, duck, red meats or cheese. They make delicious marmalade and jam and can be used in cake and biscuit mixes. For unusual petits fours, dip whole kumquats into melted bittersweet chocolate.

Kumquats combine well with bitter salad leaves like chicory and frisée and make excellent stuffings for poultry.

Limequats

These are, as the name suggests, a cross between limes and kumquats. Limequats are bright green with thin, edible skins, but they are extremely sour, so cannot be eaten raw. They should be cooked or preserved exactly like kumquats and can be served in the same way.

Whole kumquats can be cooked with fish, poultry and white meats, and spiced kumquat preserve is a Christmas treat.

Left: Not true citrus fruits, kumquats can be eaten whole – skin and all.

BERGAMOTS

These small yellow citrus fruit are seldom found in their natural state. They are best known for the essential oil contained in the rind, which is used in confectionery and perfumery, but most famously as a highly distinctive flavouring for Earl Grey tea. Bergamot oil is used in the barley sugar made in the French town of Nancy. The fruit can also be made into delicious and unusual marmalade.

Right: Seldom used for cooking, bergamots are best-known for their essential oil, which gives Earl Grey tea its unusual, aromatic scent and flavour.

TANGERINES OR MANDARINS

Sometimes known as "easy peelers", tangerines or mandarins are part of a large family of small citrus fruit. They resemble slightly flattened oranges with loose orange skin and have a fragrant aroma, which is inextricably bound up with Christmas. Who can forget the childhood delight of finding a tangerine in the toe of a Christmas stocking? The tangerine family all have aromatic skins, which can easily be detached from the segments (unlike oranges and lemons) and segments that separate easily. The flesh is sweet and perfumed, but often contains a large number of pips.

History

As the name suggests, tangerines or mandarins almost certainly originated in China and were brought to Italy in Roman times by Arab traders. Like oranges, they were regarded as a

Right: Easy to peel, satsumas have a refreshing tart flavour.

Right: These tangerines, grown in Italy, have sweet flesh, but often contain a large number of pips.

symbol of luxury and prosperity. They are now grown throughout North Africa and the Mediterranean.

Varieties

The names of many types of tangerine are commonly interchanged, so you may find a bewildering variety of fruits that are essentially the same.

Clementine The smallest of the tangerines, with bright orange skin and no pips. This, and their sweet, aromatic flesh, make clementines the most popular variety of tangerine. They are sometimes sold with the leaves still attached, which makes the fruit particularly attractive.

Mandarin Most commonly sold canned, tiny peeled tangerine segments are sold as mandarin oranges, although they are usually small satsumas. The deliciously sweet, vibrant segments make an attractive decoration for a dessert.

Satsuma These largish tangerines from Japan have loose skin and a refreshing, rather tart flavour. Satsumas contain very few pips.

Right: The cementine is the smallest and most popular variety of tangerine.

Ortanique Also known as "honey tangerines" because of their delicious sweetness, ortaniques are a hybrid, which can be found growing on the same trees as tangerines or oranges.

Tangelo These are a cross between a tangerine and a grapefruit, and have the easy-peeling qualities of the former. Tangelos are irregularly shaped and have a refreshing, tart flavour, rather like an orange.

Minneola Another tangerine–grapefruit hybrid, minneolas can be recognized by the distinctive bulge at their stalk end. They have bright orange skin and are very easy to peel. The sweet, juicy flesh has no pips.

Nutrition

All tangerines and their hybrids are extremely good sources of vitamin C and beta-carotene. They provide about 40 kilocalories per 100g/3¾oz.

Buying and Storing

Many varieties of tangerine have loose, puffy skins, which are no indication of quality. Choose fruits that feel heavy for their size; they will contain more juice. Avoid fruits with damaged skins and, if you are buying pre-packed fruits, check that none is mouldy or it will quickly taint all the other fruit.

Tangerines do not keep as long as other citrus fruit, but can be stored in the fridge for up to a week.

Canned mandarin oranges are a very useful store-cupboard item. Use them in trifles, chocolate slices and also on cheesecakes. Children love them set in orange or mandarin jelly.

It is also possible to buy canned peeled whole mandarins in syrup – the lazy cook's answer for a simply sensational dessert. Just make a caramel sauce, add the drained fruit and decorate with some fresh orange or mandarin zest. A dash of orange liqueur gilds the lily.

Preparing and Serving

All varieties of tangerine can be used in the same way as oranges. The peel is as useful as the flesh, and the zest can be candied or used to flavour sweet liqueurs. Strips of peel can be dried and used in savoury stews or included with herbs to make a bouquet garni.

Tangerine segments can be eaten on their own. Dipped in melted chocolate or crystallized, they make a delicious after-dinner sweet. Tangerine juice adds a distinctive flavour to marinades for pork and poultry; combine it with oriental aromatics like five-spice powder, ginger and soy sauce.

ORANGES

Below: Navel or navelina oranges contain a tiny embryonic fruit.

Despite their name, oranges are not always orange; they can also be yellow or mottled with red. The size can vary too – an orange can be as large as a football or as small as a cherry – and the flavour can range from sweet to intensely sour. Orange trees are beautiful all year round. Their dark glossy evergreen leaves give off a wonderful citrus scent. The beautiful waxy white, star-shaped flowers also have an intense aroma, which is captured in orange-blossom water. The fruits turn from green to bright orange or yellow, making a striking contrast with the leaves.

Like other citrus peel, orange rind contains essential oils, which are used in cooking and perfumery.

History

Oranges originated in China. They were probably known to the Ancient Greeks and may have been the mythical Golden Apples of the Hesperides. If so, they would have been bitter oranges, which were the only variety

Right: Cointreau is flavoured with the peel of bitter oranges.

known at the time. Over the centuries, traders took oranges to India and Arabia and thence to the Mediterranean region. When the first oranges reached Europe, they were so rare that they became a symbol of opulence, to be offered as luxury gifts; the Medici family adopted five oranges as their coat of arms. The oranges were too precious to be eaten raw (in any case, they would have been too sour), but were made into preserves. The first sweet oranges to arrive in Europe were brought from India by traders in the seventeenth century. They became popular throughout Europe and were served in theatres as refreshments – hence Nell Gwynn's appearance in the history books.

Varieties

Oranges fall into two groups: sweet oranges, which can be eaten raw, and bitter oranges, which cannot.

Sweet oranges

Sweet oranges can be divided into four main categories, which are available at different times of the year.

Navel and **Navelina** These seedless oranges take their name from the navel-like protuberance at the end, which contains a tiny embryonic fruit. They have thick, pebbly skins and very sweet, juicy flesh. The skin is particularly good for making candied peel.

Blonde These pale-skinned winter oranges include **Jaffa** and **Shamouti**. The large fruit have thick skins that are easy to peel. The flesh is crisp and juicy. If you are lucky, you may find **Salustianas oranges**, which are full of juice and contain no pips.

Blood oranges These small oranges have red-flushed skins and jewel-like flesh, which can range from golden to deep ruby red. These are the best oranges to use for sorbets and desserts, where colour is important. They are an essential ingredient of *sauce Maltaise*,

Peeling and segmenting oranges

1 Using a serrated knife, cut a thin slice from each end of the orange to expose the flesh.

2 Cut off the peel in a circular motion, removing the white pith.

3 Hold the fruit over a bowl to catch the juice. Cut each segment between the membranes.

4 Squeeze out all the juice.

Below: Seedless Navel oranges have very sweet juicy flesh.

an orange-flavoured mayonnaise, which takes its name from the sour but juicy Maltese blood orange.

Late oranges These include **Valencia** oranges, which have smooth, thin skins and contain few or no pips; they are the world's most popular variety. They have pale flesh and are very juicy, with a sharp flavour. Valencia are the best oranges for juicing.

Bitter oranges

Bitter oranges cannot be eaten raw; they must be cooked.

Seville or **Bigarade** oranges are used to make marmalade, jams and jellies. Vast numbers are grown in Seville, but surprisingly the Spaniards never make marmalade; almost all their oranges are exported overseas to Britain. Seville oranges are used in the classic *sauce bigarade*, which is traditionally served with roast duck. In the south of France,

these oranges are crystallized and the blossoms are distilled to make aromatic orange flower water. The aromatic oils from the peel are used to flavour such liqueurs as Grand Marnier and Cointreau. Bitter oranges have a very short season, and are only available in January.

Nutrition

An orange provides twice the adult daily requirement of vitamin C, and is high in dietary fibre. The average fruit provides about 50 kilocalories.

Buying and Storing

Choose firm oranges that feel heavy for their size – these will be juicy. Never buy oranges with damaged, shrivelled or mouldy skin. Oranges keep well; they can be stored at room temperature or in the fridge for up to two weeks. The juice and grated zest can be frozen.

Right: Bitter Seville oranges have a very short season – they are only available in January.

Right: Valencia oranges are the world's most popular variety of orange and are the best variety for juicing.

Candied orange peel

1 Choose thick-skinned oranges. Wash and dry well. Peel the oranges carefully with a swivel vegetable peeler.

2 Using a sharp knife, cut the peel into thin julienne strips.

3 For each orange, bring to the boil 250ml/8 fl oz/1 cup water with 115g/4oz/½ cup granulated sugar. Add the strips of orange peel, half-cover the pan and simmer until the syrup has reduced by three-quarters. Leave to cool completely.

4 Sift icing sugar in a thick, even layer over a baking sheet. Roll the candied peel in the sugar. Dry in a cool oven. Store the peel in a jar; it will keep for 2 to 3 months.

Preparing and Serving

Oranges are best eaten in their natural state, but can be used in an almost infinite variety of desserts, pastries and sweetmeats: fruit salads, mousses, soufflés, ice creams, sorbets and granitas, and, perhaps most famous of all, *crêpes Suzette*. They can be squeezed for juice, in which case keep the rind to use in other ways (grated zest can be ground with caster sugar for sprinkling on breakfast cereals or for use in cakes or custards, for example). The juice can be drunk or used in a marinade for poultry or fish. Fresh sliced oranges combine well with spices like cinnamon, ginger and cardamom, and a sprinkling of distilled orange flower water enhances their flavour dramatically. Candied orange peel is good in cakes, biscuits and Christmas pudding. Crystallized quartered orange slices make an attractive decoration for desserts and cakes.

Oranges go well in savoury dishes. Combine them with watercress, beetroot or chicory and thinly sliced raw red onion for a refreshing salad, or glaze carrots in orange juice and butter. Add orange juice and zest to tomato sauces and soups, or add strips of

Right: Blood oranges

Duck in bitter orange sauce

Bitter oranges is are the perfect foil for the richness of duck. For *caneton à la bigarade*, pare the rind of a Seville orange, removing only the zest and cut into julienne strips. Squeeze the orange and set the juice aside. Roast a duck, then keep it hot. Drain off the fat from the roasting tin, then deglaze the tin with a little white wine. Add 300ml/ ½ pint/1¼ cups rich chicken stock and the orange juice, reduce until syrupy, then add the orange zest, season and simmer for about 5 minutes. Beat in 25g/1oz/2 tbsp cubed chilled butter. Carve the duck, pour over the sauce, and garnish with peeled orange segments.

pared rind to hearty fish soups and meat or poultry casseroles. Peeled orange slices are also good with liver and fish(especially trout and salmon).

CITRUS
FRUIT
RECIPES

Put the squeeze on citrus fruit for some of the finest puddings and preserves in any good cook's repertoire. Lemon Surprise Pudding, Moist Orange and Almond Cake, Key Lime Pie and Lemon Meringue Pie are perennially popular, while new delights include Lemon Coeur à la Crème with Cointreau Oranges.

LEMON COEUR À LA CRÈME
WITH COINTREAU ORANGES

THIS ZESTY DESSERT IS THE IDEAL CHOICE TO FOLLOW A RICH MAIN COURSE SUCH AS ROAST PORK.

SERVES FOUR

INGREDIENTS
    225g/8oz/1 cup cottage cheese
    250g/9oz/generous 1 cup mascarpone
      cheese
    50g/2oz/¼ cup caster sugar
    grated rind and juice of 1 lemon
    spirals of orange rind, to decorate
For the Cointreau oranges
    4 oranges
    10ml/2 tsp cornflour
    15ml/1 tbsp icing sugar
    60ml/4 tbsp Cointreau

1 Put the cottage cheese in a food processor or blender and whizz until smooth. Add the mascarpone, caster sugar, lemon rind and juice and process briefly to mix the ingredients.

2 Line four coeur à la crème moulds with muslin, then divide the mixture among them. Level the surface of each, then place the moulds on a plate to catch any liquid that drains from the cheese. Cover and chill overnight.

3 Make the Cointreau oranges. Squeeze the juice from two oranges and pour into a measuring jug. Make the juice up to 250ml/8fl oz/1 cup with water, then pour into a small saucepan. Blend a little of the juice mixture with the cornflour and add to the pan with the icing sugar. Heat the sauce, stirring until thickened.

4 Using a sharp knife, peel and segment the remaining oranges. Add the segments to the pan, stir to coat, then set aside. When cool, stir in the Cointreau. Cover and chill overnight.

5 Turn the moulds out on to plates and surround with the oranges. Decorate with spirals of orange rind and serve at once.

CLEMENTINE JELLY

JELLY ISN'T ONLY FOR CHILDREN: THIS ADULT VERSION HAS A CLEAR FRUITY TASTE AND CAN BE MADE EXTRA SPECIAL BY ADDING A LITTLE WHITE RUM OR COINTREAU.

SERVES FOUR

INGREDIENTS
   12 clementines
   clear grape juice (see method
      for amount)
   15ml/1 tbsp powdered gelatine
   30ml/2 tbsp caster sugar
   whipped cream, to decorate

VARIATION
Use four ruby grapefruit instead of clementines, if you prefer. Squeeze the juice from half of them and segment the rest, discarding any bitter white pith.

1 Squeeze the juice from eight of the clementines and pour it into a jug. Make up to 600ml/1 pint/2½ cups with the grape juice, then strain the juice mixture through a fine sieve.

2 Pour half the juice mixture into a pan. Sprinkle the gelatine on top, leave for 5 minutes, then heat gently until the gelatine has dissolved. Stir in the sugar, then the remaining juice; set aside.

3 Pare the rind very thinly from the remaining fruit and set it aside. Using a small sharp knife, cut between the membrane and fruit to separate the citrus segments. Discard the membrane and white pith.

4 Place half the segments in four dessert glasses and cover with some of the liquid fruit jelly. Place in the fridge and allow to set.

5 When the jellies are set, arrange the remaining segments on top. Carefully pour over the remaining liquid jelly and chill until set. Cut the pared clementine rind into fine shreds. Serve the jellies topped with a generous spoonful of whipped cream scattered with the clementine rind shreds.

RUBY ORANGE SHERBET IN GINGER BASKETS

THIS SUPERB FROZEN DESSERT IS PERFECT FOR PEOPLE WITHOUT ICE CREAM MAKERS WHO CAN'T BE BOTHERED WITH THE FREEZING AND STIRRING THAT HOME-MADE ICES NORMALLY REQUIRE. IT IS ALSO IDEAL FOR SERVING AT A SPECIAL DINNER PARTY AS BOTH THE SHERBET AND GINGER BASKETS CAN BE MADE IN ADVANCE AND THE DESSERT SIMPLY ASSEMBLED BETWEEN COURSES.

SERVES SIX

INGREDIENTS
   grated rind and juice of
     2 blood oranges
   175g/6oz/1½ cups icing sugar
   300ml/½ pint/1¼ cups double cream
   200g/7oz/scant 1 cup Greek-style
     natural yogurt
   blood orange segments, to
     decorate (optional)
For the ginger baskets
   25g/1oz/2 tbsp unsalted butter
   15ml/1 tbsp golden syrup
   30ml/2 tbsp caster sugar
   1.5ml/¼ tsp ground ginger
   15ml/1 tbsp finely chopped mixed
     citrus peel
   15ml/1 tbsp plain flour

2 Whisk the double cream in a large bowl until the mixture forms soft peaks, then fold in the yogurt.

3 Gently stir in the orange juice mixture, then pour into a freezerproof container. Cover and freeze until firm.

6 Lightly grease two baking sheets. Using about 10ml/2 tsp of the mixture at a time, drop three portions of the ginger dough on to each baking sheet, spacing them well apart. Spread each one to a 5cm/2in circle, then bake for 12–14 minutes or until the biscuits are dark golden in colour.

1 Place the orange rind and juice in a bowl. Sift the icing sugar over the top and set aside for 30 minutes, then stir until smooth.

4 Make the baskets. Preheat the oven to 180°C/350°F/Gas 4. Place the butter, syrup and sugar in a heavy-based saucepan and heat gently until melted.

5 Add the ground ginger, mixed citrus peel and flour and stir until the mixture is smooth.

7 Remove the biscuits from the oven and allow to stand on the baking sheets for 1 minute to firm slightly. Lift off with a fish slice and drape over six greased mini pudding tins or upturned cups; flatten the top (which will become the base) and flute the edges to form a basket shape.

COOK'S TIP
When making the ginger baskets it is essential to work quickly. Have the greased tins or cups ready before you start. If the biscuits cool and firm up before you have time to drape them all, return them to the oven for a few seconds to soften them again.

8 When cool, lift the baskets off the tins or cups and place on individual dessert plates. Arrange small scoops of the frozen orange sherbet in each basket. Decorate each portion with a few orange segments, if you like.

CHOCOLATE AND MANDARIN TRUFFLE SLICE

CHOCOHOLICS WILL LOVE THIS WICKEDLY RICH DESSERT. THE MANDARINS GIVE IT A DELICIOUS TANG.

SERVES EIGHT

INGREDIENTS
    400g/14oz plain chocolate
    4 egg yolks
    3 mandarin oranges
    200ml/7fl oz/scant 1 cup crème
      fraîche
    30ml/2 tbsp raisins
    chocolate curls, to decorate
For the sauce
    30ml/2 tbsp Cointreau
    120ml/4fl oz/½ cup crème fraîche

1 Grease a 450g/1lb loaf tin and line it with clear film. Break the chocolate in to a large heatproof bowl. Place over a pan of hot water until melted.

2 Remove the bowl of chocolate from the heat and whisk in the egg yolks.

COOK'S TIP
Chocolate-tipped mandarin slices would also make a superb decoration. Use small segments; pat dry on kitchen paper, then half dip them in melted chocolate. Leave on non-stick baking paper until the chocolate has set.

3 Pare the rind from the mandarins, taking care to leave the pith behind. Cut the rind into slivers.

4 Stir the slivers of mandarin rind into the chocolate with the crème fraîche and raisins. Beat until smooth, then spoon the mixture into the prepared loaf tin and chill for 4 hours.

5 Cut the pith and any remaining rind from the mandarins, then slice thinly.

6 For the sauce, stir the Cointreau into the crème fraîche. Remove the truffle loaf from the tin, peel off the clear film and slice. Serve each slice on a dessert plate with some sauce and mandarin slices, and decorate.

LEMON AND LIME CHEESECAKE

TANGY LEMON CHEESECAKES ARE ALWAYS A HIT. THE LIME SYRUP MAKES THIS A CITRUS SENSATION.

2 Make the topping. Place the lemon rind and juice in a small saucepan and sprinkle over the gelatine. Leave to sponge for 5 minutes. Heat gently until the gelatine has melted, then set the mixture aside to cool slightly. Beat the ricotta cheese and sugar in a bowl. Stir in the cream and egg yolks, then whisk in the cooled gelatine mixture.

MAKES EIGHT SLICES

INGREDIENTS
  150g/5oz/1½ cups digestive biscuits
  40g/1½oz/3 tbsp butter
For the topping
  grated rind and juice of 2 lemons
  10ml/2 tsp powdered gelatine
  250g/9oz/generous 1 cup ricotta
    cheese
  75g/3oz/⅓ cup caster sugar
  150ml/¼ pint/⅔ cup double cream
  2 eggs, separated
For the lime syrup
  finely pared rind and juice of 3 limes
  75g/3oz/⅓ cup caster sugar
  5ml/1 tsp arrowroot mixed with
    30ml/2 tbsp water
  a little green food colouring
    (optional)

1 Lightly grease a 20cm/8in round springform cake tin. Place the biscuits in a food processor or blender and process until they form fine crumbs. Melt the butter in a large saucepan, then stir in the crumbs until well coated. Spoon into the prepared cake tin, press the crumbs down well in an even layer, then chill.

3 Whisk the egg whites in a grease-free bowl until they form soft peaks. Fold them into the cheese mixture. Spoon on to the biscuit base, level the surface and chill for 2–3 hours.

4 Meanwhile, make the lime syrup. Place the lime rind, juice and caster sugar in a small saucepan. Bring to the boil, stirring, then boil the syrup for 5 minutes. Stir in the arrowroot mixture and continue to stir until the syrup boils again and thickens slightly. Tint pale green with a little food colouring, if you like. Cool, then chill until required.

5 Spoon the lime syrup over the set cheesecake. Remove from the tin and cut into slices to serve.

LEMON SURPRISE PUDDING

THIS IS A MUCH-LOVED DESSERT MANY OF US REMEMBER FROM CHILDHOOD. THE SURPRISE IS THE UNEXPECTED SAUCE CONCEALED BENEATH THE DELECTABLE SPONGE.

SERVES FOUR

INGREDIENTS
  50g/2oz/¼ cup butter, plus extra
    for greasing
  grated rind and juice of 2 lemons
  115g/4oz/½ cup caster sugar
  2 eggs, separated
  50g/2oz/½ cup self-raising flour
  300ml/½ pint/1¼ cups milk

1 Preheat the oven to 190°C/375°F/ Gas 5. Use a little butter to grease a 1.2 litre/2 pint/5 cup baking dish.

2 Beat the lemon rind, remaining butter and caster sugar in a bowl until pale and fluffy. Add the egg yolks and flour and beat together well. Gradually whisk in the lemon juice and milk (don't be alarmed if the mixture curdles horribly!). In a grease-free bowl whisk the egg whites until they form stiff peaks.

3 Fold the egg whites lightly into the lemon mixture, then pour into the prepared baking dish.

4 Place the dish in a roasting tin and pour in hot water to come halfway up the side of the dish. Bake for about 45 minutes until golden. Serve at once.

CRÊPES SUZETTE

SIMPLY SUPERB — THAT'S THE VERDICT ON THIS PERENNIALLY POPULAR DESSERT. THESE CRÊPES DESERVE NOTHING LESS THAN THE BEST QUALITY VANILLA ICE CREAM YOU CAN FIND.

SERVES FOUR

INGREDIENTS
  8 crêpes (see Summer Berry Crêpes,
    page 116, for method)
  25g/1oz/2 tbsp unsalted butter
  50g/2oz/¼ cup caster sugar
  juice of 2 oranges
  juice of ½ lemon
  60ml/4 tbsp Cointreau or other
    orange liqueur
  best quality vanilla ice cream,
    to serve

COOK'S TIP
Crêpes freeze well and can be reheated by the method described in step 1, or simultaneously thawed and reheated in the microwave. A stack of eight crêpes, interleaved with greaseproof paper, will take 2–3 minutes on High. Be sure to cover the top crêpe with a piece of paper as well.

1 Warm the cooked crêpes between two plates placed over a saucepan of simmering water.

2 Melt the butter in a heavy-based frying pan. Stir in the caster sugar and cook over a medium heat, tilting the pan occasionally, until the mixture is golden brown. Add the orange and lemon juices and stir until the caramel has completely dissolved.

3 Add a crêpe to the pan. Using kitchen tongs, fold it in half, then in half again. Slide to the side of the pan. Repeat with the remaining crêpes.

4 When all the crêpes have been folded in the sauce, pour over the Cointreau and set it alight. Shake the pan until the flames die down. Divide the crêpes and sauce among dessert plates and serve at once with vanilla ice cream.

CITRUS FRUIT FLAMBÉ
WITH PISTACHIO PRALINE

A FRUIT FLAMBÉ MAKES A DRAMATIC FINALE FOR A DINNER PARTY. TOPPING THIS REFRESHING CITRUS FRUIT DESSERT WITH CRUNCHY PISTACHIO PRALINE MAKES IT EXTRA SPECIAL.

SERVES FOUR

INGREDIENTS
    4 oranges
    2 ruby grapefruit
    2 limes
    50g/2oz/¼ cup butter
    50g/2oz/⅓ cup light muscovado sugar
    45ml/3 tbsp Cointreau
    fresh mint sprigs, to decorate
For the praline
    oil, for greasing
    115g/4oz/½ cup caster sugar
    50g/2oz/½ cup pistachio nuts

4 Heat the butter and muscovado sugar together in a heavy-based frying pan until the sugar has melted and the mixture is golden. Strain the citrus juices into the pan and continue to cook, stirring occasionally, until the juice has reduced and is syrupy.

5 Add the fruit segments and warm through without stirring. Pour over the Cointreau and set it alight. As soon as the flames die down, spoon the fruit flambé into serving dishes. Scatter some praline over each portion and decorate with mint. Serve at once.

1 First, make the pistachio praline. Brush a baking sheet lightly with oil. Place the caster sugar and nuts in a small heavy-based saucepan and cook gently, swirling the pan occasionally until the sugar has melted.

2 Continue to cook over a fairly low heat until the nuts start to pop and the sugar has turned a dark golden colour. Pour on to the oiled baking sheet and set aside to cool. Using a sharp knife, chop the praline into rough chunks.

3 Cut off all the rind and pith from the citrus fruit. Holding each fruit in turn over a large bowl, cut between the membranes so that the segments fall into the bowl, with any juice.

COOK'S TIP
If desired, use a rolling pin or toffee hammer to break up the praline.

COLD LEMON SOUFFLÉ WITH CARAMELIZED ALMOND TOPPING

THIS TERRIFIC TO LOOK AT, REFRESHING DESSERT SOUFFLÉ IS LIGHT AND LUSCIOUS.

2 Put the lemon rind and egg yolks in a bowl. Add 75g/3oz/6 tbsp of the caster sugar and whisk until light and creamy.

3 Place the lemon juice in a small heatproof bowl and sprinkle over the gelatine. Set aside for 5 minutes, then place the bowl in a pan of simmering water. Heat, stirring occasionally, until the gelatine has dissolved. Cool slightly, then stir the gelatine mixture into the egg yolk mixture.

4 In a separate bowl, lightly whip the cream to soft peaks. Fold into the egg yolk mixture and set aside.

5 Whisk the egg whites in a grease-free bowl until stiff peaks form. Gradually whisk in the remaining caster sugar until the mixture is stiff and glossy. Quickly and lightly fold the whites into the yolk mixture. Pour into the prepared dish, smooth the surface and chill for 4–5 hours or until set.

6 Make the decoration. Brush a baking sheet lightly with oil. Preheat the grill. Scatter the almonds over the sheet and sift the icing sugar over. Grill until the nuts are golden and the sugar has caramelized. Allow to cool, then remove the mixture from the tray with a palette knife and break it into pieces.

7 When the soufflé has set, carefully peel off the paper. Pile the caramelized almonds on top of the soufflé and decorate with the physalis.

SERVES SIX

INGREDIENTS
    oil, for greasing
    grated rind and juice of
        3 large lemons
    5 large eggs, separated
    115g/4oz/½ cup caster sugar
    25ml/1½ tbsp powdered gelatine
    450ml/¾ pint/scant 2 cups
        double cream
For the decoration
    75g/3oz/¾ cup flaked almonds
    75g/3oz/¾ cup icing sugar
    3 physalis

COOK'S TIP
When peeling off the soufflé collar, hold the blade of a knife against the set soufflé so that it keeps its shape.

1 Make the soufflé collar. Cut a strip of non-stick baking paper long enough to fit around a 900ml/1½ pint/3¾ cup soufflé dish and wide enough to extend 7.5cm/3in above the rim. Fit the strip around the dish, tape, then tie it around the top of the dish with string. Brush the inside of the paper lightly with oil.

LEMON ROULADE <u>WITH</u> LEMON CURD CREAM

THIS FEATHERLIGHT ROULADE FILLED WITH A RICH LEMON CURD CREAM MAKES A MARVELLOUS DESSERT OR TEA-TIME TREAT. THE LEMON CURD CAN BE MADE AHEAD AND KEPT IN THE FRIDGE.

MAKES EIGHT SLICES

INGREDIENTS
 4 eggs, separated
 115g/4oz/½ cup caster sugar
 finely grated rind of 2 lemons
 5ml/1 tsp pure vanilla essence
 25g/1oz/¼ cup ground almonds
 40g/1½oz/⅓ cup plain flour, sifted
 45ml/3 tbsp icing sugar, for dusting
For the lemon curd cream
 300ml/½ pint/1¼ cups double cream
 60ml/4 tbsp fresh lemon curd
  (see recipe below right)

1 Preheat the oven to 190°C/375°F/ Gas 5. Grease a 33 × 23cm/13 × 9in Swiss roll tin and line with non-stick baking paper.

3 Whisk the egg whites in a grease-free bowl until they form stiff, glossy peaks. Gradually whisk in the remaining caster sugar to form a stiff meringue. Stir half the meringue mixture into the egg yolk mixture and fold in the rest.

6 Sift the icing sugar liberally over a piece of non-stick baking paper. Turn the sponge out on to it. Peel off the lining paper and spread the lemon curd cream over the surface of the sponge, leaving a border around the edge.

2 In a large bowl, beat the egg yolks with half the caster sugar until light and foamy. Beat in the lemon rind and vanilla essence, then lightly fold in the ground almonds and flour using a large metal spoon or spatula.

4 Pour into the prepared tin, level the surface with a palette knife and bake for 10 minutes or until risen and spongy to the touch. Cover loosely with a sheet of non-stick baking paper and a damp dish towel. Leave to cool in the tin.

7 Using the paper underneath as a guide, roll up the sponge from one of the long sides. Place on a serving platter, with the seam underneath. Cut the roulade into slices to serve.

FRESH LEMON CURD
Put the grated rind and juice of 3 lemons into a pan with 115g/4oz/ ½ cup caster sugar. Bring to the boil, stirring until the sugar has dissolved. Stir in 15ml/1 tbsp cornflour mixed to a paste with 15ml/1 tbsp cold water. Off the heat, whisk in 2 egg yolks. Return to a low heat, whisk for about 2 minutes; remove from the heat. Gradually whisk in 50g/2oz/¼ cup butter, at room temperature. Pour into a sterilized jar, cover and seal at once. Leave to cool, then chill. Use within 2–3 weeks. Makes 450g/1lb.

COOK'S TIP
Having filled and rolled the roulade, keep it wrapped in the non-stick baking paper and hold it together for about a minute to allow the shape to set before removing the paper and transferring the roulade to a plate.

5 Make the lemon curd cream. Whip the cream; then lightly fold in the lemon curd.

LEMON MERINGUE PIE

CRISP SHORTCRUST IS FILLED WITH A MOUTHWATERING LEMON CREAM FILLING AND HEAPED WITH SOFT GOLDEN-TOPPED MERINGUE. THIS CLASSIC OPEN TART NEVER FAILS TO PLEASE. POPULAR WITH ADULTS AND CHILDREN, IT IS THE ESSENTIAL SUNDAY LUNCH DESSERT.

2 Meanwhile make the filling. Place all the ingredients in a bowl, mix lightly and leave to soak for 1 hour.

3 Preheat the oven to 200°C/400°F/ Gas 6. Beat the filling until smooth and pour into the chilled pastry case. Bake for 20 minutes or until the filling has just set and the pastry is golden. Remove from the oven and cool on a wire rack for 30 minutes or until a skin has formed on the surface. Lower the oven temperature to 180°C/350°F/Gas 4.

4 Make the topping. Whisk the egg whites in a grease-free bowl until they form stiff peaks. Whisk in the caster sugar to form a glossy meringue. Spoon on top of the set lemon filling and spread over, making sure you spread the meringue right to the rim of the pie shell. Swirl the meringue slightly.

5 Bake the pie for 20–25 minutes or until the meringue is crisp and golden brown. Allow to cool on a wire rack for 10 minutes before serving.

SERVES SIX

INGREDIENTS
    115g/4oz/1 cup plain flour
    a pinch of salt
    50g/2oz/¼ cup butter
    50g/2oz/¼ cup lard
    15ml/1 tbsp caster sugar
    about 15ml/1 tbsp iced water
For the filling
    3 large egg yolks
    30ml/2 tbsp caster sugar
    grated rind and juice of 1 lemon
    25g/1oz/½ cup fresh
      white breadcrumbs
    250ml/8fl oz/1 cup milk
For the topping
    3 large egg whites
    115g/4oz/½ cup caster sugar

1 Sift the flour and salt into a bowl. Rub in the butter and lard until the mixture resembles fine breadcrumbs. Stir in the sugar and add enough iced water to make a soft dough. Roll out the pastry on a lightly floured surface and line a 21cm/8½in pie plate or tin. Chill until required.

FRESH LEMON TART

MADE FAMOUS BY ITS FRENCH TITLE — TARTE AUX CITRON — THIS TART SHOULD BE SERVED AT ROOM TEMPERATURE IF THE ZESTY LEMON FLAVOUR IS TO BE ENJOYED TO THE FULL.

SERVES SIX TO EIGHT

INGREDIENTS
   350g/12oz packet ready-made rich
      sweet shortcrust pastry, thawed
      if frozen
For the filling
   3 eggs
   115g/4oz/½ cup caster sugar
   115g/4oz/1 cup ground almonds
   105ml/7 tbsp double cream
   grated rind and juice of 2 lemons
For the topping
   2 thin-skinned unwaxed lemons,
      thinly sliced
   200g/7oz/scant 1 cup caster sugar
   105ml/7 tbsp water

COOK'S TIP
If you prefer not to candy the lemons, simply dust the tart with icing sugar.

1 Roll out the pastry and line a deep 23cm/9in fluted flan tin. Prick the base and chill for 30 minutes.

2 Preheat the oven to 200°C/400°F/ Gas 6. Line the pastry with non-stick baking paper and baking beans and bake blind for 10 minutes. Remove the paper and beans and return the pastry case to the oven for 5 minutes more.

3 Meanwhile, make the filling. Beat the eggs, caster sugar, almonds and cream in a bowl until smooth. Beat in the lemon rind and juice. Pour the filling into the pastry case. Lower the oven temperature to 190°C/375°F/Gas 5 and bake for 20 minutes or until the filling has set and the pastry is golden.

4 Make the topping. Place the lemon slices in a pan and pour over water to cover. Simmer for 15–20 minutes or until the skins are tender, then drain.

5 Place the sugar in a saucepan and stir in the measured water. Heat gently until the sugar has dissolved, stirring constantly, then boil for 2 minutes. Add the lemon slices and cook for 10–15 minutes until the skins become shiny and candied.

6 Lift out the candied lemon slices and arrange them over the top of the tart. Return the syrup to the heat and boil until reduced to a thick glaze. Brush this over the tart and allow to cool completely before serving.

KEY LIME PIE

THIS IS ONE OF AMERICA'S FAVOURITES. AS THE NAME SUGGESTS, IT ORIGINATED IN THE FLORIDA KEYS.

MAKES TEN SLICES

INGREDIENTS
   225g/8oz/2 cups plain flour
   115g/4oz/½ cup chilled
     butter, diced
   30ml/2 tbsp caster sugar
   2 egg yolks
   a pinch of salt
   30ml/2 tbsp cold water
   thinly pared lime rind and mint
     leaves, to decorate
For the filling
   4 eggs, separated
   400g/14oz can condensed milk
   grated rind and juice of 3 limes
   a few drops of green food
     colouring (optional)
   30ml/2 tbsp caster sugar
For the topping
   300ml/½ pint/1¼ cups double cream
   2–3 limes, thinly sliced

1 Sift the flour into a mixing bowl and rub in the butter using your fingertips until the mixture resembles fresh breadcrumbs. Add the sugar, egg yolks, salt and water. Mix to a soft dough.

2 Roll out the pastry on a lightly floured surface and use to line a deep 21cm/8½in fluted flan tin, allowing the excess pastry to hang over the edge. Prick the pastry base and chill for at least 30 minutes.

3 Preheat the oven to 200°C/400°F/Gas 6. Trim off the excess pastry from around the edge of the pastry case using a large sharp knife and line the pastry case with non-stick baking paper and baking beans.

4 Bake the pastry case blind for 10 minutes. Remove the paper and beans and return the pastry case to the oven for 10 minutes more.

5 Meanwhile, make the filling. Beat the egg yolks in a large bowl until light and creamy, then beat in the condensed milk, with the lime rind and juice until well combined. Add the food colouring, if using, and continue to beat until the mixture is thick.

COOK'S TIP
You can make the pastry in a food processor, but take care not to overprocess the dough. Use the pulse button and process for a few seconds at a time; switch off the motor the moment the dough clumps together.

6 In a grease-free bowl, whisk the egg whites to stiff peaks. Whisk in the caster sugar, then fold into the lime mixture.

7 Lower the oven temperature to 160°C/325°F/Gas 3. Pour the lime filling into the pastry case. Bake for 20–25 minutes or until it has set and is starting to brown. Cool, then chill.

8 Just before serving, whip the double cream for the topping and spoon it around the edge of the pie. Cut the lime slices once from the centre to the edge, then twist each slice and arrange between the spoonfuls of cream. Decorate with lime rind and mint leaves.

MOIST ORANGE AND ALMOND CAKE

THE KEY TO THIS RECIPE IS TO COOK THE ORANGE SLOWLY FIRST, SO IT IS FULLY TENDER BEFORE BEING BLENDED. DON'T USE A MICROWAVE TO SPEED THINGS UP — THIS MAKES ORANGE SKIN TOUGH.

SERVES EIGHT

INGREDIENTS
    1 large orange
    3 eggs
    225g/8oz/1 cup caster sugar
    5ml/1 tsp baking powder
    225g/8oz/2 cups ground almonds
    25g/1oz/¼ cup plain flour
    icing sugar, for dusting
    whipped cream and orange slices
    to serve (optional).

1 Wash the orange and pierce it with a skewer. Put it in a deep saucepan and pour over water to cover completely. Bring to the boil then lower the heat, cover and simmer for 1 hour or until the skin is very soft. Drain, then cool.

COOK'S TIP
For a treat, serve this cake with spiced poached kumquats.

2 Preheat the oven to 180°C/350°F/ Gas 4. Grease a 20cm/8in round cake tin and line it with non-stick baking paper. Cut the cooled orange in half and discard the pips. Place the orange, skin and all, in a blender or food processor and purée until smooth and pulpy.

3 In a bowl, whisk the eggs and sugar until thick. Fold in the baking powder, almonds and flour. Fold in the purée.

4 Pour into the prepared tin, level the surface and bake for 1 hour or until a skewer inserted into the centre comes out clean. Cool the cake in the tin for 10 minutes, then turn out on to a wire rack, peel off the lining paper and cool completely. Dust the top liberally with icing sugar and serve as a dessert with whipped cream, if you like. You could tuck thick orange slices under the cake just before serving.

LEMON AND LIME SYRUP CAKE

THIS CAKE IS PERFECT FOR BUSY COOKS AS IT CAN BE MIXED IN MOMENTS AND NEEDS NO ICING.
THE SIMPLE TANGY LIME TOPPING TRANSFORMS IT INTO A FABULOUSLY MOIST CAKE.

SERVES EIGHT

INGREDIENTS
    225g/8oz/2 cups self-raising flour
    5ml/1 tsp baking powder
    225g/8oz/1 cup caster sugar
    225g/8oz/1 cup butter, softened
    4 eggs, beaten
    grated rind of 2 lemons
    30ml/2 tbsp lemon juice
For the topping
    finely pared rind of 1 lime
    juice of 2 limes
    150g/5oz/⅔ cup caster sugar

1 Make the cake. Preheat the oven to 160°C/325°F/Gas 3. Grease and line a 20cm/8in round cake tin. Sift the flour and baking powder into a large bowl. Add the caster sugar, butter and eggs and beat together well until the mixture is smooth, creamy and fluffy.

2 Beat in the lemon rind and juice. Spoon the mixture into the prepared tin, then smooth the surface and make a shallow indentation in the top with the back of a spoon.

3 Bake for 1¼–1½ hours or until the cake is golden on top and spongy when lightly pressed, and a skewer inserted into the centre comes out clean.

4 Meanwhile, mix the topping ingredients together. As soon as the cake is cooked, remove it from the oven and pour the topping over the surface. Allow the cake to cool in the tin.

VARIATION
Use lemon rind and juice instead of lime for the topping if you prefer. You will need only one large lemon.

SPICED POACHED KUMQUATS

KUMQUATS ARE NOT AVAILABLE THROUGHOUT THE YEAR, BUT THEY ARE UNDOUBTEDLY AT THEIR BEST JUST BEFORE THE CHRISTMAS SEASON. THESE FRUITS CAN BE BOTTLED AND GIVEN AS PRESENTS. THEIR MARVELLOUS SPICY-SWEET CITRUS FLAVOUR COMPLEMENTS BOTH SWEET AND SAVOURY DISHES.

SERVES SIX

INGREDIENTS
   450g/1lb/4 cups kumquats
   115g/4oz/½ cup caster sugar
   150ml/¼ pint/⅔ cup water
   1 small cinnamon stick
   1 star anise
   a citrus leaf, to decorate (optional)

1 Cut the kumquats in half and discard the pips. Place the kumquats in a saucepan with the sugar, water and spices. Cook over a gentle heat, stirring until the sugar has dissolved.

2 Increase the heat, cover the pan and boil the mixture for 8–10 minutes until the kumquats are tender. To bottle the kumquats, spoon them into warm, sterilized jars, seal and label.

3 If you want to serve the spiced kumquats soon after making them, let the mixture cool, then chill it. Decorate with a citrus leaf, if you like.

COOK'S TIP
Try these delectable treats with baked ham, roast pork or slices of raised pork pie. They would also make a perfect accompaniment for moist almond or chocolate cake.

THREE-FRUIT MARMALADE

SEVILLE ORANGES HAVE A FINE FLAVOUR AND ARE THE BEST VARIETY FOR MARMALADE. SWEET ORANGES CAN BE USED AT A PINCH, BUT THEY TEND TO MAKE THE MARMALADE CLOUDY.

MAKES 2.25KG/5–5¼LB

INGREDIENTS
   2 Seville oranges
   2 lemons
   1 grapefruit
   1.75 litres/3 pints/7½ cups water
   1.5kg/3lb 6oz/6¾ cups granulated sugar
   croissants, to serve (optional)

1 Wash the fruit, halve and squeeze their juice. Pour into a large heavy-based saucepan or preserving pan. Tip the pips and pulp in a square of muslin, gather the sides into a bag and tie the neck tightly with string. Tie the bag to the handle of the pan so that it dangles in the citrus juice.

2 Cut the citrus skins into thin wedges; scrape off and discard the membranes and pith. Cut the rinds into slivers and add to the pan with the measured water. Bring to the simmer and cook gently for 2 hours until the rinds are very tender and the water has reduced by half. Test the rinds for softness by pressing a cooled piece with a finger.

3 Lift out the muslin bag, squeezing out the juice into the pan. Discard the bag. Stir the sugar into the pan and heat very gently, stirring occasionally, until all the sugar has dissolved.

4 Bring the mixture to the boil and boil for 10–15 minutes or until the marmalade registers 105ºC/220ºF.

5 Alternatively, test the marmalade for setting by pouring a small amount on to a chilled saucer. Chill for 2 minutes, then push the marmalade with your finger; if wrinkles form on the surface, it is ready. Cool for 15 minutes.

6 Stir the marmalade and pour it into warm, sterilized jars. Cover with greaseproof paper discs. Seal and label. Store in a cool dark place. Serve with warm croissants, if you like.

COOK'S TIP
Leaving the marmalade to cool slightly before potting lets it set just enough to prevent the fruit from sinking. Stir before pouring it into the jars. Cover the surface with paper discs and seal while hot.

EXOTIC FRUITS

Thanks to modern transportation methods, tropical fruits are no longer merely the stuff of travellers' tales. Rambutans, carambolas, guavas, passion fruit and pomegranates are stocked on greengrocers' shelves alongside recent rarities, which have now become commonplace, such as mangoes, fresh dates and kiwi fruit. Most supermarkets now label tropical fruits with preparation and serving suggestions, so it is easy to venture into the realms of the exotic.

BANANAS

Bananas are surely the best-known tropical fruit and one of the most healthy and versatile. Neatly packaged in their attractive easy-peel skins, hygienically enclosing the sweet, creamy-white, floury flesh, bananas are the perfect convenience food.

The banana plant, whose elongated, fan-like leaves can grow to over 3.6m/15ft long, is actually an enormous herb. "Hands" of up to 200 bananas point upwards through the leaves like fingers.

Above: Bananas, shown here in their unripe state, grow upwards in bunches on a huge plant that is actually a giant herb.

History

Bananas originated in South-east Asia and have grown in the tropics since ancient times. There is a theory that the fruit of the Tree of Knowledge in the Garden of Eden was actually a banana; certainly, a banana leaf would have protected Adam's modesty more effectively than a fig leaf. Before man began to cultivate bananas, the fruits contained so many bitter black seeds that they were almost inedible.

Varieties

Hundreds of different varieties of banana flourish in the tropics, from sweet yellow pygmy fruit to large fibrous plantains and green bananas, which can only be used for cooking.

The most common varieties of sweet banana are the long, curved yellow

Left: Lady Finger or Sugar bananas are tiny – often no more than the length of a lady's finger!

dessert fruit, which develop a speckled brown skin as they ripen. The most widely available of these is Cavendish, but unless you are an expert it is practically impossible to differentiate between individual varieties.

Lady Finger or **Sugar** These are tiny finger bananas, often no more than 7.5cm/3in long. They have creamy flesh and a very sweet flavour.

Apple These yellow bananas are also very small. They have golden flesh and when very ripe have a faint taste and aroma of apple.

Right: Perhaps the best-known tropical fruit, easy-to-peel yellow bananas, which come in a variety of sizes, are the perfect convenience food.

Right: When very ripe, small Apple bananas have a faint taste and aroma of apple.

Red bananas These bananas from Ecuador have brownish-red skins and smooth, yellowish-pink, sweet flesh with a creamy texture. Their colour makes it hard to assess the exact degree of ripeness, so they can sometimes prove rather disappointing. Allow a few blackish patches to develop on the skin before eating.

Green bananas Large green bananas are only suitable for cooking. They have crisp flesh and are often used as a substitute for potatoes, although they have a blander flavour. Fried green banana rings are good in curries.

Plantain These fruits resemble large bananas, but are flatter in shape. They have firm, pinkish flesh, which is less sweet than that of dessert bananas, but contains more starch. They are almost always used in savoury dishes and can be cooked like potatoes. Very firm plantains can be peeled, then sliced wafer-thin and deep fried like potato crisps. As plantains ripen, their flesh becomes darker and sweeter and the fruit can be used in desserts.

Right: Small (as here) or large, red bananas have the same sweet, creamy flesh.

Nutrition

Bananas are extremely nutritious, being rich in potassium, riboflavin, niacin and dietary fibre. Bananas also contain vitamins A and C and some calcium and iron. They have a high energy value (99 kilocalories per 100g/3¾oz) and are good for growing children and athletes. They are also excellent for low-salt, low-fat and cholesterol-free diets.

Buying and Storing

Bananas are harvested unripe and stored in a humid atmosphere to ripen slowly. Unripe bananas are green all over; these are inedible. Fruit with green-tinged ends are slightly underripe, with a crisp texture and refreshing taste. Perfectly ripe bananas are uniformly yellow; as the fruit continues to ripen, brown speckles appear on the skin until it is covered with brown mottling. By this stage, the flesh is soft and sweet and is best for mashing. Once the skin has become brown all over, the banana is too ripe to eat; the flesh will have collapsed, but it can still be used for cooking. Do not buy bananas with damaged skins, or those that are too ripe. Unlike other fruit, they will continue to ripen rapidly at home. Never store them in the fridge, as the skins will blacken. Kept in a fruit bowl, bananas will hasten the ripening of other fruit.

Dried bananas Drying intensifies the sweetness of bananas. Dried bananas are dark brown, sticky and extremely sweet. They are usually eaten as a highly nutritious but calorific snack, but can also be added to winter fruit salads or savoury stews.

Canned bananas Oriental food stores sell whole baby bananas, sometimes complete with blossom, canned in heavy syrup. Only for those with a very sweet tooth!

Peeling plantains

1 Using a sharp knife, top and tail the fruit. Cut in half horizontally.

2 Slit the plantain skin with a sharp knife, along the natural ridge. Take care not to cut through the flesh.

3 Ease up the edge of the skin and run your thumb tip underneath to lift up the skin. Lift off and discard the skin.

Right: Plantains are almost always used in savoury dishes and can be cooked like potatoes.

Cooking

Peel bananas just before using, removing the white threads from the flesh. Slice the bananas and, if not serving immediately, brush with lemon juice to prevent discoloration.

Dessert bananas are delicious eaten raw, but cooking brings out the sweetness and enhances the flavour. Raw bananas can be made into ice cream, milk shakes and trifles. Sliced bananas can be added to fruit salads or used to garnish sweet and savoury dishes. In Indonesia and the Far East, they are served as an accompaniment to rice dishes such as *nasi goreng* and curries. They combine well with other tropical ingredients, especially brown sugar, coconut, exotic fruits like pineapple, passion fruit and mango, and rum.

Bananas can be baked in their skins, then split and served with melted butter and lemon juice. Alternatively, cook them over the dying embers of a barbecue until the skins turn black. Split them, sprinkle with rum and serve with double cream. Another rich dessert is banoffi pie, a very sweet concoction of bananas and toffee. A less sweet, but equally delicious combination is grilled bananas wrapped in bacon. Banana fritters are always popular; cut the fruit into chunks, coat in batter and deep fry, or wrap in filo

Above: Dried bananas are dark brown, sticky and very sweet.

pastry, brush with melted butter and deep fry. Mashed bananas make deliciously moist cakes and teabreads.

Green bananas and plantains are starchier than sweet bananas and contain less sugar, so they are served as a vegetable. They can be boiled, baked, mashed, fried or grilled, and are an essential ingredient of many African and West Indian dishes. Banana leaves are often used as a wrapping for savoury fillings and add a pleasant aromatic flavour to both chicken and fish.

BABACOS

The babaco is a hybrid of the papaya. Pointed at the stem end and blunt at the other, this large five-sided fruit reveals a soft white core when halved. When unripe, the waxy skin is pale green, maturing to yellow. When ripe, the pale orangey-pink flesh is succulent and juicy, with a faint aroma of fresh strawberries, and the flavour resembles that of a rather bland papaya.

History

The babaco is native to Ecuador. European botanists discovered it about seventy years ago, and it is now widely grown in New Zealand, and in the Channel Islands.

Nutrition

The fruit contains valuable enzymes that help to digest fat and proteins and can be used to tenderize meat. It is a good source of vitamin C.

Buying and Storing

Babacos keep well. Yellow fruit are ready to eat straight away and should be stored in the fridge, where they will keep for about five days. Pale green babacos can be kept for a few days at room temperature until yellow and ripe.

Preparing and Cooking

Babacos can be sliced, skin and all, and eaten raw. The delicate flavour can be livened up with lemon or lime juice and sugar. The flesh can be diced and used raw in salads, or squeezed to make a refreshing juice. Babacos can also be poached in syrup and served as a dessert with cream, custard or vanilla or stem ginger ice cream, but you will need to flavour the syrup with lime juice

and aromatics. On a savoury note, the fruit makes excellent sauces, chutneys and relishes. Stewed babaco can be served as an accompaniment to roast chicken, pork and ham.

Babaco for breakfast

For a deliciously different breakfast experience, try serving your favourite cereal with chilled cooked babaco. Make a syrup by boiling equal quantities of water and sugar with the juice of a lemon or lime and a split vanilla pod, a cinnamon stick or a grating of nutmeg. Dice the babaco (there is no need to peel it) and poach gently in the syrup for about 10 minutes, until tender. Chill well before using.

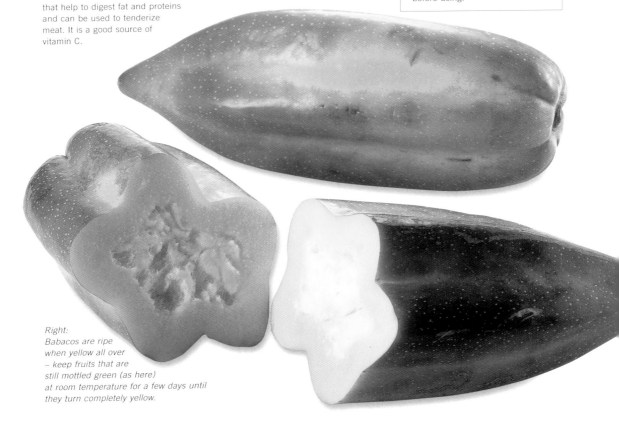

*Right:
Babacos are ripe
when yellow all over
– keep fruits that are
still mottled green (as here)
at room temperature for a few days until
they turn completely yellow.*

BREADFRUIT

The fruit of a very tall tree, these large round to egg-shaped fruits weigh from 300g/11oz to 3kg/6½lb. They have thick, warty, greenish skin and white starchy flesh with a bread-like texture, which sometimes contains up to 200 edible seeds and sometimes none at all. Breadfruit form part of the staple diet in the tropics.

History

Native to the Pacific and East Indies, breadfruit came to fame in the famous 1787 mutiny on the *Bounty*, when, during the voyage to the West Indies, Captain William Bligh gave the last remaining fresh water to his precious cargo of breadfruit in preference to the crew. After being cast adrift, and enduring immense hardship, the overbearing captain arrived in Timor and was again sent out to collect breadfruit, earning himself the name "Breadfruit Bligh".

Nutrition

Breadfruit is very starchy. It is high in fibre and contains small amounts of vitamin C and folic acid.

Below: Breadfruit

Preparing and Cooking

Breadfruit are normally eaten as a vegetable. When really ripe, they can be eaten raw, but they are more usually cooked. They can be peeled and boiled, roasted or fried like potatoes, or baked whole in the oven.

CARAMBOLAS

Native to Indonesia and the Moluccas, carambolas or star fruit are now widely available in supermarkets. The uncut yellow or pale amber fruit has a waxy skin and is cilindrical in shape, with concave sides and five ridged edges; it resembles an elongated Chinese lantern. When the fruit is sliced crossways, the slices are perfect star shapes, which are wonderful for decorative purposes. Although the fruit often tastes less exciting than it looks, it is refreshing and juicy to eat.

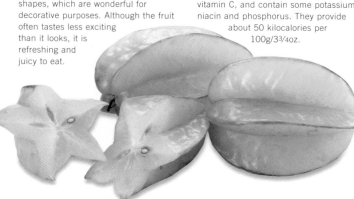

History

Carambolas originated in the Malay Archipelago, between South-east Asia and Australia, but they are now also grown in Africa, Brazil, the West Indies and the United States.

Nutrition

Carambolas are a very good source of vitamin C, and contain some potassium, niacin and phosphorus. They provide about 50 kilocalories per 100g/3¾oz.

Buying and Storing

Some carambolas have more flavour than others; there is no way of telling before you taste, so they are best used simply as an attractive decoration or in conjunction with other exotic fruits. Choose firm, undamaged fruits and hope for the best. They will keep in the fridge for up to a week.

Preparing and Serving

A good carambola will be sweet and tangy enough to eat on its own, complete with skin. Slice the fruit crossways and, if you wish, cut out the flat central seeds with a sharp knife. The fruits are generally eaten raw as part of a fruit salad, or made into jams, but they can also be poached in a syrup enlivened with lime juice.

Left: Carambolas make a wonderful garnish. When cut crossways, the slices are perfect star shapes, hence their other name – star fruit.

CHERIMOYAS, CUSTARD APPLES AND SOURSOPS

Native to South America and the West Indies, cherimoyas are the fruit of shrubs belonging to the annona species. The large heart-shaped or oval fruit is made up of many corpels, or concave sections, with scaly yellowish-green or tan skin, rather like a pine cone or a half-prepared globe artichoke. Inside, the fruit has creamy-white, custard-like flesh with a sweet-sour flavour (hence the name soursop) reminiscent of pineapples and bananas, and large black seeds.

Varieties

There are many different varieties of cherimoya, of which custard apples and soursops are the most widely available.
Custard apples These are heart-shaped or oval and can weigh up to 450g/1lb.

Below: Heart-shaped soursops have a tangy, acidic flavour.

They have light tan or greenish quilted skin, which develops brown patches as the fruit ripens; the flesh is particularly mellow and custard-like.
Soursop Also called prickly custard apples or bullock's hearts, soursops are the largest of this group of fruits. They have dark green skins covered in numerous short spines. The white juicy flesh of the soursop has a tangy, acidic flavour. Once they are ripe, soursops rapidly ferment and quickly become inedible.

Nutrition

Cherimoyas are high in vitamin C and iron, and provide 92 kilocalories per 100g/3¾oz.

Buying and Storing

Cherimoyas are fragile, so choose compact fruit with unblemished skin and tightly packed corpels; once these have separated, the fruit is past its best. Press gently to check that the fruit has a slight "give". Cherimoyas should be eaten as soon as possible after buying, but can be kept in the bottom of the fridge for a day or two. Unripe fruit should be kept in a brown paper bag at room temperature until they are ready to eat.

Preparation and Serving

All types of cherimoya can be eaten fresh. Simply cut the fruit in half

Above: Custard apples have delicious mellow flesh, which is soft – almost like custard (hence their name).

lengthways and scoop the flesh straight from the shell with a spoon, discarding the inedible seeds. For a special treat, add a dollop of cream.

Cherimoya flesh makes a delicious fruit sauce when blended with bananas and cream, or it can be blended with four times its volume of water to make a refreshing drink; stir in sugar to taste. The fruits can also be made into jams, jellies and sorbets.

CURUBA

Also known as the "banana passion fruit", the curuba is like an elongated passion fruit, with soft yellowish skin. The orange pulp has a sharp flavour and needs a little sugar to make it palatable. The skin can be peeled off in the same way as a banana. Curubas marry well with other tropical fruits and can be used in the same way as you would passion fruit.

Right: Curuba have a sharp flavour and can be used like passion fruit.

DATES

Dates are the fruit of the date palm, which grows in sub-tropical and desert areas throughout North Africa, the Arab States, California and Australia. The finger-shaped fruit grows in clusters of several dozen at the top of the tall trees, ripening from green to burnished brown. Date palms are prolific; the average annual yield of a single palm is 50kg/110lb.

Until a few years ago, only dried dates were available outside their native lands, but now fresh dates are exported, although only a few of the many varieties reach the shops.

History

Dates are one of the world's oldest cultivated fruits. It is probable that the Babylonians grew them as long as 8,000 years ago; certainly records show that they have been cultivated for over 5,000 years. In early times, the date palm was regarded as the "tree of life". Every part of it was used; the buds and fruit were eaten or dried and ground into flour, the sap was drunk, the fibres were woven and the date stones were used as fuel or fodder for donkeys and camels. Even today, dates are still known as the "bread of the desert".

Left: Boxed halawi dates.

Above: Date palms grow throughout North Africa, the Arab States, California and Australia.

The Ancient Greeks and Romans were also fond of dates and often combined them with meat in their cooking.

Varieties

Of the many varieties of date, only a few are exported, and these are seldom sold by name. The most popular variety is the golden brown *deglet noor* ("date of the light") from North Africa and Israel; you may also find the very sweet *halawi* or the fragrant *khaleseh*, which can be recognized by its orange-brown skin. The finest dates are the large crinkly-skinned *medjool* from Egypt and California, whose flesh is intensely mellow and sweet.

Nutrition

Dates are extremely nutritious. They contain more natural sugar than any other fruit and deliver a substantial amount of dietary fibre and potassium, as well as providing many vitamins and mineral salts. They provide 144 kilocalories per 100g/3¾oz.

Buying and Storing

Fresh dates These should be plump and moist, with a smooth skin and a slightly crunchy texture. They are sold loose or in punnets. Dates are ripe when they are burnished brown. Unripe dates are more golden; they can be eaten in this state, but the flesh will be crisp and less honeyed than ripe dates. To ripen, keep the dates at room temperature. Fresh dates can be frozen whole, but check that they have not been previously frozen (they almost always have been).

Semi-dried dates These are sold in a cluster on the stem. They have wrinkled skins and a chewy texture.

Dried dates These are the old familiar Christmas favourites, sticky and intensely sweet, and are often sold sitting on a frilly doily inside a long box decorated with palm trees and camels. Since the advent of fresh dates, their popularity has declined. Dried dates are also sold pressed into blocks for use in cooking. Some oriental supermarkets stock tiny, wrinkled red dates and smoky black dates with the flavour of a bonfire, which are only suitable for cooking. Semi-dried and dried dates will keep for months, but do not store them near strong-smelling foods like onions, as they absorb odours.

Below: Dried deglet noor dates in their familiar long box.

Stuffed dates

1 Cut the dates in half and pick out the stones.

2 Fill the cavities of the dates with cream cheese and sandwich the halves together.

3 Alternatively, mould a little marzipan to fill the cavities, roll the date halves in granulated sugar and top each with a walnut half.

Right: Dried dates pressed into a block. For cooking, this type of date may need to be softened in hot water before using.

Above: Crinkly skinned Medjool dates have intensely sweet flesh.

Below: Fresh dates, which are often frozen in their country of origin, then thawed before being sold.

Preparation and Cooking

Fresh dates can be eaten just as they are. If you prefer to peel them, gently pinch the skin at the stem end until the fruit pops out. They can be stoned and filled with plain or coloured marzipan or nuts, or rolled in sugar to serve as decorative petits fours.

Fresh dates also make good additions to fruit salads and winter compotes. Surprisingly, they are also good in savoury dishes; in North Africa, they are used in *tagines* (fragrant stews) and curries, or as a sauce or stuffing for fish, meat or poultry.

Above: Dried Chinese dates are only suitable for cooking.

Dates have a particular affinity with cheese. Serve them on a cheese board, or halve and stone them and sandwich together with cream cheese.

Dried dates are good in moist cakes and hot sticky puddings, and combine very well with nuts, particularly walnuts and almonds. For cooking, dried dates should be stoned and chopped, using scissors dipped in hot water.

DRAGON FRUIT

Dragon fruit, or pitihayas, come in both yellow and pink versions. Pink dragon fruit are large, fuschia-pink fruit about 10cm/4in long, covered with pointed green-tipped scales, rather like the leaves of a globe artichoke. Inside, they are spectacularly beautiful, with translucent pearly-white flesh dotted with a mass of edible black seeds, which add an appealing crunch. The flesh is sweet and refreshing, with a slightly acidic melon-like flavour. It has the texture of kiwi fruit.

Yellow dragon fruit look more like prickly pears or mini-pineapples. They taste exactly like the pink variety.

Nutrition

Dragon fruit are rich in vitamin C and dietary fibre.

Buying and Storing

Yellow dragon fruit are ripe when golden all over. Both pink and yellow varieties should yield when gently squeezed in the hand. They are best eaten as soon as they are ripe, but the fruits can be kept in the fridge for up to three days.

Preparing and Serving

Dragon fruit are best eaten on their own, sprinkled with lemon or lime juice to enhance the flavour. They should be served chilled. Cut them in half lengthways, then scoop out the flesh from the shell. The shells can be used as unusual serving dishes.

Above: Brightly coloured dragon fruit have sweet refreshing flesh.

DURIANS

The disgusting, all-pervading, sewage-like smell is legendary and has given rise to the alternative name: civet fruit. When ripe, the flavour of the flesh, however, is delicious.

Durians are large fruit, which can weigh up to 4.5kg/10lb. Round or oval, they have a woody, olive green outer layer covered with stubby, sharp spikes, which turns yellow as they ripen. They consist of three to five segments containing aromatic creamy-white flesh with the texture of rich custard; the flavour is sweet, a little like strawberries, with a creamy after-taste. The large brown seeds are edible if cooked.

History

Durians originated in Malaysia or Borneo and from there spread to South-east Asia in prehistoric times. Despite their unspeakable smell, they have always been considered an aphrodisiac.

Nutrition

Durians are starchy fruits. They contain a small amount of fat and are a good source of potassium and vitamin C.

Buying and Storing

It is essential to eat durians very fresh; don't attempt to store them, however briefly, or your house will smell of blocked drains. Never buy fruit with damaged skin, or the smell will be

unbearable. Do not buy durians abroad and attempt to bring them home, as they are banned by most airlines! Take care not to drip juice on to clothing or table linen as it stains indelibly. Despite all these dire warnings, don't be put off trying this exotic fruit; it really does taste wonderful.

Preparing and Serving

Durians are best eaten raw. Use a large sharp knife to slit the skin at the segment joints, press out the segments and scoop out the flesh and seeds with a spoon. The rich, custardy flesh can be eaten just as it is, or puréed to make ice cream or milk shakes. Durian flesh is also used for making jam and cakes, and is available canned. The richness of the pulp also makes an excellent foil to hot, spicy foods like curries and chilli dishes. Durian seeds can be roasted or boiled and eaten like nuts.

Left: The horrible, all-pervading sewage-like smell of Durians is legendary, however, when ripe, the flavour of the flesh is delicious.

FEIJOAS

Although a distant member of the guava family, feijoas resemble small slightly pear-shaped passion fruit, with a dark green skin that yellows as the fruit ripens. The thin, tough skin protects a soft jelly-like pulp containing tiny hard seeds, which are edible. Despite its alternative name of "pineapple guava", the feijoa tastes more like an aromatic strawberry. Treat it like guava.

History

Originally from South America, the feijoa takes its name from the Portuguese botanist Dom da Silva Feijoa, who discovered it in Brazil. It is also nowadays cultivated in New Zealand.

Nutrition

Feijoas are an excellent source of vitamin C and are rich in iodine. They provide 20 kilocalories per 100g/3³⁄₄oz.

Right: Feijoas taste a little like aromatic fresh strawberries.

GINUP

The bright green dimpled skin of the ginup gives rise to its alternative name of "Spanish lime", but it is related to neither the lime nor the lychee, which it resembles in flavour. Ginups are small round tropical fruits, about 3cm/1¹⁄₄in in diameter, which grow on trees in bunches like grapes. The tough green skin protects a jelly-like pink pulp containing a large central seed. The flesh is juicy and sweet, with a slightly acidic note. Despite its pale colour, ginup juice stains horribly and if you get it on your clothes or table linen, it will never come out.

GRANADILLAS

Granadillas, or grenadillas, are the largest members of the passion fruit family and can weigh several pounds. In their unripe state, these large specimens are used as vegetables, but they are seldom exported. The granadillas you will find in the shops are smooth, round, orange-skinned fruits, with greyish pulp containing small hard seeds. They look more attractive than passion fruit, but taste less fragrant. Granadillas can be eaten and used in exactly the same way as passion fruit.

Right: Granadillas

GUAVAS

Similar in shape to pears or plums, guavas can be as small as 2.5cm/1in or as large as 10cm/4in in diameter. They have thin, pale green skins, which turn light yellow as they ripen; the flesh varies from white through to deep pink or salmon red. It contains a number of flattish, hard but edible seeds. Guavas are highly scented with an aromatic sweet-acid flavour, not unlike that of quinces.

Above: Guavas are delicious eaten raw.

Guavas are available tinned in syrup and made into sweet fruit drinks.

Varieties

There are several varieties of guava, the most common being the familiar yellow fruit. **Strawberry** or **cherry guavas** are smaller, with reddish-purple skins.

Nutrition

Guavas are exceptionally rich in vitamin C and are also a good source of niacin, potassium and dietary fibre. They provide 62 kilocalories per 100g/3¾oz.

Preparing and Cooking

Ripe guavas are delicious eaten raw. They can be poached in syrup, but must be simmered gently as the flesh easily disintegrates. The flesh can be puréed to use in ice creams and sorbets, or made into jams and jellies (alone, or with other fruits) or sweet drinks. Like quinces, they have an affinity with apples; a few slices of peeled guava added

Preparing guavas

To eat guavas raw, cut in half and squeeze over a little lime juice. Scoop out the flesh from the skin.

to an apple pie or apple sauce impart a special fragrance.

Guavas can also be used in savoury dishes and are particularly good in a sauce for duck or game birds. They make an interesting addition to salads, and can be stuffed with cream cheese and served as a starter.

JACKFRUIT

Jackfruit are related to breadfruit. The large, irregularly shaped oval fruits can weigh 20kg/44lb, but you will only find smaller specimens in the shops. They have a rough, spiny skin, which ripens from green to brown, and each fruit contains large white edible seeds. Ripe jackfruit have a pungent, musty odour.

History

Jackfruit come originally from the rainforests of India and Malaysia, and are now grown in Asia, Africa, America and Australia.

Preparing and Cooking

Ripe jackfruit can be peeled and eaten raw; the pulp is

sweet and rather bland. They are better boiled, roasted or fried, to be served as a vegetable or in a curry. The seeds can be eaten boiled, fried or roasted like chestnuts.

Below: Jackfruit are huge – they can weigh up to 20kg/44lb.

JAMAICAN PLUMS

Also known as "hoy" or "hog" plum, golden apple, limbu and mombin, this fruit belongs to the same family as the mango and is grown in the West Indies, Central and South America, South-east Asia and India. The golden yellow to deep red and purple fruits are small, about 4cm/1½ in long and 2.5cm/1in in diameter. They grow several to a branch and, like mangoes, have soft skin and contain a large central stone. The firm, yellow flesh, which is juicy, deliciously fragrant and sweet, is more akin to pineapple or apple than mango. The distinctive flavour has a slightly acidic tang. Unfortunately, these fruits are fragile and do not travel well, but you may find them in Indian shops. Jamaican plums can be eaten raw, sweetened with a little brown sugar or sprinkled with rum or liqueur and served with cream. They combine well with other fruits in a fruit salad, and can also be poached, pickled or made into jams, jellies and sorbets. They make a good addition to curries.

Right: Unripe Jamaican plums

JUJUBES

Also known as Chinese jujubes, apples or dates, these small greeny-brown fruits and have been cultivated in northern China for more than 4,000 years and are now grown extensively in India (where they are known as bec or bor), Asia, Southern Europe and more recently in Northern America and Australia. Jujubes, which ripen in the

Left: Jujubes

autumn, can be oblong, egg-shaped or round. They have crisp pearly-white flesh enclosing a single stone, with the sweet flavour and texture of an unripe pear. Most fruits are deep brown when ripe, but can be bought while still firm, but orange-red with just a hint of brown and left at room temperature for a day or two to ripen.They can be eaten raw, stewed with orange juice, candied or made into jams and jellies.

KIWANOS

This strange-looking fruit is also known as horned melon, horned cucumber and jelly melon. The oval fruits have thick, bright golden-orange skin covered in sharp spikes. The skin conceals a bright green, jelly-like flesh encasing edible seeds, rather like a passion fruit, with a subtle taste of cucumber, banana and lime.

History

Originally from Africa, kiwanos are now grown commercially in New Zealand, Portugal and the United States.

Preparing and Cooking

Cut the fruit in half, then spoon the pulp straight from the shell. It makes a refreshing drink or it can be added to fruit salads or cocktails. The shells can be used as serving dishes. Blend the pulp with natural yogurt, honey and vanilla ice cream to make an unusual milk shake.

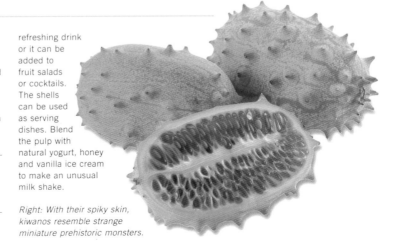

Right: With their spiky skin, kiwanos resemble strange miniature prehistoric monsters.

KIWI FRUIT

These cylindrical fruit, 7.5–10cm/3–4in in length, are covered with a light brown fuzzy skin, which looks very dull in comparison with the beautiful bright green interior, with its crown of tiny edible black seeds arranged around a white core. The flavour is delicate, yet refreshing and tangy.

History

Kiwi fruit were formerly known as Chinese gooseberries, in recognition of the fact that they originated in the Yangtze Valley. They are now extensively grown in New Zealand, Australia, South America and even Italy and France.

Nutrition

A single kiwi fruit contains more than a day's vitamin C requirement for an adult, plus vitamin E, and provides only 50 kilocalories per 100g/3¾oz.

Buying and Storing

Choose plump, unwrinkled fruit with unblemished skins. Kiwis are ripe when they yield to gentle pressure like a ripe pear; however, hard, unripe fruit can easily be ripened at home. Store at room temperature, but not in a bowl with other fruits, since the enzymes

Right: Kiwi fruit are delicious eaten raw – scoop out the flesh with a teaspoon.

in kiwi fruit cause them to ripen very quickly. Firm, unripe kiwis will keep for several weeks if stored in a cool place.

Preparing and Serving

The skin of a kiwi fruit is edible, but the fuzzy texture is not particularly pleasant, so it is best to peel the fruit with a small sharp knife. For the most attractive effect, slice kiwis horizontally.

When *nouvelle cuisine* was in its heyday, slices of kiwi fruit appeared as a garnish for almost every dish, however inappropriate. Kiwi fruit are certainly decorative, but they are good eaten as a fruit in their own right. They make an attractive addition to fruit salads, open fruit tarts and pavlovas, or can be puréed to make a sorbet or coulis. They go well with

white meats, Parma ham, poultry and fish, especially salmon and shellfish.

Kiwi fruit contain enzymes that make an excellent meat tenderizer. Rub the peeled skin or slices of kiwi into both sides of a cheaper cut of meat and leave for 20 minutes; the meat will become tender enough to grill.

The same enzymes, however, will prevent gelatine from setting and will curdle milk products, so do not attempt to make ice cream with raw kiwi. Cooking destroys the enzymes, but also the delicate flavour and texture.

KUBOS

Looking rather like wine-red guavas, kubos are pear-shaped fruit with thick bitter skin and refreshingly sweet, slightly tangy, creamy-white flesh

spattered with tiny, edible, crunchy black seeds. The texture is a little like that of an unripe pear. To eat, cut the fruit in half lengthways and scoop out

the pulp with a spoon, or spoon the pulp over ice cream. The flesh can be combined with other fruits and makes a good addition to fruit salads.

LONGANS

Distant relatives of the lychee, longans are small, round, undistinguished-looking fruit. The brittle light brown skin encloses translucent, jelly-like flesh around a single large inedible stone.

They taste similar to lychees, but have a pleasant peppery tang. Longans are grown throughout South-east Asia and China where they are particularly popular; the Chinese name means

"dragon's eye". Fresh longans can be peeled and eaten like lychees, on their own or in fruit salads, sweet-and-sour dishes and stir-fries. Oriental food stores sell longans canned in syrup.

LOQUATS

Native to China and south Japan, the loquat is one of the few sub-tropical fruits that belong to the apple and pear family, and is sometimes known as a Japanese medlar. The name comes from the Cantonese *luk-kwyit*, meaning "rush-orange", which describes the colour of the loquat's flesh. The fruits are small and plum-shaped, with apricot-coloured skin and white or yellowy-orange flesh surrounding inedible brown stones. They have a sweet scent and a delicate mango-like flavour, which is greatly enhanced by a squeeze of lime or lemon juice.

Buying and Storing

Ripe loquats are speckled with brown patches; perfect, apricot-like fruit are

Right: Loquats are one of the few sub-tropical fruits that belong to the apple and pear family.

still unripe. These can be ripened at home by being kept in a fruit bowl for a few days.

Preparing and Serving

Loquats can be eaten raw, complete with skin, or poached in a light syrup. They go well with other fruits, like

apples, pears and peaches, and make a wonderful ice cream to accompany these fruits. Loquats make good jams, jellies and chutneys (leave in a few of the seeds to impart a bitter almond flavour); they can also be cooked with brown sugar and wine vinegar to make a sauce for poultry.

LYCHEES

The leathery, scaly, reddish skin or "shell" of the lychee encloses pearly white, translucent flesh that is firm and jelly-like. This sweet, fragrant flesh is wrapped around a large, shiny, inedible brown seed. Canned lychees are on sale

Left: Lychees

– and are often served as a dessert in Chinese restaurants – but they have none of the fragrance and subtlety of the fresh fruit.

History

Lychees have been cultivated in China for thousands of years. They have been considered a symbol of romance ever since the time a concubine of one of the Chinese emperors insisted on having teams of horses carry lychees hundreds of miles across country for her pleasure.

Nutrition

Lychees are rich in vitamin C. They provide about 65 kilocalories per 100g/3¾oz.

Buying and Storing

Choose lychees whose shells are as pink or red as possible. Greenish fruits are underripe, while brown fruit is past

their prime. Although the shells act as protection, lychees quickly dry out, so do not buy too many at a time and eat them as soon as possible after purchase. They will keep in the fridge for up to a week.

Preparing and Serving

Fresh lychees are best eaten raw as a refreshing end to a meal. Diners simply remove the shells, then nibble or suck the flesh off the stones.

Lychees can also be stoned and added to fruit salads, or poached in lemon-scented syrup and then served chilled, alone or with ice cream or other poached fruits. For an unusual appetizer, serve stoned fresh lychees stuffed with cream cheese and nuts.

Use these succulent fruits in savoury dishes too – they are good in Chinese sweet-and-sour dishes and also in salads (particularly when combined with avocado). They also make an interesting accompaniment to cold meats like pork and duck.

MANGOES

Among the most delicious and luxurious of all tropical fruits, different varieties of mangoes are grown throughout the tropics, from the Caribbean to Africa, South-east Asia, Australia and India. Although they come in many different shapes, sizes and colours, mangoes are typically curved oblong fruits with green, pinkish-gold or red skin and glorious orange, highly perfumed flesh surrounding a very large, hairy, inedible flat stone. The meltingly soft flesh is always juicy and sweet, although it sometimes has an acid overtone. Some mangoes have fibrous flesh; others are succulent and buttery. Certain varieties are said to have a flavour of fresh mint, lemon, banana or pineapple, but in reality mangoes have their own distinctive taste, unlike any other fruit.

Below: Mangoes have meltingly soft flesh that is juicy and sweet.

History

The history of the mango goes back over 6,000 years and is closely connected with Hinduism. Buddha was said to have been presented with a mango grove so that he could rest in its shade. Mangoes are native to Malaysia and India, and they form part of the local legend and folklore. The name comes from the Tamil *man-key* ("fruit of the tree"). Nineteenth-century traders introduced the fruit to the West Indies, Africa and South America.

Varieties

There are over 2,500 varieties of mango. They can be round-, oval-, heart- or kidney-shaped and can weigh between 150g/5oz and 675g/1½lb. All mangoes are green when unripe, but some remain green when they ripen, while others turn golden or bright red, or a combination of these colours.

Popular varieties include the **Alphonso** or **Alphonsine** from India, which has supple, buttery flesh and a heady, sweet flavour. West Indian varieties include the small **Julie** and the round, juicy **Bombay**. Cultivated varieties like **Parvin, Kent** and **Tommy Atkins** have thinner skins than wild mangoes and are less fibrous. **Ruby mangoes**, from the Gambia, have an excellent flavour but are rather fibrous. To eat one of these glowing red fruit, squeeze it gently between your hands, then pierce the skin and suck out the juice.

Nutrition

Ripe mangoes are rich in vitamins, especially A and C, and are a good source of beta-carotene. They provide about 59 kilocalories per 100g/3¾oz.

Buying and Storing

Colour is not necessarily an indication of ripeness in a mango; some remain solidly green even when ripe. Buy unblemished fruit without any black blotches on the skin, as these indicate that the fruit is overripe and will have mushy flesh. The best test of a mango is its aroma, which should be highly perfumed. The fruit should be just yielding when gently pressed.

Mangoes will ripen at home if left in a warm place. To hasten ripening, place them in a brown paper bag with a banana or kiwi fruit. Eat the mangoes as soon as they are ripe.

Canned mangoes Mango slices are available canned in syrup. These are extremely sweet and are best drained before eating. They can be puréed to make a coulis or ice cream.

Above: Parvin

Preparing a mango

1 Place the mango narrow side down on a chopping board. Cut off a thick lengthways slice, keeping the knife as close to the stone as possible. Turn the mango round and repeat on the other side. Cut off the flesh adhering to the stone and scoop out the flesh from the mango slices.

2 To make a "hedgehog", prepare the mango as above and score the flesh on each thick slice with criss-cross lines at 1cm/1/2in intervals, taking care not to cut through the skin.

3 Turn the mango halves inside out and serve.

Right: Thin-skinned Tommy Atkins mangoes

Dried mangoes

These can be added to chutneys and relishes, or mixed with other dried fruits in cake and teabread recipes.

Preparing and Serving

Mangoes are so delicious that they are best savoured in their raw state, perhaps with a squeeze of lime or lemon. The main disadvantage of this is that they are extremely difficult to eat elegantly. Indeed, it is said that the only way to eat them is in the bath. The secret of retaining a modicum of dignity is to remove the stone before attempting to eat the juicy flesh.

Whichever way you cut a mango, some flesh will always be left clinging to the stone. On no account waste this – wait until no one can see you, then cut off the skin and suck the aromatic pulp off the stone for a real treat!

Mangoes make an exotic addition to fruit salads and can be puréed to make sorbets and ice creams. They go well with other tropical flavours, like passion fruit and rum. They are excellent served with cured meats like Parma ham or smoked chicken, and make a refreshing accompaniment to spicy dishes and curries. Prawns or other shellfish combine well with mango.

Ripe mangoes can be mixed with chillies to make a delicious salsa, while unripe green fruit are traditionally used to make mango chutney and pickles, which go well with cold meats and curries. In the West Indies and Asia, unripe mangoes are used as a vegetable and are baked or stewed with chicken and meat dishes.

Right: Kent is another of the 2,500 varieties of mango.

MANGOSTEENS

Despite their name, mangosteens have nothing to do with mangoes. Nor are they related to lychees, although their pearly white flesh looks very similar.

Mangosteens are apple-shaped with rather leathery, reddish-brown skin, which is deep purple when ripe. The flesh is divided into five segments, each containing a large seed. The segments are enclosed in dark pink pith, which should be removed before eating. Mangosteens have a sweet, refreshing flavour, rather like that of a plum, but more highly perfumed.

History

Mangosteens are indigenous to South-east Asia. The trees are slow to grow; it is fifteen years before they bear fruit. They are now grown commercially in parts of Thailand, Central America and Australia.

Preparing and Serving

The flavour of mangosteens is too fragrant and delicate to be impaired by cooking. Eat them just as they are, or add to fruit salad. Peeled mangosteens look spectacular surrounded by a ribbon of strawberry or raspberry coulis.

Above: Mangosteens have a highly perfumed flavour. Eat the pearly white fruit segments just as they are, or add them to fruit salad.

Serving a mangosteen

1 Using a small sharp knife, cut the skin around the equator of the shell, then lift off the top half of the shell and spoon out the flesh.

2 Alternatively, simply cut the mangosteens in half and scoop out the flesh with a spoon.

MARACOYAS

Also known as yellow passion fruit, the maracoya is a largish fruit with vibrant green, thick shiny skin that turns yellow as it ripens. Inside is a mass of translucent orange pulp enclosing hard grey seeds, just like a passion fruit, but sharper and less aromatic. Use in exactly the same way as passion fruit, adding plenty of sugar.

Right: Maracoyas

PASSION FRUIT

Passion fruit takes its name from its exotic flower, which is said to symbolize the Passion of Christ. Native to the Americas, these round or oval fruits have a leathery purplish-brown skin (some, like those from Brazil, are yellow in colour), which wrinkles when the fruits are fully ripe. Inside, the edible seeds are surrounded by intensely fragrant, translucent, greenish-orange pulp with a distinctive sour-sweet flavour and a wonderful scent. The fruits can be as small as a cherry or as large as an orange, but the ones most commonly available in the shops are about 7.5cm/3in long.

Left: Passion fruit

Nutrition

The fruits contain vitamins A and C and are a good source of dietary fibre. They contain 34 kilocalories per 100g/3¾oz.

Buying and Storing

Choose fruit that feel heavy for their size, with firm, slightly wrinkled skins. Very wrinkly passion fruit with extremely dark skins will have dried out. Passion fruit can be ripened at room temperature; do not keep them in the fridge. The pulp can be frozen in ice cube trays, then packed into plastic bags. The juice is sold in cartons.

Preparing and Serving

The simplest way to eat passion fruit is on its own; cut the fruit in half and scoop out the pulp and seeds with a spoon. Both are edible, but the pulp can be sieved to make a smooth coulis or refreshing drink. Passion fruit enhances the flavour of all other fruits and makes a delicious topping for a pavlova or cheesecake.

Sieved pulp can be made into ice creams and sorbets, or added to yogurt. Passion fruit jelly goes well with roast meats, or it can be spread on bread or toast. The juice makes an excellent marinade for rich meats like venison and game birds.

PAPAYAS

The papaya, or paw-paw, is native to tropical America, but it is now grown in most tropical or sub-tropical regions of the world. The large pear-shaped fruits grow to about 20cm/8in in length. Some varieties remain green when ripe, but most turn deep yellow or orange. Papayas have beautiful deep salmon-pink flesh, with an abundance of grey-black seeds in the central cavity, which are edible. The soft, juicy, sweet flesh tastes like a cross between melons and peaches.

Right: Papayas

Nutrition

Papayas are rich in vitamin A and calcium, and contain large quantities of the enzyme papain, which breaks down protein and can be used to tenderize meat. Papain also makes these fruit very easy to digest. They provide about 45 kilocalories per 100g/3¾oz.

Buying and Storing

Choose uniformly yellow fruit. Sniff them; they should have a delicate scent. Papayas bruise easily, so do not buy any with damaged or shrivelled skins. If the fruit is not ripe, check the skin around the stem end; it should be yellow, otherwise the papaya will never ripen. Ripe papayas should be eaten immediately. Fruit that is not quite ripe should be left at room temperature until soft and yellow. The flesh can be cubed or puréed and frozen.

Preparing and Serving

Simply cut the ripe papaya in half lengthways and scoop out the seeds from the cavity. You can eat them (they have a peppery flavour), but they are not particularly pleasant. Squeeze a little lime or lemon juice on the flesh before serving.

Papayas can be used in the same way as melons, served solo with a good squeeze of lime, or sprinkled with ground ginger and served with cured meats like Parma ham or smoked chicken. The cubed flesh can be added to fruit salads, piled on top of pavlovas, made into ice creams and sorbets, or served with yogurt and stem ginger. It also goes well with savoury dishes like seafood and chicken curries. Finely chopped papaya is perfect with chillies in a fresh salsa. The skins can be used to tenderize cheaper cuts of meat. The papain, however, prevents gelatine from setting, so do not attempt to make a fruit jelly, cold soufflé or mousse with papaya.

Slightly unripe papayas can be used in salads, while fruit that is still hard is ideal for relishes and chutneys. Large fruit can be stuffed like marrows and baked as a vegetable dish.

PERSIMMONS

Persimmons, also known as "kaki" or "date" plums, arouse strong feelings. People either love them or loathe them. When fully ripe these fruits, which originated in Japan, are exceptionally beautiful; the name means "food of the Gods". They resemble large orange tomatoes, but have a wide, pale brown calyx and translucent, inedible skin. At their best, they have very sweet, honeyed flesh; unripe persimmons, however, are almost inedible, horribly sour and astringent.

Nutrition

Persimmons, rich in vitamin A, yield potassium, calcium and iron. They contain about 30 kilocalories per 100g/3¾oz.

Above: Persimmon

Buying and Storing

Persimmons should be plump and extremely soft and pulpy, with undamaged skins. A perfect specimen will look as though it is about to burst, but this is exactly as it should be. Handle with great care and eat immediately, or store briefly in the bottom of the fridge. To ripen, place in a brown paper bag with a banana.

Preparing and Cooking

The fruit are best eaten raw; slice off the top and spoon out the flesh. Serve with cream or yogurt, use to make mousses, custards and ice creams or purée the flesh to make a sauce for ham, pork and game. Slightly unripe fruit can be poached in syrup or peeled and cooked like apple sauce.

Sharon fruit

Developed in the Sharon Valley in Israel, this non-astringent variety of persimmon can be eaten while still firm and does not require peeling. Sharon fruit are less highly flavoured than standard persimmons, and benefit from a squeeze of lemon or lime juice, but are treated in much the same way. They can be added to salads and make an attractive garnish for avocado vinaigrette.

To dry persimmons

Peel the fruit, leaving the calyxes and stems intact. Arrange on a rack over a baking sheet and dry in a very low oven. The sugar which is naturally present in the persimmons will crystallize on the outside. Dried persimmons taste like a mixture of dried figs, prunes and dates. They can be used in place of these fruits and added to cakes and puddings.

PEPINOS

This beautiful fruit, with its smooth golden skin heavily streaked with purple, is sometimes called a "tree melon". Native to Peru, the pepino is a relative of the tomato, potato and aubergine family (*Solanacae*), but looks rather like a melon. The pale yellow flesh is quite tart, with a flavour suggestive of lemon, pineapple and melon. The sweet seeds of this fruit are edible.

Nutrition

Pepino fruits are rich in vitamin C, and also yield some vitamin A. They contain about 25 kilocalories per 100g/3¾oz.

Preparing and Serving

Pepinos can be peeled and eaten raw, but they are best poached with sugar or honey to counteract their acidity. Serve the fruit like melon, add pepino cubes to fruit salad or serve with vanilla ice cream.

Right: Pepinos

PHYSALIS

Sometimes also known as "Cape gooseberries", physalis are distantly related to tomatoes, peppers, aubergines and potatoes, although you would never guess this by looking at them. The small, orange-gold berries are encased in a papery beige husk, similar to a Chinese lantern. They have a rather tart, mildly scented flavour reminiscent of a ripe dessert gooseberry with a hint of strawberry.

History

Although physalis are native to South America, the fruits seem to have been known to the Greeks as early as the third century AD. Physalis were introduced to England in the eighteenth century, but did not become popular until two centuries later. The early settlers in South Africa cultivated physalis in the Cape of Good Hope, which gave rise to their common name, Cape gooseberries.

Preparing and Serving

Physalis are delicious eaten raw; the inedible papery husk is simply peeled back and used as a "handle", leaving the luscious berries free to be devoured as they are or dipped in fondant icing or melted chocolate. As such, they are very popular as petits fours and make attractive decorations for cheesecakes, pavlovas and gâteaux.

Physalis can also be cooked – they make the most delicious-tasting jams and jellies.

Above: Physalis

Dipping physalis in fondant icing

1 Peel back the papery husk like petals and fold into "wings".

2 Holding each physalis by the husk, dip into warm fondant icing.

3 Transfer to a plate lined with non-stick baking paper and leave to cool.

PINEAPPLES

Pineapples are probably the most recognizable of all fruit. In fact, they are multiple fruits consisting of dozens of lozenge-shaped protuberances, each one being the fruit of a single flower, which together make up a single pineapple. Resembling a large pine cone topped with a spiky grey-green plume of leaves, a whole pineapple makes a spectacular addition to a fruit platter. The warm, distinctive aroma of the fruit is also very pleasing.

Pineapples are very versatile fruit, their sweet, acidic taste lending itself to sweet and savoury dishes.

History

Native to South and Central America, pineapples had been cultivated for centuries before Christopher Columbus "discovered" them on his voyage to the West Indies in 1493. Astonished by the extraordinary appearance and flavour of the fruit, he brought some back to Europe, where they were regarded with wonder and awe. Due to their rarity and high cost, they became a symbol of hospitality, and stone pineapples often featured on the gateposts of houses to welcome guests.

The first pineapples, ripened in glasshouses, were presented to Louis XV of France, whose passion for the fruit made them even more highly prized. Pineapples are now grown in every tropical region of the world.

Varieties

There are hundreds of pineapple varieties, ranging from very large to miniature fruits. They are seldom sold by name, although **Sweet Gold** is becoming familiar in some stores and markets. The colour of the skin varies from orange to greenish-yellow, while the degree of juiciness and sweetness depends upon the season.

Nutrition

Pineapples, which are rich in both vitamin C and dietary fibre, provide about 46 kilocalories per 100g/3¾oz. They contain bromelain, an enzyme that aids digestion, so are the perfect

Above: Crystallized pineapple

Left: Large, small and baby pineapples

Making pineapple wedges with plumes

1 Place the fruit upright, hold it firmly and slice it in half vertically with a sharp serrated knife, cutting down through the plume into the flesh. Cut each piece in half again to make four wedges.
2 Run a small sharp knife between the rind and flesh. Slice off the core on each wedge, then slice the fruit into neat pieces, leaving these in place.

fruit to finish a rich meal. The enzyme breaks down protein so can be used to tenderize meat, but will prevent gelatine from setting.

Buying and Storing

Choose a plump pineapple that feels heavy for its size, with a fresh, stiff plume. To test for ripeness, gently pull out one of the bottom leaves; it should come out easily. Avoid lifeless-looking, bruised or withered fruit with browning leaves. Use the fruit as soon as possible after purchase. Do not store whole pineapples in the fridge, although peeled, sliced or cubed pineapple can be chilled in an airtight container for up to three days. Fresh, peeled and sliced pineapple is available and should also be kept chilled.
Dried and crystallized pineapple Both can be eaten as a snack or used to make cakes and puddings.
Canned pineapple Chunks and rings are available in syrup or juice. They are useful store cupboard items, but lack the aromatic flavour of fresh pineapple. Crushed pineapple is also available.

Preparing and Cooking

Pineapples are delicious on their own, served in wedges or rings. Some people like to add a splash of Kirsch, but a good pineapple should need no enhancement (although, surprisingly, a grinding of black pepper does wonders for the flavour). They go very well with other fruits; a hollowed-out pineapple shell complete with plume makes a spectacular container for fruit salad or tropical fruit sorbets.

Sliced pineapple can be made into a variety of hot desserts. Sauté in butter and brown sugar, make crisp fritters or combine with other fruits on skewers to make grilled fruit kebabs.

Tropical flavours, such as ginger, vanilla, cinnamon, allspice, coconut and rum, go extremely well with pineapple. Perhaps the most famous combination of pineapple, coconut and rum is the pina colada cocktail.

Pineapples' refreshing sweet-sour flavour makes them perfect for savoury dishes and they are often used in Chinese cooking. Traditionally, pineapple is cooked with gammon and pork, but it also goes well with lamb, poultry and fish, particularly in spicy dishes and curries.

Below: Dried pineapple can be eaten as a snack or chopped to use in cake and pudding recipes.

Peeling a pineapple

1 Cut the pineapple across into slices of the desired width.

2 Use a small, sharp knife to cut off the rind.

3 Hold each slice upright and cut out the "eyes".

4 Remove the central core of each slice with an apple corer.

POMEGRANATES

This attractive, apple-shaped fruit has leathery reddish-gold skin and a large calyx or crown. Inside is a mass of creamy-white edible seeds, each encased in a translucent sac of deep pink or crimson pulp and held together by segments of bitter, inedible, yellow membrane that extend outwards to the skin. The seeds gave the fruit its name, which means "grain apple". Eating a pomegranate is quite hard work, as each fleshy seed must be picked out individually, but their delicate, slightly tart flavour and refreshing, juicy texture make the effort worthwhile. Be warned, however, that pomegranate juice stains indelibly.

History

Originally from Persia, pomegranates have been linked with many cultures and religions for centuries and have been a symbol of fertility since ancient times because of their numerous seeds. Venus, the goddess of Love, was said to have given pomegranates as presents to her favourites.

Until the Renaissance, pomegranates were used primarily for medicinal purposes in Europe, although they have always featured in the cooking of Middle Eastern countries. Nowadays, they are widely cultivated, from France, Spain and Israel to America and all over Asia.

Nutrition

Pomegranate seeds are rich in vitamin C and are a good source of dietary fibre. They provide about 72 kilocalories per 100g/3¾oz.

Buying and Storing

A pomegranate that feels heavy for its size is likely to be full of juice. Choose glossy fruit and avoid those whose skin looks hard and dry. They will keep in the fridge for up to a week. Dried pomegranate seeds are used in Middle Eastern cooking.

Preparing and Serving

If you have the patience, pomegranates are fun to eat raw; cut them open and pick out the seeds with a pin. Either suck out the juice and discard the

Below: Inside pomegranates is a mass of seeds, each encased in deep pink pulp.

Preparing a pomegranate

1 Cut off a thin slice from one end.

2 Stand the fruit upright. Cut downwards through the skin at intervals, using a small sharp knife.

3 Bend back the segments and use your fingers to push the seeds into a bowl.

4 Remove all the bitter pith and membrane from the seeds.

seeds or eat the jelly-like cells, seeds
and all. The seeds make a decorative
addition to fruit salads and can be used
as a pretty topping for creamy desserts,
ice cream or cheesecake. They have a
particular affinity with almonds and
make a jewel-like garnish for couscous.
In India and Pakistan, the seeds are
used in meat dishes.

Pomegranate juice Pomegranate juice
must be extracted gently; electric or
mechanical juicers will over-crush the
seeds and make the juice bitter. The
juice is delicious in some refreshing

long drinks, such as pomegranate-
flavoured lemonade, or it can be used
to make a syrup to colour and flavour
alcoholic drinks and cocktails.
Commercially produced pomegranate
syrup is called grenadine.

The juice can also be used for
sorbets and sauces, and makes a
delicious pink jelly for savoury dishes,
particularly those from the Middle East.
Use it to marinate pheasant, turkey or
chicken, or to make a sauce for chicken
or turkey, which can then be garnished
with pomegranate seeds.

PRICKLY PEARS

Sometimes known as "Indian figs",
prickly pears are the fruit of a cactus.
They certainly live up to their name,
the skin being covered in tiny, painful
prickles. Prickly pears are generally
7.5cm/3in long, with greenish-orange
skin and orangey-pink flesh with a
melon-like texture. The flavour is sweet
and aromatic. The small seeds can be
eaten raw, but become hard when they
are cooked.

Buying and Storing

Prickly pears are orangey-yellow when
ripe. Choose unblemished fruit and
ripen at room
temperature if
necessary.

Preparing and Cooking

Prickly pears are usually peeled and
eaten raw with a squeeze of lime or
lemon and perhaps a little cream.

Prickly pears go well with other fruit
and are good in fruit salads. They can
be made into jams or mixed with oranges
to make an unusual marmalade. Mix raw
sieved pulp with ginger to make a sauce
for gammon or cooked ham, or serve
slices of prickly pear instead of melon
with cured meats like Parma ham. Try
adding stewed prickly pear segments to
a fruit compote, or make a sauce or ice
cream with the sieved purée. Candied
or crystallized slices of prickly pear can
be used to decorate cakes and many
desserts, such as cheesecake.

*Right: Prickly pears have a sweet and
aromatic flavour.*

Preparing prickly pears
1 The pear prickles are usually
removed before the fruits are
sold, but if not, wearing gloves,
scrub each fruit with a stiff brush.

2 Using a sharp knife, cut a thin
slice from each end of the prickly
pear, then make a shallow cut just
through the skin from end to end
on either side of the fruit.

3 Now simply peel off the skin.

RAMBUTANS

Rambutans are related to lychees and are sometimes referred to as "hairy lychees". Originally from Malaysia, but now grown in tropical Central America and South-east Asia, they are larger than lychees (about 5cm/2in in diameter) and look quite different, but have a similar texture. Their taste is similar, too, but slightly sharper. Rambutans resemble small hairy animals, their reddish-brown leathery skins being covered with soft curly spines or hairs.

Preparing and Serving

Rambutans can be used in exactly the same way as lychees. To prepare, cut around the equator of the rambutan with a sharp knife, penetrating the skin only. Lift off the top half of the skin, leaving the fruit on the half shell, like an egg in a (rather hairy) egg cup. They can be added to fruit salads, served with ice cream (coffee ice cream is particularly compatible) or made into

jams or jellies, but are best eaten on their own. For an unusual appetizer, wrap peeled and stoned rambutans in Parma ham and serve speared on

Above: Rambutans

cocktail sticks. Rambutans are also available canned in syrup.

SAPODILLAS

The unprepossessing appearance of this drab oval fruit from Central America belies its delicious taste, which resembles that of vanilla-flavoured banana custard. Inside the rough, light brown skin of the ripe fruit, the honey-coloured flesh is sweet and luscious, with a core containing inedible, hard black pips.

Right: Sapodillas are sweet and luscious – like vanilla-flavoured banana custard.

Buying and Storing

Ripe sapodillas should have wrinkled brown skins and "give" slightly when pressed. Unripe fruit has smooth skin with a greenish tinge. Avoid this – unripe fruit is full of tannin and the flesh is unpleasantly grainy and mouth-puckeringly unpalatable. Instead, leave the fruit to ripen for up to a week in a fruit bowl. Ripe sapodillas can be kept in the fridge for up to a month.

Preparing and Serving

Sapodillas can be eaten just as they are – simply cut them in half, scoop out the flesh and discard the pips. A squeeze of lime or lemon enhances the flavour. The flesh can be mashed and stirred into cream or custard, or made into ice creams, fools and mousses. It can be added to cakes and teabreads and

makes an unusual pancake filling. Mix puréed sapodilla flesh with home-made mayonnaise or lime vinaigrette to make a sauce or dressing to be served with cold fish or chicken.

The milky sap of the sapodilla tree is used to make chicle gum, the main component of chewing gum.

SNAKE FRUIT

Also known as salak, this large member of the lychee family acquired its nickname from its beautifully patterned scaly brown snake-like skin. The creamy flesh is divided into four segments, each enclosing a very large inedible brown stone. The flesh is denser and less juicy than a lychee and has a distinctive apple flavour. Although the hard shells protect the fruit, the flesh quickly dries out, so eat them as soon as possible after purchase.

Snake fruit can be peeled and then eaten just as they are, or added to fruit salads. They are delicious poached in a light lemon- or vanilla-scented syrup and served chilled, alone or with vanilla ice cream or sorbet as a refreshing end to a meal.

Right: Snake fruit – so named because the patterned, scaly brown shell resembles snake skin.

TAMARILLOS

Also known as "tree tomatoes", tamarillos look like large egg-shaped tomatoes with thick, smooth, wine-red skins. Each fruit has two lobes containing a multitude of black seeds.

Buying and Storing

Tamarillos with a greenish tinge will be unripe. Ripe fruit is bright purplish- or orangey-red and is soft to the touch. The fruit will keep in the fridge for several days.

Preparing and Cooking

Tamarillos can only be eaten raw when they are completely ripe. At this stage the flavour is tangy, sweet and sour, while unripe fruit has a quite unpleasant tannin taste.

To enjoy tamarillos at their best, cut them in half, sprinkle with a little sugar and leave overnight in the fridge. The next day, scoop out the chilled pulp with a spoon. Do not attempt to eat the skin, which is horribly bitter. Remove it by plunging the fruit into boiling water for about a minute, then slipping it off, or peel the fruit with a sharp vegetable peeler or knife.

Raw tamarillos can be used in fruit salads or puréed and made into jam and ice cream. They can be stewed or dredged with brown sugar and grilled. They make excellent chutney and a delicious sweet-sour sauce to go with fish or poultry.

Above: Tamarillos are members of the same family as tomatoes, aubergines and potatoes.

EXOTIC
FRUIT
RECIPES

*Who can resist the colours, textures and flavours of
exotic fruits? Now that many varieties are widely
available all year, there's every excuse for taking the
taste trip and trying such delights as Lychee and
Elderflower Sorbet, Passion Fruit Crème Caramels
with Dipped Physalis or Exotic Fruit Sushi.*

COLD MANGO SOUFFLÉS TOPPED
WITH TOASTED COCONUT

FRAGRANT, FRESH MANGO IS ONE OF THE MOST DELICIOUS EXOTIC FRUITS AROUND, WHETHER IT IS SIMPLY SERVED IN SLICES OR USED AS THE BASIS FOR AN ICE CREAM OR SOUFFLÉ.

MAKES FOUR

INGREDIENTS
    4 small mangoes, peeled, stoned
      and chopped
    30ml/2 tbsp water
    15ml/1 tbsp powdered gelatine
    2 egg yolks
    115g/4oz/½ cup caster sugar
    120ml/4fl oz/½ cup milk
    grated rind of 1 orange
    300ml/½ pint/1¼ cups double cream
    toasted flaked or coarsely shredded
      coconut, to decorate

COOK'S TIP
Cool and creamy, these go down a treat
after a curry. Add some juicy pieces of
fresh mango on the side if you like.

1 Place a few pieces of mango in the base of each of four 150ml/¼ pint/⅔ cup ramekins. Wrap a greased collar of non-stick baking paper around the outside of each dish, extending well above the rim. Secure with adhesive tape, then tie tightly with string.

2 Pour the water into a small heatproof bowl and sprinkle the gelatine over the surface. Leave for 5 minutes or until spongy. Place the bowl in a pan of hot water, stirring occasionally, until the gelatine has dissolved.

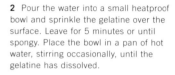

3 Meanwhile, whisk the egg yolks with the caster sugar and milk in another heatproof bowl. Place the bowl over a saucepan of simmering water and continue to whisk until the mixture is thick and frothy. Remove from the heat and continue whisking until the mixture cools. Whisk in the liquid gelatine.

4 Purée the remaining mango pieces in a food processor or blender, then fold the purée into the egg yolk mixture with the orange rind. Set the mixture aside until starting to thicken.

5 Whip the double cream to soft peaks. Reserve 60ml/4 tbsp and fold the rest into the mango mixture. Spoon into the ramekins until the mixture is 2.5cm/1in above the rim of each dish. Chill for 3–4 hours or until set.

6 Carefully remove the paper collars from the soufflés. Spoon a little of the reserved cream on top of each soufflé and decorate with some toasted flaked or coarsely shredded coconut.

PASSION FRUIT CRÈME CARAMELS
WITH DIPPED PHYSALIS

PASSION FRUIT HAS AN AROMATIC FLAVOUR THAT REALLY PERMEATES THESE CRÈME CARAMELS.
USE SOME OF THE CARAMEL TO DIP PHYSALIS TO CREATE A UNIQUE DECORATION.

MAKES FOUR

INGREDIENTS
185g/6½oz/generous ¾ cup
  caster sugar
75ml/5 tbsp water
4 passion fruit
4 physalis
3 eggs plus 1 egg yolk
150ml/¼ pint/⅔ cup double cream
150ml/¼ pint/⅔ cup creamy milk

1 Place 150g/5oz/⅔ cup of the caster sugar in a heavy-based saucepan. Add the water and heat the mixture gently until the sugar has dissolved. Increase the heat and boil until the syrup turns a dark golden colour.

2 Meanwhile, cut each passion fruit in half. Scoop out the seeds from the passion fruit into a sieve set over a bowl. Press the seeds against the sieve to extract all the juice. Spoon a few of the seeds into each of four 150ml/¼ pint/⅔ cup ramekins. Set the juice aside.

3 Peel back the papery casing from each physalis and dip the orange berries into the caramel. Place on a sheet of non-stick baking paper and set aside. Pour the remaining caramel carefully into the ramekins.

4 Preheat the oven to 150°C/300°F/Gas 2. Whisk the eggs, egg yolk and remaining sugar in a bowl. Whisk in the cream and milk, then the passion fruit juice. Strain through a sieve into each ramekin, then place the ramekins in a baking tin. Pour in hot water to come halfway up the sides of the dishes; bake for 40–45 minutes or until just set.

5 Remove the custards from the tin and leave to cool, then cover and chill for 4 hours before serving. Run a knife between the edge of each ramekin and the custard and invert each in turn on to a dessert plate, shaking the ramekins firmly to release the custards. Decorate each with a dipped physalis.

LYCHEE AND ELDERFLOWER SORBET

THE FLAVOUR OF ELDERFLOWERS IS FAMOUS FOR BRINGING OUT THE ESSENCE OF GOOSEBERRIES,
BUT WHAT IS LESS WELL KNOWN IS HOW WONDERFULLY IT COMPLEMENTS LYCHEES.

SERVES FOUR

INGREDIENTS
    175g/6oz/¾ cup caster sugar
    400ml/14fl oz/1⅔ cups water
    500g/1¼lb fresh lychees, peeled
      and stoned
    15ml/1 tbsp elderflower cordial
    dessert biscuits, to serve

COOK'S TIP
Switch the freezer to the coldest setting
before making the sorbet – the faster the
mixture freezes, the smaller the ice
crystals that form and the better the final
texture will be. To ensure rapid freezing,
use a metal freezerproof container and
place it directly on the freezer shelf.

1 Place the caster sugar and water in a
saucepan and heat gently until the
sugar has dissolved. Increase the heat
and boil for 5 minutes, then add the
lychees. Lower the heat and simmer for
7 minutes. Remove from the heat and
allow to cool.

2 Purée the fruit and syrup in a
blender or food processor. Place a sieve
over a bowl and pour the purée into it.
Press through as much of the purée as
possible with a spoon.

3 Stir the elderflower cordial into the
strained purée, then pour the mixture
into a freezerproof container. Freeze
for 2 hours, until ice crystals start to
form around the edges.

4 Remove the sorbet from the freezer
and process briefly in a food processor
or blender to break up the crystals.
Repeat this process twice more, then
freeze until firm. Transfer to the fridge
for 10 minutes to soften slightly before
serving in scoops, with biscuits.

EXOTIC FRUIT SUSHI

THIS IDEA CAN BE ADAPTED TO INCORPORATE A WIDE VARIETY OF FRUITS, BUT TO KEEP TO THE EXOTIC THEME TAKE YOUR INSPIRATION FROM THE TROPICS. THE SUSHI NEEDS TO CHILL OVERNIGHT TO ENSURE THE RICE MIXTURE FIRMS PROPERLY, SO BE SURE YOU START THIS IN GOOD TIME.

SERVES FOUR

INGREDIENTS
150g/5oz/⅔ cup short grain
   pudding rice
350ml/12fl oz/1½ cups water
400ml/14fl oz/1⅔ cups coconut milk
75g/3oz/⅓ cup caster sugar
a selection of exotic fruit, such as
   1 mango, 1 kiwi fruit, 2 figs and
   1 star fruit, thinly sliced
30ml/2 tbsp apricot jam, sieved
For the raspberry sauce
225g/8oz/2 cups raspberries
25g/1oz/¼ cup icing sugar

COOK'S TIP
To cut the rice mixture into bars, turn
out of the tin, cut in half lengthways,
then make 7 crossways cuts for 16 bars.
Shape into ovals with damp hands.

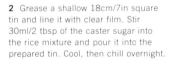

1 Rinse the rice well under cold
running water, drain and place in a
saucepan with 300ml/½ pint/1¼ cups of
the water. Pour in 175ml/6fl oz/¾ cup
of the coconut milk. Cook over a very
low heat for 25 minutes, stirring often
and gradually adding the remaining
coconut milk, until the rice has
absorbed all the liquid and is tender.

2 Grease a shallow 18cm/7in square
tin and line it with clear film. Stir
30ml/2 tbsp of the caster sugar into
the rice mixture and pour it into the
prepared tin. Cool, then chill overnight.

3 Cut the rice mixture into 16 small
bars, shape into ovals and flatten the
tops. Place on a baking sheet lined with
non-stick baking paper. Arrange the
sliced fruit on top, using one type of
fruit only for each sushi.

4 Place the remaining sugar in a small
pan with the remaining 50ml/4 tbsp
water. Bring to the boil, then lower the
heat and simmer until thick and syrupy.
Stir in the jam and cool slightly.

5 To make the sauce, purée the
raspberries with the icing sugar in a
food processor or blender. Press
through a sieve, then divide among four
small bowls. Arrange a few different
fruit sushi on each plate and spoon over
a little of the cool apricot syrup. Serve
with the raspberry sauce.

LEMON GRASS SKEWERS WITH LIME CHEESE

GRILLED FRUITS MAKE A FINE FINALE TO ANY MEAL, AND THE LEMON GRASS SKEWERS NOT ONLY LOOK GOOD, BUT GIVE THE FRUIT A SUBTLE LEMON TANG. THE FRUITS USED HERE MAKE AN IDEAL EXOTIC MIX, BUT ALMOST ANY SOFT FRUIT CAN BE SUBSTITUTED.

SERVES FOUR

INGREDIENTS
    4 long fresh lemon grass stalks
    1 mango, peeled, stoned and cut
        into chunks
    1 papaya, peeled, seeded and cut
        into chunks
    1 star fruit, cut into thick slices
        and halved
    8 fresh bay leaves
    a nutmeg
    60ml/4 tbsp maple syrup
    50g/2oz/⅓ cup demerara sugar
For the lime cheese
    150g/5oz/⅔ cup curd cheese or
        low-fat soft cheese
    120ml/4fl oz/½ cup double cream
    grated rind and juice of ½ lime
    30ml/2 tbsp icing sugar

1 Prepare the barbecue or preheat the grill. Cut the top of each lemon grass stalk into a point with a sharp knife. Discard the outer leaves, then use the back of the knife to bruise the length of each stalk to release the aromatic oils. Thread each stalk, skewer-style, with the fruit pieces and bay leaves.

2 Support a piece of foil on a baking sheet and roll up the edges to make a rim. Grease the foil, lay the kebabs on top and grate a little nutmeg over each. Drizzle the maple syrup over and dust liberally with the demerara sugar. Grill for 5 minutes, until lightly charred.

3 Meanwhile, make the lime cheese. Mix together the cheese, cream, grated lime rind and juice and icing sugar in a bowl. Serve at once with the lightly charred fruit kebabs.

COOK'S TIP
Only fresh lemon grass will work as skewers for this recipe. It is now possible to buy lemon grass stalks in jars. These are handy for curries and similar dishes, but are too soft to use as skewers.

COCONUT JELLY WITH STAR ANISE FRUITS

SERVE THIS DESSERT AFTER ANY ORIENTAL-STYLE MEAL WITH PLENTY OF REFRESHING EXOTIC FRUIT.

SERVES FOUR

INGREDIENTS
    250ml/8fl oz/1 cup cold water
    75g/3oz/⅓ cup caster sugar
    15ml/1 tbsp powdered gelatine
    400ml/14fl oz/1⅔ cups coconut milk
For the syrup and fruit
    250ml/8fl oz/1 cup water
    3 star anise
    50g/2oz/¼ cup caster sugar
    1 star fruit, sliced
    12 lychees, peeled and stoned
    115g/4oz/1 cup blackberries

1 Pour the water into a saucepan and add the caster sugar. Heat gently until the sugar has dissolved. Sprinkle over the gelatine and continue to heat the mixture gently until the gelatine has dissolved, stirring occasionally. Stir in the coconut milk, remove from the heat and set aside to cool.

2 Grease an 18cm/7in square cake tin. Line with clear film. Pour in the coconut milk mixture and chill until set.

3 To make the syrup, combine the water, star anise and sugar in a pan. Bring to the boil, stirring, then lower the heat and simmer for 10–12 minutes until syrupy. Place the prepared fruit in a heatproof bowl and pour over the hot syrup. Cool, then chill.

4 To serve, cut the coconut jelly into diamonds and remove from the tin. Arrange the coconut jelly on individual plates, adding a few of the fruits and their syrup to each portion.

COOK'S TIP
Coconut milk is available in cans or as a powder. If using the coconut powder, reconstitute it with cold water according to the packet instructions.

PAPAYA BAKED <u>WITH</u> GINGER

*GINGER ENHANCES THE FLAVOUR OF PAPAYA IN THIS RECIPE, WHICH TAKES NO MORE THAN
TEN MINUTES TO PREPARE! DON'T OVERCOOK PAPAYA OR THE FLESH WILL BECOME VERY WATERY.*

<u>SERVES FOUR</u>

INGREDIENTS

  2 ripe papayas
  2 pieces stem ginger in syrup,
    drained, plus 15ml/1 tbsp syrup
    from the jar
  8 amaretti or other dessert biscuits,
    coarsely crushed
  45ml/3 tbsp raisins
  shredded, finely pared rind and juice
    of 1 lime
  25g/1oz/¼ cup pistachio
    nuts, chopped
  15ml/1 tbsp light muscovado sugar
  60ml/4 tbsp crème fraîche, plus
    extra to serve

VARIATION
Use Greek yogurt and almonds instead of
crème fraîche and pistachio nuts.

1 Preheat the oven to 200°C/400°F/
Gas 6. Cut the papayas in half and
scoop out their seeds. Place the halves
in a baking dish and set aside. Cut the
stem ginger into fine matchsticks.

2 Make the filling. Combine the
crushed amaretti biscuits, stem ginger
matchsticks and raisins in a bowl.

3 Stir in the lime rind and juice, two-
thirds of the nuts, then add the sugar
and the crème fraîche. Mix well.

4 Fill the papaya halves and drizzle
with the ginger syrup. Sprinkle with
the remaining nuts. Bake for about
25 minutes or until tender. Serve with
extra crème fraîche.

EXOTIC FRUIT SALAD WITH PASSION FRUIT DRESSING

PASSION FRUIT MAKES A SUPERB DRESSING FOR ANY FRUIT, BUT REALLY BRINGS OUT THE FLAVOUR OF EXOTIC VARIETIES. YOU CAN EASILY DOUBLE THE RECIPE, THEN SERVE THE REST FOR BREAKFAST.

SERVES SIX

INGREDIENTS
    1 mango
    1 papaya
    2 kiwi fruit
    coconut or vanilla ice cream, to serve
For the dressing
    3 passion fruit
    thinly pared rind and juice of 1 lime
    5ml/1 tsp hazelnut or walnut oil
    15ml/1 tbsp clear honey

COOK'S TIP
A clear golden honey scented with orange blossom or acacia blossom would be perfect for the dressing.

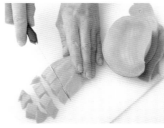

1 Peel the mango, cut it into three slices, then cut the flesh into chunks and place it in a large bowl. Peel the papaya and cut it in half. Scoop out the seeds, then chop the flesh.

2 Cut both ends off each kiwi fruit, then stand them on a board. Using a small sharp knife, cut off the skin from top to bottom. Cut each kiwi fruit in half lengthways, then cut into thick slices. Combine all the fruit in a large bowl.

3 Make the dressing. Cut each passion fruit in half and scoop the seeds out into a sieve set over a small bowl. Press the seeds well to extract all the juices. Lightly whisk the remaining dressing ingredients into the passion fruit juice, then pour the dressing over the fruit. Mix gently to combine. Leave to chill for 1 hour before serving with scoops of coconut or vanilla ice cream.

TROPICAL FRUIT GRATIN

THIS OUT-OF-THE-ORDINARY GRATIN IS STRICTLY FOR GROWN-UPS. A COLOURFUL COMBINATION OF FRUIT IS TOPPED WITH A SIMPLE SABAYON BEFORE BEING FLASHED UNDER THE GRILL.

SERVES FOUR

INGREDIENTS
2 tamarillos
½ sweet pineapple
1 ripe mango
175g/6oz/1½ cups blackberries
120ml/4fl oz/½ cup sparkling
   white wine
115g/4oz/½ cup caster sugar
6 egg yolks

VARIATION
Although boiling drives off the alcohol in the wine, children do not always appreciate the flavour, so substitute orange juice if making the gratin for them. White grape juice or pineapple juice would also work well.

1 Cut each tamarillo in half lengthways and then into thick slices. Cut the rind and core from the pineapple and take spiral slices off the outside to remove the eyes. Cut the flesh into chunks. Peel the mango, cut it in half and cut the flesh from the stone in slices.

2 Divide all the fruit, including the blackberries, among four 14cm/5½in gratin dishes set on a baking sheet and set aside. Heat the wine and sugar in a saucepan until the sugar has dissolved. Bring to the boil and cook for 5 minutes.

3 Put the egg yolks in a large heatproof bowl. Place the bowl over a pan of simmering water and whisk until pale. Slowly pour on the hot sugar syrup, whisking all the time, until the mixture thickens. Preheat the grill.

4 Spoon the mixture over the fruit. Place the baking sheet holding the dishes on a low shelf under the hot grill until the topping is golden. Serve hot.

GRILLED PINEAPPLE WITH PAPAYA SAUCE

PINEAPPLE COOKED THIS WAY TAKES ON A SUPERB FLAVOUR AND IS SENSATIONAL WHEN SERVED WITH THE PAPAYA SAUCE.

SERVES SIX

INGREDIENTS
1 sweet pineapple
melted butter, for greasing
   and brushing
2 pieces drained stem ginger in
   syrup, cut into fine matchsticks,
   plus 30ml/2 tbsp of the syrup
   from the jar
30ml/2 tbsp demerara sugar
a pinch of ground cinnamon
fresh mint sprigs, to decorate
For the sauce
1 ripe papaya, peeled and seeded
175ml/6fl oz/¾ cup apple juice

1 Peel the pineapple and take spiral slices off the outside to remove the eyes. Cut it crossways into six slices, each 2.5cm/1in thick. Line a baking sheet with a sheet of foil, rolling up the sides to make a rim. Grease the foil with melted butter. Preheat the grill.

2 Arrange the pineapple slices on the lined baking sheet. Brush with butter, then top with the ginger matchsticks, sugar and cinnamon. Drizzle over the stem ginger syrup. Grill for 5–7 minutes or until the slices are golden and lightly charred on top.

3 Meanwhile, make the sauce. Cut a few slices from the papaya and set aside, then purée the rest with the apple juice in a blender or food processor.

4 Press the purée through a sieve placed over a bowl, then stir in any juices from cooking the pineapple. Serve the pineapple slices with a little sauce drizzled around each plate. Decorate with the reserved papaya slices and the mint sprigs.

COOK'S TIP
Try the papaya sauce with savoury dishes, too. It tastes great with grilled chicken and game birds as well as pork and lamb.

JAMAICAN FRUIT TRIFLE

This trifle is actually based on a Caribbean fool that consists of fruit stirred into thick vanilla-flavoured cream. This version is not so rich, redressing the balance with plenty of fruit, and with crème fraîche replacing some of the cream.

2 Whip the double cream to very soft peaks, then lightly but thoroughly fold in the crème fraîche, sifted icing sugar, vanilla essence and rum.

3 Fold the drained chopped pineapple into the cream mixture. Place the chopped papayas and mangoes in a large bowl and pour over the lime juice. Gently stir the fruit mixture to combine. Shred the pared lime rind.

4 Divide the fruit mixture and the pineapple cream among eight dessert plates. Decorate with the lime shreds, toasted coconut and a few small pineapple leaves, if you like, and serve at once.

SERVES EIGHT

INGREDIENTS

1 large sweet pineapple, peeled and cored, about 350g/12oz
300ml/½ pint/1¼ cups double cream
200ml/7fl oz/scant 1 cup crème fraîche
60ml/4 tbsp icing sugar, sifted
10ml/2 tsp pure vanilla essence
30ml/2 tbsp white or coconut rum
3 papayas, peeled, seeded and chopped
3 mangoes, peeled, stoned and chopped
thinly pared rind and juice of 1 lime
25g/1oz/⅓ cup coarsely shredded or flaked coconut, toasted

1 Cut the pineapple into large chunks, place in a food processor or blender and process briefly until chopped. Tip into a sieve placed over a bowl and leave for 5 minutes so that most of the juice drains from the fruit.

COOK'S TIP

It is important to let the pineapple purée drain thoroughly, otherwise, the pineapple cream will be watery. Don't throw away the drained pineapple juice – mix it with fizzy mineral water for a wonderfully refreshing drink.

POMEGRANATE JEWELLED CHEESECAKE

THIS LIGHT CHEESECAKE IS FLAVOURED WITH COCONUT AND HAS A STUNNING POMEGRANATE GLAZE.

SERVES EIGHT

INGREDIENTS
225g/8oz oat biscuits
75g/3oz/⅓ cup unsalted
   butter, melted
For the filling
45ml/3 tbsp orange juice
15ml/1 tbsp powdered gelatine
250g/9oz/generous 1 cup mascarpone
   cheese
200g/7oz/scant 1 cup full-fat
   soft cheese
75g/3oz/¾ cup icing sugar, sifted
200ml/7fl oz/scant 1 cup coconut
   cream
2 egg whites
For the topping
2 pomegranates, peeled and
   seeds separated
grated rind and juice of 1 orange
30ml/2 tbsp caster sugar
15ml/1 tbsp arrowroot, mixed to a
   paste with 30ml/2 tbsp Kirsch
a few drops of red food colouring
   (optional)

2 For the filling, pour the orange juice into a heatproof bowl, then sprinkle the gelatine on top and set aside for 5 minutes until sponged. Place the bowl in a pan of hot water and stir until the gelatine has dissolved.

3 In a bowl, beat together both cheeses and the icing sugar, then gradually beat in the coconut cream. Whisk the egg whites in a grease-free bowl to soft peaks. Quickly stir the melted gelatine into the coconut mixture and fold in the egg whites. Pour over the biscuit base, level and chill until set.

4 Make the cheesecake topping. Place the pomegranate seeds in a saucepan and add the orange rind and juice and caster sugar. Bring to the boil, then lower the heat, cover and simmer for 5 minutes. Add the arrowroot paste and heat, stirring constantly, until thickened. Stir in the food colouring, if using. Allow to cool, stirring occasionally.

5 Pour the glaze over the top of the set cheesecake, then chill. To serve, run a knife between the edge of the tin and the cheesecake, then remove the side of the tin.

1 Grease a 23cm/9in springform cake tin. Crumb the oat biscuits in a food processor or blender. Add the melted butter and process briefly to combine. Spoon into the prepared tin, press the mixture in well, then chill.

COOK'S TIP
If you do not have a blender or a food processor, crumb the biscuits by placing them in a large, strong plastic bag and crushing them with a rolling pin. For the best results, crush the crumbs as finely as you possibly can.

BANANA AND MASCARPONE CREAMS

IF YOU ARE A FAN OF COLD BANANA CUSTARD, YOU'LL LOVE THIS RECIPE. IT IS A GROWN-UP VERSION OF AN OLD FAVOURITE. NO ONE WILL GUESS THAT THE SECRET IS READY-MADE CUSTARD.

SERVES FOUR TO SIX

INGREDIENTS
   250g/9oz/generous 1 cup mascarpone
      cheese
   300ml/½ pint/1¼ cups fresh ready-
      made custard
   150ml/¼ pint/⅔ cup Greek yogurt
   4 bananas
   juice of 1 lime
   50g/2oz/½ cup pecan nuts,
      coarsely chopped
   120ml/4fl oz/½ cup maple syrup

VARIATIONS
Use clear honey instead of maple syrup
and walnuts instead of pecans, if you
like. Also, try layering in some crumbled
biscuits, such as amaretti or ratafia,
shortbread crumbs or crushed meringues.
Or add a handful of finely grated dark or
white chocolate.

1 Combine the mascarpone, custard
and yogurt in a large bowl and beat
together until smooth. Make this mixture
up to several hours ahead, if you
like. Cover and chill, then stir before using.

2 Slice the bananas diagonally and
place in a separate bowl. Pour over the
lime juice and toss together until the
bananas are coated in the juice.

3 Divide half the custard mixture
among four or six dessert glasses and
top each portion with a generous
spoonful of the banana mixture.

4 Spoon the remaining custard mixture
into the glasses and top with the rest of
the bananas. Scatter the nuts over the
top. Drizzle maple syrup over each dessert
and chill for 30 minutes before serving.

BANANAS WITH LIME AND CARDAMOM SAUCE

SERVE THESE BANANAS SOLO, WITH VANILLA ICE CREAM, OR SPOON THEM OVER FOLDED CRÊPES.

SERVES FOUR

INGREDIENTS
   6 small bananas
   50g/2oz/¼ cup butter
   seeds from 4 cardamom
      pods, crushed
   50g/2oz/½ cup flaked almonds
   thinly pared rind and juice
      of 2 limes
   50g/2oz/⅓ cup light
      muscovado sugar
   30ml/2 tbsp dark rum
   vanilla ice cream, to serve

VARIATION
If you prefer not to use alcohol in your
cooking, replace the rum with orange
juice or even pineapple juice.

1 Peel the bananas and cut them in
half lengthways. Heat half the butter in
a large frying pan. Then add half the
bananas, and cook until the undersides
are golden. Turn carefully, using a fish
slice. Cook until golden.

2 As they cook, transfer the bananas to
a heatproof serving dish. Cook the
remaining bananas in the same way.

3 Melt the remaining butter, then add
the cardamom seeds and almonds.
Cook, stirring, until golden.

4 Stir in the lime rind and juice, and
then the sugar. Cook, stirring, until the
mixture is smooth, bubbling and slightly
reduced. Stir in the rum. Pour the
sauce over the bananas and serve
immediately, with vanilla ice cream.

TOFFEE BANANAS

ALTHOUGH THE METHOD FOR THIS RECIPE SOUNDS SIMPLE, IT CAN BE A BIT TRICKY TO MASTER. YOU NEED TO WORK FAST, ESPECIALLY WHEN DIPPING THE FRUIT IN THE CARAMEL, AS IT WILL COOL AND SET QUITE QUICKLY. THE LUSCIOUS RESULTS, HOWEVER, ARE WORTH THE EFFORT.

2 Heat the groundnut, sunflower or corn oil in a deep pan until it registers 180°C/350°F or until a cube of bread, added to the oil, turns pale brown in 45 seconds.

3 Using a fork, remove a piece of banana from the batter, allowing the excess batter to drain back into the bowl. Gently lower the piece of banana into the hot oil. Add more pieces of battered banana in the same way; do not overcrowd the pan. Fry for about 2 minutes or until the coating is golden.

4 As they are cooked, remove the banana fritters from the oil with a slotted spoon and place on kitchen paper to drain. Cook the rest of the battered bananas in the same way.

5 When all the banana pieces have been fried, make the caramel. Mix the sugar, sesame seeds and water in a pan. Heat gently, stirring occasionally, until the sugar has dissolved. Raise the heat slightly and continue cooking, without stirring, until the syrup becomes a light caramel. Remove from the heat.

6 Have ready a bowl of iced water. Working quickly, drop one fritter at a time into the hot caramel. Flip over with a fork, remove immediately and plunge the piece into the iced water. Remove from the water quickly (using your fingers for speed, but taking care) and drain on a wire rack while coating the rest. Serve immediately.

SERVES FOUR

INGREDIENTS
    4 firm bananas
    75g/3oz/¾ cup plain flour
    50g/2oz/½ cup cornflour
    10ml/2 tsp baking powder
    175ml/6fl oz/¾ cup water
    5ml/1 tsp sesame oil
    groundnut, sunflower or corn oil, for
        deep frying
For the caramel
    225g/8oz/1 cup granulated sugar
    30ml/2 tbsp sesame seeds
    60ml/4 tbsp water

1 Peel the bananas, then cut them diagonally into thick slices. Sift the flours and baking powder into a large bowl. Quickly beat in the water and sesame oil, taking care not to overmix. Stir in the bananas until coated.

HOT DATE PUDDINGS <u>WITH</u> TOFFEE SAUCE

FRESH DATES MAKE THIS PUDDING LESS RICH THAN THE CONVENTIONAL DRIED DATE VERSION, BUT IT IS STILL A BIT OF AN INDULGENCE! IT IS PREFERABLE TO PEEL THE DATES AS THE SKINS CAN BE TOUGH: SIMPLY SQUEEZE THEM BETWEEN YOUR THUMB AND FOREFINGER AND THE SKINS WILL POP OFF.

<u>SERVES SIX</u>

INGREDIENTS
   50g/2oz/¼ cup butter, softened
   75g/3oz/½ cup light muscovado sugar
   2 eggs, beaten
   115g/4oz/1 cup self-raising flour
   2.5ml/½ tsp bicarbonate of soda
   175g/6oz/1 cup fresh dates, peeled,
   stoned and chopped
   75ml/5 tbsp boiling water
   10ml/2 tsp coffee and chicory
   essence
For the toffee sauce
   75g/3oz/½ cup light muscovado sugar
   50g/2oz/¼ cup butter
   60ml/4 tbsp double cream
   30ml/2 tbsp brandy

1 Preheat the oven to 180°C/350°F/ Gas 4. Place a baking sheet in the oven to heat up. Grease six individual pudding moulds or tins. Cream the butter and sugar in a mixing bowl until pale and fluffy. Gradually add the eggs, beating well after each addition.

2 Sift the flour and bicarbonate of soda together and fold into the creamed mixture. Put the dates in a heatproof bowl, pour over the boiling water and mash with a potato masher. Add the coffee and chicory essence, then stir the paste into the creamed mixture.

3 Spoon the mixture into the prepared moulds or tins. Place on the hot baking sheet and bake for 20 minutes.

4 Meanwhile, make the toffee sauce. Put all the ingredients in a pan and heat very gently, stirring occasionally, until the mixture is smooth. Increase the heat and boil for 1 minute.

5 Turn the warm puddings out on to individual dessert plates. Spoon a generous amount of sauce over each portion and serve at once.

COOK'S TIP
The sauce is a great standby. Try it on poached apple or pear slices, over ice cream or with a steamed pudding.

RUM AND BANANA WAFFLES

TO SAVE TIME, THESE SCRUMPTIOUS DESSERT WAFFLES CAN BE MADE IN ADVANCE, WRAPPED TIGHTLY, FROZEN, AND THEN WARMED THROUGH IN THE OVEN JUST BEFORE SERVING.

SERVES FOUR

INGREDIENTS
    225g/8oz/2 cups plain flour
    10ml/2 tsp baking powder
    5ml/1 tsp bicarbonate of soda
    15ml/1 tbsp caster sugar
    2 eggs
    50g/2oz/¼ cup butter, melted
    175ml/6fl oz/¾ cup milk, plus extra
        if needed
    300ml/½ pint/1¼ cups buttermilk
    5ml/1 tsp pure vanilla essence
    single cream, to serve
For the bananas
    6 bananas, thickly sliced
    115g/4oz/1 cup pecan nuts, broken
        into pieces
    50g/2oz/⅓ cup demerara sugar
    75ml/5 tbsp maple syrup
    45ml/3 tbsp dark rum

1 Sift the dry ingredients into a large mixing bowl. Make a well in the centre. Add the eggs, melted butter and milk. Whisk together, gradually incorporating the flour mixture, until smooth.

COOK'S TIP
If you don't own a waffle iron, prepare the batter as directed, but make small pancakes in a heavy-based frying pan. Alternatively, use ready-made waffles, which are available from most large supermarkets, and reheat as directed on the packet before serving with the hot banana topping.

2 Add the buttermilk and vanilla to the batter and whisk well. Cover and leave to stand for 30 minutes. Preheat the oven to 150°C/300°F/Gas 2.

3 Place a hand-held waffle iron over the heat. Stir the batter and add more milk if required (the consistency should be quite thick). Open the waffle iron and pour some batter over two-thirds of the surface. Close it and wipe off any excess batter.

4 Cook for 3–4 minutes, carefully turning the waffle iron over once during cooking. If using an electric waffle maker, follow the manufacturer's instructions for cooking.

VARIATIONS
Use other fruits for the waffle topping, if you like. Small chunks of fresh or drained, canned pineapple, thin wedges of peaches or nectarines or even orange slices would be delicious alternatives to the sliced banana.

5 When the batter stops steaming, open the iron and lift out the waffle with a fork. Put it on a heatproof plate and keep it hot in the oven. Repeat with the remaining batter to make eight waffles in all. Preheat the grill.

6 Cook the bananas. Spread them out on a large shallow baking tin and top with the nuts. Scatter over the demerara sugar. Mix the maple syrup and rum together and spoon over.

7 Grill for 3–4 minutes or until the sugar begins to bubble. Serve on top of the waffles with single cream.

MANGO AND TAMARILLO PASTRIES

THESE FRUIT-TOPPED LITTLE PASTRIES GO DOWN A TREAT WITH A CUP OF AFTERNOON TEA.

MAKES EIGHT

INGREDIENTS
    225g/8oz ready-rolled puff pastry
       (30 × 25cm/12 × 10in rectangle)
    1 egg yolk, lightly beaten
    115g/4oz/½ cup white marzipan
    40ml/8 tsp ginger or apricot conserve
    1 mango, peeled and thinly sliced off
       the stone
    2 tamarillos, halved and sliced
    caster sugar, for sprinkling

1 Preheat the oven to 200°C/400°F/
Gas 6. Unroll the pastry and cut it into
8 rectangles. Place on baking sheets.

VARIATION
Use apricot slices instead of tamarillos,
or a mix of plums and peaches.

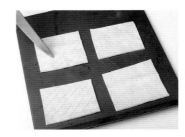

2 Using a sharp knife, score the
surface of each piece of pastry into a
diamond pattern, then brush with the
egg yolk to glaze. Cut eight thin slices
of marzipan and lay one slice on each
pastry rectangle. Top each with a
teaspoon of the ginger or apricot
conserve and spread over evenly.

3 Top the pastry rectangles with
alternate slices of mango and tamarillo.
Sprinkle with some of the caster sugar,
then bake for 15–20 minutes until the
pastry is well puffed up and golden.
Remove the pastries to a wire rack to
cool. Sprinkle with more caster sugar
before serving.

EXOTIC FRUIT TRANCHE

THIS IS A GOOD WAY TO MAKE THE MOST OF A SMALL SELECTION OF EXOTIC FRUIT.

SERVES EIGHT

INGREDIENTS
  175g/6oz/1½ cups plain flour
  50g/2oz/¼ cup unsalted butter
  25g/1oz/2 tbsp white vegetable fat
  50g/2oz/¼ cup caster sugar
  2 egg yolks
  about 15ml/1 tbsp cold water
  115g/4oz/scant ½ cup apricot
    conserve, sieved and warmed
For the filling
  150ml/¼ pint/⅔ cup double cream,
    plus extra to serve
  250g/9oz/generous 1 cup mascarpone
    cheese
  25g/1oz/¼ cup icing sugar, sifted
  grated rind of 1 orange
  450g/1lb/3 cups mixed prepared
    fruits, such as mango, papaya, star
    fruit, kiwi fruit and blackberries
  90ml/6 tbsp apricot conserve, sieved
  15ml/1 tbsp white or coconut rum

1 Sift the flour into a bowl and rub in the butter and white vegetable fat until the mixture resembles fine breadcrumbs. Stir in the caster sugar. Add the egg yolks and enough cold water to make a soft dough. Thinly roll out the pastry between two sheets of clear film and use the pastry to line a 35 × 12cm/14 × 4½in fluted tranche tin. Allow the excess pastry to hang over the edge of the tin and chill for 30 minutes.

2 Preheat the oven to 200°C/400°F/ Gas 6. Prick the base of the pastry case and line with non-stick baking paper and baking beans. Bake for 10–12 minutes. Lift out the paper and beans and return the pastry case to the oven for 5 minutes. Trim off the excess pastry and brush the inside of the case with the warmed apricot conserve to form a seal. Leave to cool on a wire rack.

3 Make the filling. Whip the cream to soft peaks, then stir it into the mascarpone with the icing sugar and orange rind. Spread in the cooled pastry case and top with the prepared fruits. Warm the apricot conserve with the rum and drizzle or brush over the fruits to make a glaze. Serve with extra cream.

COOK'S TIP
If you don't have a tranche tin, line a 23cm/9in flan tin with the pastry.

MANGO PIE

THIS RECIPE COMES STRAIGHT FROM THE CARIBBEAN AND CAPTURES ALL THE SUNSHINE FLAVOURS OF
THAT EXOTIC SETTING. FOR THE TASTIEST PIE, BE SURE THAT THE MANGOES ARE GOOD AND RIPE.

SERVES SIX

INGREDIENTS
    175g/6oz/1½ cups plain flour
    a pinch of salt
    75g/3oz/⅓ cup unsalted butter,
      chilled and diced
    25g/1oz/2 tbsp white vegetable fat,
      chilled and diced
    15ml/1 tbsp caster sugar, plus extra
      for sprinkling
    about 45ml/3 tbsp cold water
    beaten egg, to glaze
    vanilla ice cream, to serve
For the filling
    2 ripe mangoes
    45ml/3 tbsp fresh lime juice
    115g/4oz/½ cup caster sugar
    15ml/1 tbsp arrowroot mixed to a
      paste with 15ml/1 tbsp water

1 Sift the flour and salt into a large mixing bowl. Rub in the butter and white vegetable fat with your fingertips until the mixture resembles fine breadcrumbs, then stir in the caster sugar. Add just enough of the cold water to make a dough.

VARIATIONS
Make the pie using one mango and one papaya, peeled, seeded and sliced. Add a little ground cinnamon and some freshly grated nutmeg to the filling for a sweet spice flavour.

COOK'S TIP
If the top of the pie begins to brown too much during baking, simply cover it loosely with a piece of foil.

2 Knead lightly, then roll out two-thirds of the pastry and line a 18cm/7in pie dish. Wrap the remaining pastry in clear film and chill both the pastry and the pastry case for 30 minutes.

3 Meanwhile, make the filling. Peel the mangoes and slice the flesh off the stone. Reserve half the sliced mango, and coarsely chop the rest.

4 Place the chopped mango in a saucepan with the lime juice and caster sugar. Cover and cook for 10 minutes or until soft. Pour in the arrowroot paste and cook, stirring all the time, until thickened. Set the filling aside to cool.

5 Preheat the oven to 190°C/375°F/ Gas 5. Pour the cooled mango sauce into the chilled pastry case and top with the reserved mango slices. Roll out the remaining pastry to make a pie lid.

6 Dampen the rim of the pastry case and add the pastry lid. Crimp the edges to seal, then cut a cross in the centre to allow the steam to escape.

7 Glaze the pastry with the beaten egg and sprinkle lightly with caster sugar. Bake for 35–40 minutes until the pastry is golden brown. Cool slightly on a wire rack. Serve warm with vanilla ice cream.

BANANA AND PECAN BREAD

BANANAS AND PECAN NUTS JUST SEEM TO BELONG TOGETHER. THIS IS A REALLY MOIST AND DELICIOUS TEA BREAD. SPREAD IT WITH CREAM CHEESE OR JAM, OR SERVE AS A DESSERT WITH WHIPPED CREAM.

MAKES A 900G/2LB LOAF

INGREDIENTS
115g/4oz/½ cup butter, softened
175g/6oz/1 cup light muscovado
   sugar
2 large eggs, beaten
3 ripe bananas
75g/3oz/¾ cup pecan nuts,
   coarsely chopped
225g/8oz/2 cups self-raising flour
2.5ml/½ tsp ground mixed spice

1 Preheat the oven to 180°C/350°F/ Gas 4. Generously grease a 900g/2lb loaf tin and line it with non-stick baking paper. Cream the butter and muscovado sugar in a large mixing bowl until the mixture is light and fluffy. Gradually add the eggs, beating after each addition, until well combined.

2 Peel and then mash the bananas with a fork. Add them to the creamed mixture with the chopped pecan nuts. Beat until well combined.

COOK'S TIP
If the mixture shows signs of curdling when you add the eggs, stir in a little of the flour to stabilize it.

3 Sift the flour and mixed spice together and fold into the banana mixture. Spoon into the tin, level the surface and bake for 1–1¼ hours or until a skewer inserted into the centre of the loaf comes out clean. Cool for 10 minutes in the tin, then invert the tin on a wire rack. Lift off the tin, peel off the lining paper and cool completely.

DATE AND WALNUT BROWNIES

THESE RICH BROWNIES ARE GREAT FOR AFTERNOON TEA, BUT THEY ALSO MAKE A FANTASTIC DESSERT. REHEAT SLICES BRIEFLY IN THE MICROWAVE OVEN AND SERVE WITH CRÈME FRAÎCHE.

MAKES TWELVE

INGREDIENTS
350g/12oz plain chocolate, broken
   into squares
225g/8oz/1 cup butter, diced
3 large eggs
115g/4oz/½ cup caster sugar
5ml/1 tsp pure vanilla essence
75g/3oz/¾ cup plain flour, sifted
225g/8oz/1½ cups fresh dates,
   peeled, stoned and chopped
200g/7oz/1¾ cups walnut pieces
icing sugar, for dusting

COOK'S TIP
When melting the chocolate and butter, keep the water in the pan beneath hot, but do not let it approach boiling point. Chocolate is notoriously sensitive to heat; it is vital not to let it get too hot or it may stiffen into an unmanageable mass.

1 Preheat the oven to 190°C/375°F/ Gas 5. Generously grease a 30 × 20cm/ 12 × 8in baking tin and line with non-stick baking paper.

2 Put the chocolate and butter in a large heatproof bowl. Place the bowl over a pan of hot water and leave until both have melted. Stir until smooth, then lift the bowl out and cool slightly.

3 In a separate bowl, beat the eggs, sugar and vanilla. Then beat into the chocolate mixture and fold in the flour, dates and nuts. Pour into the tin.

4 Bake for 30–40 minutes, until firm and the mixture comes away from the sides of the tin. Cool in the tin, then turn out, remove the paper and dust with icing sugar.

MANGO CHUTNEY

THIS CLASSIC CHUTNEY IS CONVENTIONALLY SERVED WITH CURRIES AND INDIAN POPPADOMS, BUT IT IS ALSO DELICIOUS WITH BAKED HAM OR A TRADITIONAL CHEESE PLOUGHMAN'S LUNCH.

2 Place these in a large saucepan, add the vinegar and cover. Cook over a low heat for 10 minutes.

3 Stir in the muscovado sugar, chilli, ginger, garlic, bruised cardamoms and coriander. Add the bay leaf and salt. Bring to the boil slowly, stirring often.

4 Lower the heat and then simmer, uncovered, for 30 minutes or until the mixture is thick and syrupy.

MAKES 450G/1LB

INGREDIENTS
    3 firm green mangoes
    150ml/¼ pint/⅔ cup cider vinegar
    130g/4½oz/⅔ cup light
      muscovado sugar
    1 small red finger chilli or jalapeño
      chilli, split
    2.5cm/1in piece of fresh root ginger,
      peeled and finely chopped
    1 garlic clove, finely chopped
    5 cardamom pods, bruised
    2.5ml/½ tsp coriander
      seeds, crushed
    1 bay leaf
    2.5ml/½ tsp salt

1 Peel the mangoes and cut the flesh off the stone. Slice the mango flesh lengthways, then cut across into small chunks or thin wedges.

5 Ladle into hot sterilized jars, seal and label. Store for 1 week before eating. Keep chilled after opening.

PAPAYA AND LEMON RELISH

THIS CHUNKY RELISH IS BEST MADE WITH A FIRM, UNRIPE PAPAYA. IT SHOULD BE LEFT FOR A WEEK BEFORE EATING TO ALLOW ALL THE FLAVOURS TO MELLOW. STORE THE UNOPENED JARS IN A COOL PLACE, AWAY FROM SUNLIGHT. SERVE WITH ROAST MEATS OR WITH A ROBUST CHEESE AND CRACKERS.

MAKES 450G/1LB

INGREDIENTS

    1 large unripe papaya
    1 onion, thinly sliced
    40g/1½oz/⅓ cup raisins
    250ml/8fl oz/1 cup red wine vinegar
    juice of 2 lemons
    150ml/¼ pint/⅔ cup elderflower
      cordial
    165g/5½oz/¾ cup golden
      granulated sugar
    1 cinnamon stick
    1 fresh bay leaf
    2.5ml/½ tsp hot paprika
    2.5ml/½ tsp salt

1 Peel the papaya and cut it lengthways in half. Remove the seeds with a small spoon. Cut the flesh into small chunks and place in a large saucepan.

2 Add the onion slices and raisins to the papaya chunks, then stir in the vinegar. Bring to a boil, lower the heat and simmer for 10 minutes.

3 Add all the remaining ingredients and bring to the boil, stirring all the time. Check that all the sugar has dissolved, then lower the heat and simmer for 50–60 minutes or until the relish is thick and syrupy.

4 Ladle into hot sterilized jars. Seal and label and store for 1 week before using. Keep chilled after opening.

MELONS, GRAPES, FIGS AND RHUBARB

Some fruits are in a class of their own. Melons, grapes and figs have little in common, apart from the fact that they are all fruits, and rhubarb cannot even lay claim to that characteristic: it is technically a vegetable. Without these treasures, however, the food world would be a poorer place. Melons are the cool fruits, grapes the sybarites' choice, figs the sweetest treats and rhubarb the perfect excuse for custard!

MELONS

Sweet melons are members of a large family of fruits and vegetables which grow on trailing vines and include cucumbers, squashes and marrows. They come in a huge number of varieties (possibly thousands) and range in size from a single portion to melons which are large enough to provide a dozen servings. They have a hard, often beautifully patterned rind and very juicy, refreshing flesh enclosing a central cavity filled with a large number of pale, pointed, edible seeds.

History

Melons originated in Africa or Asia and have been known in China for at least 3,000 years. These early melons were bitter, rather like cucumbers, and could not be eaten raw. Hybridization resulted in sweeter fruits, which the Moors brought to Spain from Persia or Africa. They were taken to Italy, and by the fifteenth century reached France, where they were propagated

enthusiastically by the Avignon popes. Christopher Columbus took melons to the New World; when his men had eaten the fruit, they discarded the seeds, which produced large melon crops. These popular fruits are now grown in most warm parts of the world.

Varieties

Melons fall into two main categories – summer fruit, which includes all those varieties with cross-hatched skin that looks like brown netting, and winter melons, which have smooth or finely ridged pale or bright yellow rind and delicate, pale flesh, which can be rather lacking in taste.

Summer melons

Cantaloupe This summer melon takes its name from the Italian town of Cantalupo near Rome, where the fruits were grown in profusion on the papal estate. Most cantaloupes are slightly elongated with craggy pale green or golden rinds, marked into segments, and have aromatic orangey-yellow flesh.

Charentais Charentais have smooth, grey-green rinds and very fragrant orange flesh. A ripe charentais gives off a heady, delicious aroma. Most of the charentais melons are grown around Cavaillon in France, and are sometimes sold under this name. The French writer Alexandre Dumas so loved these melons that he offered the municipality of Cavaillon all his published and future works in exchange for a life annuity of twelve melons a year.

Galia A relative of the Ogen, Galia is a round melon with a raised pattern of fine netting on the skin. The skin turns from green to golden as it ripens, and the fragrant flesh is green and juicy.

Musk melons These summer melons, also known as "nutmeg" melons, are round or oval, with a raised pattern of lacy netting on the rind. The skins can be green or orange, and the sweet, highly aromatic flesh ranges from orangey-pink to pale green. They take their name from the Romans' habit of sprinkling the fruit with powdered musk to accentuate the flavour. Musk melons are often grown in hothouses.

Ogen A hybrid developed in Israel, this Cantaloupe melon has a smooth pale green skin, marked with green or orange lines, which turns golden when the fruit is ripe. The juicy flesh is sweet and aromatic.

Pineapple or **Khoob melons** These large oval melons have orangey-yellow netted skin and beautiful, juicy orange flesh, which has the aroma and faint flavour of pineapple.

Above: Ein d'Or, one of the winter melons, has golden skin and delicately flavoured flesh.

Winter melons

In addition to the winter melons listed below, there are the golden **Ein d'Or** and the **Piel de Sapo,** with rough-ridged, dark green skin and green-to-orange flesh. Its name means "toad's skin".
Casaba is a walnut-shaped melon with ridged, deep yellow skin and pale creamy flesh.
Crenshaws are pointed at the stem end and have smooth golden skins. They have the best flavour of all winter melons, with sweet juicy salmon-pink flesh and a pleasantly scented aroma.
Honeydew is the most common winter melon. Sadly, its name is often more flavoursome than its taste.
Watermelons See page 231.

Nutrition

Melons have a very high water content, so are low in calories (30 kilocalories per 100g/3³/₄oz). The more orange the flesh, the more beneficial carotenes it contains.

Left: The aromatic orangey-yellow flesh of Cantaloupes is delicious served with cured meats.

Buying and Storing

Melons should feel heavy for their size and give off a pleasant, sweet aroma; they should not smell too musky, as this is a sign that they are overripe. Gently press the stalk end with your thumb; it should "give" slightly, but check that the fruit has not started to rot. The rind should be thick and unblemished with a good colour for its type.

To ripen a melon, keep it at room temperature. Ripe melons are best kept in a cool, airy place. The fridge is fine, but wrap the melon in clear film or a polythene bag first, or the smell will permeate other foods. Melon balls or cubes can be frozen in rigid containers for up to three months, either as they are or in a light syrup.

Preparing and Serving

Aromatic ripe melons are best eaten raw, on their own, in a fruit salad (use the melon shell as a container) or as an hors d'oeuvre with Parma ham or salami. Melons can be served in long slices, balls or cubes. They should always be chilled. A sprinkling of salt and pepper or ground ginger enhances the flavour. Small round varieties can be halved horizontally, seeded and served as they are or with a filling such as raspberry coulis or ice cream. They can also be filled with port, although purists frown on this practice. For single-portion melons, cut off a lid and scoop out the seeds. Always scoop out melons into a sieve set over a bowl to catch all the juice. The seeds can be dried and roasted in the oven to make a delicious snack.

Melon goes well with sweet or savoury ingredients. It makes a refreshing salad if mixed with cucumber and tossed in lemon juice, a light cream cheese or

Above: Piel de Sapo whose name means "toad's skin".

Left: Galia melons are fragrant and juicy.

yogurt dressing, or a vinaigrette made with lemon juice. Add cubes of blue cheese, such as Cambozola or Dolcelatte. Melon cubes also enhance cold chicken, prawns and other seafood bound in a light mayonnaise.

For the simplest and prettiest of desserts, scoop out balls of different-coloured melon flesh (white, yellow, orange – perhaps even red watermelon), pile into a glass bowl and serve chilled, with a sprinkling of sugar if needed and a decoration of mint sprigs or nasturtium flowers. Melons make very refreshing sorbets, fools, mousses and ice creams. Spiced with pieces of stem ginger, they also make excellent jams.

Chunks of melon can be made into a cool pickle that goes well with hot and cold meats or cold ham and poultry. The rind can also be pickled; remove the hard, outer, coloured layer of rind, leaving the white inner rind.

*Above:
Honeydew melons*

Preparing melons for serving

1 If the melons are small, either cut off the lids or cut the melons in half, then scoop out the seeds into a sieve set over a bowl. Pour any juice from the bowl back into the melons; serve them plain or with a filling of other fruit like strawberries and raspberries.

2 For a prettier effect, "vandyke" the melon. Make a 2.5cm/1in diagonal cut where you want the lid to be. Turn the knife and cut down on the opposite diagonal to make an inverted V. Continue to cut zig-zags all round the fruit in this way, then lift off the lid. Remove the seeds.

3 For melon slices, cut a large melon in half lengthways. Scoop out the seeds and cut the melon into long wedges.

4 To make melon "boats", slice the melon as in step 3. Run a flexible knife between the melon rind and flesh to release the flesh. Slice the flesh on the rind into 2cm/3/4in chunks. Push alternate chunks in opposite directions to give a staggered effect.

WATERMELONS

Watermelons are huge round or oval fruits that weigh up to 12kg/26½lb – much larger than sweet melons. They have solid dark green or paler striped skins, and vibrant pink or red flesh studded with large, flat, black, edible seeds. The flesh is very watery, and can taste rather insipid, but a slice of chilled watermelon really is one of the most refreshing experiences imaginable.

History

Watermelons are thought to have originated in India, but may have come from tropical Africa. They were enjoyed by the Ancient Egyptians, but were unknown in Europe until the thirteenth century. They became a symbol of the martyrdom of San Lorenzo in Italy; every year on 10 August in Florence, the patron saint of cooks is celebrated with an orgy of watermelon-eating.

Varieties

Smaller varieties of watermelon are now available, weighing from 2.5–4.5kg/ 5½–10lb. These include **Sugar Baby,** a particularly sweet, round variety with very dark green skin and red flesh. **Tiger** has a paler green skin, striped with yellow or green, as its name suggests. **Golden watermelons** have bright yellow flesh and a more delicate (or dull) flavour than the red-fleshed varieties. They do, however, look very pretty when mixed with red watermelons.

Nutrition

The high water content of watermelons means that they are low in calories; only 30 kilocalories per 100g/3¾oz. They contain some vitamins B and C.

Buying and Storing

Watermelons should be firm and evenly coloured and feel heavy. Tap them with your knuckles; they should not sound hollow. The side where the melon has rested should be yellowish, not white or green. Watermelons are usually sold cut into wedges. Do not buy those with faded flesh, or with white seeds; these are unripe. Whole and cut watermelons can be wrapped in clear film and kept in the fridge for at least a week.

Preparing and Serving

Watermelons are generally cut into wedges and eaten on their own as a thirst-quencher. Cubes or balls make an attractive addition to fruit salads and melon medleys, and they can be made into sorbets (add plenty of lemon for flavour). In some African countries, unripe watermelons are prepared like marrows as a vegetable dish. The rind can be pickled, and is sometimes candied. The seeds can be toasted and eaten when crunchy but discard the outer shell.

Left: Tiger watermelons are – as the name suggests – striped.

GRAPES

These best known of all vine fruits grow in pendulous bunches on a stalk. The skins can be green, pale yellow, purple, bluish or red; green grapes are known as "white" and purple as "black". Some grapes have a bloom; others have almost waxy skins. Inside, the pulp is translucent and usually contains a few pips, although there are several varieties of seedless grapes.

Some varieties are grown as dessert or table grapes, others are cultivated exclusively for wine-making. Some varieties are also grown for drying into raisins, currants and sultanas. Generally speaking, table grapes are not used for wine-making and vice versa, but there are one or two dual-purpose varieties.

Right: Alphonse Lavalle grapes are firm and crisp to eat.

History

Grapes are among the oldest cultivated fruits and were known to man long before Noah planted his vineyard on Mount Ararat. Wild grapes were already established in the Caucasus in the Stone Age, and it was not long before man discovered

Left: Red and white grape juice is refreshing to drink on its own, or topped up with fizzy mineral water.

how to ferment them into wine. It is certain that the Ancient Egyptians made wine, although they used it for temple rituals rather than social drinking. The Ancient Greeks and Romans, however, were enthusiastic consumers of wine and grapes, and planted a huge number of vineyards. They also learnt the technique of drying the fruit.

It was the Gauls who first put wine into wooden casks and later medieval monks became very expert wine-makers. They also pressed grapes into *verjus,* a sour liquid resembling vinegar. In nineteenth-century England, the Victorians were hugely enthusiastic about grapes and cultivated magnificent specimens in hothouses. At the same time, in France, a *uvarium* or grape spa offered medicinal and slimming cures consisting entirely of grapes.

Varieties

A wide variety of table grapes is available, both seedless and seeded,

the finest by far being **Muscat.** Seedless grapes contain less tannin than the seeded fruit and are easier to eat. The main varieties are listed below.

WHITE GRAPES

Italia The nearest inexpensive alternative to Muscat grapes, Italia are very large, roundish, seeded fruit with greenish-yellow skins and a luscious musky flavour.
Perlette Small, seedless, thin-skinned grapes with a rather tart flavour.
Sultana These small, elongated grapes with thin, greenish-gold, bloomy skins and sweet, juicy pulp grow in compact conical bunches. The varieties Perlette and Thompson are both hybrids of Sultana.
Thompson Seedless Medium-size elongated fruit with thin, bloomy skins and very sweet, juicy pulp.

BLACK GRAPES

Alphonse Lavalle These large, round, seeded grapes grow in a compact bunch. They have thick, purplish-black skin, with firm, crisp pulp.
Cardinal Large oval fruit with reddish-purple skin and firm, fleshy pulp, which can sometimes lack flavour. They grow in large, unevenly shaped bunches.
Flame Seedless A smallish grape with thin, wine-red skin and very sweet, juicy pulp. These are mostly grown in Chile.
Napoleon The thick, dark purple skin on these large grapes has a heavy white bloom. The flesh is particularly sweet, although not very juicy.

MUSCAT GRAPES

Without doubt, these are the king of grapes, with a wonderful perfumed flavour, almost like nectar. The very best are hothouse-grown and are displayed in shops cocooned in padded paper to preserve their beautiful bloom. All Muscats are large; the white varieties are pale green or golden, while black Muscats can be either red or black. The best Muscat grape of all is the white **Chasselas,** whose skin turns almost bronze when ripe.

Muscat grapes are used for making sweet Muscat dessert wines, which encapsulate the honeyed flavour of the grapes.

Nutrition

Grapes are highly nutritious, containing natural sugars, potassium, iron and dietary fibre. They provide about 80 kilocalories per 100g/3¾oz.

Buying and Storing

Now that grapes are available all year round, many are sold underripe. The best way to judge a bunch of grapes is to taste a stray fruit; there is nearly always one that has fallen off the bunch. A perfect bunch of grapes should be of equal size and shape, with the bloom still on. White grapes should have a golden or amber tinge; avoid any

Right: Black Muscat grapes can either be black (as here) or red.

Below: Wonderfully perfumed, white Muscat are the king of grapes.

Left: Italia grapes, which can be green (as here) or black, have a luscious musky flavour and are the nearest inexpensive alternative to Muscat grapes.

Peeling and de-seeding grapes

1 Put the grapes in a heatproof bowl and pour over enough boiling water to cover. Leave for about 20 seconds.

2 Drain off the hot water, rinse the grapes in cold water, then peel off the skins with your fingers.

3 Cut each grape in half and pick out the pips with the tip of a sharp knife.

Right: Grown mostly in Chile, rich-coloured Flame seedless grapes are sweet and juicy, with thin easy-to-eat skins.

Above: Immensely popular, Thompson seedless grapes are very sweet, with thin bloomy skins.

that are uniformly vivid green. Black varieties should not be tinged with green. It is easier to spot overripe grapes, as they will fall off the bunch and often show traces of browning or mould. Do not buy wrinkled grapes, or bunches with tiny specimens attached; these will be very sour.

Store grapes in a bowl in a cool, dry place; they will keep for at least a week. To store them for longer, place in a

sealed polythene bag and keep in the salad drawer of the fridge for up to two weeks. Remove the grapes from the fridge and keep at room temperature for at least an hour before serving so that the flavour can develop fully.

Grape juice Naturally sweet, clear red and white grape juice, from crushed grapes, is delicious served chilled on its own or topped up with sparkling mineral water.

Grapeseed oil Grape pips are pressed into a very pale oil with a delicate, almost neutral flavour. This healthy oil is extremely rich in polyunsaturated fats. It can be used for cooking, but is best used in its natural state, in salad dressings, for example. It is the perfect oil to choose for making mayonnaise as it has such a mild flavour, and it never separates.

Above: Large, golden muscatel raisins from Muscat grapes are often dried and sold on their stems.

DRIED GRAPES

The best of these are sun-dried, without undergoing any chemical processes. Dried grapes – raisins, currants and sultanas – sometimes contain bits of stalk and the occasional pip, so pick them over carefully before using.

Artificially dried grapes are usually cleaner, but may need to be plumped up in boiling water for a few seconds before being added to cake mixtures.

Raisins The best raisins are made from Muscat grapes and they come from California and Spain. These large, deep amber fruit are tender and sweet and can be eaten on their own, with cheese and nuts, or used in rice and couscous dishes. Smaller, black raisins are used for making cakes and puddings, muesli and mincemeat. All raisins benefit from being plumped up in brandy before using.

Currants These small dried fruits are made from Turkish and Greek seedless black grapes.

Sultanas These small golden dried fruit are made from seedless white grapes. They are deliciously moist, with a tender texture and delicate flavour.

Serving and Cooking

Grapes are best eaten on their own as a snack or dessert, or at the end of a meal with cheese or nuts. To make an unusual sandwich, try Brie with halved grapes. They make a good addition to fruit salad and some savoury salads, combined with crunchy vegetables and walnuts. White and black grapes make attractive garnishes, particularly in small clusters frosted with egg white and sugar. They can be used to make jams and jellies; a few small grapes look beautiful suspended in a clear jelly.

Their slight acidity makes grapes a good foil for rich meats like foie gras and calves' liver. They can also be used to stuff quail, chicken or guinea fowl, or to make a sauce for poultry or ham. A classic French dish is

sole Véronique, rolled fillets of sole poached in white wine and garnished with white grapes. It is best to peel and de-seed grapes before cooking and to poach them lightly in wine or syrup so that they keep their shape. For savoury dishes, they can be sautéed in butter.

> ### Caramelizing grapes
> **1** Combine 200g/7oz/scant 1 cup granulated sugar and 60ml/4 tbsp water in a small heavy-based saucepan. Stir over a low heat until the sugar has dissolved. Bring to the boil, add 5ml/1 tsp lemon juice and boil until the syrup turns a deep golden brown.
> **2** Carefully add 15ml/1 tbsp hot water (protecting your hand with an oven glove as the mixture will "spit") and shake the pan to mix. Spear a pair of grapes on a fork by the stem and dip them into the caramel to coat. Slide the caramelized grapes off the fork and leave on an oiled baking sheet for about 10 minutes until the caramel cools and hardens.

Above: Clockwise from top left, sultanas, currants and raisins.

FIGS

These oval or pear-shaped fruits are among the most luscious of all and can be eaten fresh or dried. They are not juicy in the conventional sense, nor do they have a particularly strong flavour, but they are succulent and sweet, conjuring up images of sun-filled Mediterranean gardens.

Figs come in three main varieties – white, black and red – and range in colour from palest green to dark gold, burnished brown or deep purple. The entire fig is edible (although some people prefer to peel them), from the soft thin skin to the sweet succulent red or purplish flesh and the myriad tiny seeds. Skin colour makes little difference to the taste of a fig. Their high natural sugar content makes them the sweetest of all fruits. The flavour varies, depending on where they were grown and how ripe they are when consumed.

History

Figs were said to grow in the Garden of Eden and their leaves, it is alleged, were used to cover the nakedness of Adam and Eve. Over the centuries, prudes have delighted in defacing works of art depicting naked bodies with carefully placed fig leaves.

Below: Although green in colour, these figs are classified as white.

Figs most probably originated in Asia Minor and were one of the first fruits to be cultivated. They were certainly known to the Ancient Egyptians at the time of the Pharaohs and were brought to the Mediterranean long before the arrival of the Ancient Greeks and Romans, rapidly becoming an important part of the Mediterranean diet. The world's oldest known living fig tree is said to be growing in a Sicilian garden.

Figs are now widely cultivated and exported from France, Greece, Turkey and Brazil.

Above: Turkish purple figs

Varieties

You will seldom find figs in shops or markets labelled according to their variety; instead they are classified by colour – white, black and red. In reality, they come in a wide range of colours. In Italy, you are most likely to find the green **Kadota,** while in France you may come across **Buissone, Barbillone** and **Dauphine Violette.** Imported figs from Turkey are generally purple with deep red flesh.

Nutrition

Figs consist of 83 per cent sugars. They are a good source of calcium and are high in fibre, and contain vitamins A, B and C. They are well known for their laxative and digestive

properties. A single fig provides approximately 30 kilocalories.

Buying and Storing

Ripe figs are very delicate and do not travel well, so it is often difficult to find imported fruit at a perfect stage of maturity. Look for unblemished fruit that is soft and yielding when gently squeezed but still holds its shape. Figs should have a faint, delicate aroma; if they smell sour, they are overripe and will taste sour too. If you are buying figs in their country of origin, you may find some with split skins. Provided you are going to eat them immediately, this does not matter. Be careful not to squash the figs on the way home, or you will end up with a squishy mess.

Ripe figs should ideally be eaten on the day they are bought, but can be stored in the salad drawer of the fridge for up to three days. Remove them well before serving, as chilling spoils the delicate flavour. Underripe fruit can be kept at room temperature for a day or two until the skin softens, but they will never develop the wonderful flavour of figs that have ripened naturally on the tree in the sun.

Right: Dried figs are sometimes sold strung together in a ring.

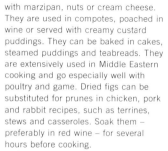

DRIED FIGS

Dried figs are made from very ripe autumn fruits, usually golden Smyrna figs or deep purple Mission figs from Turkey. They are spread out on hurdles to dry in the sun and must be turned several times before they are dried completely. This process flattens the figs into the familiar cushion shape. Dried figs contain large amounts of sugar and are highly nutritious. The best have a soft texture and are sold loosely packed so that they remain plump. Less high quality figs are commonly sold in blocks or strung together like a necklace. Store them in a cool and dry place. Eat dried figs as they are, or stuff them

with marzipan, nuts or cream cheese. They are used in compotes, poached in wine or served with creamy custard puddings. They can be baked in cakes, steamed puddings and teabreads. They are extensively used in Middle Eastern cooking and go especially well with poultry and game. Dried figs can be substituted for prunes in chicken, pork and rabbit recipes, such as terrines, stews and casseroles. Soak them – preferably in red wine – for several hours before cooking.

Dried figs are also used to make syrup of figs, the intensely sweet laxative traditionally loathed by most children. They can also be combined with juniper berries to make a drink called *figuette*.

CANNED OR BOTTLED FIGS

These are usually green Kadota figs preserved in heavy syrup. Canned or bottled figs are very sweet and are best served in a fruit compote. A dollop of whipped cream or Greek yogurt will temper the sweetness.

Preparing and Cooking

The best way to enjoy a fig is to pick a perfectly sun-ripened fruit straight off the tree. Wash it briefly and pat it dry very gently. Serve it whole. Always serve figs at room temperature, never chilled. They look particularly attractive on a bed of fig leaves, especially if each fruit is slit into four and opened out to resemble a flower. The centres can be

Left: Dried figs – the best, soft-textured fruits are sold loosely packed.

*Above: Dried figs
– dusted with
cornflour to
keep the
fruits
separate.*

or ice cream. They also go well with
savoury dishes like duck and lamb. To
poach figs, put them in a saucepan and
cover with syrup, red or white wine or
port. Add your chosen flavourings –
honey, cinnamon, vanilla and lemon are
all suitable. Bring to the boil, lower the
heat, cover and simmer gently for about
15 minutes, until the figs are tender.
Using a slotted spoon, transfer the figs
to a serving dish, then boil the poaching
liquid until it is thick and syrupy before
pouring it over the fruit.

To cook figs in butter, cut them in
half vertically, then arrange them cut-
side up in a heatproof dish. Put a knob
of butter on each fig half. Sprinkle with
port or Marsala and a good pinch of
cinnamon or nutmeg, and grill until
lightly browned. Serve with meat or
poultry, or brush with honey before
grilling and serve as a dessert.

To caramelize figs, dip the fruit in
water, then roll in caster or vanilla sugar
until completely coated. Place in a
shallow baking dish and bake in a
preheated oven at 220°C/425°F/Gas 7
for about 15 minutes, or until the sugar
has caramelized. Leave to cool, then
chill before serving.

stuffed, if you like. Cream cheese mixed
with honey and chopped nuts, fresh
raspberries or raspberry mousse
make delicious fillings.

Fresh figs are usually eaten raw
as a dessert fruit, or as an
hors d'oeuvre with Parma
ham or salami. They have
an affinity with nuts such
as walnuts, pistachios
and almonds and make
an excellent addition to a
cheese platter along with
grapes and nuts.

They can be stuffed with
sweet or savoury fillings like
cream or blue cheese, celery
and walnuts or marzipan, and
are especially delicious filled
with mascarpone and berries.
Figs can also be successfully
cooked in compotes, preserves
and jams. For desserts,
they can be
poached in wine,
honey or syrup,
they can also be
caramelized or
made into tarts

*Above: Almost too sweet
on their own, green
bottled figs are best
served with cream or
natural yogurt.*

Making fig flowers

Cut each fig downwards into
quarters, starting from the stalk
end and leaving the quarters
attached at the base. Gently pull
the sections apart to open them
out like the petals of a flower.
Serve the figs plain or pile in your
chosen creamy filling.

RHUBARB

Strictly speaking, rhubarb is not a fruit, but a vegetable; it is the fleshy stalk of the rhubarb plant, a relative of sorrel and dock. The stems are succulent, but too sour to eat raw, and the leaves contain oxalic acid, which makes them highly poisonous. The normal growing season is late spring to late summer, but early forced rhubarb, grown under ceramic pots, is available throughout the spring months. Maincrop rhubarb stalks vary from green to purplish-pink; the forced variety has spindly, tender bright pink or red stems, crowned with yellow leaves, and tastes much nicer.

History

Rhubarb originated in northern Asia and Siberia. It has been cultivated for centuries, but was originally used as a medicinal and ornamental plant. It was not until the eighteenth century that British gardeners began to grow rhubarb for cooking.

Preparing rhubarb

1 Using a large knife, cut off and discard the leaves and the root end of the stalk. Peel off any stringy fibres with a swivel-blade vegetable peeler.

2 Cut the rhubarb into pieces.

Nutrition

Rhubarb is one of the lowest calorie foods, providing only 7 kilocalories per 100g/3¾oz. It contains significant amounts of calcium, potassium and thiamine (vitamin B1) and has natural laxative properties.

Buying and Storing

Choose crisp, firm stalks that look bright and release sap when you snap them. Rhubarb can be stored for a few days in the bottom of the fridge, but wilts quite quickly. It freezes well: cut the stalks into short lengths, blanch briefly in boiling water, refresh in iced water and freeze in polythene bags.

Preparing and Cooking

All rhubarb needs to be sweetened when it is cooked, usually with sugar. This can be added at the outset, or when it has been cooked until tender. Use a stainless steel pan and only a spoonful or two of water. Poach gently until the fruit is tender. Rhubarb makes a wonderful pie or tart filling, and a delicious crumble, especially when mixed with banana.

Puréed rhubarb can be made into ice cream, sorbets, mousses and fools. Citrus fruits and spices, particularly ginger, vanilla and cinnamon, complement the flavour of rhubarb. Rhubarb can be combined with any of these to make excellent jams and chutneys. Because it is a vegetable, rhubarb goes well with savoury dishes like scrambled eggs, but you will still need to add sugar. It adds piquancy to rich casseroles, particularly pork, lamb and duck. Its sharp acidity makes it a good substitute for sorrel in sauces, especially to serve with oily fish, such as mackerel.

Above: Early forced rhubarb, grown under covered pots, is pink and tender.

Below: Tougher, maincrop rhubarb is grown in the open.

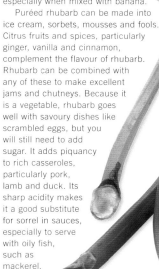

MELON, GRAPE, FIG AND RHUBARB RECIPES

Whether alone or with other fruits, melons, rhubarb, figs and grapes make wonderful desserts, pies, cakes and preserves. Don't miss Red Grape and Cheese Tartlets, One-crust Rhubarb Pie or Greek Yogurt and Fig Cake.

MELON TRIO WITH GINGER BISCUITS

THE EYE-CATCHING COLOURS OF THESE THREE DIFFERENT MELONS REALLY MAKE THIS DESSERT, WHILE THE CRISP BISCUITS PROVIDE A PERFECT CONTRAST IN TEXTURE.

SERVES FOUR

INGREDIENTS
¼ watermelon
½ honeydew melon
½ charentais melon
60ml/4 tbsp stem ginger syrup
For the biscuits
    25g/1oz/2 tbsp unsalted butter
    25g/1oz/2 tbsp caster sugar
    5ml/1 tsp clear honey
    25g/1oz/¼ cup plain flour
    25g/1oz/¼ cup luxury glacé
      mixed fruit, finely chopped
    1 piece of stem ginger in syrup,
      drained and finely chopped
    30ml/2 tbsp flaked almonds

1 Remove the seeds from the melons, cut them into wedges, then slice off the rind. Cut all the flesh into chunks and mix in a bowl. Stir in the ginger syrup, cover and chill until ready to serve.

2 Meanwhile, make the biscuits. Preheat the oven to 180°C/350°F/ Gas 4. Melt the butter, sugar and honey in a saucepan. Remove from the heat and stir in the remaining ingredients.

3 Line a baking sheet with non-stick baking paper. Space four spoonfuls of the mixture on the paper using half the mixture, leaving room for spreading. Flatten the mixture slightly into rounds and bake for 15 minutes or until the tops are golden.

4 Let the biscuits cool on the baking sheet for 1 minute, then lift each one in turn, using a fish slice, and drape over a rolling pin to cool and harden. Repeat with the remaining ginger mixture to make eight biscuits in all.

5 Serve the melon chunks with some of the syrup and the ginger biscuits.

COOK'S TIP
For an even prettier effect, scoop the melon flesh into balls with the large end of a melon baller.

PORT-STEWED RHUBARB WITH VANILLA DESSERTS

RHUBARB IS ONE OF THOSE FRUITS THAT SELDOM REALIZES ITS FULL POTENTIAL. IT HAS QUITE A SHORT SEASON, SO IT IS WORTH FREEZING SOME FOR USE LATER IN THE YEAR.

2 Meanwhile, pour the water into a ramekin and sprinkle the gelatine over the surface. Set aside to sponge for 5 minutes. Place the ramekin in a pan of hot water and leave until the gelatine is dissolved, stirring occasionally.

3 Add the gelatine mixture to the hot milk mixture and stir until dissolved. Remove the vanilla pod and pour the mixture into the moulds or tins. Cool, then chill overnight or until set.

4 Put the sugar into a pan and add the water, orange rind and juice, and the cinnamon stick. Bring to the boil over a low heat, stirring occasionally until the sugar has dissolved. Increase the heat and boil for 1 minute.

5 Add the port, let the syrup return to the boil, then lower the heat and simmer for 15 minutes or until it has reduced and thickened. Remove the orange rind and cinnamon stick, add the rhubarb, cover and simmer gently for 2–3 minutes without stirring. Cool.

6 To serve, run a knife around the edge of each vanilla dessert to loosen it, then unmould on to a dessert plate. Serve each dessert with a spoonful or two of the rhubarb with its syrup.

COOK'S TIP

Rhubarb yields a lot of juice when cooked, so make sure the syrup has reduced well before adding the fruit.

SERVES FOUR

INGREDIENTS

  115g/4oz/½ cup granulated sugar
  150ml/¼ pint/⅔ cup water
  pared rind and juice of 1 orange
  1 cinnamon stick
  300ml/½ pint/1¼ cups ruby port
  275g/10oz/2 cups rhubarb, cut into
    2.5cm/1in pieces
For the vanilla desserts
  ¾ vanilla pod
  175ml/6 fl oz/¾ cup double cream
  175ml/6fl oz/¾ cup creamy milk
  45ml/3 tbsp caster sugar
  30ml/2 tbsp water
  7.5ml/1½ tsp powdered gelatine

1 Start by making the vanilla desserts. Grease four individual pudding moulds or tins. Split the vanilla pod and scrape the seeds into a small saucepan. Add the pod, cream, milk and caster sugar. Simmer gently for 5 minutes, stirring.

FIG AND WALNUT TORTE

THIS RECIPE IS BASED ON THE TRADITIONAL MIDDLE EASTERN SPECIALITY, BAKLAVA. IT IS SWEET, STICKY AND DELICIOUS, AND THE FIGS ADD A REFRESHING TOUCH. SINCE IT IS QUITE RICH, PLAN ON CUTTING THE TORTE INTO FAIRLY SMALL DIAMONDS — LOVELY WITH A CUP OF STRONG BLACK COFFEE.

MAKES 20–25 PIECES

INGREDIENTS

75g/3oz/⅓ cup butter, melted, plus
extra for greasing
175g/6oz/1½ cups walnuts,
finely chopped
115g/4oz/1 cup ground almonds
75g/3oz/⅓ cup caster sugar
10ml/2 tsp ground cinnamon
9 large sheets of filo pastry, thawed
if frozen, each cut into two
30 × 20cm/12 × 8in rectangles
4 fresh figs, sliced
Greek yogurt, to serve
For the syrup
350g/12oz/1½ cups caster sugar
4 whole cloves
1 cinnamon stick
2 strips of lemon rind

1 Preheat the oven to 160°C/325°F/
Gas 3. Generously grease a 30 × 20cm/
12 × 8in shallow baking tin with melted
butter. Mix together the walnuts, ground
almonds, sugar and cinnamon in a bowl
and set aside.

2 Fit a sheet of filo pastry in the base
of the baking tin. Brush with some of
the melted butter and place another
sheet of filo on top. Repeat this until
you have layered up eight sheets.

COOK'S TIP
Paper-thin filo pastry is delicate and
dries out quickly. Work with one sheet
at a time, and keep the other sheets
covered or they will dry out.

3 Spoon half the nut mixture evenly
over the filo pastry, right to the edges,
and top with the fig slices.

4 Place two filo sheets on top of the
figs, brushing each with more melted
butter as before, then evenly spoon
over the remaining nut mixture.

5 Layer the remaining filo sheets on
top, buttering each one. Brush any
remaining melted butter over the top of
the torte, then score the surface with a
sharp knife to give a diamond pattern.
Bake for 1 hour until golden.

6 Meanwhile, make the syrup. Place all
the ingredients in a saucepan and mix
well. Heat, stirring, until the sugar has
dissolved. Bring to the boil, lower the
heat and simmer for 10 minutes until
syrupy, stirring occasionally.

7 Allow the syrup to cool for about
15 minutes, then strain it evenly over
the hot torte.

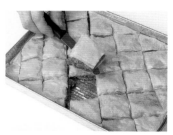

8 Allow to cool and soak for 2–3 hours,
then cut the torte into diamonds or
squares and serve with Greek yogurt.
Store the torte in an airtight tin for up to
three days.

VARIATION
If you like, replace the chopped walnuts
with coarsely chopped pistachio nuts, or
use finely chopped cashew nuts for an
ultra-rich flavour.

RED GRAPE AND CHEESE TARTLETS

FRUIT AND CHEESE IS A NATURAL COMBINATION IN THIS SIMPLE RECIPE. LOOK OUT FOR THE PALE, MAUVE-COLOURED OR RED GRAPES THAT TEND TO BE SLIGHTLY SMALLER THAN BLACK GRAPES. THESE ARE OFTEN SEEDLESS AND HAVE THE ADDED ADVANTAGE OF BEING SWEETER.

MAKES SIX

INGREDIENTS
 350g/12oz sweet shortcrust pastry,
  thawed if frozen
 225g/8oz/1 cup curd cheese
 150ml/¼ pint/⅔ cup double cream
 2.5ml/½ tsp pure vanilla essence
 30ml/2 tbsp icing sugar
 200g/7oz/2 cups red grapes, halved,
  seeded if necessary
 60ml/4 tbsp apricot conserve
 15ml/1 tbsp water

VARIATIONS
Use cranberry jelly or redcurrant jelly for the glaze. There will be no need to sieve either of these. Also vary the fruit topping, if you like. Try blackberries, blueberries, raspberries, sliced strawberries, kiwi fruit slices, banana slices or well-drained pineapple slices.

1 Preheat the oven to 200°C/400°F/ Gas 6. Roll out the pastry and line six deep 9cm/3½in fluted individual tartlet tins. Prick the bases and line with non-stick baking paper and baking beans. Bake for 10 minutes, remove the paper and beans, then return the cases to the oven for 5 minutes until golden and fully cooked. Remove the pastry cases from the tins and cool on a wire rack.

2 Meanwhile, beat the curd cheese, double cream, vanilla essence and icing sugar in a bowl. Divide the mixture among the pastry cases. Smooth the surface and arrange the halved grapes on top.

3 Sieve the apricot conserve into a pan. Add the water and heat, stirring, until smooth. Spoon over the grapes. Cool, then chill before serving.

ONE-CRUST RHUBARB PIE

THIS METHOD CAN BE USED FOR ALL SORTS OF FRUIT AND IS REALLY FOOLPROOF. IT DOESN'T MATTER HOW ROUGH THE PIE LOOKS WHEN IT GOES INTO THE OVEN; IT COMES OUT LOOKING FANTASTIC!

SERVES SIX

INGREDIENTS
  350g/12oz shortcrust pastry, thawed
    if frozen
  1 egg yolk, beaten
  25g/1oz/3 tbsp semolina
  25g/1oz/¼ cup hazelnuts,
    coarsely chopped
  30ml/2 tbsp golden granulated sugar
For the filling
  450g/1lb rhubarb, cut into
    2.5cm/1in pieces
  75g/3oz/⅓ cup caster sugar
  1–2 pieces stem ginger in syrup,
    drained and finely chopped

COOK'S TIP
Egg yolk glaze brushed on to pastry gives
it a nice golden sheen. However, be
careful not to drip the glaze on the
baking sheet, or it will burn and be
difficult to remove.

1 Preheat the oven to 200°C/400°F/
Gas 6. Roll out the pastry to a circle
35cm/14in across. Lay it over the rolling
pin and transfer it to a large baking
sheet. Brush a little egg yolk over the
pastry. Scatter the semolina over the
centre, leaving a wide rim all round.

2 Make the filling. Place the rhubarb
pieces, caster sugar and chopped
ginger in a large bowl and mix well.

3 Pile the rhubarb mixture into the
middle of the pastry. Fold the rim
roughly over the filling so that it almost
covers it. Some of the fruit will remain
visible in the centre.

4 Glaze the pastry rim with any
remaining egg yolk and scatter the
hazelnuts and golden sugar over. Bake
for 30–35 minutes or until the pastry is
golden brown. Serve warm.

FRESH FIG FILO TART

FIGS COOK WONDERFULLY WELL AND TASTE SUPERB IN THIS TART — THE RIPER THE FIGS, THE BETTER.

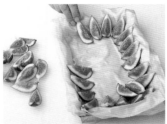

2 Using scissors, cut off any excess pastry, leaving a little overhanging the edge. Arrange the figs in the filo case.

3 Sift the flour into a bowl and stir in the caster sugar. Add the eggs and a little of the milk and whisk until smooth. Gradually whisk in the remaining milk and the almond essence. Pour the mixture over the figs; bake for 1 hour or until the batter has set and is golden.

SERVES SIX TO EIGHT

INGREDIENTS
  five 35 × 25cm/14 × 10in sheets filo
    pastry, thawed if frozen
  25g/1oz/2 tbsp butter, melted, plus
    extra for greasing
  6 fresh figs, cut into wedges
  75g/3oz/¾ cup plain flour
  75g/3oz/⅓ cup caster sugar
  4 eggs
  450ml/¾ pint/1¾ cups creamy milk
  2.5ml/½ tsp almond essence
  15ml/1 tbsp icing sugar, for dusting
  whipped cream or Greek yogurt,
    to serve

1 Preheat the oven to 190°C/375°F/ Gas 5. Grease a 25 × 16cm/10 × 6¼in baking tin with butter. Brush each filo sheet in turn with melted butter and use to line the prepared tin.

4 Remove the tart from the oven and allow it to cool in the tin on a wire rack for 10 minutes. Dust with the icing sugar and serve with whipped cream or Greek yogurt.

GREEK YOGURT <u>AND</u> FIG CAKE

BAKED FRESH FIGS, THICKLY SLICED, MAKE A DELECTABLE BASE FOR A FEATHERLIGHT SPONGE.
FIGS THAT ARE A BIT ON THE FIRM SIDE WORK BEST FOR THIS PARTICULAR RECIPE.

SERVES SIX TO EIGHT

INGREDIENTS
   6 firm fresh figs, thickly sliced
   45ml/3 tbsp clear honey, plus extra
     for glazing
   200g/7oz/scant 1 cup butter,
     softened
   175g/6oz/¾ cup caster sugar
   grated rind of 1 lemon
   grated rind of 1 orange
   4 eggs, separated
   225g/8oz/2 cups plain flour
   5ml/1 tsp baking powder
   5ml/1 tsp bicarbonate of soda
   250ml/8fl oz/1 cup Greek yogurt

1 Preheat the oven to 180°C/350°F/ Gas 4. Grease a 23cm/9in cake tin and line the base with non-stick baking paper. Arrange the figs over the base of the tin and drizzle over the honey.

2 In a large mixing bowl, cream the butter and caster sugar with the lemon and orange rinds until the mixture is pale and fluffy, then gradually beat in the egg yolks.

3 Sift the dry ingredients together. Add a little to the creamed mixture, beat well, then beat in a spoonful of Greek yogurt. Repeat this process until all the dry ingredients and Greek yogurt have been incorporated.

4 Whisk the egg whites in a grease-free bowl until they form stiff peaks. Stir half the whites into the cake mixture to slacken it slightly, then fold in the rest. Pour the mixture over the figs in the tin, then bake for 1¼ hours or until golden and a skewer inserted in the centre of the cake comes out clean.

5 Turn the cake out on to a wire rack, peel off the lining paper and cool. Drizzle extra honey over the figs to glaze before serving.

MELON AND STAR ANISE JAM

MELON AND GINGER ARE CLASSIC COMPANIONS. THE ADDITION OF STAR ANISE IMPARTS A WONDERFUL ORIENTAL FLAVOUR TO THE JAM. IT'S SPLENDID ON TOASTED FRUIT AND SPICE MUFFINS.

MAKES 450G/1LB

INGREDIENTS
2 charentais or cantaloupe melons,
   peeled and seeded
450g/1lb/2 cups granulated sugar
2 star anise
4 pieces stem ginger in syrup,
   drained and finely chopped
finely grated rind and juice of
   2 lemons

COOK'S TIPS
Use this jam in savoury dishes instead
of honey to add a spicy, non-cloying
sweetness. Jams require a large amount of
sugar for proper jelling – don't cut back.

1 Cut the melons into small cubes and
layer with the granulated sugar in a
large non-metallic bowl. Cover with
clear film and leave overnight so the
melons can release their juices.

2 Tip the melons and juice into a large
saucepan and add the star anise,
ginger, lemon rind and juice.

3 Bring to the boil, then lower the heat.
Simmer for 25 minutes or until the
melon has become transparent and the
setting point has been reached. Test for
this by spooning a small amount of the
juice on to a chilled plate. If it wrinkles
when you push a finger through the
cooled liquid, it is ready to be potted.

4 Spoon the jam into hot sterilized jars.
Seal, label and store in a cool, dry
place. Once a jar has been opened,
keep it in the fridge.

FIG AND DATE CHUTNEY

THIS RECIPE IS USUALLY MADE WITH DRIED FIGS AND DATES, BUT IT WORKS PERFECTLY WELL WITH
FRESH FRUIT AND HAS A SUPERB FLAVOUR. TRY IT WITH CREAM CHEESE ON BROWN BREAD.

MAKES 450G/1LB

INGREDIENTS

1 orange
5 large fresh figs, coarsely chopped
350g/12oz/2½ cups fresh dates,
  peeled, stoned and chopped
2 onions, chopped
5cm/2in piece of fresh root ginger,
  peeled and finely grated
5ml/1 tsp dried crushed chillies
300g/11oz/1½ cups golden
  granulated sugar
300ml/½ pint/1¼ cups spiced
  preserving vinegar
2.5ml/½ tsp salt

1 Finely grate the rind of the orange,
then cut off the remaining pith and
segment the orange.

2 Place the orange segments in a
large heavy-based saucepan with the
chopped figs and dates. Add the rind,
then stir in the onions, grated ginger,
dried chillies, golden granulated sugar,
spiced preserving vinegar and salt.
Bring to the boil, stirring gently until
all the sugar has dissolved.

3 Lower the heat and simmer gently
for 1 hour or until the mixture has
thickened and become pulpy, stirring
often to prevent the mixture from
sticking to the base of the pan.

4 Spoon the chutney into hot sterilized
jars. Seal while still hot and label once
the jars are cold. Store for 1 week
before using. Once a jar has been
opened, keep it in the fridge.

VARIATION
If you would rather use dried figs and
dates to make the chutney, you will
need to increase the amount of spiced
preserving vinegar by 150ml/¼ pint/
⅔ cup to 450ml/¾ pint/scant 2 cups.
Stone the dates and coarsely chop the
figs and dates.

VEGETABLES

DISCOVERING VEGETABLES

AS A CHILD, there were two basic types of vegetables for me: the ones my mother cooked and the ones given to us at school. My mother only ever bought fresh vegetables and she knew how to cook them, so they were simple but good. Vegetables at school were overcooked and invariably tasteless. Travel then broadened my outlook.

From my first teenage sojourns around Europe, I recall, even now, the vegetable stalls in a Barcelona market, piled high with tomatoes, peppers and aubergines. The exotic-looking produce of the Orient, Asia and Caribbean countries cannot fail to spark off an inquisitive and creative enthusiasm in those who are unfamiliar with them and even basic ingredients – potatoes, onions and carrots – do not look like sorry, everyday necessities when they are displayed with pride.

History

Vegetables, whether the root, stems, seeds or fruit, have been an essential part of our diet since the early existence of mankind, and many of our familiar vegetables were cultivated in prehistoric times. The Egyptians grew onions, garlic, radishes, lettuce and broad beans; and later the Greeks and Romans grew artichokes and fennel. By the Middle Ages a wealth of vegetables was available, with recipes for them recorded in the first cookery books.

Early explorers returned with exotic ingredients, the spoils of their travels, to their native countries and created a huge appetite for new tastes among the wealthy classes of Europe. Marco Polo travelled to China and carried aromatic spices on his return to Europe. Christopher Columbus and subsequent explorers found potatoes, tomatoes, peppers, squashes and maize. Today we have the option of buying exactly what we want, when we want it. It's a luxury we pay for but one that means you are never stuck for an ingredient whatever the time of year. On the other hand there's much to be said for enjoying vegetables in their season. Vegetables from local growers will be the freshest you can buy and gardeners love the way their produce

Above: Roast Asparagus Crêpes with a cheese sauce

Right: Rocket

traces the seasons, never minding that it means gluts at some times of the year and only cabbages and roots at other times.

Nutrition

Vegetables are really good for you – all nutritionists agree. Vegetables protect against disease, they are an important source of many vitamins and minerals, and we should eat more. The nutritional value of vegetables varies according to type, freshness, preparation and cooking method. In general it can be said that along with fruit they are the main source of vitamin C. Some of the B-group vitamins are also found in

Right: Green, red, orange and yellow peppers

vegetables, particularly in green vegetables and pulses. Carrots and the dark green vegetables also include carotene which is used by the body to manufacture vitamin A. Vegetable oils are a useful source of vitamin E.

Vegetables can also contain calcium, iron, potassium and magnesium, as well as some trace elements which are also required in small quantities.

Starchy vegetables are an important

Above: Cherry tomatoes

Below: Tomato and Basil Tart

source of energy-giving carbohydrate and they may include useful quantities of fibre.

Freshly picked vegetables have the highest nutritional content, but this diminishes with staleness and exposure to sunlight. Use fresh vegetables as soon as possible after purchase and always avoid stale limp specimens. The peel and the layer directly beneath it contain the highest concentration of nutrients, so it is best to avoid

Right: Swiss chard is striking to look at as well as being delicious to eat.

peeling your vegetables or to remove the thinnest layer for maximum nutrient retention. Minerals and vitamins C and B are water soluble and they are lost by seepage into cooking water or the liquid over which vegetables are steamed. To minimize loss of nutrients, do not cut up vegetables finely as this creates a greater surface area for seepage. Vitamin C is also destroyed by long cooking and by exposure to alkalines. Raw and lightly cooked vegetables provide the best nutritional value and source of fibre. Any cooking liquid should, whenever possible, be used in stocks, gravies or sauces.

Vegetables can play a starring role in a recipe or they may be combined with other ingredients in a harmony of flavours. Over the following pages you will find an eclectic mix of classic dishes from around the world, some family favourites that have stood the test of time and others that I have devised over years of cooking. All the recipes make the most of each vegetable, so that their particular virtues can be appreciated to the full. The recipes are not designed for vegetarians although there are plenty of recipes which are vegetarian. In many instances, simply substituting vegetable stock for chicken stock will ensure that the recipe is acceptable.The great thing about cooking with vegetables is, however, that once you have got the hang of using them, a recipe really becomes unnecessary. You will discover how you most enjoy carrots, asparagus or less-common vegetables and this in turn will inspire you to experiment with vegetables you have not used before.

EQUIPMENT

There is almost no limit to the amount of equipment you could purchase for preparing and cooking vegetables – the only limit will be the depth of your pocket and the size of your kitchen. The most important tool, inevitably, is a good kitchen knife, and for cooking you'll need two or three different sized saucepans and a good sieve. Good equipment not only makes the cook's job easier, but also more of a pleasure, so take stock of the tools you have at the moment and then gradually buy additional pieces. You don't need to buy everything immediately – it's always preferable to buy the more pricey but better made appliances, whether it's food processors, saucepans, knives or a potato peeler.

Peeling and Slicing

Knives

There are dozens of different knives, designed for a variety of tasks. For preparing and chopping vegetables, you ideally should have two types of knife, a general-purpose knife for cutting or chopping hard vegetables, such as potatoes and cabbage, and a smaller paring knife for peeling vegetables and slicing or chopping smaller ones like courgettes and onions. A serrated knife is useful for tomatoes, cucumbers and peppers with tough or slippery skins.

Potato Peeler

Peeling potatoes with a knife means that much of the goodness from the potato, contained just under the skin, is lost along with the peel, and a good potato peeler not only makes the job easier, but means you don't waste this valuable part of the potato.

Swivel-bladed peelers are probably the most effective peelers and, once you have the hang of them, are also very quick and efficient. Make sure to buy one that feels comfortable to hold, or buy a fixed-blade peeler. Left-handed people will need to buy the left-handed version.

Slicing and Grating

Grater

if you don't own a food processor, you'll need a good quality grater for grating carrots, celeriac, onions and other hard vegetables. Although most vegetables are grated coarsely, choose a type, such as the box grater, that has a variety of grating surfaces so that it can be used for grating Parmesan or nutmeg, or for zesting lemons.

Mandoline

Professional cooks often prefer the mandoline for slicing firm foods like potatoes, celeriac and carrots, as the result is much finer. The best and most expensive are in stainless steel and have several blades for a

Left: A variety of kitchen knives

Left: Mandoline

variety of thicknesses and shapes. More commonly available though are the wooden ones, which generally have two adjustable blades.

Mashers

Potato masher

Essential for mashing potatoes and other root vegetables that can't be puréed any other way. Strong stainless-steel mashers are the most efficient, but if you use non-stick pans, buy a strong plastic masher instead or you will damage the pans.

Garlic Press

This is another simple but useful labour-saving device. Cheaper aluminium garlic presses are usually just as efficient as the more expensive varieties made of stainless steel with comfortable rubber handles. However, more expensive ones normally have self-cleaning devices, which saves you the bother of picking out bits of garlic.

Below: Stainless steel steamer

Right: Pans

Saucepans and Sieves

Your saucepans are the single most important items when it comes to vegetable cookery, and if you're starting from scratch, it is worth investing in good quality pans. Among the best are stainless-steel pans with strong insulated handles and a heavy base. A heavy base is essential, as it ensures the heat is properly distributed, and food doesn't scorch or cook unevenly. A set of three saucepans, with lids, will normally be sufficient for general cooking, but in addition a large pan with two handles can be tremendously useful for making soups and stocks.

Colanders and Sieves

A good quality colander or sieve is almost as essential as a good saucepan. A colander is probably best as it can stand alone and has two handles.

Frying pan

A cast-iron frying pan is probably the most versatile for vegetable recipes, as these are the traditional pans used for sautéing. Stainless-steel and non-stick pans, however, are both useful.

Cast-iron/flameproof casserole

These are tremendously useful for any recipe that needs sautéing on the hob before going into the oven. They are by definition extremely heavy, so make sure to buy only those with two handles.

Wok

Though not essential for stir-frying, woks are by far the best option for this type of cooking. Make sure you buy the appropriate wok for your cooker – round-bottomed for gas hobs and flat-bottomed for an electric hob.

Steamers

If you intend to steam your vegetables regularly, invest in a steamer set, which contains two or three compartments that stack on top of each other. Alternatively, Chinese bamboo steamers can be stacked over a medium-size saucepan.

Electrical Appliances

Food processor

The food processor has become an almost essential piece of kitchen equipment, and is hugely versatile. Ideally choose a heavy-duty model with a pulse button. Most now come complete with grating and slicing blades, but if not, make sure you purchase them as well; they take the effort out of some of the most laborious tasks in the kitchen.

Hand blender

Useful for making vegetable purées, sauces, vegetable pâtés and soups.

Right: Food processor

Blender/liquidizer

These are even better than food processors for making soups and purées. Choose a model where the blades are set as low as possible as these are useful for baby foods, and also for making mayonnaise where you start with just one or two egg yolks.

PURCHASING, PREPARING AND COOKING

BUYING VEGETABLES

The single golden rule for buying vegetables is "use your instinct". All vegetables should be firm and blemish free, without any soft spots or mould. Most vegetables are available all the year round, but even with modern air transport, the best vegetables are those that are recently picked which is why local seasonal vegetables are always going to have the finest flavour. This is especially true of tomatoes, beans, peas, sweetcorn and tomatoes. Farm shops, or better still, pick-your-own farms mean you can buy many seasonal vegetables in their prime. If this is not an option, large supermarkets with a fast turnover tend to sell better quality vegetables simply because they have daily deliveries and they also have a commercial interest in making sure that their produce is of top quality.

STORING VEGETABLES

This depends entirely on the particular vegetable and while onions and potatoes can be successfully stored for months, more tender vegetables, like mushrooms or tomatoes are best eaten as soon as possible. The following are a few basic rules and guidelines:

• If possible, buy vegetables as you need them. If buying for the week, plan your meals so that the more tender vegetables, like courgettes and peas are eaten sooner rather than later.
• Whenever storing vegetables, always remove them from any polythene bags or clear film.
• Unless stated otherwise, store vegetables in the salad drawer of the fridge and eat as soon as possible or within 2-3 days.
• Always store potatoes in a dark, cool and dry place. If potatoes are exposed to the light, they will develop green patches which can be poisonous.
• Don't store onions in the fridge as they will go soft: store in a cool, dry place, like a larder or outhouse.
• Keep garlic in a cool, dry place. If the temperature is too warm, the cloves will turn to a grey powder and if the air is damp, the garlic will sprout.

• If celery has become limp, revive it by wrapping in absorbent kitchen paper and standing in a jar of water.
• Ripen avocados at room temperature. If ripe already, keep in the fridge for up to 2 days.
• Dried beans should always be kept in labelled jars in a dry place. They will keep for about 12 months but after that tend to become tough, lose their flavour and take longer to cook, so throw away beans that are more than a year old.

PREPARING VEGETABLES

Preparation depends largely on the vegetable concerned, the type of recipe and your own preference. Potatoes for mashing, chipping, salads, sautéeing and roasting usually need peeling, but new potatoes or potatoes for baking need only be scrubbed. Similarly, many recipes call for fresh tomatoes that are peeled, cored and seeded, and yet for hors d'oeuvres, tomatoes need no preparation at all, save to be sliced – and cherry tomatoes don't even need that! Chillies are the only vegetable for which there is a preparation rule – always wear gloves or wash your hands thoroughly, as the capsaicin contained within them can irritate the skin, especially the eyes.

Washing Vegetables

Because the skin of many vegetables, is full of vitamins it is always preferable to wash your vegetables under cold running water, rather than peel them.

Young root vegetables

Rinse new potatoes, baby carrots or turnips under cold running water. Use a sponge or a scrubbing brush, to remove any stubborn areas of dirt.

Main crop potatoes

Older potatoes need more vigorous scrubbing in order to dislodge lumps of mud. Remove eyes and any blemishes with a knife or the tip of a potato peeler.

Mushrooms

Wipe mushrooms with a damp cloth, as washing makes them soggy.

Leeks

Leeks notoriously contain grit and earth between their layers, so need very careful rinsing.

1 Trim the roots and cut away the dark green leaves. Remove and discard the outer layer of leek and then cut a slit along its length.

2 Wash under running water, pulling the sections apart so that the water washes out all the earth.

Washing Salads

Almost all salad leaves that have not specifically been bought labelled as ready to eat, should be washed, since they may well harbour earth, grit or small insects. This is particularly the case with lettuce from the garden and to a lesser extent organic produce, where nature has been allowed to follow her natural course.

Preparing salad leaves

1 Remove any discoloured or damaged leaves, then separate the leaves.

2 Swirl the salad leaves gently in a bowl of cold water to make sure any earth or insects are dislodged. If the leaves are robust enough you could then use a salad spinner to dry them, otherwise pat them dry in a soft tea towel. Make sure that there is no moisture left on them before adding to the salad.

3 All salad leaves should be washed this way, but spinach can often be gritty and so needs particular attention, as does lollo rosso, and it is often recommended to rinse in several bowls of cold water to make sure any earth clinging to the leaves is removed. It is also wise to remove the centre stalk from the larger leaves.

Peeling Vegetables

Almost all root vegetables may need peeling at some time. Potatoes, carrots and turnips only need peeling if old, but sweet potatoes, yams and taros nearly always need to be peeled, either before or after cooking. Other vegetables, such as courgettes and cucumbers, can be peeled for effect, but marrows and other large squash will always require peeling.

A swivel-bladed or a fixed-blade peeler can be used for peeling potatoes, carrots, parsnips, turnips and other root vegetables.

As peeling only shaves away a thin layer of skin you keep most of the valuable nutrients that lie in or just below the skin. Vegetables such as celery and asparagus may need their tough, woody ends peeling.

Potatoes can be peeled after boiling. Once they are cool enough to handle, peel off the skin using a small knife.

Sweet potatoes, salsify and celeriac are among the vegetables that oxidize and turn brown if exposed to air. To prevent this from happening, place the peeled vegetables in a bowl of cold water to which 15ml/1 tbsp lemon juice has been added.

Cucumbers don't need to be peeled, but some producers use a wax coating to give a shine to the vegetable and if you haven't washed the cucumber you may wish to remove this by peeling. If you're handy with a potato peeler or canelle knife it's possible to remove thin strips of peel to give an attractive striped effect. The same technique can be used on courgettes and fruit.

Skinning Tomatoes and Peppers

It is worth the effort of skinning tomatoes for sauces and other cooked tomato dishes, where bits of tomato skin would spoil the effect. Cut a cross in the top of the tomato, and then plunge into boiling water. Leave for 30-60 seconds (it will depend on the ripeness of the fruit) and then remove and peel away the skin, using a knife. If using cold, in a salad or gazpacho, plunge into cold water, to prevent the tomato cooking any further.

Place the peppers under a hot grill until the skin blisters and blackens. You can cut them into quarters if necessary. Either wrap the pieces in clingfilm or put them into a plastic bag and tie the end. Leave for about 20 minutes or until the peppers are cool enough to handle. The skin should peel off easily and the seeds can be scraped out.

Chopping Vegetables

Most vegetables need to be chopped to various degrees of fineness before cooking and eating. Vegetables will taste the same however you chop them, but remember that although the smaller you chop your vegetables, the quicker they will cook, it will also be easier to overcook them!

Fine chopping

Finely chopping onion can be fiddly, but not if you follow this simple technique.

1 Peel the onion, leaving on the root end, and cut it in half, straight through the root. Place the onion flat down on a chopping board and make a series of horizontal cuts to the root, but not through it.

2 Make vertical lengthways cuts in the onion half, again not cutting to the root. Then cut across the onion to produce finely chopped pieces.

Carrot julienne

Cut a carrot lengthwise into 5cm/2in lengths and then cut each of the lengths into 5mm/¼in slices. Stack the slices and cut in matchsticks to form julienne.

Shredding vegetable leaves

Individual leaves of cabbage, lettuce and spinach can be cut into neat shreds with this method.

1 Stack the leaves, six to eight at a time, and then roll them up tightly parallel with the central rib.

2 With a sharp knife slice the leaves to make shreds of the required thickness.

COOKING VEGETABLES

Some vegetables can be cooked many different ways; others are less versatile, although no less delicious for that.

Boiling

Boiling is one of the most popular techniques for cooking vegetables. Take care not to overcook though, as then all the nutrients will be lost in the water.

Blanching and Refreshing

Vegetables are blanched either when they need further cooking, such as stir-frying, roasting, or reheating in butter, or if they are to be used in salad. After blanching, vegetables are 'refreshed' to stop them cooking any further.

1 Immerse the vegetables in a large pan of boiling water. Bring the water back to the boil for 1–2 minutes, then drain immediately.

2 Refresh the vegetables by quickly immersing them in iced water for a few seconds. Drain well.

Sweating

Sweating is a common preliminary step in vegetable cooking, particularly for onions and leeks. It is important to cook the vegetables extremely gently.

Steaming

Tender vegetables, like baby carrots, pumpkin and mangetouts are best cooked by the steaming method.

Set the vegetables in a steamer over a pan of rapidly simmering water. Cover, and cook until tender.

Shallow Frying and Sautéing

The oil and/or butter used in frying adds another dimension to the dish.

Add the sliced or chopped vegetables to the pan once the oil is hot or the butter has melted and stir regularly.

Stir-frying

Stir-frying is a quick and healthy method of cooking. Make sure that vegetables are cut to an appropriate size so that they cook evenly.

Deep-frying

Potatoes are among the favourite vegetables for deep-frying, but other vegetables can be deep-fried too. Try deep-frying thinly sliced spring greens to make Chinese style 'seaweed', or other root vegetables, such as yams and sweet potatoes.

Heat oil for deep-frying to 185°C/360°F or until a cube of bread sizzles when added to the pan. It is best to use an appropriate chip pan with wire basket so that the vegetables can be removed quickly and easily. Potato or sweet potato chips should be soaked in cold water and then drained and patted dry before adding to the pan. Fry until soft, drain for a few minutes and then plunge again into the hot oil until crisp and golden.

Fritters and Tempura

Batter, made from flour, eggs, milk, beer or water, often combined with breadcrumbs or another dry coating, helps protect more tender vegetables when deep-frying.

Cut the vegetables into even-sized shapes and coat with the batter then the breadcrumbs, if using. Lower gently into the pan. Cook in small batches, so that the fritters don't stick together.

ONIONS AND LEEKS

Where would we be without the onion family?
Whether it's the merest hint of chives in a dressing, leeks in a
sauce, garlic adding its unmistakable tang or full-bodied onion
soup, this is the vegetable family that gives so much flavour to
our savoury dishes.

ONIONS

There are bound to be vegetables you like better than others but a cook would be lost without onions. There are many classic recipes specifically for onion dishes so they can be appreciated in their own right. Onion tarts or French onion soup, for instance, have a sublime flavour and are widely enjoyed. But also, there is hardly a recipe where onions, or their cousins – garlic, leeks or shallots – are not used. Gently fried until soft, or fried more fiercely until golden brown, they contribute a unique and wonderful savoury flavour to dishes.

History

Onions, along with shallots, leeks, chives and garlic, belong to the *Allium* family which, including wild varieties, has some 325 members. All have the characteristic onion smell which is caused by volatile acids beneath the plants' skin.

Archaeological and historical records show that onions have been eaten for thousands of years. They are believed to have come originally from the Middle East and their easy cultivation suggests that their use spread quickly. There are references to the onion in the Bible and it was widely eaten in Egypt. There was, we are told, an inscription on the Great Pyramid stating that the slaves who built the tomb ate their way through 1,600 talents worth of onions, radishes and garlic – presumably a lot, given that the Great Pyramid was made using more than two million 2^1/$_2$-tonne blocks of stone.

By the Middle Ages, onions were a common vegetable throughout Europe and would have been used in soups, stews and sauces.

Varieties

As they keep well in a cool place, most people keep a handy stock of onions, usually a general-purpose type that can be sautéed or browned. However, onions come in a variety of different colours and strengths of flavour, and for certain recipes particular onions are needed.

Above right: Spanish onions
Opposite above: Yellow onions
Opposite below: Red onions

Spanish onions: Onions raised in warm areas are milder in taste than onions from cooler regions, and Spanish onions are among the mildest cultivated onions. They are a beautiful pale copper colour and are noticeably larger than yellow onions. They have a delicate and sweet flavour which makes them ideal for serving raw in salads, thinly sliced, while their size makes them suitable for stuffing and baking whole.

Yellow onions: These are the widely available onions you find everywhere and, though called yellow onions, their skins are more golden brown. They are the most pungent of all the onions and are a good, all-purpose variety. The smallest ones, referred to as baby, button or pickling onions, are excellent for pickling but can also be added whole to a casserole or sautéed in butter to make a delicious vegetable accompaniment.

Red onions: Sometimes called Italian onions, these mild onions have an attractive appearance and are now widely available from most good greengrocers and supermarkets. Beneath their ruby red skins the flesh is blushed with red. They are generally smaller than yellow onions, and have a mild, sweet flavour. They are excellent thinly sliced and used raw in salads and *antipasti* dishes.

White onions: These come in all sorts of interesting shapes and sizes – squat, round and oval, big and small. The very small white onions, with shimmery silver skins, are mild and best added whole to stews or served in a creamy sauce. Larger white onions can be mild or strong – there is no way of telling. Like yellow onions, white onions are extremely versatile whether used raw or cooked. The very small white onions, called Paris Silverskin, are the ones used for dry martinis and for commercial pickling.

Vidalia onions: These popular American onions are a speciality of and named after a town in Georgia, USA. They are a large, pale yellow onion and are both deliciously sweet and juicy. Used in salads, or roasted with meat or with other vegetables, they are superb.

Bermuda onions: These are similar in size to Spanish onions but are rather more squat. They have a mild flavour and are good thinly sliced, fried until golden and served with steaks or burgers.

often dry, discoloured or damaged. Unless slicing onions for stir-fries, for which it is   customary to slice the onion into wedges, always slice the onion through the rings, widthways. Make whole rings, or for half-rings, cut in half lengthways through the root before slicing (*see below*). For finely chopped onion, slice again lengthways.

Spring onions or scallions: These are also true onions but harvested very young while their shoots are still green and fresh. They have a mild, delicate taste and both the small white bulb and the green tops can be used in salads, omelettes and stir-fries, or indeed any dish which requires a mild onion flavour.

Nutrition

As well as tasting good, onions are good for you. They contain vitamins B and C together with calcium, potassium and iron. Like garlic, they also contain cycloallin, an anticoagulant which helps protect against heart disease.

Buying and Storing

It used to be a common sight to see an onion seller on a bicycle with many strings of onions hanging from every available support including his own neck. Nowadays strings of onions are hard to come by although, if you do find them in shops, they are a good way of buying and storing the vegetable.

Onions, more than almost any other vegetable, keep well provided they are stored in a cool, dry place, such as a larder or outhouse. Do not store them in the refrigerator as they will go soft, and never keep cut onions in the refrigerator – or anywhere else – unless you want onion-flavoured milk and an onion-scented home. Onions do not keep well once cut and it is worth buying onions in assorted sizes so that you do not end up having bits left over. Unused bits of onion can be added to stocks; otherwise throw them away.

Preparing

Onions contain a substance which is released when they are cut and causes the eyes to water, quite painfully sometimes. There are all sorts of ways which are supposed to prevent this, including cutting onions under running water, holding a piece of bread between your teeth or wearing goggles!

As well as the outer brown leaves, remove the next layer of onion, as it is

Cooking

The volatile acids in onions are driven off during cooking, which is why cooked onion is never as strong as raw onion. The method of cooking, even the way of frying an onion, affects its eventual taste. Boiled onion or chopped onion added neat to soups or casseroles has a stronger, more raw taste. Frying or sautéing briefly, or sweating (frying in a little fat with the lid on) until soft and translucent gives a mild flavour. When fried until golden brown, onions develop a distinct flavour, both sweet and savoury, that is superb in curries and with grilled meats and is essential for French onion soup.

Opposite above : Vidalia onions
Opposite below: White onions
Above left: Large and small spring onions

SHALLOTS

Shallots are not baby onions but a separate member of the onion family. They have a delicate flavour, less intense than most onions and they also dissolve easily into liquids, which is why they are favoured for sauces. Shallots grow in small, tight clusters so that when you break one open there may be two or three bunched together at the root.

Their size makes them convenient for any recipe where only a little onion is required. Use shallots when only a small amount of onion is needed or when only a fine onion flavour is required. Shallots are a pleasant, if perhaps extravagant, alternative to onions, but where recipes specify shallots (especially sauce recipes), they should be used if possible.

Although classic cookery frequently calls for particular ingredients, the art of improvisation should not be ignored. For instance, Coq au Vin is traditionally made with walnut-size white onions, but when substituted with shallots, the result is delightful.

History

Shallots are probably as ancient as onions. Roman commentators wrote eloquently about the excellence of shallots in sauces.

Varieties

Shallots are small slender onions with long necks and golden, copper-coloured skins. There are a number of varieties, although there is unlikely to be a choice in the supermarkets. In any case, differences are more in size and colour of skin than in flavour.

Buying and Storing

Shallots should be firm without any green shoots. They will keep well for several months in a cool dry place.

Preparing and Cooking

Skin shallots in the same way as onions, i.e. top and tail them and then peel off the outer skin. Pull apart the bulbs. Slice them carefully and thinly using a sharp knife – shallots are so small, it is easy to slip and cut yourself. When cooking them whole, fry over a very gentle heat without browning too much.

CHIVES

In culinary terms, chives are really classed as a herb, but as members of the onion family they are worth mentioning here. As anyone who has grown them knows, chives are tufts of aromatic grass with pretty pale lilac flowers, which are also edible.

Preparing and Serving

Chives are often snipped with scissors and added to egg dishes, or used as a garnish for salads and soups, adding a pleasant but faint onion flavour. Along with parsley, tarragon and chervil, they are an essential ingredient of *fines herbes*.

Chives are also a delicious addition to soft cheeses – far nicer than commercially bought cheeses, where the flavour of chives virtually disappears. Stir also into soft butter for an alternative to garlic butter. This can then be spread on to bread and baked like garlic bread.

If adding to cooked dishes, cook only very briefly, otherwise their flavour will be lost.

CHINESE CHIVES

Sometimes called garlic chives, these chives have a delicate garlic flavour, and if you see them for sale in a Chinese supermarket, they are worth buying as they add a delicate onion flavour to stir-fries and other oriental dishes.

Preparing and Serving

Use them as you would chives – both the green and white parts are edible. They are also delicious served on their own as a vegetable accompaniment.

Buying and Storing

For both types of chives, look for plump, uniformly green specimens with no brown spots or signs of wilting. They can be stored for up to a week in the fridge. Unopened flowers on Chinese chives are an indication that the plant is young and therefore more tender than one with fully opened flowers.

Opposite: Shallots
Above left: Chives
Above right: Chinese chives

GARLIC

Garlic is an ingredient that almost anyone who does any cooking at all, and absolutely everyone who enjoys cooking, would not be without.

History

Garlic is known to have been first grown in around 3200 BC. Inscriptions and models of garlic found in the pyramids of Ancient Egypt show that garlic was not only an important foodstuff but that it had ceremonial significance as well. The Greeks and Romans likewise believed garlic to have magical qualities. Warriors would eat it for strength before going into battle, gods were appeased with gifts of garlic, and cloves of garlic were fastened round the necks of babies to ward off evil. So, vampire mythology has ancient precedents.

The Greeks and Romans also used garlic for its therapeutic qualities. Not only was it thought to be an aphrodisiac but also it was believed to be good for eczema, toothache and snake bites.

Although garlic found its way all over Europe – vats of butter, very strongly flavoured with garlic, have been found by archaeologists working in Ireland which date back 200-300 years – basically, its popularity today derives from our liking for Mediterranean, Indian and Asian food, where garlic plays a very important part in many dishes.

Nutrition

As is often the case, what was once dismissed as an old wives' tale is, after thorough scientific inquiry, found to be true. Garlic is a case in point; most authorities accept that it has many therapeutic properties. The most significant of these is that it lowers blood cholesterol, thus helping prevent heart disease. Also, raw garlic contains a powerful antibiotic and there is evidence that it has a beneficial effect against cancer and strokes, and increases the absorption of vitamins. Many garlic enthusiasts take their garlic in tablet form, but true devotees prefer to take it as it comes.

Right: A string of pink-skinned garlic

Varieties

There are numerous varieties of garlic, from the large "elephant" garlic, to small tight bulbs. Their papery skin can be white, pink or purple. Colour makes no difference to taste but the particular attraction of the large purple bulbs is that they make a beautiful display in the kitchen.

As a general rule, the smaller the garlic bulb, the stronger it is likely to be. However, most garlic sold in shops is not classified in either shape or form (unless it is elephant garlic) and in practice you will simply pick up whatever you need, either loose, in bunches or on strings.

Garlic grown in a hot climate is likely to be the most pungent, and fresh new season's garlic has a subtle, mild flavour that is particularly good if it is to be used raw, for example, in salads and for dressings.

Above: Elephant garlic is shown beside normal-size bulbs.

Buying and Storing

Garlic bulbs should be firm and round with clear, papery skins. Avoid any that are beginning to sprout. Garlic bulbs keep well stored in a cool, dry place; if the air is damp they will sprout and if it is too warm the cloves will eventually turn to grey powder.

Preparing and Cooking

First break the garlic bulb into cloves and then remove the papery skin. You can blanch this off with hot water but using a fingernail or knife is just as effective. When a garlic clove is split lengthways a shoot is revealed in the centre, which is occasionally green, and some people remove this whatever the colour. Cloves are the little segments which make up the bulb and most recipes call for one or more cloves of garlic. (Don't use a bulb when the recipe just calls for a clove!)

Crush cloves either with the blade of a knife or use a garlic crusher. Crushed garlic cooks more evenly and distributes its flavour in food better than when it is used sliced or finely chopped (stir-fries are the exception). Prepare the garlic according to the strength of flavour required: thinly sliced garlic is milder than chopped, which in turn is milder than crushed garlic and, of course, cooking mutes the pungency.

Garlic Breath

The taste and smell of garlic tends to linger on the breath and can be a problem to get rid of. Chewing parsley is a well-known remedy but is only moderately successful. Chewing the seeds of cardamom pods is also said to work but is rather unpleasant. The best suggestion is to eat garlic with your friends so that nobody notices!

LEEKS

Leeks are very versatile, having their own distinct yet subtle flavour. They are excellent in pies and casseroles with other ingredients, braised in cream and served by themselves, or simmered in butter as an accompanying vegetable.

Leeks are also wonderful in soups and broths and have rightly earned the title "king of the soup onions". Cock-a-leekie from Scotland and Crème Vichyssoise, invented by the chef of New York's Ritz-Carlton, are two classic leek soups, but many other soups call for leeks.

History

Leeks, like onions and garlic, have a long history. They were grown widely in Ancient Egypt and were also eaten and enjoyed throughout the Greek and Roman period. In England, there is evidence that leeks were enjoyed during the Dark Ages. There is little mention of them during the Middle Ages, and history suggests that between the sixteenth and eighteenth centuries eating leeks was not considered fashionable.

However, while they may not have enjoyed a good reputation among the notoriously fickle aristocracy, the rural communities probably continued to eat leeks. They grow in all sorts of climates and are substantial enough to make a reasonable meal for a poor family. It was probably during this time that they were dubbed "poor man's asparagus" – a name which says more about people's snobbery about food than it does about leeks.

Many place names in England, such as Leckhampstead and Leighton Buzzard are derived from the word leek and, of course, the leek has been a national emblem of Wales for hundreds of years.

Varieties

There are many different varieties of leeks but among them there is little difference in flavour. Commercially grown leeks tend to be about 25cm/10in long and about 2cm/³⁄₄in in diameter. Leeks nurtured in home gardens can be left to grow to an enormous size but these may develop a woody centre.

the first layer of white; then cut a slit from one end to the other through to the centre of the leek *(see below)*. Wash under cold running water, pulling the sections apart so that the water rinses out any stubborn pieces of earth. If you slice the leeks – either slice thickly or thinly – place them in a colander and rinse thoroughly under cold water.

RAMP

Among the many wild onions and leeks, the Canadian ramp is perhaps the best known. Also called the wild leek, it looks a little like a spring onion, but has a stronger and more assertive garlic-onion flavour. Choose unblemished, clear white specimens with bright, fresh leaves and keep in a cool place, wrapped in a polythene bag to store.

Prepare and cook as you would spring onions, by trimming the root end and then slicing thinly. Use in cooking or in salads but remember the onion flavour is stronger, so use sparingly.

Buying and Storing

Buy leeks which look fresh and healthy. The white part should be firm and unblemished and the leaves green and lively. As leeks do not keep particularly well, it is best to buy them as and when you need them. If you need to store them, trim away the top of the leaves and keep them in the salad drawer of the fridge or in a cool place. After several days they will begin to shrivel.

Preparing

It is important to wash leeks thoroughly before cooking as earth and grit lodges itself between the white sections at the base. To prepare leeks, cut away the flags (leaves) and trim the base. Unless the leek is extremely fresh or home grown, you will probably have to remove

Cooking

Leeks can be steamed or boiled and then added to your recipe, or fry sliced leeks gently in butter for a minute or so and then cover with a lid to sweat so they cook without browning. Unlike onions, leeks shouldn't be allowed to brown; they become tough and unappetizing. They can be stir-fried, however, with a little garlic and ginger. If they begin to cook too fiercely, splash in a little stock and soy sauce and simmer until tender.

Left: Leeks
Above left: Ramp

ONION AND LEEK RECIPES

You'll never be at a loss for a meal idea when it comes to onions and leeks. Individual Onion Tarts with Goat's Cheese, or Baked Onions Stuffed with Feta make fabulous starters, or for a main course try Leek Soufflé or Chicken with Shallots. Garlic doesn't have to have just a walk-on role either — give it star billing as with Roast Garlic with Croûtons. It's a dish your friends won't forget.

BAKED ONIONS STUFFED WITH FETA

FETA CHEESE COMBINED WITH PINE NUTS AND FRESH CORIANDER MAKES A PIQUANT STUFFING WHICH OFFERS A WONDERFUL CONTRAST OF FLAVOUR WITH THE MELLOW RED ONION. FOR THE BEST TASTE MAKE SURE THAT YOU USE AUTHENTIC GREEK FETA CHEESE.

SERVES FOUR

INGREDIENTS
    4 large red onions
    15ml/1 tbsp olive oil
    25g/1oz/¼ cup pine nuts
    115g/4oz feta cheese, crumbled
    25g/1oz/½ cup white breadcrumbs
    15ml/1 tbsp chopped fresh coriander
    salt and freshly ground black pepper

1 Preheat the oven to 180°C/350°F/ Gas 4 and lightly grease a shallow oven- proof dish. Peel the onions and cut a thin slice from the top and base of each. Place in a large saucepan of boiling water and cook for 10–12 minutes until just tender. Remove with a slotted spoon. Drain on kitchen paper and leave to cool slightly.

2 Using a small knife or your fingers, remove the inner sections of the onions, leaving about two or three outer layers. Finely chop the inner sections and place the shells in the ovenproof dish.

3 Heat the oil in a medium-size frying pan and fry the chopped onions for 4–5 minutes until golden, then add the pine nuts and stir-fry for a few minutes.

4 Place the feta cheese in a small bowl and stir in the onions and pine nuts, the breadcrumbs and coriander. Season well with salt and pepper and then spoon the mixture into the onion shells. Cover loosely with foil and bake in the oven for about 30 minutes removing the foil for the last 10 minutes.

5 Serve as a starter or as a light lunch with warm olive bread.

ONION TARTS WITH GOAT'S CHEESE

A VARIATION OF A CLASSIC FRENCH DISH, TARTE À L'OIGNON, THIS DISH USES YOUNG GOAT'S CHEESE INSTEAD OF CREAM, AS IT IS MILD AND CREAMY AND COMPLEMENTS THE FLAVOUR OF THE ONIONS. THIS RECIPE MAKES EITHER EIGHT INDIVIDUAL TARTS OR ONE LARGE 23CM/9IN TART.

SERVES EIGHT

INGREDIENTS
For the pastry
    175g/6oz/1½ cups plain flour
    65g/2½oz/generous ¼ cup butter
    25g/1oz goat's cheddar or Cheddar
        cheese, grated
For the filling
    15–25ml/1–1½ tbsp olive or
        sunflower oil
    3 onions, finely sliced
    175g/6oz young goat's cheese
    2 eggs, beaten
    15ml/1 tbsp single cream
    50g/2oz goat's cheddar, grated
    15ml/1 tbsp chopped fresh tarragon
    salt and freshly ground black pepper

1 To make the pastry, sift the flour into a bowl and rub in the butter until the mixture resembles fine breadcrumbs. Stir in the cheese and add enough cold water to make a dough. Knead lightly, put in a polythene bag and chill. Preheat the oven to 190°C/375°F/Gas 5.

2 Roll out the dough on a lightly floured surface, and then cut into eight rounds using a 11.5cm/4½in pastry cutter, and line eight 10cm/4in patty tins. Prick the bases with a fork and bake in the oven for 10–15 minutes until firm but not browned. Reduce the oven temperature to 180°C/350°F/Gas 4.

3 Heat the olive or sunflower oil in a large frying pan and fry the onions over a low heat for 20–25 minutes until they are a deep golden brown. Stir occasionally to prevent them burning.

4 Beat the goat's cheese with the eggs, cream, goat's cheddar and tarragon. Season with salt and pepper and then stir in the fried onions.

5 Pour the mixture into the part-baked pastry cases and bake in the oven for 20–25 minutes until golden. Serve warm or cold with a green salad.

GARLIC MUSHROOMS

GARLIC AND MUSHROOMS MAKE A WONDERFUL COMBINATION. THEY MUST BE SERVED PIPING HOT, SO IF POSSIBLE USE A BALTI PAN OR CAST-IRON FRYING PAN AND DON'T STAND ON CEREMONY – SERVE STRAIGHT FROM THE PAN.

SERVES FOUR

INGREDIENTS
   30ml/2 tbsp sunflower oil
   25g/1oz/2 tbsp butter
   5 spring onions, thinly sliced
   3 garlic cloves, crushed
   450g/1lb button mushrooms
   40g/1½oz/¾ cup white breadcrumbs
   15ml/1 tbsp chopped fresh parsley
   30ml/2 tbsp lemon juice
   salt and freshly ground black pepper

1 Heat the oil and butter in a balti pan, wok or cast-iron frying pan. Add the spring onions and garlic and stir-fry over a medium heat for 1–2 minutes.

2 Add the whole button mushrooms and fry over a high heat for 4–5 minutes, stirring and tossing with a large wide spatula or wooden spoon, all the time.

3 Stir in the breadcrumbs, parsley, lemon juice and seasoning. Stir-fry for a few minutes until the lemon juice has virtually evaporated and then serve.

ROAST GARLIC <u>WITH</u> CROÛTONS

YOUR GUESTS WILL BE ASTONISHED TO BE SERVED A WHOLE ROAST GARLIC BULB FOR A STARTER. ROAST GARLIC HAS A HEAVENLY FLAVOUR AND IS SO IRRESISTIBLE THEY WILL FORGIVE YOU THE NEXT DAY!

SERVES FOUR

INGREDIENTS
   4 small garlic bulbs
   45ml/3 tbsp olive oil
   45ml/3 tbsp water
   a sprig of rosemary
   a sprig of thyme
   1 bay leaf
   sea salt and freshly ground
     black pepper
To serve
   slices of French bread
   olive or sunflower oil, for frying
   175g/6oz young goat's cheese or soft
     cream cheese
   10ml/2 tsp chopped fresh herbs, e.g.
     marjoram, parsley and chives

1 Preheat the oven to 190°C/375°F/ Gas 5. Place the garlic bulbs in a small ovenproof dish and pour over the oil and water. Add the rosemary, thyme and bay leaf and sprinkle with sea salt and pepper. Cover with foil and bake in the oven for 30 minutes.

2 Remove the foil, baste the garlic heads with the juices from the dish and bake for a further 15–20 minutes until they feel soft when pressed.

3 Heat a little oil in a frying pan and fry the French bread on both sides until golden. Blend the cheese with the mixed herbs and place in a serving dish.

4 Open out each garlic bulb slightly. Serve the garlic on small plates with the croûtons and soft cheese. Each garlic clove should be squeezed out of its papery shell, spread over a croûton and eaten with the cheese.

THAI NOODLES <u>WITH</u> CHINESE CHIVES

THIS RECIPE REQUIRES A LITTLE TIME FOR PREPARATION, BUT THE COOKING TIME IS VERY SHORT.
EVERYTHING IS COOKED SPEEDILY IN A HOT WOK AND SHOULD BE EATEN AT ONCE.

SERVES FOUR

INGREDIENTS
  350g/12oz dried rice noodles
  1cm/½ in fresh root ginger, grated
  30ml/2 tbsp light soy sauce
  45ml/3 tbsp vegetable oil
  225g/8oz Quorn, cut into small cubes
  2 garlic cloves, crushed
  1 large onion, cut into thin wedges
  115g/4oz fried bean curd, thinly sliced
  1 green chilli, seeded and sliced
  175g/6oz/¾ cup beansprouts
  115g/4oz Chinese chives, cut into
    5cm/2in lengths
  50g/2oz/½ cup roasted peanuts,
    ground
  30ml/ 2 tbsp dark soy sauce
  30ml/2 tbsp chopped fresh coriander
  1 lemon, cut into wedges

1 Place the noodles in a large bowl, cover with warm water and soak for 20–30 minutes, then drain. Blend together the ginger, light soy sauce and 15ml/1 tbsp of the oil in a bowl. Stir in the Quorn and set aside for 10 minutes. Drain, reserving the marinade.

2 Heat 15ml/1 tbsp of the oil in a wok or frying pan and fry the garlic briefly. Add the Quorn and stir-fry for 3–4 minutes. Then transfer to a plate and set aside.

5 When hot, spoon on to serving plates and garnish with the remaining ground peanuts, coriander and lemon wedges.

COOK'S TIP
Quorn makes this a vegetarian meal, however thinly sliced pork or chicken could be used instead. Stir-fry it initially for 4–5 minutes.

3 Heat the remaining oil in the wok or frying pan and stir-fry the onion for 3–4 minutes until softened and tinged with brown. Add the bean curd and chilli, stir-fry briefly and then add the noodles. Stir-fry for 4–5 minutes.

4 Stir in the beansprouts, Chinese chives and most of the ground peanuts, reserving a little for the garnish. Stir well, then add the Quorn, the dark soy sauce and the reserved marinade.

LEEK SOUFFLÉ

SOME PEOPLE THINK OF A SOUFFLÉ AS A DINNER PARTY DISH, AND A RATHER TRICKY ONE AT THAT. HOWEVER, OTHERS FREQUENTLY SERVE THEM FOR FAMILY MEALS BECAUSE THEY ARE QUICK AND EASY TO MAKE, AND PROVE TO BE VERY POPULAR AND SATISFYING.

SERVES TWO TO THREE

INGREDIENTS
    15ml/1 tbsp sunflower oil
    40g/1½oz/3 tbsp butter
    2 leeks, thinly sliced
    about 300ml/½ pint/1¼ cups milk
    25g/1oz/¼ cup plain flour
    4 eggs, separated
    75g/3oz Gruyère or Emmenthal
        cheese, grated
    salt and freshly ground black pepper

1 Preheat the oven to 180°C/350°F Gas 4 and butter a large soufflé dish. Heat the oil and 15g/½oz/1 tbsp of the butter in a saucepan or flameproof casserole and fry the leeks over a gentle heat for 4–5 minutes until soft but not brown, stirring occasionally.

2 Stir in the milk and bring to the boil. Cover and simmer for 4–5 minutes until the leeks are tender. Strain the liquid through a sieve into a measuring jug.

3 Melt the remaining butter in a saucepan, stir in the flour and cook for 1 minute. Remove pan from the heat. Make up the reserved liquid with milk to 300ml/ ½ pint/1¼ cups. Gradually stir the milk into the pan to make a smooth sauce. Return to the heat and bring to the boil, stirring. When thickened, remove from the heat. Cool slightly and then beat in the egg yolks, cheese and the leeks.

4 Whisk the egg whites until stiff and, using a large metal spoon, fold into the leek and egg mixture. Pour into the prepared soufflé dish and bake in the oven for about 30 minutes until golden and puffy. Serve immediately.

TAGLIATELLE WITH LEEKS AND PARMA HAM

*LEEKS ARE A VERY VERSATILE VEGETABLE. THEIR DELICATE, MILDLY ONIONY FLAVOUR MAKES THEM
IDEAL TO USE IN STIR-FRIES, RISOTTOS, EGG DISHES, SOUPS AND SAUCES. IF USING OLDER LEEKS, MAKE
SURE THEY HAVE NOT DEVELOPED A WOODY CORE.*

SERVES FOUR

INGREDIENTS
  5 leeks
  40g/1½oz/3tbsp butter or margarine
  225g/8oz tagliatelle, preferably
    green and white
  20ml/4 tsp dry sherry
  30ml/2 tbsp lemon juice
  10ml/2 tsp chopped fresh basil
  115–150g/4–5oz Parma ham,
    torn into strips
  175g/6oz fromage frais
  salt and freshly ground black pepper
  fresh basil leaves, to garnish
  Parmesan cheese, to serve

4 Stir the sherry, lemon juice, basil and seasoning into the leek mixture and cook for 1–2 minutes so that the flavours can blend together. Add the Parma ham and fromage frais, stir and cook for about 1–2 minutes until heated through.

5 Drain the pasta and place in a warmed serving dish. Pour the leek and Parma ham mixture on top and mix lightly together. Garnish each serving with basil leaves and serve with shavings of Parmesan cheese.

1 Trim the leeks and then cut a slit from top to bottom, rinse well under cold water and cut into thin slices.

2 Melt the butter or margarine in a saucepan or flameproof casserole, add the leeks and fry over a gentle heat for 3–4 minutes until tender but not too soft.

3 Add the tagliatelle to a large saucepan of boiling water and cook according to the instructions on the packet (about 3–5 minutes for fresh pasta; 8 minutes for dried pasta).

BAKED LEEKS WITH CHEESE AND YOGURT TOPPING

LIKE ALL VEGETABLES, THE FRESHER LEEKS ARE, THE BETTER THEIR FLAVOUR, AND THE FRESHEST LEEKS AVAILABLE SHOULD BE USED FOR THIS DISH. SMALL, YOUNG LEEKS ARE AROUND AT THE BEGINNING OF THE SEASON AND ARE PERFECT TO USE HERE.

SERVES FOUR

INGREDIENTS

8 small leeks, about 675g/1½lb
2 small eggs or 1 large one, beaten
150g/5oz fresh goat's cheese
85ml/3fl oz/⅓ cup natural yogurt
50g/2oz Parmesan cheese, grated
25g/1oz/½ cup fresh white or brown breadcrumbs
salt and freshly ground black pepper

1 Preheat the oven to 180°C/350°F/ Gas 4 and butter a shallow ovenproof dish. Trim the leeks, cut a slit from top to bottom and rinse well under cold water.

2 Place the leeks in a saucepan of water, bring to the boil and simmer gently for 6–8 minutes until just tender. Remove and drain well using a slotted spoon, and arrange in the prepared dish.

3 Beat the beaten egg with the goat's cheese, yogurt and half the Parmesan cheese, and season well with salt and black pepper.

4 Pour the cheese and yogurt mixture over the leeks. Mix the breadcrumbs and remaining Parmesan cheese together and sprinkle over the sauce. Bake in the oven for 35–40 minutes until the top is crisp and golden brown.

CHICKEN <u>WITH</u> SHALLOTS

SERVES FOUR

INGREDIENTS

   1 small chicken, about 1.3kg/3lb,
     or 4 chicken pieces
   seasoned plain flour, for coating
   30ml/2 tbsp sunflower oil
   25g/1oz butter
   115g/4oz unsmoked streaky
     bacon, chopped
   2 garlic cloves
   450ml/¾ pint/1¾ cups red wine
   1 bay leaf
   2 thyme sprigs
   250g/9oz shallots
   115g/4oz/1½ cups button mushrooms,
     halved if large
   10ml/2 tsp plain flour
   salt and freshly ground black pepper

1 Preheat the oven to 180°C/350°F/
Gas 4. Remove any excess skin or fat
from the chicken and cut into four or
eight pieces. Place a little seasoned flour
in a large plastic bag, add the chicken
pieces and shake to coat evenly.

2 Heat half the oil and half the butter in
a large flameproof casserole and fry the
bacon and garlic for 3–4 minutes. Add
the chicken pieces and fry until lightly
browned. Add the wine, bay leaf and
thyme and bring to the boil. Cover and
cook in the oven for 1 hour.

3 Peel the shallots and boil them in
salted water for 10 minutes. Heat the
remaining oil in a small frying pan and
fry the shallots for 3–4 minutes until
beginning to brown. Add the mushrooms
and fry for a further 2–3 minutes.

4 Stir the shallots and mushrooms into
the casserole with the chicken and cook
for a further 8–10 minutes. Using a fork,
blend the flour with the remaining butter
to make a thick paste.

5 Transfer the chicken pieces, shallots
and mushrooms to a serving dish and
keep warm. Bring the liquid to the boil
and then add small pieces of the flour
paste, stirring vigorously after each
addition. When all the paste has been
added and the sauce is thick, either pour
over the chicken pieces or return the
chicken to the casserole and serve.

GLAZED SHALLOTS

SERVES FOUR

INGREDIENTS

   350–400g/12–14oz shallots
   15ml/1 tbsp olive oil
   25g/1oz butter
   15ml/1 tbsp sugar
   about 175ml/6fl oz/¾ cup water
   salt and freshly ground black pepper

1 Peel the shallots and break in two if
the bulbs are joined. Heat the oil and
butter in a heavy-based saucepan and
gently fry the shallots over a moderate
heat for 5–6 minutes until patches of
brown begin to appear. Stir occasionally.

2 Sprinkle the shallots with the sugar
and cook, stirring, for 1 minute.

3 Add enough water to just cover the
shallots and then cover and simmer over
a low heat for about 25–35 minutes until
completely tender, adding a little extra
water if necessary, then remove the lid
and continue simmering gently until the
liquid has reduced to a thin syrup. Stir
occasionally. Season with salt, if liked.

4 Spoon the shallots into a serving dish
and pour over the syrup. Sprinkle with
black pepper. Serve with roast meat or a
baked vegetable dish.

SHOOTS AND STEMS

Here are some of Nature's most tender vegetables. Asparagus,
fennel, samphire and the American fiddlehead fern have the taste
of early summer, while the globe artichoke arrives later but is no
less delicious for its tardiness. Celery and beansprouts are
available all year round and, like other shoots and stems, add a
fresh taste to a meal.

ASPARAGUS

Asparagus is most definitely a luxury
vegetable. Its price, even in season, sets
it apart from cabbages and cauliflowers,
and it has a taste of luxury too. The
spears, especially the thick green
spears, at their best in early summer,
have an intense, rich flavour that is
impossible to describe but easy to
remember. If the gods eat, they will eat
asparagus – served simply with a good
hollandaise sauce!

History

The ancient Greeks enjoyed eating wild
asparagus but it was not until the Roman
period that we know it was cultivated.
Even then asparagus was highly thought
of; it is recorded that Julius Caesar liked
to eat it with melted butter. There is little
mention of asparagus being eaten in
England until the seventeenth century.
Mrs Beeton has 14 recipes for asparagus
and from the prices quoted in her
cookbook it is apparent that it was
expensive even in Victorian times.

Nutrition

Asparagus provides vitamins A, B2 and
C and is also a very good source of
potassium, iron and calcium. It is a
well-known diuretic.

Varieties

There are many varieties of asparagus
and many different ways of raising it too.
Spanish and some Dutch asparagus is
white with ivory tips; it is grown under
mounds of soil and cut just as the tips
begin to show. The purple variety is
mostly grown in France, where the
spears are cut once the tips are about
4cm/1 1/2 in above the ground. As a
consequence, the stalks are white and
the tops tinged with green or purple. In
contrast, both English and American
asparagus grow above the ground and
the spears are entirely green. Arguments
continue over which has the better
flavour, with most growers expressing a
preference for their own asparagus!

   Thin, short asparagus are called sprue
and are excellent when briefly steamed
or stir-fried and added to salads. In Italy,
they are served by themselves, scattered
with grated Parmesan cheese.

Preparing

The bottom of the asparagus stalk is usually hard and woody, so will probably need cutting off. If the bottom parts of the stem also feel hard, pare them away with a potato peeler *(see below)*. However, if the asparagus is very fresh this will not be necessary, and sprue rarely needs trimming at all.

Buying and Storing

Asparagus has a relatively short growing season from late spring to early summer. Nowadays, it is available in the shops almost all year round but outside the season it will have been imported. It is still good, but it is expensive and will not have the flavour of home-produced asparagus, because it starts to lose its flavour once it is cut.

When buying asparagus, the tips should be tightly furled and fresh looking, and the stalks fresh and straight. If the stalks are badly scarred or droopy, it indicates that they have been hanging around for too long and it is not worth buying. Asparagus will keep for several days if necessary. Untie the bundles and store in the salad drawer of the fridge.

Cooking

The problem when cooking asparagus is that the stalks take longer to cook than the tender tips, which need to be only briefly steamed. Ideally, use an asparagus kettle. Place the asparagus spears with the tips upwards in the wire basket and then lower into a little boiling salted water in the kettle. Cover and cook until the stems are tender.

Alternatively, if you do not have an asparagus kettle, place the bundle upright in a deep saucepan of boiling salted water. (The bundle can be wedged into place with potatoes.) Cover with a dome of foil and cook for 5–10 minutes or until the spears are tender. The cooking time depends largely on the thickness of the spears but take care not to overcook; the spears should still have a "bite" to them.

Asparagus can also be roasted in a little olive oil. This cooking method intensifies the flavour and is gratifyingly simple. Serve with just a sprinkling of sea salt – it's quite delicious! If you are steaming asparagus, serve simply with melted butter, which perfectly complements the luxury of the vegetable.

Left: Asparagus
Above: White asparagus

GLOBE ARTICHOKES

Globe artichokes have an exquisite flavour and are a very sociable food to eat. They grow in abundance in Brittany, and during July and August farmers can frequently be seen selling them by the roadside. The globes are huge hearty specimens and are extremely fresh, so they make a good buy.

History

It is not known for certain whether or not artichokes were eaten in antiquity.

Although they are mentioned by writers, they could have been referring to the cardoon, which is the uncultivated form of artichoke. Cardoons grew wild in many southern European countries and, as far as we know, cultivated artichokes first became a popular food in Italy. However, Goethe did not share the Italians' liking for the vegetable and remarks in his book, *Travels Through Italy*, that "the peasants eat thistles", something he didn't care for at all.

Nowadays, artichokes are grown all over southern Europe and in California. People in Italy, France and Spain eat artichokes while the vegetable is still young, before the choke has formed and the entire artichoke is still edible. Most unfortunately, such young delicacies are not exported but look out for them if you are in these countries.

Buying and Storing

It is only worth buying artichokes when they are in season, although they are available in supermarkets almost all year round. In winter, however, they are sad-looking specimens, small and rather dry, and are really not worth the bother of cooking. At their best, artichokes should be lively looking with a good bloom on their leaves, the inner leaves wrapped tightly round the choke and heart inside. Artichokes will keep for 2–3 days in the salad drawer of the fridge but are best eaten as soon as possible.

Preparing and Cooking

First twist off the stalk which should also remove some of the fibres at the base and then cut the base flat and pull away any small base leaves. If the leaves are very spiky, trim them with scissors if you like *(see above)*, then rinse under running water. Cook in boiling water, acidulated with the juice of half a lemon. Large artichokes need to be simmered for 30–40 minutes until tender. To test if they are done, pull off one of the outer leaves. It should come away easily and the base of the leaf should be tender.

altogether. Then pull or cut away the fine prickly choke and discard to reveal the heart, which can be eaten with a knife and fork.

CARDOONS

This impressively large vegetable is closely related to the globe artichoke and has a superb flavour, a cross between artichokes and asparagus. Cultivated plants frequently grow to 2 metres/6 feet in height, and once mature, cardoons, like celery, are blanched as they grow. This process involves wrapping the stalks with newspaper and black bags for several weeks so that when harvested in late autumn, before the frosts, the stalks are a pale green.

The cardoon is a popular vegetable in southern Europe but less commonly available elsewhere. In Spain, for instance, it is much appreciated and often appears on the table, poached and served with chestnuts or walnuts. Only the inner ribs and heart of the vegetable are used.

Artichokes and Drink

Artichokes contain a chemical called cynarin, which in many people affects the taste buds by enhancing sweet flavours. Among other things, this will spoil the taste of wine. Consequently, don't waste good wine with artichokes but drink iced water instead, which should taste pleasantly sweet.

Eating Artichokes

Artichokes are fun to eat. They have to be eaten with fingers, which does away with any pomp and ceremony. One artichoke per person is usually about right as a first course, but if you are serving other vegetables with the artichoke you could serve one artichoke between two, so that people can share the fun of pulling off the leaves and dipping them into garlic butter or vinaigrette.

The dipping sauces are an essential part of eating artichokes; people can either spoon a little on to their plates or you could give everyone a little bowl each. After dipping, draw the leaf through your

teeth, eating the fleshy part and piling the remains of the leaf on your plate. When most of the leaves have been eaten, a few thin pointed leaves remain in the centre, which can be pulled off

Opposite: Globe artichokes
Top left: Baby globe artichokes
Above: Cardoons

CELERY

It is said that the very act of eating celery has a slimming effect because chewing it uses up more calories than the vegetable itself contains. Although it may be insubstantial, celery nevertheless has a distinct and individual flavour, sharp and savoury, which makes it an excellent flavouring for soups and stuffings, as well as good on its own or in salads. The astringent flavour and crunchy texture of celery contrasts well with the other ingredients in salads such as Waldorf salad or walnut and avocado salad.

History

Celery has been eaten in Britain for several hundred years, having been introduced from Italy where it was commonly eaten in salads.

Nutrition

Celery is very low in calories but contains potassium and calcium.

Varieties

Most greengrocers and supermarkets, depending on the time of year, sell both green and white celery and you would be excused for not knowing the difference. When celery is allowed to grow naturally, the stalks are green. However, by banking up earth against the shoots celery is blanched: the stalks are protected from sunlight and remain pale and white. Consequently, white celery is often "dirty" – covered loosely in soil – while green celery will always be clean. White celery, which is frost hardy, is only available in winter. It is more tender and less bitter than green celery and is generally considered superior. Celery is therefore thought of as a winter vegetable and is traditionally used at Christmas time, for stuffing and as a sauce to go with turkey or ham.

Buying and Storing

White celery is in season during the winter months. If possible, buy "dirty" celery which hasn't been washed. It has a better flavour than the pristine but rather bland supermarket variety. Look for celery with green fresh-looking leaves and straight stems. If the leaves or any

outer stalks are missing, it is likely to be rather old, so worth avoiding.

Celery will keep for several days in the salad drawer of the fridge. Limp celery can be revived by wrapping it in absorbent paper and standing it in a jar of water.

Preparing

Wash if necessary and pull the stalks apart, trimming the base with a sharp knife. Cut into thick or thin slices according to the recipe. When served raw and whole, the coarse outer "strings" should be removed from each stalk by pulling them up from the base.

Cooking and Serving

Serve celery raw and finely sliced in salads, mixed with cream cheese or soured cream. Braised celery is tasty, either whole or sliced. Celery has a distinctive, savoury, astringent flavour so it is excellent in soups or stuffings.

CELERIAC

Strictly speaking, celeriac is a root vegetable, being the root of certain kinds of celery. It is knobbly with a patchy brown/white skin and has a similar but less pronounced flavour than celery. Grated and eaten raw, it has a crunchy texture, but when cooked it is more akin to potatoes. Thin slices of potato and celeriac cooked *au gratin* with cream is a popular way of serving this vegetable.

Buying and Preparing

If possible, buy smallish bulbs of celeriac. Celeriac flesh discolours when exposed to light, so as soon as you have peeled, sliced, diced or grated it, plunge it into a bowl of acidulated water (water with lemon juice added).

Cooking

Celeriac can be used in soups and broths, or can be diced and boiled and eaten in potato salads.

Opposite: Green celery
Above right: White celery
Right: Celeriac

FIDDLEHEAD FERN

Sometimes called the ostrich fern, these shoots are a rich green colour and are normally about 5cm/2in long. They have an unusual flavour, something like a cross between asparagus and okra, and have a slightly chewy texture, which makes them a popular choice for oriental dishes.

Preparing and Cooking

To prepare and cook, trim the ends and then steam or simmer in a little water or sauté in butter until tender. Use in salads or you could serve as a first course with a hollandaise sauce.

Right: Fiddlehead ferns.
Below left: Alfalfa sprouts.
Below right: Mung bean sprouts.

ORIENTAL SHOOTS

BAMBOO SHOOTS

In the Far East, edible bamboo shoots are sold fresh in the market. The young shoots are stripped of their brown outer skins and the insides are then eaten. Although fresh bamboo shoots can occasionally be found in oriental stores, the most readily available variety is sold in cans. The flavour is undoubtedly spoilt. Fresh bamboo shoots have a mild but distinct taste, faintly reminiscent of globe artichokes, while canned ones really taste of nothing at all. However, the texture, which, in Chinese cuisines particularly, is as important as the flavour, is not so impaired, and bamboo shoots have a pleasantly crunchy bite.

Preparing and Cooking

Peel away the outer skin and then cook in boiling water for about half an hour. They should feel firm, but not "rock" hard. Once cooked, slice thinly and serve by themselves as a side dish, with garlic butter or a sauce, or add to stir-fries, spring rolls or any oriental dish

where you need a contrast of textures. Since canned bamboo shoots have been preserved in brine, always rinse well before using.

BEAN SPROUTS

Bean sprouts are rather a neglected vegetable, used almost carelessly for

oriental dishes but otherwise passed over as being insipid and not very interesting. This is a reputation they don't deserve, as they have a lovely fresh flavour and are also good for you.

All sorts of seeds can be sprouted, but the bean family are favourites among the sprouted vegetables. The bean sprouts most commonly available in the shops are sprouted mung beans, but aduki beans, alfalfa, lentils and soybeans can all be sprouted and taste delicious. Most health food shops will have instructions on sprouting your own beans. Only buy seeds intended for sprouting.

Nutrition

Beans sprouts contain a significant amount of protein, Vitamin C and many of the B vitamins. They have an excellent flavour too, best appreciated eaten raw in salads or sandwiches, and for slimmers they are an ideal food, low in calories, yet with sufficient substance to be filling, and with a flavour and texture that can be enjoyed without a dressing.

Buying and Storing

Bean sprouts should only be bought when absolutely fresh. They don't keep for long and they will taste sour if past their best. The sprouts should be firm, not limp, and the tips should be green or yellow; avoid any that are beginning to turn brown.

Cooking

If stir-frying, add the bean sprouts at the last minute so they only cook for the minimum period to keep plenty of crunch and retain their nutritional value.

PALM HEARTS

Fresh palm hearts are the buds of cabbage palm trees and are considered a delicacy in many parts of the world. They are available canned from oriental stores, but are most prized when fresh. These should be blanched before being cooked to eliminate any bitterness. They can be braised or sautéed and then served hot with a Hollandaise sauce, or cold with a simple vinaigrette.

WATER CHESTNUTS

Water chestnut is the common name for a number of aquatic herbs and their nutlike fruit, the best known and most popular variety being the Chinese water chestnut, sometimes known as the Chinese sedge. The plants require exactly the same conditions as rice –

high temperatures, shallow water and good soil. In spring, the corms are planted in paddy fields which are then flooded to a depth of some 10cm/4in. These are drained in autumn, and the corms are harvested and stored over the winter. Water chestnuts are much used in Chinese cooking and have a sweet crunchy flavour with nutty overtones.

They are edible cooked or raw and are excellent in all sorts of Chinese dishes.

Above: Sprouting mung beans
Below (clockwise from top left): canned water chestnuts, canned bamboo shoots, fresh water chestnuts, canned palm hearts

FENNEL

The vegetable fennel is closely related to
the herb and spice of the same name. It
is called variously Florence fennel, sweet
fennel, *finocchio dulce* or Italian fennel.

Like the herb, Florence fennel has the
distinct flavour of anise, a taste that
seems to go particularly well with fish, so
the vegetable is often served with fish
dishes while the herb or spice is
commonly used in fish stocks, sauces
or soups. The leaves are edible and can
be used in soups and stocks as well as
for garnishing.

History

Florence fennel has only been popular in
Britain for the last 20 years, although it
has a long history of cultivation, having
been eaten by the Ancient Egyptians,
Greeks and Romans. In Italy, fennel
has been eaten for several centuries:
many of the best fennel recipes come
from Italy and also from other parts of
the Mediterranean.

Buying and Storing

If possible, buy small tender bulbs. The
bulbs should be clean and white with no
bruises or blemishes and the feathery
leaves should be green and lively. Fennel
will keep for a day or two in the salad
drawer of the fridge.

Preparing

Unless the bulbs are very young and
tender, remove the first layer of skin, as it
is likely to be tough (this can be used for
a stock). Fennel can then be sliced into
slivers by cutting downwards or into
rings by cutting across the bulb. When
used raw in salads, it needs to be cut
into smaller pieces.

Cooking and Serving

Fennel can be served raw if it is thinly
sliced and then dressed with a light
vinaigrette. In salads, its flavour
contrasts well with apple, celery and
other crunchy ingredients. Fennel is also
excellent braised with onions, tomatoes
and garlic.

Right: Florence fennel
Opposite: Marsh samphire

SAMPHIRE

There are two types of samphire. Marsh samphire grows in estuaries and salt marshes while rock samphire, sometimes called sea fennel, grows on rocky shores. The two are understandably confused since they are both connected with the sea, yet they are completely different plants.

The type likely to be sold by a fishmonger is marsh samphire. It is also known as glasswort and is sometimes called sea asparagus, as its shoots are similar to sprue, small asparagus shoots.

Although marsh samphire grows easily and is commonly found all over Europe and North America, it is not cultivated and is only available for a short time while it is in season, normally in late summer and early autumn.

Samphire has a distinctly salty, iodine flavour and a pleasant crisp texture. The flavour is reminiscent of the sea and goes particularly well with fish and seafood. However, samphire can be enjoyed simply steamed and dipped into melted butter.

Buying and Storing

When in season, good fishmongers get regular stocks of marsh samphire, and it should look bright and fresh. Buy it when you need it, as it will not keep long.

Preparing and Cooking

If necessary, wash marsh samphire under cold running water. It is best steamed over a pan of boiling water for no more than 3 minutes. Otherwise, blanch in boiling water for 3–5 minutes and then drain. Samphire can be eaten raw but blanching it removes some of the saltiness.

To eat samphire, draw the shoots through the teeth to peel the succulent part from the thin central core.

SHOOT AND STEM RECIPES

If the season's right, you owe it yourself — and your guests — to make the most of shoots and stems. What could be a more perfect way to start a meal than with fresh Asparagus with Tarragon Hollandaise? Alternatively roast asparagus, French-style, for Roast Asparagus Crêpes. Other favourites include Celery, Avocado and Walnut Salad and Fennel and Mussel Provençal, while for something new, try Samphire with Chilled Fish Curry or Celeriac and Blue Cheese Roulade.

ASPARAGUS TART WITH RICOTTA

THIS DELICIOUS TART COMBINES THE SUBTLE FLAVOUR OF ASPARAGUS WITH THE MILD TASTE OF CREAMY RICOTTA CHEESE TO GREAT EFFECT. SERVE WITH A GREEN SALAD AND TINY NEW POTATOES FOR A PERFECT WEEKEND LUNCH.

SERVES FOUR

INGREDIENTS
For the pastry
  175g/6oz plain flour
  75g/3oz butter or margarine
  a pinch of salt
For the filling
  225g/8oz asparagus
  2 eggs, beaten
  225g/8oz/1 cup ricotta cheese
  30ml/2 tbsp Greek-style yogurt
  40g/1½oz Parmesan cheese, grated
  salt and freshly ground black pepper

1 Preheat the oven to 200°C/400°F/Gas 6. Rub the butter or margarine into the flour and salt until the mixture resembles fine breadcrumbs. Stir in enough cold water to form a smooth dough and knead lightly on a floured surface.

2 Roll out the pastry and then line a 23cm/9in flan ring. Press firmly into the tin and prick all over with a fork. Bake in the oven for about 10 minutes until the pastry is pale but firm. Remove from the oven and reduce the temperature to 180°C/350°F/Gas 4.

3 To make the filling, trim the asparagus if necessary. Cut 5cm/2in from the tops and chop the remaining stalks into 2.5cm/1in pieces. Add the stalks to a saucepan of boiling water and after 1 minute add the asparagus tips. Simmer for 4–5 minutes until almost tender, then drain and refresh under cold water.

4 Beat together the eggs, ricotta cheese, yogurt, Parmesan cheese and seasoning. Stir in the asparagus stalks and pour the mixture into the pastry case. Arrange the asparagus tips on top, pressing them down slightly.

5 Bake in the oven for 35–40 minutes until golden. Serve warm or cold.

ASPARAGUS WITH TARRAGON HOLLANDAISE

THIS IS THE IDEAL STARTER FOR AN EARLY SUMMER DINNER PARTY WHEN THE NEW SEASON'S ASPARAGUS IS JUST IN AND AT ITS BEST. MAKING HOLLANDAISE SAUCE IN A BLENDER OR FOOD PROCESSOR IS INCREDIBLY EASY AND VIRTUALLY FOOLPROOF!

SERVES FOUR

INGREDIENTS
  500g/1¼lb fresh asparagus
  salt
For the hollandaise sauce
  2 eggs yolks
  15ml/1 tbsp lemon juice
  115g/4oz/½ cup butter
  10ml/2 tsp finely chopped fresh
    tarragon
  salt and freshly ground black pepper

1 Prepare the asparagus, lay it in a steamer or in an asparagus kettle and place over a saucepan of rapidly boiling water. Cover and steam for 6–10 minutes until tender (the cooking time will vary depending on the thickness of the asparagus stems).

2 To make the hollandaise sauce, place the egg yolks, lemon juice and seasoning in a blender or food processor and process briefly. Melt the butter in a small pan until foaming and then, with the machine running, pour it on to the egg mixture in a slow, steady stream.

3 Stir in the tarragon by hand or process it (for a sauce speckled with green or a pale green sauce, respectively).

4 Arrange the asparagus on small plates and pour over some hollandaise sauce. Serve the remaining sauce in a jug.

ASPARAGUS SOUP

HOME-MADE ASPARAGUS SOUP HAS A DELICATE FLAVOUR, QUITE UNLIKE THAT FROM A CAN. THIS SOUP IS BEST MADE WITH YOUNG ASPARAGUS, EARLY IN THE SEASON, WHICH IS TENDER AND BLENDS WELL. SERVE IT WITH WAFER-THIN SLICES OF BREAD.

SERVES FOUR

INGREDIENTS
450g/1lb young asparagus
40g/1½ oz/3 tbsp butter
6 shallots, sliced
15g/½ oz/2 tbsp plain flour
600ml/1 pint/2½ cups vegetable
    stock or water
15ml/1 tbsp lemon juice
250ml/8fl oz/1 cup milk
120ml/4fl oz/½ cup single cream
10ml/2 tsp chopped fresh chervil
salt and freshly ground black pepper

1 Trim the stalks of the asparagus if necessary. Cut 4cm/1½in off the tops of half the asparagus and set aside for a garnish. Slice the remaining asparagus.

2 Melt 25g/1oz/2 tbsp of the butter in a large saucepan and gently fry the sliced shallots for 2–3 minutes until soft but not brown, stirring occasionally.

3 Add the sliced asparagus and fry over a gentle heat for about 1 minute. Stir in the flour and cook for 1 minute. Stir in the stock or water and lemon juice, and season to taste. Bring to the boil and then simmer, partially covered, for 15–20 minutes until the asparagus is very tender.

4 Cool slightly and then process the soup in a food processor or blender until smooth. Then press the purée through a sieve placed over a clean saucepan. Add the milk by pouring and stirring it through the sieve with the asparagus so as to extract the maximum amount of asparagus purée.

5 Melt the remaining butter and fry the reserved asparagus tips gently for about 3–4 minutes to soften.

6 Heat the soup gently for 3–4 minutes. Stir in the cream and the asparagus tips. Continue to heat gently and serve sprinkled with the chopped fresh chervil.

ROAST ASPARAGUS CRÊPES

ROAST ASPARAGUS IS DELICIOUS AND GOOD ENOUGH TO EAT JUST AS IT COMES. HOWEVER, FOR A REALLY SPLENDID STARTER, TRY THIS SIMPLE RECIPE. EITHER MAKE SIX LARGE OR TWELVE COCKTAIL-SIZE PANCAKES TO USE WITH SMALLER STEMS OF ASPARAGUS.

SERVES SIX

INGREDIENTS
90–120ml/6–8 tbsp olive oil
450g/1lb fresh asparagus
175g/6oz/¾ cup mascarpone cheese
60ml/4 tbsp single cream
25g/1oz Parmesan cheese, grated
sea salt
For the pancakes
175g/6oz 1½ cup plain flour
2 eggs
350ml/12fl oz/1½ cups milk
vegetable oil, for frying
a pinch of salt

1 To make the pancake batter, mix the flour with the salt in a large bowl, food processor or blender, then add the eggs and milk and beat or process to make a smooth, fairly thin batter.

2 Heat a little oil in a large frying pan and add a small amount of batter, swirling the pan to coat the base evenly. Cook over a moderate heat for about 1 minute, then flip over and cook the other side until golden. Set aside and cook the rest of the pancakes in the same way; the mixture makes about six large or 12 smaller pancakes.

3 Preheat the oven to 180°C/350°F/Gas 4 and lightly grease a large shallow ovenproof dish or roasting tin with some of the olive oil.

4 Trim the asparagus by placing on a board and cutting off the bases. Using a small sharp knife, peel away the woody ends, if necessary.

5 Arrange the asparagus in a single layer in the dish or tin, trickle over the remaining olive oil, rolling the asparagus to coat each one thoroughly. Sprinkle with salt and then roast in the oven for 8–12 minutes until tender (the cooking time depends on the stem thickness).

6 Blend the mascarpone cheese with the cream and Parmesan cheese and spread a generous tablespoonful over each of the pancakes, leaving a little extra for the topping. Preheat the grill.

7 Divide the asparagus spears among the pancakes, roll up and arrange in a single layer in an ovenproof dish. Spoon over the remaining cheese mixture and then place under a moderate grill for 4–5 minutes, until heated through and golden brown. Serve at once.

CELERIAC GRATIN

ALTHOUGH CELERIAC HAS A RATHER UNATTRACTIVE APPEARANCE WITH ITS HARD, KNOBBLY SKIN, IT IS A VEGETABLE THAT HAS A VERY DELICIOUS SWEET AND NUTTY FLAVOUR. THIS IS ACCENTUATED IN THIS DISH BY THE ADDITION OF THE MILDLY FLAVOURED EMMENTAL CHEESE.

SERVES FOUR

INGREDIENTS
    450g/1lb celeriac
    juice of ½ lemon
    25g/1oz/2 tbsp butter
    1 small onion, finely chopped
    30ml/2 tbsp plain flour
    300ml/½ pint/1¼ cups milk
    25g/1oz Emmental cheese, grated
    15ml/1 tbsp capers
    salt and cayenne pepper

1 Preheat the oven to 190°C/375°F/ Gas 5. Peel the celeriac and cut into 5mm/¼in slices, immediately plunging them into a saucepan of cold water acidulated with the lemon juice.

2 Bring the water to the boil and simmer the celeriac for 10–12 minutes until just tender. Drain and layer the celeriac in a shallow ovenproof dish.

3 Melt the butter in a small saucepan and fry the onion over a gentle heat until soft but not browned. Stir in the flour, cook for 1 minute and then slowly stir in the milk to make a smooth sauce. Stir in the cheese, capers and seasoning to taste and then pour over the celeriac. Cook in the oven for 15–20 minutes until the top is golden brown.

VARIATION
For a less strongly flavoured dish, alternate the layers of celeriac with potato. Slice the potato, cook until almost tender, then drain well before assembling the dish.

CELERIAC AND BLUE CHEESE ROULADE

CELERIAC ADDS A DELICATE AND SUBTLE FLAVOUR TO THIS ATTRACTIVE DISH. THE SPINACH ROULADE MAKES AN ATTRACTIVE CONTRAST TO THE CREAMY FILLING BUT YOU COULD USE A PLAIN OR CHEESE ROULADE BASE INSTEAD. BE SURE TO ROLL UP THE ROULADE WHILE IT IS STILL WARM AND PLIABLE.

SERVES SIX

INGREDIENTS
  15g/½oz/1 tbsp butter
  225g/8oz cooked spinach, drained
    and chopped
  150ml/¼ pint/⅔ cup single cream
  4 large eggs, separated
  15g/½oz Parmesan cheese, grated
  a pinch of nutmeg
  salt and freshly ground black pepper
For the filling
  225g/8oz celeriac
  lemon juice
  75g/3oz St Agur cheese
  115g/4oz/½ cup plain fromage frais
  freshly ground black pepper

1 Preheat the oven to 200°C/400°F/Gas 6 and line a 34 x 24cm/13 x 9in Swiss roll tin with non-stick baking paper.

2 Melt the butter in a saucepan and add the spinach. Cook gently until all the liquid has evaporated, stirring frequently. Remove the pan from the heat and stir in the cream, egg yolks, Parmesan cheese, nutmeg and seasoning.

3 Whisk the egg whites until stiff, fold them gently into the spinach mixture and then spoon into the prepared tin. Spread the mixture evenly and use a palette knife to smooth the surface.

4 Bake in the oven for 10–15 minutes until the roulade is firm to the touch and lightly golden on top. Carefully turn out on to a sheet of greaseproof or non-stick baking paper and peel away the lining paper. Roll it up with the paper inside and leave to cool slightly.

5 To make the filling, peel and grate the celeriac into a bowl and sprinkle well with lemon juice. Blend the blue cheese and fromage frais together and mix with the celeriac and a little black pepper.

6 Unroll the roulade, spread with the filling and roll up again. Serve at once or wrap loosely and chill.

BRAISED CELERY WITH GOAT'S CHEESE

THE SHARP FLAVOUR OF THE CELERY IN THIS DISH IS PERFECTLY COMPLEMENTED BY THE MILD YET TANGY GOAT'S CHEESE. THIS RECIPE IS AN EXAMPLE OF QUICK AND EASY PREPARATION TO MAKE A DELICIOUS ACCOMPANIMENT TO GRILLED MEAT OR STUFFED PANCAKES.

SERVES FOUR

INGREDIENTS
   25g/1oz/2 tbsp butter
   1 head of celery, thinly sliced
   175g/6oz mild medium-fat
     goat's cheese
   45–60ml/3–4 tbsp single cream
   salt and freshly ground black pepper

1 Preheat the oven to 180°C/350°F/
Gas 4 and lightly butter a medium-size
shallow ovenproof dish.

2 Melt the butter in a heavy-based
saucepan and fry the thinly sliced celery
for 2–3 minutes, stirring frequently. Add
45–60ml/3–4 tbsp water to the pan, heat
gently and then cover and simmer over a
gentle heat for 5–6 minutes, until the
celery is nearly tender and the water has
almost evaporated.

3 Remove the pan from the heat and
stir in the goat's cheese and cream.
Taste and season with salt and pepper,
then turn into the prepared dish.

4 Cover the dish with some buttered
greaseproof paper and bake for about
10–12 minutes. Serve at once.

CELERY, AVOCADO AND WALNUT SALAD

THE CRUNCHINESS OF THE CELERY AND WALNUTS CONTRASTS PERFECTLY WITH THE SMOOTH AVOCADO. SERVE IT WITH A SOURED CREAM DRESSING AS SUGGESTED, OR SIMPLY DRESSED WITH A LITTLE OLIVE OIL AND FRESHLY SQUEEZED LEMON JUICE.

SERVES FOUR

INGREDIENTS
   3 bacon rashers (optional)
   8 tender white or green celery stalks,
     very thinly sliced
   3 spring onions, finely chopped
   50g/2oz/½ cup chopped walnuts
   1 ripe avocado
   lemon juice
For the dressing
   120ml/4fl oz/½ cup soured cream
   15ml/1 tbsp olive oil
   a pinch of cayenne pepper

1 Dry-fry the bacon, if using, until
golden and then chop into small pieces
and place in a salad bowl with the celery,
spring onions and walnuts.

2 Halve the avocado and, using a very
sharp knife, cut into thin slices. Peel
away the skin from each slice and then
sprinkle generously with lemon juice and
add to the celery mixture.

3 Lightly beat the soured cream, olive
oil and cayenne pepper together in a jug
or small bowl. Either fold carefully into
the salad or serve separately.

STUFFED ARTICHOKES

THE AMOUNT OF STUFFING NEEDED FOR THIS DISH DEPENDS ON THE SIZE OF THE ARTICHOKES — IF THEY ARE SMALL YOU COULD SERVE ONE PER PERSON. TO INCREASE THE AMOUNT OF STUFFING, ADD EXTRA MOZZARELLA AND LEEK RATHER THAN BACON.

SERVES FOUR

INGREDIENTS
2 large or 4 medium globe artichokes,
    trimmed
lemon juice
For the stuffing
25g/1oz/2 tbsp butter
2–3 small leeks, sliced
2–3 bacon rashers, chopped (optional)
75g/3oz mozzarella cheese, cubed
25–40g/1–1½oz/½–¾ cup fresh brown
    or white breadcrumbs
5ml/1 tsp chopped fresh basil
salt and freshly ground black pepper
fresh basil leaves, to garnish

1 Place the artichokes in a large saucepan of salted water. Bring to the boil, cover and cook for 35–40 minutes or until a lower leaf comes away easily.

3 Drain the artichokes, upside-down, and, when cool enough to handle, cut in half from top to bottom using a sharp knife. Remove the inner leaves, pull out and discard the choke and then sprinkle the inside and base liberally with lemon juice to prevent discoloration.

4 Preheat the grill. Spoon a little of the stuffing into each artichoke half and place them in a single layer in an ovenproof dish. Set under a moderately hot grill and grill for 5–6 minutes until the stuffing is golden brown. Serve garnished with basil leaves.

2 To make the stuffing, melt the butter in a saucepan and gently fry the leeks for 2–3 minutes. Add the bacon, if using, and continue frying until the leeks are soft and the bacon lightly golden brown. Remove the pan from the heat and stir in the mozzarella cubes, breadcrumbs, chopped fresh basil and seasoning to taste.

SAMPHIRE WITH CHILLED FISH CURRY

EVEN IF YOU'RE A BIG CURRY FAN, DON'T BE TEMPTED TO ADD TOO MUCH CURRY PASTE TO THIS DISH.
YOU NEED ONLY THE MEREST HINT OF MILD CURRY PASTE SO THAT THE FLAVOUR OF THE SAMPHIRE AND
FISH CAN STILL BE APPRECIATED.

SERVES FOUR

INGREDIENTS
  175g/6oz samphire
  350g/12oz fresh salmon steak or fillet
  350g/12oz lemon sole fillets
  fish stock or water
  115g/4oz large peeled prawns
  25g/1oz/2 tbsp butter
  1 small onion, very finely chopped
  10ml/2 tsp mild curry paste
  5–10ml/1–2 tsp apricot jam
  150ml/¼ pint/⅔ cup soured cream
  a sprig of mint, to garnish (optional)

1 Trim the samphire and blanch in boiling water for about 5 minutes until tender. Drain and set aside.

2 Place the salmon and lemon sole in a large frying pan, cover with fish stock or water and bring to the boil. Reduce the heat, cover and cook for 6–8 minutes until the fish is tender.

COOK'S TIP
As the samphire has a fresh salty tang of the sea, there is no need to add extra salt to this recipe.

3 Transfer the fish to a plate and, when cool enough to handle, break the salmon and sole into bite-size pieces, removing any skin and bones. Place in a mixing bowl with the prawns.

4 Melt the butter in a saucepan and gently fry the onion for 3–4 minutes until soft but not brown. Add the curry paste, cook for 30 seconds, then remove from the heat. Stir in the jam. Allow to cool and then stir in the soured cream.

5 Pour the curry cream over the fish. Arrange the samphire around the edge of a serving plate and spoon the fish into the centre. Garnish with a sprig of mint.

FENNEL AND MUSSEL PROVENÇAL

SERVES FOUR

INGREDIENTS

2 large fennel bulbs
1.75kg/4–4½lb fresh mussels in
    their shells, well scrubbed under
    cold water and beards removed
175ml/6fl oz/¾ cup water
a sprig of thyme
25g/1oz/2 tbsp butter
4 shallots, finely chopped
1 garlic clove, crushed
250ml/8fl oz/1 cup white wine
10ml/2 tsp plain flour
175ml/6fl oz/¾ cup single cream
15ml/1 tbsp chopped fresh parsley
salt and freshly ground black pepper
a sprig of dill, to garnish

1 Trim the fennel, cut into slices
5mm/¼in thick and then cut into
1cm/½in sticks. Cook in a little salted
water until just tender, then drain.

2 Discard any mussels that are
damaged or do not close. Put in a large
saucepan, add the water and thyme,
cover tightly, bring to the boil and cook
for about 5 minutes until the mussels
open, shaking occasionally.

3 Transfer the mussels to a plate and
discard any that are unopened. When
cool enough to handle, remove them
from their shells, reserving a few in their
shells for the garnish.

4 Melt the butter in a saucepan and fry
the shallots and garlic for 3–4 minutes
until softened but not browned. Add the
fennel, fry briefly for 30–60 seconds and
then stir in the wine and simmer gently
until the liquid is reduced by half.

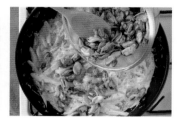

5 Blend the flour with a little extra wine
or water. Add the cream, parsley and
seasoning to the saucepan and heat
gently. Stir in the blended flour and the
mussels. Cook over a low heat until the
sauce thickens. Season and pour into a
warmed serving dish. Garnish with dill
and the reserved mussels in their shells.

BRAISED FENNEL WITH TOMATOES

SERVES FOUR

INGREDIENTS

3 small fennel bulbs
30–45ml/2–3 tbsp olive oil
5–6 shallots, sliced
2 garlic cloves, crushed
4 tomatoes, peeled and chopped
about 175ml/6fl oz/¾ cup dry
    white wine
15ml/1 tbsp chopped fresh basil or
    2.5ml/½ tsp dried
40–50g/1½–2oz/¾–1cup fresh white
    breadcrumbs
salt and freshly ground black pepper

1 Preheat the oven to 150°C/300°F/
Gas 2. Trim the fennel bulbs and cut into
slices about 1cm/½ in thick.

2 Heat the olive oil in a large saucepan
and fry the shallots and garlic for about
4–5 minutes over a moderate heat until
the shallots are slightly softened. Add the
tomatoes, stir-fry briefly and then stir in
150ml/¼ pint/⅔ cup of the wine, the basil
and seasoning. Bring to the boil, add the
fennel, then cover and cook for 5 minutes.

3 Arrange the fennel in layers in an
ovenproof dish. Pour over the tomato
mixture and sprinkle the top with half the
breadcrumbs. Bake in the oven for about
1 hour. From time to time, press down on
the breadcrumb crust with the back of a
spoon and sprinkle over another layer of
breadcrumbs and a little more of the
wine. The crust slowly becomes golden
brown and very crunchy.

ROOTS

Roots are the mainstays of our winter meals. Parsnips, turnips,
swedes and potatoes combine to make wonderful warming stews.
Jerusalem artichokes are another winter favourite and, as winter
turns to spring, young carrots and Jersey Royal potatoes appear.
Exotic roots such as sweet potatoes and yams are available
almost all year round, and look out too for salsify — a root
vegetable that can be enjoyed whatever the season.

POTATOES

History

The potato originates from South America. Most people learned at school that Sir Walter Raleigh brought the tubers to England from Virginia, but this never convinced historians as the potato was completely unknown in North America until the eighteenth century. They now believe that Sir Francis Drake was responsible. In 1586, after battling against the Spaniards in the Caribbean, Drake stopped to pick up provisions from Cartegena in northern Colombia – and these included tobacco and potato tubers. En route home, he stopped off at Roanoke Island, off the coast of Virginia. The first group of English colonists had been sponsored to settle there by Sir Walter Raleigh but by this time they had had enough. Drake brought them back to England, along with some of Raleigh's men and, of course, the provisions – including the potato tubers.

Potatoes apparently fascinated Queen Elizabeth and intrigued horticulturists, but they were not an overnight success among the people. The wealthy frequently reviled them as being flavourless and the food of the poor. People distrusted the fact that they reached maturity while underground, believing them to be the work of the devil. In Scotland, Presbyterian ministers darkly advised their congregations that there was no mention of potatoes in the Bible, and thus the eating of them was an ungodly act!

In spite of such a bad press, potatoes nevertheless were slowly recognized for their merit. By 1650 they were the staple food of Ireland, and elsewhere in Europe potatoes began to replace wheat as the most important crop, both for people and for livestock. In an early English cookery book, *Adam's Luxury and Eve's Cookery*, there are 20 different recipes for cooking and serving potatoes.

The first mention of potatoes in North America is in 1719 in Londonderry, New Hampshire. They arrived not from the south, but via Irish settlers who brought their potatoes with them.

The current popularity of potatoes is probably thanks to a Frenchman called Antoine-Auguste Parmentier. A military pharmacist of the latter part of the eighteenth century, Parmentier recognized the virtues of the potato, both for its versatility and as an important food for the poor, and set out to improve its image. He persuaded Louis XVI to allow him ostentatiously to grow potatoes on royal land around the palace in Versailles to impress the fashion-conscious Parisians. He also produced a court dinner in which each course contained potatoes. Gradually, eating potatoes became chic, first among people in the French court and then in French society. Today, if you see *Parmentier* in a recipe or on a menu, it means "with potato".

Nutrition

Potatoes are an important source of carbohydrate. Once thought to be fattening, we now know that, on the contrary, potatoes can be an excellent part of a calorie-controlled diet – provided, of course, they are not fried in oil or mashed with too much butter. Potatoes are also a very good source (and during winter sometimes the main source) of vitamin C, and they also contain potassium, iron and vitamin B.

Varieties

There are more than 400 varieties of potato but unless you are a gardener, you will find only some 15 varieties generally available. Thanks to labelling laws, packaged potatoes carry their names which makes it easier to learn to differentiate between the varieties and find out which potato is good for what.

New Potatoes

Carlingford: Available as a new potato or as main crop, Carlingford has a close white flesh.

Jersey Royal: Often the first new potato of the season, Jersey Royals have been shipped from Jersey for over a hundred years and have acquired an enviable reputation among everyone who enjoys good food. Boiled or steamed and then served with butter and a sprinkling of parsley, they cannot be beaten.

Jersey Royals are kidney-shaped, with yellow firm flesh and a distinctive flavour. Don't confuse Jersey Royals with Jersey Whites, which are actually Maris Pipers, grown in Jersey.

Maris Bard: A regularly shaped, slightly waxy potato with white flesh.

Maris Peer: This variety has dry firm flesh and a waxy texture and doesn't disintegrate when cooked – consequently, it is good in salads.

Main Crop Potatoes

Desirée: A potato with a pink skin and yellow soft-textured flesh. It is good for baking, chipping, roasting and mashing.

Estima: A good all-rounder with yellow flesh and pale skin.

Golden Wonder: A russet-skinned potato that was the original favourite for making crisps. It has an excellent, distinctive flavour, and should you find them for sale, buy them at once for baked potatoes. They are also good boiled or roasted.

Kerr's Pink: A good cooking potato with pink skin and creamy flesh.

King Edward: Probably the best known of British potatoes, although not the best in flavour. King Edwards are creamy white in colour with a slightly floury texture.

Red King Edwards are virtually identical except for their red skin. Both are good roasted or baked. However, the flesh disintegrates when boiled, so while good for mashing do not use King Edwards if you want whole boiled potatoes.

Maris Piper: This is a widely grown variety of potato, popular with growers and cooks because it is good for all kinds of cooking methods – baking, chipping, roasting and mashing. It has a pale, smooth skin and creamy white flesh.

Oppoisite: Maris Bard potatoes
Above: Kerr's pink (left) and Maris Piper (right) potatoes
Right: Romano potatoes

Pentland Dell: A long, oval-shaped potato with a floury texture that does tend to disintegrate when boiled. It is popular for roasting as the outside becomes soft when par-boiled and then crisps up with the fat during roasting.

Romano: The Romano has a distinctive red skin with creamy flesh and is a good all-rounder, similar to Desirée.

Wilja: Introduced from Holland, this is a pale, yellow-fleshed potato with a good, sweet flavour and waxy texture.

Other Varieties

Although most of these varieties are also main crop, they are less widely available than those listed above but they are increasingly sold in supermarkets. They are recommended for salads but are also excellent sautéed or simply boiled.

Cara: A large main crop potato, which is excellent baked or boiled but is a good all-rounder.

Finger Potatoes: Thumb-size, long baby potatoes are sometimes called finger potatoes or fingerlings. Among the many varieties are the German Lady's Finger. Since they are new crop potatoes, they need simply be boiled and then served either in salads or with a little butter and a sprinkling of parsley.

La Ratte: A French potato with a smooth skin and waxy yellow flesh. It has a chestnut flavour and is good in salads.

Linzer Delikatess: These small, kidney-shaped potatoes look a little like Jersey Royals but have a pale smooth skin. They do not have much taste and are best in salads where their flavour can be enhanced with other ingredients.

Pink Fir Apple: This is an old English variety, with pink skin and smooth yellow flesh. It is becoming increasingly popular and has a distinctive flavour.

Opposite above: Cara (left) and Estima (right) potatoes
Opposite below: Linzer Delikatess potatoes
Above: Desirée (left) and King Edward (right) potatoes
Right: Finger potatoes

Purple Congo: If you want to startle your friends, serve some of these striking purple-blue potatoes. There are several varieties of blue potato, ranging from a pale lavender to a purple-black, but one of the most popular is the Purple Congo, which is a wonderful deep purple. They are best boiled and served simply with a little butter, and do retain their colour when cooked.

Truffe de Chine: Another deep purple, almost black potato, of unknown origin but now grown in France. It has a nutty, slightly mealy flavour and is best served in a salad with a simple dressing. Like the Purple Congo, it retains its colour after being cooked.

Recommended Varieties for Cooking

Baking: As for roasting, use potatoes with a floury texture, such as Golden Wonder,

Pentland Dell, King Edward and Maris Piper.

Boiling: Jersey Royal, Maris Bard and Maris Peer, or any of the Egyptian or Belgian new crop varieties. In addition, Pink Fir Apple, La Ratte and Linzer Delikatess are excellent.

Chipping: King Edward, Golden Wonder, Romano, Maris Piper and Desirée.

Mashing: Golden Wonder, Maris Piper, King Edward, Wilja, Romano and Pentland Dell.

Roasting: Pentland Dell, Golden Wonder, Maris Piper, King Edward, Desiree and Romano are among the best roasting potatoes. Ideally, use potatoes with a floury texture.

Salads: All the small, specialist potatoes, such as La Ratte, Pink Fir Apple and Linzer Delikatess as well as Finger Potatoes and small new potatoes.

Sautéing: Any waxy type of potato, such as Maris Bard, Maris Peer, any of the specialist potatoes, and Romano and Maris Piper.

Buying and Storing

Potatoes should always be stored in a dark, cool, dry place. If they are stored exposed to the light, green patches will develop which can be poisonous, and they will go mouldy if kept in the damp. When buying potatoes in bulk, it is best to buy them in paper sacks rather than plastic bags as humid conditions will cause them to go rotten. Similarly, if you buy potatoes in polythene bags, remove them when you get home and place them in a vegetable rack or in a paper bag, in a dark place.

Main crop potatoes will keep for several months in the right conditions but will gradually lose their nutritional value. New potatoes should be eaten within two or three days as they will go mouldy if stored for too long.

Preparing

Most of the minerals and vitamins that are contained in potatoes are found in or just below the skin. It is therefore better to eat potatoes in their skins. New potatoes need only be washed under running water; older potatoes need to be scrubbed.

If you peel potatoes, use a peeler that removes only the very top surface (see below left) or, alternatively, for salads and cold dishes, boil the potatoes in their skins and peel when cool.

Cooking

Baking: Cook baked potatoes in a low oven for well-browned and crunchy skins and fluffy flesh. Baked potatoes can be cooked more quickly in a microwave oven; for a crunchy texture to the skin place them in a hot oven for 10 minutes.

Boiling: It is impossible to generalize on how long to boil as it depends so much on the variety of potato. Try to cut your potatoes to an even size (new potatoes should not need to be cut), salt the water if liked, cover and cook over a moderate heat. Don't boil potatoes too fiercely; old ones especially may disintegrate and leave you with a pan of starchy water.

Chips: Home-cooked chips are a treat worth making occasionally instead of the convenient but otherwise disappointing oven chips. However, they are fatty and therefore not good for you when eaten in great quantities or too frequently.

To make them, cut the potatoes into even-size chips and place in a bowl of cold water for about 10 minutes before frying. Drain and then dry in a piece of muslin or a dish towel before frying. Fry only as many chips as will comfortably sit in the fat. Halfway through cooking, drain them and allow the oil to come back to temperature before plunging the chips back in. This browns the chips and they don't soak up excessive amounts of oil. Be warned; the cooking smells from making chips tend to linger!

Mashing: Boil the potatoes until tender, drain thoroughly and then tip them back into the pan; mash with a little milk and butter using a potato masher (see below right), and season to taste with a little salt, if necessary, and pepper. Never use a food processor or liquidizer: the potatoes will turn into an inedible thick grey paste. You may lightly whisk potatoes with a fork after mashing to fluff them up but no more – for once modern machines have not improved on the basic utensil.

Roast potatoes: The best roast potatoes are made using a floury textured potato such as Maris Piper or King Edward. Wash and then cut them into even-size chunks and par-boil in lightly salted water until they begin to go tender and the outside looks soft. Drain them through a sieve or colander and then tip them back into the saucepan, put the lid on and shake the pan two or three times. This roughens up the surface of the potato. Place the potatoes in a dish of hot oil or fat, or round a joint of meat, and turn them over so that they are evenly coated. Roast them in the oven for 40-50 minutes until golden. Serve as soon as possible once cooked as the outsides become leathery if they are kept in a warm oven for too long.

Sautéing: There are various ways to sauté potatoes and no one way is better than another. For sautéed sliced potatoes, par-boil whole potatoes for 5–10 minutes until they begin to soften. Drain them thoroughly and then slice into thick rounds. Using sunflower oil or a mixture of sunflower and olive oil (not butter as it will burn), fry them in a large frying pan. Turn the potatoes occasionally and cook until evenly browned. For sautéed, diced potatoes, cut the potatoes into small cubes, blanch for 2 minutes and then drain well. Either fry them on the stove or cook them in a little oil in the oven; turn them once or twice to brown evenly.

Steaming: New potatoes are excellent steamed. Place them on a bed of mint in a steamer or a colander over a pan of boiling water for 15-20 minutes.

Opposite above: Purple Congo potatoes
Opposite below:Truffe de Chine (left) and
Pink Fir Apple (right) potatoes

PARSNIPS

There's something very old-fashioned about parsnips. They conjure up images of cold winter evenings and warm comforting broths supped in front of a blazing wood fire. Nowadays parsnips are available all year round, but many people still feel they belong to winter, adding their characteristic flavour to soups and stews.

Parsnips are related to carrots and they are similarly sweet but have a distinct earthy flavour that blends well with other root vegetables and is also enhanced with spices and garlic.

History

Parsnips have a very long history. The Romans grew and cooked them to make broths and stews. When they conquered Gaul and Britain, the Romans discovered that root vegetables grown in northerly areas had a better flavour than those grown in the south – they may have been the first to decree that parsnips should be eaten after the first frost!

Throughout the Dark Ages and early Middle Ages, parsnips were the main starchy vegetable for ordinary people (the potato had yet to be introduced). Parsnips were not only easy to grow but were a welcome food to eat during the lean winter months. They were also valued for their sugar content. Sweet parsnip dishes like jam and desserts became part of traditional English cookery, and they were also commonly used for making beer and wine. Parsnip wine is still one of the most popular of the country wines, with a beautiful golden colour and a rich sherry-like flavour.

Nutrition

Parsnips contain moderate amounts of vitamins A and C, along with some of the B vitamins. They are also a source of calcium, iron and potassium.

Buying and Storing

Parsnips are really a winter vegetable, although nowadays they are available all year round. Tradition has it that parsnips are best after the first frost, but many people like the very young tender parsnips available in the early summer. When buying parsnips, choose small or

medium-size specimens as the large ones tend to be rather fibrous. They should feel firm and be a pale ivory colour without any sprouting roots. Store parsnips in a cool place, ideally an airy larder or cool outhouse, where they will keep well for 8–10 days.

Preparing

Very small parsnips require little or no peeling; just trim the ends and cook according to your recipe. Medium-size and large parsnips need to be peeled. Larger parsnips also need to have the woody core removed; if it is cut out before cooking, the parsnips will cook more quickly and evenly.

Cooking

Roast parsnips are best if par-boiled for a few minutes before adding to the roasting dish. Very young parsnips can be roasted whole but larger ones are best halved or quartered lengthways. Roast in butter or oil for about 40 minutes in an oven preheated to 200°C/400°F/Gas 6.

To boil parsnips, cut them into pieces about 5cm/2in long and boil for 15–20 minutes until tender. When boiled briefly like this, they keep their shape, but when added to a casserole or stew they will eventually disintegrate. Don't worry if this happens; parsnips need plenty of cooking so that the flavour can blend with the other ingredients in the pot.

JERUSALEM ARTICHOKES

Jerusalem artichokes are related to the sunflower and have nothing to do with Jerusalem. One explanation for their name is that they were christened girasole, "Jerusalem", because their yellow flowers turned towards the sun. The Italian name for the Jerusalem artichoke is *girasole articocco*.

These small knobbly tubers have a lovely distinct flavour and are good in Palestine soup, a popular classic recipe. They are also delicious baked or braised.

History

Jerusalem artichokes are thought to have come from the central United States and Canada, where they were cultivated by Native Americans as long ago as the fifteenth century. However, many writers have alluded to the fact that they cause "wind", which tempers their popularity.

Buying and Storing

Jerusalem artichokes are at their best during winter and early spring. They are invariably knobbly but if possible buy neat ones with the minimum of knobs to save waste. The skins should be pale brown without any dark or soft patches. If they are stored in a cool dark place they will keep well for up to 10 days.

Preparing

The white flesh of artichokes turns a purplish brown when exposed to light, so when peeling or slicing them raw, place them in a bowl of acidulated water (water to which the juice of about half a lemon has been added). Because artichokes are so knobbly, it is often easier to boil them in acidulated water in their skins and peel them afterwards – the cooked skins should slip off easily.

Cooking

Jerusalem artichokes can be cooked in many of the ways in which you would cook potatoes or parsnips. They are excellent roasted, sautéed or dipped in batter and fried, but first par-boil them for 10-15 minutes until nearly tender. For creamed artichokes, mix with potatoes in equal amounts; this slightly blunts their flavour, making a tasty side dish which is not too overpowering.

Opposite: Parsnips
Below: Jerusalem artichokes

TURNIPS AND SWEDES

Turnips and swedes are both members of the cabbage family and are closely related to each other – so closely that it is not surprising that their names are often confused. For instance, swedes are sometimes called Swedish turnips or swede-turnips and in Scotland, where they are thought of as turnips, they are called neeps.

Nowadays, the confusion is not quite so acute. Many greengrocers and super-markets sell early or baby turnips or, better still, French turnips – *navets*.

Both are small and white, tinged either with green or in the case of *navets*, with pink or purple. Consequently, people are learning to tell their swedes from their turnips and are also discovering what a delicious vegetable the turnip is.

History

Turnips have been cultivated for many centuries, principally as an important livestock feed but also for humans. Although they were not considered the food of gourmets, they have been grown

by poorer families as a useful addition to the winter table.

Swedes were known as turnip-rooted cabbages until the 1780s, when Sweden began exporting the vegetable to Britain and the shorter name resulted.

Until recently, turnips and swedes have not enjoyed a very high reputation among cooks in many parts of the world. This is partly because they are perceived as cattle food and partly because few people have taken the trouble to find acceptable ways of cooking them. Schools and other

institutions tend to boil and then mash them to a watery pulp, and for many people this is the only way they have eaten either vegetable.

The French, in contrast, have had far more respect for the turnip, at least. For centuries they have devised recipes for their delicate *navets*, roasting them, caramelizing them in sugar and butter or simply steaming and serving with butter. Young, tender turnips have also been popular all over the Mediterranean region for many years, and there are many dishes using turnips with fish, poultry, or teamed with tomatoes, onions and spinach.

Nutrition

Both turnips and swedes are a good source of calcium and potassium.

Varieties

French **navets**, small, round, squashed-shaped turnips tinged with pink or purple, are increasingly available in greengrocers and supermarkets in the spring. Less common, but even more prized by the French, are the long carrot-shaped turnips, called **vertus**. English turnips are generally larger and are mainly green and white.

Both have the characteristic peppery flavour, but this is less pronounced in *navets* which are generally sweeter.

Swedes generally have a more substantial, fuller-bodied flavour than turnips but at their best have a subtle, pleasant taste. **Marian** is a yellow-fleshed variety with a distinct "swede" flavour, whereas white fleshed swedes, such as **Merrick**, have a watery, "turnip-like" flavour.

Buying and Storing

Turnips: If possible, buy French *navets* or failing that, the smallest and youngest turnips, available in the shops from spring. They should be firm, smooth and unblemished, ideally with fresh green tops. Store in a cool dry place.
Swedes: Unlike turnips, swedes generally seem to come large. However, if it is possible, choose small swedes with smooth and unblemished skins as large ones are likely to be tough and fibrous. Store as for turnips.

Preparing and Cooking

Turnips: Young turnips should not need peeling; simply trim, then simmer or steam until tender. They are delicious raw, thinly sliced or grated into salads.

Peel older turnips (see below) and then slice or dice before cooking. Remember, turnips are members of the cabbage family and older specimens particularly can show signs of that unpleasant cabbage rankness if overcooked. To avoid this, blanch turnips if they are to be served as a vegetable dish, or add sparingly to soups and casseroles, so that the rank flavour is dispersed.

Swedes: Peel to remove the skin and then cut into chunks (see below). Swedes will disintegrate if overcooked, and they are unpleasantly raw tasting if not cooked sufficiently. The only answer is to check frequently while they are cooking. Swedes are particularly good when teamed with other root vegetables in soups and casseroles, adding a pleasant, slightly nutty flavour.

*Opposite: Navets and turnips
Below: Swedes*

CARROTS

After potatoes, carrots are without doubt our best-known and best-loved root vegetable. In the days when vegetables were served merely as an accessory to meat, carrots always made an appearance – often overcooked but still eaten up because, we were told, they helped you to see in the dark.

Carrots have many different flavours, depending on how they are cooked. Young, new season carrots braised in butter and a splash of water are intensely flavoured and sweet; when steamed, they are tender and melting. Carrots grated into salads are fresh and clean tasting, while in casseroles they are savoury with the characteristic "carrot" flavour. In soups they are fragrant and mild, and in cakes their flavour can hardly be detected, yet their sweetness adds richness.

History

Until the Middle Ages, carrots were purple. The orange carrots came from Holland, from where they were exported during the seventeenth and eighteenth centuries. Although purple and white carrots continued to be eaten in France, nowadays they are something of a rarity.

Nutrition

The carrot contains large amounts of carotene and vitamin A, along with useful amounts of vitamins B3, C and E. When eaten raw, they also provide good quantities of potassium, calcium, iron and zinc, but these are reduced when carrots are boiled.

The idea that carrots are good for your night sight originated in the Second World War. Early radar stations were established along the south and east coasts of England in 1939 to detect aggressors in the air or at sea. The Germans attributed this sudden remarkable night vision to the British habit of eating carrots. Indeed, the vitamin A in carrots forms retinol, a lack of which brings on night blindness.

Buying and Storing

Home-grown carrots are so much nicer than the shop-bought ones. Almost all vegetables have a better flavour if grown organically, but this is particularly true of carrots.

When buying carrots, look out for the very young, pencil-thin ones, which are beautifully tender either eaten raw or steamed for just a few minutes. Young carrots are commonly sold with their feathery tops intact, which should be fresh and green. Older carrots should be firm and unblemished. Avoid tired-looking carrots as they will have little nutritional value.

Carrots should not be stored for too long. They will keep for several days if stored in a cool, airy place or in the salad drawer of the fridge.

Preparing

Preparation depends on the age of the carrots. The valuable nutrients lie either in or just beneath the skin, so if the carrots are young, simply wash them under cold running water. Medium-size carrots may need to be scraped and large carrots will need either scraping or peeling.

Cooking

Carrots are excellent cooked or raw. Children often like raw carrots as they have a very sweet flavour. They can be cut into julienne strips, with a dressing added, or grated into salads and coleslaw – their juices run and blend wonderfully with the dressing. Carrots can be cooked in almost any way you choose. As an accompaniment, cut them into julienne strips and braise in butter and cider, or cook in the minimum of stock and toss in butter and a sprinkling of caraway seeds.

Roasted carrots are delicious, with a melt-in-the-mouth sweetness. Par-boil large ones first, but younger carrots can be quickly blanched or added direct to the roasting tin with a joint of meat.

HORSERADISH

Horseradish is grown for its pungent root, which is normally grated and mixed with cream or oil and vinegar and served with roast beef. Fresh horseradish is available in many supermarkets in the spring, and you can make your own horseradish sauce by simply peeling the root and then mixing 45ml/3 tbsp grated horseradish with 150m/¹/₄ pint/²/₃ cup whipping cream and adding a little Dijon mustard, vinegar and sugar to taste. As well as being excellent with hot or cold beef, horseradish sauce is delicious with smoked trout or mackerel or spread thinly on sandwiches with a fine pâté.

Left: Carrots
Right: Horseradish

BEETROOT

Experience of vinegar-sodden beetroot has doubtless put many people off beetroot. Those who love it know to buy their beetroot fresh, so that they can cook it themselves. It can be served in a number of different ways: baked and served with soured cream, braised in a creamy sauce, grated in a salad or used for the classic soup *borscht*.

History

Beetroot is closely related to sugar beet and mangelwurzels. As the demand for sugar increased over the centuries, when sugar could successfully be extracted from beet, sugar production became a big industry in Britain and Europe.

Mangelwurzels were eaten in parts of Europe and in England in times of famine, although they were primarily grown as cattle fodder.

Beetroot, however, has probably been eaten since Roman times. By the mid-nineteenth century it was clearly a very popular vegetable, and Mrs Beeton in her famous cookbook has 11 recipes for it, including a beetroot and carrot jam and beetroot fritters.

Nutrition

Beetroot is an excellent provider of potassium. The leaves, which have the flavour of spinach, are high in vitamin A, iron and calcium.

Buying and Storing

If possible, buy small beetroots which have their whiskers intact and have at least 5cm/2in of stalk at the top; if they are too closely cropped they will bleed during cooking. Beetroots will keep for several weeks if stored in a cool place.

Preparing

To cook beetroot whole, first rinse under cold running water. Cut the stalks to about 2.5cm/1in above the beetroot and don't cut away the root or peel it – or the glorious deep red colour will bleed away. When serving cold in salads, or where the recipe calls for chopped or grated beetroot, peel away the skin using a potato peeler or sharp knife.

Cooking

To bake in the oven, place the cleaned beetroot in a dish with a tight-fitting lid, and add 60-75ml/4-5 tbsp of water. Lay a double layer of foil over the dish before covering with the lid, then bake in a low oven for 2-3 hours or until the beetroot is tender. Check occasionally to ensure the pan doesn't dry out and to see whether the beetroot is cooked. It is ready when the skin begins to wrinkle and can be easily rubbed away with your fingers. Alternatively, simply wrap the beetroot in a double layer of foil and cook as above. To boil beetroot, prepare as above and simmer for about 1½ hours.

BEET GREENS

The tops of several root vegetables are not only edible, but are also extremely nutritious. Beet greens are particularly good, being very high in vitamins A and C, and indeed they have more iron and calcium than spinach itself. They are delicious, but not easily available unless you grow your own. If you are lucky enough to get some, boil the greens for a few minutes, then drain well and serve with butter or olive oil.

Left: Beetroot
Opposite above: Scorzonera
Opposite below: Salsify

SALSIFY AND SCORZONERA

These root vegetables are closely related to one another as well as to members of the same family as dandelion and lettuce. All have long tapering roots.

Salsify has a white or pale brownish skin and scorzonera, sometimes called black salsify, has a black skin. They both have pale creamy flesh and a fairly similar flavour reminiscent of artichokes and asparagus. Salsify is said to have the superior flavour and has been likened to oysters (it is sometimes referred to as the oyster plant), although many people fail to detect this.

Both salsify and scorzonera make an unusual and pleasant accompaniment, either creamed or fried in butter. They can also be also used in soups.

History

Salsify is native to the Mediterranean but now grows in most areas of Europe and North America. Scorzonera is a southern European plant.

Both roots are classified as herbs and, like many wild plants and herbs, their history is bound up with their use in medicines. The roots, together with their leaves and flowers, were used for the treatment of heartburn, loss of appetite and various liver diseases.

Buying and Storing

Choose specimens that are firm and smooth and, if possible, still with their tops on, which should look fresh and lively. Salsify will keep for several days stored in a cool dark place.

Preparing

Salsify and scorzonera are difficult to clean and peel. Either scrub the root under cold running water and then peel after cooking, or peel with a very sharp stainless steel knife (see below). As the flesh discolours quickly, place the trimmed pieces into acidulated water with added lemon juice.

Cooking

Cut into short lengths and simmer for 20–30 minutes until tender. Drain well and sauté in butter, or serve with lemon juice, melted butter or chopped parsley.

Alternatively, they can be puréed for soups, or mashed. Cooked and cooled salsify and scorzonera can be served in a mustard or garlic vinaigrette along with a simple salad.

EXOTIC ROOTS

Throughout the tropical regions of the world all sorts of tubers are grown and used for a fabulous variety of dishes. Yams, sweet potatoes, cassava and taro, to name but a few, are for many people a staple food, not only cooked whole as a vegetable accompaniment, but ground or pounded for bread and cakes. There is an enormous variety of these tropical and subtropical tubers, and while they cannot be cultivated in a moderate climate, the more common tubers are now widely available in specialist shops and in most supermarkets.

SWEET POTATOES

Sweet potatoes are another one of those vegetables that once tasted, are never forgotten. They are, as their name suggests, sweet, but they also have a slightly spicy taste. It's this distinct sweet and savoury flavour which makes them such an excellent foil to many savoury dishes and they are fittingly paired with meat dishes that need a touch of sweetness, like turkey or pork.

History

Sweet potatoes are native to tropical America, but today they are grown all over the tropical world. They have been grown in South America from before the Inca civilizations and were introduced into Spain before the ordinary potato. They also have a long history of cultivation in Asia spreading from Polynesia to New Zealand during the fourteenth century.

They are an important staple food in the Caribbean and southern United States, and many famous recipes feature them. Candied sweet potatoes are served with turkey at Thanksgiving all over the United States, while Jamaica and the West Indies abound with sweet potato dishes, from the simple baked potato to Caribbean pudding, a sweet and spicy dish with sweet potatoes, coconut, limes and cinnamon.

Sweet potatoes appear to have been introduced to England even earlier than regular potatoes. Henry VIII was said to have been very partial to them baked in a pie, believing they would improve his love life! If Henry VIII was eating sweet potatoes in the early/mid-sixteenth century, then it is probable that he received them via the Spanish, who, thanks to Christopher Columbus, were busy conquering the New World, thus experiencing a whole range of tropical vegetables and fruit.

Varieties

The skin colour ranges from white to pink to reddish brown. The red-skinned variety, which has a whitish flesh, is the one most commonly used in African and Caribbean cooking.

Buying and Storing

Choose small or medium-size ones if possible as larger specimens tend to be rather fibrous. They should be firm and evenly shaped; avoid those that seem withered, have damp patches or are sprouting. They will keep for several days in a cool place.

Preparing and Cooking

If baking, scrub the potatoes well and cook exactly as you would for ordinary potatoes. To boil, either cook in their skins and remove these after cooking, or peel and place in acidulated water (water to which lemon juice has been added). This prevents them turning brown and it is worth boiling them in lightly acidulated water for the same reason. Sweet potatoes can be cooked in any of the ways you would cook ordinary potatoes – roast, boiled, mashed or baked. However, the the flavour of sweet potatoes does not enhance creamy or gratin-type dishes.

It is preferable to roast or sauté sweet potatoes with onions and other savoury ingredients to bring out their flavour, or mash them and serve them American-style over chunks of chicken for a crusted chicken pie.

YAMS

Yams have been a staple food for many cultures for thousands of years. There are today almost countless varieties, of different shapes, sizes and colours and different names are used by different people. Most varieties are thought to have been native to China, although they found their way to Africa at a very early period and became a basic food, being easy to grow in tropical and sub-tropical conditions, and containing the essential carbohydrate of all staple foods.

Although cush-cush or Indian yam was indigenous to America, most yams were introduced to the New World as a result of the slave trade during the sixteenth century. Today with a huge variety of this popular vegetable available, there are innumerable recipes for yam, many probably not printed and published, but handed down by word of mouth from mother to daughter and making their appearance at mealtimes all over the hot regions of the world.

Varieties

The greater yam, as the name suggests, can grow to a huge size. A weight of 62kg/150lb has been recorded. The ones you are likely to find in shops will be about the size of a small marrow, although smaller yams are also available such as the sweet yam, which looks like a large potato and is normally covered with whiskery roots. All sizes have a coarse brown skin and can be white or red fleshed.

In Chinese stores, you may find the Chinese yam, which is a more elongated, club-like shape whose skin is covered with fine whiskers.

Buying and Storing

Look out for firm yams with unbroken skins. The flesh inside should be creamy and moist, and if you buy from a grocery, the shopkeeper may well cut open a yam so you can check that it is fresh. They can be stored for several weeks in a cool, dark place.

Preparing and Cooking

Peel away the skin thickly to remove the outer skin and the layer underneath that contains the poison dioscorine. This in fact is destroyed by cooking, but discard the peel carefully. Place the peeled yam in salted water as it discolours easily.

Yams, like potatoes, are used as the main starchy element in a meal, boiled and mashed, fried, sautéed or roasted. They tend to have an affinity with spicy sauces and are delicious cut into discs, fried and sprinkled with a little salt and cayenne pepper. African cooks often pound boiled yam to make a dough which is then served with spicy stews and soups.

TARO/EDDO/DASHEEN

Like yams, taro is another important tuber in tropical areas. For thousands of years it has been a staple food for many people. It has under many different names; in South-east Asia, South and Central America, all over Africa and in the Caribbean it is called variously eddo and dasheen.

There are two basic varieties of taro – a large barrel-shape tuber and a smaller variety, which is often called eddo or dasheen. They are all a dark mahogany brown with a rather shaggy skin, looking like a cross between a beetroot and a swede.

Although they look very similar, taro belongs to a completely different family from yam, and in flavour and texture is noticeably different. When boiled, it has a completely unique flavour, something like a floury water chestnut.

Buying and Storing

Try to buy small specimens; the really small smooth bulbs are tiny attachments to the larger taro and are either called eddoes or, rather sweetly, "sons of taro". Stored in a cool, dark place, they should keep for several weeks.

Opposite: Sweet potatoes
Above left: Yams

Preparing

Taros, like yams, contain a poison just under the skin which produces an allergic reaction. Consequently, either peel taros thickly, wearing rubber gloves, or cook in their skins. The toxins are completely eliminated by boiling, and the skins peel off easily, once cooked.

Cooking

Taros soak up large quantities of liquid during cooking, and this can be turned to advantage by cooking in well-flavoured stock or with fresh tomatoes and other vegetables. For this reason, they are excellent in soups and casseroles, adding bulk and flavour in a very similar way to potatoes. They can also be steamed or boiled, deep-fried or puréed for fritters but must be served hot as they become sticky if allowed to cool.

CALLALOO

Callaloo are the leaves of the taro plant, poisonous if eaten raw but used widely in Asian and Caribbean cooking. They are cooked thoroughly, then used for wrapping meat and vegetables. Callaloo can also be shredded and cooked together with pork, bacon, crab, prawns, okra, chilli, onions and garlic, along with lime and coconut milk to make one of the Caribbean's most famous dishes, named after the leaves themselves, the delicious Callaloo.

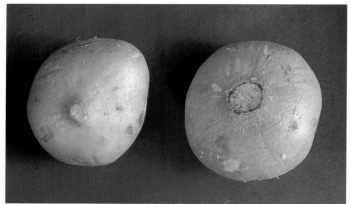

JICAMA

Also known as the Mexican potato, this large root vegetable is a native of central America. It has a thin brown skin and white, crunchy flesh which has a sweet, nutty taste. It can be eaten cooked in the same way as potatoes or sliced and added raw to salads.

Buy specimens that are firm to the touch. Jicama in good condition will keep for about two weeks if stored in a polythene bag in the fridge.

Top: Taros (eddoes or dasheens)
Above: Jicama
Left: Callaloo

CASSAVA/MANIOC/JUCA

This is another very popular West Indian root, included in numerous Caribbean dishes. It is native to Brazil, and found its way to the West Indies surprisingly via Africa, where it also became a popular vegetable. Known as cassava in the West Indies, it is called manioc or mandioc in Brazil, and juca or yucca is used in other parts of South America.

Cassava is used to make tapioca; and in South America a sauce and an intoxicating drink are prepared from the juice. However, in Africa and the West Indies it is eaten as a vegetable either boiled, baked or fried, or cooked and pounded to a dough to make *fufu*, a traditional savoury African pudding.

Right: Cassava
Below left: Ginger
Below right: Galangal

GINGER ᴬᴺᴰ GALANGAL

GINGER

Ginger is probably the world's most important and popular spice and is associated with a number of different cuisines – Chinese, Indian and Caribbean, to name but a few. Although it was known in Europe during the Roman period, it was still rare until the spice routes opened up trade in the sixteenth and seventeenth centuries. Like many spices, ginger has the quality of complementing and enhancing both sweet and savoury food, adding a fragrant spiciness to all sorts of dishes. However, while ground ginger is best in recipes which will be baked, and stem ginger, where the ginger is preserved in syrup, tastes wonderful in desserts, for savoury dishes, it is best always to use fresh root ginger.

Nowadays, the pale, knobbly roots of fresh root ginger are available in most supermarkets.Only buy a small quantity, as you will not need a great deal and it will not keep indefinitely.

To prepare, simply peel away the skin with a sharp knife and grate or thinly slice according to the recipe.

GREATER GALANGAL

Galangal looks similar to ginger except that the rhizome is thinner and the young shoots are bright pink. The roots should be prepared in the same way as fresh root ginger and can be used in curries and satay sauces.

ROOTS
RECIPES

For tasty, nourishing meals, you don't need to look further than roots, whether it is carrots, beetroot or the ever popular potato. Potatoes Dauphinois or Artichoke Rösti are the stuff of winter evenings — warm and filling, simple to make, great to eat. For something with a more exotic flavour, try Yam Fritters or Mediterranean Chicken with Turnips.

PATATAS BRAVAS

THIS IS A CLASSIC SPANISH TAPAS DISH OF DEEP-FRIED CUBES OF POTATO WITH A SPICY TOMATO SAUCE. SERVING TAPAS IS A GOOD WAY OF PROVIDING YOUR GUESTS WITH A WONDERFUL RANGE OF FLAVOURS AND TEXTURES.

SERVES FOUR

INGREDIENTS
   675g/1½lb potatoes, such as Maris
      Piper or Estima
   oil, for deep frying
For the sauce
   15ml/1 tbsp olive oil
   1 small onion, chopped
   1 garlic clove, crushed
   400g/14oz can tomatoes
   10ml/2 tsp Worcestershire sauce
   5ml/1 tsp wine vinegar
   about 5ml/1 tsp Tabasco sauce

1 Peel then cut the potatoes into small cubes. Place in a large bowl of cold water to remove the excess starch.

2 Heat the oil in a medium-size frying pan and fry the onion and garlic for 3–4 minutes until the onion is soft and just beginning to brown.

3 Pour the tomatoes into a blender or food processor, process until smooth then pour into the pan with the onion. Simmer, uncovered, over a moderate heat for 8–10 minutes until the mixture is thick and reduced, stirring occasionally.

4 Heat the oil in a deep fryer. Drain the potatoes and pat dry with kitchen paper. Fry the potatoes in the hot oil, in batches if necessary, until golden brown. Drain on kitchen paper.

5 Stir the Worcestershire sauce, the vinegar and Tabasco into the tomato mixture. Add the potatoes, stirring well so that all the potatoes are coated with the sauce. Spoon into individual serving dishes and serve at once.

POTATOES DAUPHINOIS

SERVES FOUR

INGREDIENTS
   675g/1½lb potatoes, peeled and
      thinly sliced
   1 garlic clove
   25g/1oz/2tbsp butter
   300ml/½ pint/1¼ cups single cream
   50ml/2fl oz/¼ cup milk
   salt and white pepper

1 Preheat the oven to 150°C/300°F/ Gas 2. Place the potato slices in a bowl of cold water to remove the excess starch. Drain and pat dry with kitchen paper.

2 Cut the garlic in half and rub the cut side around the inside of a wide shallow ovenproof dish then butter the dish. Blend the cream and milk in a jug.

3 Cover the base of the dish with a layer of potatoes. Dot a little butter over the potato layer, season with salt and pepper and then pour over a little of the cream and milk mixture.

4 Continue making layers, until all the ingredients have been used up, ending with a layer of cream.

5 Bake in the oven for about 1¼ hours. If the dish browns too quickly and seems to be drying out then cover with a lid or with a piece of foil. The potatoes are ready to eat when they are very soft and the top is golden brown.

COOK'S TIP
For a slightly speedier version of this recipe, par-boil the potato slices for 3–4 minutes. Drain and assemble as above. Cook at 160°C/325°F/Gas 3 for 45–50 minutes until the potatoes are completely tender.

PARSNIP AND CHESTNUT CROQUETTES

THE SWEET NUTTY TASTE OF CHESTNUTS BLENDS PERFECTLY WITH THE SIMILARLY SWEET BUT EARTHY FLAVOUR OF PARSNIPS. FRESH CHESTNUTS NEED TO BE PEELED BUT FROZEN CHESTNUTS ARE EASY TO USE AND ARE NEARLY AS GOOD AS FRESH FOR THIS RECIPE.

MAKES TEN TO TWELVE

INGREDIENTS
    450g/1lb parsnips, cut roughly into
      small pieces
    115g/4oz/1 cup frozen chestnuts
    25g/1oz/2 tbsp butter
    1 garlic clove, crushed
    15ml/1 tbsp chopped fresh coriander
    1 egg, beaten
    40–50g/1½–2oz fresh white
      breadcrumbs
    vegetable oil, for frying
    salt and freshly ground black pepper
    sprig of coriander, to garnish

1 Place the parsnips in a saucepan with enough water to cover. Bring to the boil, cover and simmer for 15–20 minutes until completely tender.

2 Place the frozen chestnuts in a pan of water, bring to the boil and simmer for 8–10 minutes until very tender. Drain, place in a bowl and mash roughly.

3 Melt the butter in a small saucepan and cook the garlic for 30 seconds. Drain the parsnips and mash with the garlic butter. Stir in the chestnuts and chopped coriander, then season well.

4 Take about 30-45ml/2-3 tbsp of the mixture at a time and form into small croquettes, about 7.5cm/3in long. Dip each one into the beaten egg and then roll in the fresh white breadcrumbs.

5 Heat a little oil in a frying pan and fry the croquettes for 3–4 minutes until golden, turning frequently so they brown evenly. Drain on kitchen paper and then serve at once, garnished with coriander.

PARSNIP, AUBERGINE <u>AND</u> CASHEW BIRYANI

<u>SERVES FOUR TO SIX</u>

INGREDIENTS

275g/10oz/1½ cups basmati rice
1 small aubergine, sliced
3 each parsnips and onions
2 garlic cloves
2.5cm/1in piece fresh root
   ginger, peeled
about 60ml/4 tbsp vegetable oil
175g/6oz/1½ cups unsalted
   cashew nuts
40g/1½oz/generous ¼ cup sultanas
1 red pepper, seeded and sliced
5ml/1 tsp ground cumin
5ml/1 tsp ground coriander
2.5ml/½ tsp chilli powder
120ml/4fl oz/½ cup natural yogurt
300ml/½ pint/1¼ cups vegetable
   or chicken stock
25g/1oz/2 tbsp butter
salt and freshly ground black pepper
2 hard-boiled eggs, quartered and
   sprigs of coriander, to garnish

1 Soak the rice for 40 minutes. Salt the aubergine and leave for 30 minutes. Rinse, pat dry and cut into bite-size pieces. Peel and core the parsnips. Cut into 1cm/⅓in pieces. Chop 1 onion and then combine it with the garlic and ginger in a food processor. Add 30–45ml/2–3 tbsp water and process the mixture again.

2 Slice the remaining onions. Heat 45ml/3 tbsp of oil in a flameproof casserole; fry gently for 15 minutes until they are golden. Remove and drain. Add 40g/1½oz of the cashew nuts to the pan and stir-fry for 2 minutes. Add the sultanas and fry until they swell. Remove and drain.

3 Add the aubergine and pepper to the pan and stir-fry for 4–5 minutes. Drain on kitchen paper. Fry the parsnips for 4–5 minutes. Stir in the remaining cashew nuts and fry for 1 minute. Transfer to the plate with the aubergines.

4 Add the remaining 15ml/1 tbsp of oil to the pan. Add the onion paste. Cook, stirring over a moderate heat for 4–5 minutes until the mixture turns golden. Stir in the cumin, coriander and chilli powder. Cook, stirring, for 1 minute, then reduce the heat and add the yogurt.

5 Bring the mixture slowly to the boil and stir in the stock, parsnips, aubergines and peppers. Season, cover and simmer for 30–40 minutes until the parsnips are tender and then transfer to an ovenproof casserole.

6 Preheat the oven to 150°C/300°F/ Gas 2. Drain the rice and add to 300ml/ ½ pint/1¼ cups of salted boiling water. Cook gently for 5–6 minutes until it is tender but slightly undercooked.

7 Drain the rice and pile it in a mound on top of the parsnips. Make a hole from the top to the base using the handle of a wooden spoon. Scatter the reserved fried onions, cashew nuts and sultanas over the rice and dot with butter. Cover with a double layer of foil and then secure in place with a lid.

8 Cook in the oven for 35–40 minutes. To serve, spoon the mixture on to a warmed serving dish and garnish with coriander sprigs and quartered eggs.

MEDITERRANEAN CHICKEN <u>WITH</u> TURNIPS

Turnips are popular in all parts of the Mediterrean, cooked with tomatoes and spinach in simple vegetarian dishes, or teamed with fish or poultry for a more substantial meal. This recipe comes from the eastern Mediterranean.

SERVES FOUR

INGREDIENTS

    30ml/2 tbsp sunflower oil
    8 chicken thighs or 4 chicken pieces
    4 small turnips
    2 onions, chopped
    2 garlic cloves, crushed
    6 tomatoes, peeled and chopped
    250ml/8fl oz/1 cup tomato juice
    250ml/8fl oz/1 cup chicken stock
    120ml/4fl oz/½ cup white wine
    5ml/1 tsp paprika
    a good pinch of cayenne pepper
    20 black olives, stoned
    ½ lemon, cut into wedges
    salt and freshly ground black pepper
    fresh parsley, to garnish
    couscous, to serve

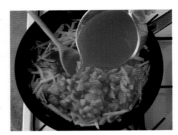

1 Preheat the oven to 160°C/325°F/ Gas 3. Heat 15ml/1 tbsp of the oil in a large frying pan and fry the chicken pieces until lightly browned. Peel the turnips and cut into julienne strips.

2 Transfer the chicken to a large casserole. Add the remaining oil to the pan and fry the onions and garlic for 4–5 minutes until lightly golden brown, stirring occasionally.

3 Add the turnip and stir-fry for about 2–3 minutes. Add the tomatoes, tomato juice, stock, wine, paprika, cayenne and seasoning. Bring to the boil. Pour over the chicken. Stir in the olives and lemon.

4 Cover tightly and cook in the oven for 1–1¼ hours until the chicken is tender.

5 Garnish with fresh parsley and serve on a bed of couscous.

SWEDE CRISPS

Tender slices of swede with a crunchy breadcrumb coating provide a feast for the senses. The slightly peppery flavour of swede is complemented by the spicy breadcrumb mixture.

SERVES FOUR

INGREDIENTS

    1 small swede
    50g/2oz/1 cup fresh brown or white
      breadcrumbs
    15ml/1 tbsp plain flour
    2.5ml/½ tsp paprika
    2.5ml/½ tsp ground coriander
    2.5ml/½ tsp ground cumin
    a pinch of cayenne pepper
    1 egg, beaten
    salt and freshly ground black pepper
    oil, for deep frying
    mango chutney, to serve

1 Peel the swede, cut in half and slice thinly. Cook in a pan of boiling water for 3–5 minutes until just tender. Drain well.

2 Mix together the breadcrumbs, flour, paprika, coriander, cumin, cayenne pepper and seasoning. Dip the swede slices first in the egg and then in the breadcrumb mixture.

3 Heat the oil in a deep fryer or wok and fry the swede discs, in batches if you need to, for 4–5 minutes until golden on the outside and soft inside. Drain on kitchen paper, to absorb the oil, and serve with mango chutney.

COOK'S TIP
Fry the discs until the swede is tender, so that the crunchiness of the breadcrumb coating contrasts with the soft vegetable.

GLAZED CARROTS WITH CIDER

THIS RECIPE IS EXTREMELY SIMPLE TO MAKE. THE CARROTS ARE COOKED IN THE MINIMUM OF LIQUID TO BRING OUT THE BEST OF THEIR FLAVOUR, AND THE CIDER ADDS A PLEASANT SHARPNESS.

SERVES FOUR

INGREDIENTS
    450g/1lb young carrots
    25g/1oz/2 tbsp butter
    15ml/1 tbsp brown sugar
    120ml/4fl oz/½ cup cider
    60ml/4 tbsp vegetable stock or water
    5ml/1 tsp Dijon mustard
    15ml/1 tbsp finely chopped
        fresh parsley

1 Trim the tops and bottoms of the carrots. Peel or scrape them. Using a sharp knife, cut them into julienne strips.

2 Melt the butter in a frying pan, add the carrots and sauté for 4–5 minutes, stirring frequently. Sprinkle over the sugar and cook, stirring for 1 minute or until the sugar has dissolved.

3 Add the cider and stock or water, bring to the boil and stir in the Dijon mustard. Partially cover the pan and simmer for about 10–12 minutes until the carrots are just tender. Remove the lid and continue cooking until the liquid has reduced to a thick sauce.

4 Remove the saucepan from the heat, stir in the parsley and then spoon into a warmed serving dish. Serve as an accompaniment to grilled meat or fish or with a vegetarian dish.

COOK'S TIP
If the carrots are cooked before the liquid in the saucepan has reduced, transfer the carrots to a serving dish and rapidly boil the liquid until thick. Pour over the carrots and sprinkle with parsley.

CARROT, APPLE AND ORANGE COLESLAW

THIS DISH IS AS DELICIOUS AS IT IS EASY TO MAKE. THE GARLIC AND HERB DRESSING PROVIDES THE NECESSARY CONTRAST TO THE SWEETNESS OF THE SALAD.

SERVES FOUR

INGREDIENTS
    350g/12oz young carrots,
        finely grated
    2 eating apples
    15ml/1 tbsp lemon juice
    1 large orange
For the dressing
    45ml/3 tbsp olive oil
    60ml/4 tbsp sunflower oil
    45ml/3 tbsp lemon juice
    1 garlic clove, crushed
    60ml/4 tbsp natural yogurt
    15ml/1 tbsp chopped mixed fresh
        herbs: tarragon, parsley, chives
    salt and freshly ground black pepper

1 Place the carrots in a large serving bowl. Quarter the apples, remove the core then slice thinly. Sprinkle with the lemon juice to stop discolouration then add to the carrots.

2 Using a sharp knife, remove the peel and pith from the orange and then separate into segments.

3 To make the dressing, place all the ingredients in a jar with a tight-fitting lid and shake vigorously to emulsify.

4 Just before serving, pour the dressing over the salad and toss together well.

CARROT AND CORIANDER SOUP

NEARLY ALL ROOT VEGETABLES MAKE EXCELLENT SOUPS AS THEY PURÉE WELL AND HAVE AN EARTHY
FLAVOUR WHICH COMPLEMENTS THE SHARPER FLAVOURS OF HERBS AND SPICES. CARROTS ARE
PARTICULARLY VERSATILE AND THIS SIMPLE SOUP IS ELEGANT IN BOTH FLAVOUR AND APPEARANCE.

SERVES FOUR TO SIX

INGREDIENTS
   450g/1lb carrots, preferably young
     and tender
   15ml/1 tbsp sunflower oil
   40g/1½oz/3 tbsp butter
   1 onion, chopped
   1 celery stalk, sliced plus 2–3 pale
     leafy celery tops
   2 small potatoes, chopped
   1 litre/1¾ pints/4 cups chicken stock
   10–15ml/2–3 tsp ground coriander
   15ml/1 tbsp chopped fresh coriander
   200ml/7fl oz/⅞ cup milk
   salt and freshly ground black pepper

1 Trim the carrots, peel if necessary and cut into chunks. Heat the oil and 25g/1oz/2 tbsp of the butter in a large flameproof casserole or heavy-based saucepan and fry the onion over a gentle heat for 3–4 minutes until they are slightly softened but not browned.

2 Cut the celery stalk into slices. Add the celery and potatoes to the onion in the pan, cook for a few minutes and then add the carrots. Fry over a gentle heat for 3–4 minutes, stirring frequently, and then cover. Reduce the heat even further and sweat for about 10 minutes. Shake the pan or stir occasionally so the vegetables do not stick to the base.

3 Add the stock, bring to the boil and then partially cover and simmer for a further 8–10 minutes until the carrots and potatoes are tender.

4 Remove 6–8 tiny celery leaves for garnish and finely chop the remaining celery tops (about 15ml/1 tbsp once chopped). Melt the remaining butter in a small saucepan and fry the ground coriander for about 1 minute, stirring all the time.

5 Reduce the heat and then add the chopped celery and fresh coriander and fry for about 1 minute. Set aside.

6 Purée the soup in a food processor or blender and pour into a clean saucepan. Stir in the milk, coriander mixture and seasoning. Heat gently, taste and adjust the seasoning. Serve garnished with the reserved celery.

COOK'S TIP
For a more piquant flavour, add a little lemon juice just before serving.

PAN-FRIED SWEET POTATOES WITH BACON

THIS IS A COMFORTING DISH TO EAT ON A COLD WINTER'S EVENING. BACON AND ONION COUNTERACT THE SWEETNESS OF THE POTATO, AND THE CAYENNE PEPPER GIVES THE NECESSARY EXTRA "KICK".

SERVES FOUR

INGREDIENTS

675–900g/1½–2lb sweet potatoes
juice of 1 lemon
15ml/1 tbsp plain flour
a good pinch of cayenne pepper
about 45ml/3 tbsp sunflower oil
1 large onion, chopped
115g/4oz streaky bacon, chopped
50g/2oz/1 cup fresh brown or
  white breadcrumbs
salt

1 Peel the sweet potatoes and cut into chunks about 4cm/1½in square. Place in a pan of boiling water with the lemon juice and a little salt, and simmer for 8–10 minutes until cooked but not soft.

2 Mix together the flour, cayenne pepper and a pinch of salt. Drain the potatoes and then dust with the seasoned flour, coating the pieces well.

3 Heat 15ml/1tbsp of the oil in a large frying pan and fry the onion for about 2 minutes. Add the bacon and fry over a gentle heat for 6–8 minutes until the onion and bacon are golden. Transfer to a plate using a slotted spoon.

4 Add the breadcrumbs and fry, stirring, for about 1–2 minutes until golden. Add to the plate with the bacon.

5 Heat the remaining oil in the pan and fry the potatoes for 5–6 minutes, turning occasionally, until evenly browned. Stir in the breadcrumb and bacon mixture and cook for 1 minute. Serve at once.

ARTICHOKE RÖSTI

SERVES FOUR TO SIX

INGREDIENTS
    450g/1lb Jerusalem artichokes
    juice of 1 lemon
    450g/1lb potatoes
    about 50g/2oz/4 tbsp butter
    salt

1 Peel the Jerusalem artichokes and place in a saucepan of water together with the lemon juice and a pinch of salt. Bring to the boil and cook for about 5 minutes until barely tender.

2 Peel the potatoes and place in a separate pan of salted water. Bring to the boil and cook until barely tender – the potatoes will take slightly longer than the artichokes.

3 Drain and cool both the artichokes and potatoes, and then grate them into a bowl. Mix them with your fingers, without breaking them up too much.

4 Melt the butter in a large heavy-based frying pan. Add the artichoke mixture, spreading it out with the back of a spoon. Cook gently for about 10 minutes.

5 Invert the "cake" on to a plate and slide back into the pan. Cook for about 10 minutes until golden. Serve at once.

ARTICHOKE TIMBALES WITH SPINACH SAUCE

SERVES SIX

INGREDIENTS
    900g/2lb Jerusalem artichokes
    juice of 1 lemon
    25g/1oz/2 tbsp butter
    15ml/1 tbsp oil
    1 onion, finely chopped
    1 garlic clove, crushed
    50g/2oz/1 cup white breadcrumbs
    1 egg
    60–75ml/4–5 tbsp vegetable stock
      or milk
    15ml/1 tbsp chopped fresh parsley
    5ml/1 tsp finely chopped sage
    salt and freshly ground black pepper
For the sauce
    225g/8oz fresh spinach, prepared
    15g/½oz/1 tbsp butter
    2 shallots, finely chopped
    150ml/¼ pint/⅔ cup single cream
    175ml/6fl oz/¾ cup vegetable stock
    salt and freshly ground black pepper

1 Preheat the oven to 180°C/350°F/Gas 4. Grease six 150ml/¼ pint/⅔ cup ramekin dishes, and then place a circle of non-stick baking paper in each base.

2 Peel the artichokes and put in a saucepan with the lemon juice and water to cover. Bring to the boil and simmer for about 10 minutes until tender. Drain and mash with the butter.

3 Heat the oil in a small frying pan and fry the onion and garlic until soft. Place in a food processor with the white breadcrumbs, egg, stock or milk, herbs and seasoning. Process to a smooth purée, add the artichokes and process again. Do not over-process.

4 Put the mixture in the prepared dishes and smooth the tops. Cover with non-stick baking paper, place in a roasting tin half-filled with boiling water and bake for 35–40 minutes until firm.

5 To make the sauce, cook the spinach without water, in a large covered saucepan, for 2–3 minutes. Shake the pan occasionally. Strain and press out the excess liquid.

6 Melt the butter in a small saucepan and fry the shallots gently until slightly softened but not browned. Place in a food processor or blender with the spinach and process to make a smooth purée. Pour back into the pan, add the cream and seasoning, and keep warm over a very low heat. Do not allow the mixture to boil.

7 Allow the timbales to stand for a few minutes after cooking and then turn out on to warmed serving plates. Spoon the warm sauce over them and serve.

COOK'S TIP
When puréeing the artichokes in a food processor or blender, use the pulse button and process for a very short time. The mixture will become cloying and unpalatable if it is over-processed.

YAM FRITTERS

YAMS HAVE A SLIGHTLY DRIER FLAVOUR THAN POTATOES AND ARE PARTICULARLY GOOD WHEN MIXED WITH SPICES AND THEN FRIED. THE FRITTERS CAN ALSO BE MOULDED INTO SMALL BALLS AND DEEP FRIED. THIS IS A FAVOURITE AFRICAN WAY OF SERVING YAMS.

MAKES ABOUT 18–20

INGREDIENTS
  675g/1½lb yams
  milk, for mashing
  2 small eggs, beaten
  45ml/3 tbsp chopped tomato flesh
  45ml/3 tbsp finely chopped
    spring onions
  1 green chilli, seeded and
    finely sliced
  flour, for shaping
  40g/1½oz/¾ cup white breadcrumbs
  vegetable oil, for shallow frying
  salt and freshly ground black pepper

1 Peel the yams and cut into chunks. Place in a saucepan of salted water and boil for 20–30 minutes until tender. Drain and mash with a little milk and about 45ml/3 tbsp of the beaten eggs.

2 Add the chopped tomato, spring onions, chilli and seasoning and stir well to mix thoroughly.

3 Using floured hands, shape the yam and vegetable mixture into round fritters, about 7.5cm/3in in diameter.

4 Dip each in the remaining egg and then coat evenly with the breadcrumbs. Heat a little oil in a large frying pan and fry the fritters for about 4–5 minutes until golden brown. Turn the fritters over once during cooking. Drain well on kitchen paper and serve.

EDDO, CARROT AND PARSNIP MEDLEY

EDDO (TARO), LIKE YAMS, IS WIDELY EATEN IN AFRICA AND THE CARIBBEAN, OFTEN AS A PURÉE. HERE, IT IS ROASTED AND COMBINED WITH MORE COMMON ROOT VEGETABLES TO MAKE A COLOURFUL DISPLAY.

SERVES FOUR TO SIX

INGREDIENTS
  450g/1lb eddoes (taros)
  350g/12oz parsnips
  450g/1lb carrots
  25g/1oz/2 tbsp butter
  45ml/3 tbsp sunflower oil
For the dressing
  30ml/2 tbsp fresh orange juice
  30ml/2 tbsp demerara sugar
  10ml/2 tsp soft green peppercorns
  salt
  fresh parsley, to garnish

1 Preheat the oven to 200°C/400°F/ Gas 6. Thickly peel the eddoes, making sure to remove all the skin as this can be an irritant. Cut into pieces about 5 x 2cm/2 x ¾in by 2cm/¾in, and place in a large bowl.

2 Peel the parsnips, halve lengthways and remove the inner core if necessary. Cut into the same size pieces as the eddo and add to the bowl. Blanch in boiling water for 2 minutes and then drain. Peel or scrub the carrots, and halve or quarter them according to their size.

3 Place the butter and sunflower oil in a roasting tin and heat in the oven for 3–4 minutes. Add the vegetables, turning them in the oil to coat evenly. Roast in the oven for 30 minutes.

4 Meanwhile, blend the orange juice, sugar and soft green peppercorns in a small bowl. Remove the roasting tin from the oven and allow to cool for a minute or so and then carefully pour the mixture over the vegetables, stirring to coat them all. (If the liquid is poured on too soon the hot oil will spit.)

5 Return the tin to the oven and cook for a further 20 minutes or until the vegetables are crisp and golden. Then transfer to a warmed serving plate and sprinkle with a little salt. Garnish with fresh parsley to serve.

GREENS

Whatever the season, there is something for everyone when it comes to greens. Cauliflowers, kale, broccoli and Brussels sprouts are all members of the cabbage family and like the cabbage itself are among the most nutritious of all vegetables. Spinach too is full of vitamins and minerals and is wonderfully versatile, and if you want to ring the changes, Oriental cabbages, such as Chinese leaves or pak choi are widely available and quite delicious.

SPINACH

For many people, spinach is inextricably linked with Popeye, the cartoon character who used to eat huge amounts of it. It is a wonderfully versatile vegetable, popular worldwide, with nearly every cuisine featuring spinach somewhere in its repertoire. The Italians are particularly partial to spinach and have hundreds of dishes using the vegetable. The words *à la florentine* mean the dish contains spinach.

As well as being delicious on its own, chopped or puréed spinach can be mixed with a range of other ingredients with superb results. It has a particular affinity with dairy products and in the Middle East, feta or helim cheese is used to make boreks or other spinach pies. The Italians mix spinach with ricotta or Parmesan cheese for a huge range of recipes, and the English use eggs and sometimes Cheddar for a spinach soufflé.

History

Spinach was first cultivated in Persia several thousand years ago. It came to Europe via the Arab world; the Moors introduced it to Spain, and Arabs in the Middle East took it to Greece. It first appeared in England in the fourteenth century, probably via Spain, and it is mentioned in the first known English cookery book, where it is referred to as *spynoches*. This echoes the Spanish word for spinach which is *espinacas*. It fast became a popular vegetable, which is probably because it is quick and easy to grow and similarily quick and easy to cook.

Nutrition

Spinach is an excellent source of vitamin C if eaten raw, as well as vitamins A and B, calcium, potassium and iron. Spinach was originally thought to provide far more iron than it actually does, but the iron is "bound" up by oxalic acid in cooked spinach, which prevents the body from absorbing most of it. Even so, it is still an extremely healthy vegetable whether eaten cooked or raw.

Buying and Storing

Spinach grows all year round, so you should have no difficulty in buying it fresh. Frozen spinach is rather a poor substitute, mainly because it has so little flavour, so it is worth the effort to use the fresh product.

Spinach leaves should be green and lively; if they look tired and the stalks are floppy, shop round until you find some in better condition. Spinach reduces significantly when cooked; about 450g/1lb will serve two people. Store it in the salad drawer of the fridge, where it will keep for 1–2 days.

Preparing

Wash well in a bowl of cold water and remove any tough or over-large stalks.

Cooking

Throw the leaves into a large pan with just the water that clings to the leaves and place over a low heat with a sprinkling of salt. Cover the pan so the spinach steams in its own liquid, and shake the pan occasionally to prevent the spinach sticking to the base. It cooks in 4–6 minutes, wilting down to about an eighth of its original volume. Drain and press out the remaining liquid with the back of a spoon.

Spinach can be used in a variety of ways. It can be chopped and served with lots of butter, or similarly served with other spring vegetables such as

BRUSSELS SPROUTS

baby carrots or young broad beans. For frittatas, chop the spinach finely, stir in a little Parmesan cheese, a good sprinkling of salt and pepper and a dash of cream, if liked, and stir into the omelette before cooking. Alternatively, purée it for sauces or blend it for soups. Spinach is also delightful eaten raw, served with chopped bacon or croûtons. A fresh spinach salad is delicious as the leaves have just the right balance of flavour – sharp but not overpowering.

Below: Spinach
Below right: Brussels sprouts

Brussels sprouts have a pronounced and sweet nutty flavour, which is quite unlike cabbage, although the two are related. They are traditionally served at Christmas with chestnuts and indeed have a definite affinity for certain nuts – particularly the sweet-flavoured nuts, e.g. almonds pair well rather than hazelnuts or walnuts.

History

The brussels sprout was cultivated in Flanders (now Belgium) throughout the Middle Ages. Sprouts are basically miniature cabbages which grow in a knobbly row on a long tough stalk. The Germans call sprouts *rosenkohl* – rose cabbage – a pretty and descriptive name as they look like small rosebuds.

Buying and Storing

Buy Brussels sprouts as fresh as you can as older ones are more likely to have that strong unpleasant "cabbage" flavour. They should be small and hard with tightly wrapped leaves. Avoid any that

are turning yellow or brown or have loose leaves.

Brussels sprouts will keep for several days in a cool place such as a larder or the salad drawer of a fridge, but it is far better to buy them as you need them.

Preparing

Cut away the bottom of the stalk and remove the outer leaves. Some people cut a cross through the bottom of the stalk although this is not really necessary. If you haven't been able to avoid buying big Brussels sprouts, cut them in half or into quarters, or slice them thinly for stir-frying.

Cooking

As with cabbage, either cook Brussels sprouts very briefly or braise slowly in the oven. Cook in small amounts of very fast boiling water for about 3 minutes until just tender. To stir-fry Brussels sprouts, slice into three or four pieces and then fry in a little oil and butter – they taste great with onions and ginger.

CAULIFLOWER

Cauliflower is a member of the cabbage family, *Brassica oleracea*. Like all the cabbages, cauliflower suffers terribly from overcooking. A properly cooked cauliflower has a pleasant fresh flavour but when overcooked it turns grey and becomes unpalatably soft, taking on a nasty rank flavour with an unpleasant aftertaste. Children often like raw cauliflower even though they may not connect it with the same vegetable served up at school.

History

Cauliflower is thought to have come originally from China and thence to the Middle East. The Moors introduced it to Spain in the twelfth century and from there it found its way to England via established trading routes. The early cauliflower was the size of a tennis ball but they have gradually been cultivated to the enormous sizes we see today. Ironically, baby cauliflowers are back in fashion.

Varieties

Green and occasionally some purple cauliflowers are available in the shops. The purple variety was originally grown in Sardinia and Italy but is increasingly grown elsewhere. They look pretty and unusual but are otherwise similar to white cauliflowers.

Dwarf varieties of cauliflowers are now commonly available in shops, as well as baby white cauliflowers.

Romanescoes: These attractive green or white vegetables look like a cross between broccoli and cauliflower, but are more closely related to cauliflowers. They taste very much like cauliflowers, but since they are quite small, they are less likely to be overcooked and consequently retain their excellent flavour.

Broccoflower: A cross between broccoli and cauliflower, this looks like a pale green cauliflower. It has a mild flavour and should be cooked in the same way as you would cauliflower.

Right: Baby cauliflower.
Opposite above: Romanescoes.
Opposite below: Green cauliflower.

Nutrition

Cauliflower contains potassium, iron and zinc, although cooking it reduces the amounts. Additionally it is a good source of vitamins A and C.

Buying and Storing

In perfect condition, a cauliflower is a creamy white colour with the outer leaves curled round the flower. The head should be unblemished with no black or discoloured areas and the outer leaves should look fresh and crisp. Store cauliflowers in a cool place for no longer than 1–2 days; after that they deteriorate and valuable nutrients will be lost.

Preparing

To cook a cauliflower whole, first trim away the coarse bottom leaves (leave the inner ones on, if liked). Really large cauliflowers are best halved or broken into florets, as the outside will overcook before the inside is tender. Some people trim away the stalk, but others like this part and only trim off the very thick stalk at the bottom of the plant.

Cooking

Cauliflowers are excellent steamed, either whole or in florets. Place in a steamer or colander over a pan of boiling water, cover and steam until just tender and immediately remove from the heat. The florets can then be fried in olive oil or butter for a few minutes to give a lightly browned finish.

When cooking a cauliflower whole, start testing it after 10 minutes; it should feel tender but still have plenty of "bite" left in it. Cauliflower is a popular vegetable accompaniment, either served with just a little butter, or with a tomato or cheese sauce. It is also good stir-fried with onions and garlic together with a few tomatoes and capers.

Cauliflower is excellent in salads or used for crudités. Either use it raw or blanch it in boiling water for 1–2 miutes, then refresh under cold running water.

Small cauliflowers and romanescoes are intended to be cooked whole, and can be steamed or boiled, covered with a lid, in the minimum of water for about 4–5 minutes until just tender.

SPROUTING BROCCOLI AND CALABRESE

Varieties

Calabrese broccoli: This is the vegetable that today we commonly call broccoli, with large beautiful, blue-green heads on succulent stalks. It is named after the Italian province of Calabria where this variety was first developed.

Purple sprouting broccoli: The original variety – it has long thin stalks with small flowerheads that are normally purple but can be white or green. Heads, stalks and tender leaves are all edible. The purple heads turn green when cooked but the others keep their colour. This variety is more seasonal than the readily available calabrese; it is usually available from late winter onwards.

Buying and Storing

If possible, buy loose broccoli rather than the pre-wrapped bundles, because it is easier to check that it is fresh and also because wrapped vegetables tend to deteriorate more quickly.

Purple sprouting broccoli can also be - sold loose or prepacked. Check that the stalk, flowerhead and leaves all look fresh and that the flowerlets are tightly closed and bright green. Neither type will keep for long.

Broccoli or calabrese is a relatively modern vegetable and is one of the most popular. It is quick and easy to prepare with little or no waste and similarly easy to cook. It is attractive, whether served raw or cooked, and you can buy it in the quantity you require, unlike cauliflower or cabbage.

History

Before calabrese came into our shops, people bought and ate purple sprouting broccoli. This is basically an "untidy" version of calabrese, with long shoots and clusters of flowerheads at the end – the broccoli we know today has neat tidy heads. The stalks of purple sprouting broccoli have a faint asparagus flavour.

The Romans cooked purple sprouting broccoli in wine or served it with sauces and it is still a popular vegetable today in Italy, cooked in the oven with anchovies and onions or served with pasta in a garlic and tomato sauce.

Preparing and Cooking

Trim the ends of the stalks and pull off any discoloured leaves.

Calabrese broccoli: Break into even-size pieces, dividing the stem and flowerhead lengthways if they are thick. Cook in a little boiling water for 4–5 minutes until just tender and then drain. Do not steam this variety of broccoli as its vibrant green colour tends to turn grey.

Purple sprouting broccoli: Either steam in long, even-size lengths in a steamer or, if you have an asparagus kettle, cook as you would asparagus. Alternatively, tie the stems loosely together and stand in a little water – if necessary, wedge it in with a potato or rolled up piece of foil. Cover with a dome of foil and steam for about 4–5 minutes until tender.

Serving

Serve both varieties simply with butter and lemon juice or with a hollandaise or Béarnaise sauce as an accompaniment. They are also excellent stir-fried.

Opposite above: Purple cauliflower
Opposite below: Purple sprouting broccoli
Left: Calabrese broccoli
Below: Turnip tops

TURNIP TOPS

Turnip tops, like beet greens, are both delicious and nutritious. They are not widely available but if you are able to buy some or if you grow your own, slice them (see below), boil or steam for a few minutes, drain and serve with butter.

CABBAGE

Cabbage, sliced and cooked, can be one of two things: deliciously crisp, with a mild pleasant flavour – or overcooked and truly horrible! Cabbage and other brassicas contain the chemical hydrogen sulphide, which is activated during cooking at about the point the vegetable starts to soften. It eventually disappears, but during the in-between time, cabbage will acquire its characteristic rank smell and flavour. So, either cook cabbage briefly, or cook it long and slowly, preferably with other ingredients so that flavours can mingle.

History

Cabbage has a long and varied history. However, because there are so many varieties of cabbage under the general heading of "brassica", it is difficult to be sure whether the variety the Greeks and Romans enjoyed is the same as today's round cabbage, or something more akin to kale or even Chinese cabbage.

The round cabbages we know today were an important food during the Dark Ages, and by the Middle Ages they were in abundance, as you will see if you study the paintings of that period. They often show kitchen tables or baskets at market positively groaning with fruit and vegetables, and cabbages in all their shapes and sizes were usually featured.

Medieval recipes suggest cooking the cabbage with leeks, onions and herbs. In the days when all except the very wealthy cooked everything in one pot, it is fair to assume that cabbages were cooked long and slowly until fairly recently.

Varieties

Savoy cabbage: This is a variety of green cabbage with crimped or curly leaves. It has a mild flavour and is particularly tender, thus needing less cooking than other varieties.

Spring greens: These have fresh loose heads with a pale yellow-green heart. Available in spring, they are delicious sliced, steamed and simply served with butter.

Right: Savoy cabbage
Opposite above: Green cabbage
Opposite below: Spring greens

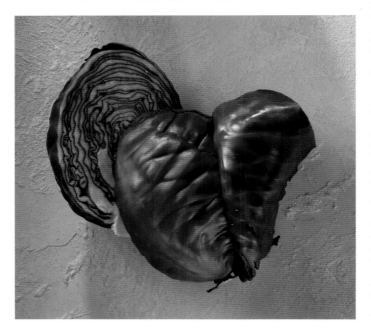

Green cabbage: The early green, or spring, cabbages are dark green, loose leafed and have a slightly pointed head. They have little or no heart as they are picked before this has had time to develop. Nevertheless, they are a very good cabbage; all but the very outside leaves should be tender. As the season progresses, larger, firmer and pale green cabbages are available. These are a little tougher than the spring cabbages and need longer cooking.

Red cabbage: This beautifully coloured cabbage has smooth firm leaves. The colour fades during cooking unless a little vinegar is added to the water. Red cabbage can be pickled or stewed with spices and other flavourings.

White cabbage: Sometimes called Dutch cabbages, white cabbages have smooth firm pale green leaves. They are available throughout the winter. They are good cooked or raw. To cook, slice them thinly, then boil or steam and serve with butter. To serve raw, slice thinly and use in a coleslaw.

Buying and Storing

Cabbages should be fresh looking and unblemished. When buying, avoid any with wilted leaves or those that look or feel puffy. Savoys and spring greens will keep in a cool place for several days; firmer cabbages will keep happily for much longer.

Preparing

Remove the outer leaves, if necessary, and then cut into quarters. Remove the stalk and then slice or shred according to your recipe or to taste.

Cooking

For green or white cabbages, place the shredded leaves in a pan with a knob of butter and a couple of tablespoons of water to prevent burning. Cover and cook over a medium heat until the leaves are tender, occasionally shaking the pan or stirring.

Red cabbage is cooked quite differently and is commonly sautéed in oil or butter and then braised in a low oven for up to $1^1/_2$ hours with apples, currants, onions, vinegar, wine, sugar and spices.

KALE AND CURLY KALE

Kale is the name used for a variety of green-leafed vegetable of the brassica family. Most kales have thick stems and robust leaves that do not form a head. Many kales have curly leaves, which are the variety most commonly eaten. Large coarse-leafed kales are grown for cattle and sheep feeds.

History

Kale is thought to be one of the very first cultivated brassicas. Colewort, the wild ancestor, still grows along the coasts of western Europe.

Varieties

Collards: Collards, or collard greens, are a very popular green vegetable in the southern United States. They are grown in summer and autumn for harvesting in spring and are a good source of vitamin A.
Curly kale: With its crimped and curly leaves, this is the most commonly available kale, although even though it can be quite hard to come by. If you are a big fan but don't grow your own, try farm shops in early spring.
Purple or silver kale: This is really an ornamental variety, and is grown almost exclusively for display.

Preparing and Cooking

Kale is probably the strongest tasting of the brassicas and is best cooked simply, paired with a bland-flavoured vegetable, such as potatoes. To prepare, break the leaves from the central stalk and cut out any thick stalk from the leaf. This can then be rolled and sliced or cooked whole. Boil the leaves in a little salted water for 3–5 minutes until tender. Owing to its robust nature, kale is frequently teamed with fairly hot spices and is consequently popular in many Indian dishes.

Opposite above: White cabbage
Opposite below: Red cabbage
Above: Curly kale
Left: Collards

GARDEN AND WILD LEAVES

VINE LEAVES

All leaves from vines that produce grapes can be eaten when young. They make an ideal wrapping for various meats and vegetables as they are surprisingly strong and of course edible. Most countries that produce wine will have dishes where vine leaves appear. *Dolmades*, commonly eaten in Greece and the Middle East is perhaps the best-known dish, but in France, Spain and Italy there are recipes using vine leaves to wrap small birds, like quail or snipe.

Vine leaves possess a faintly lemony cabbage flavour which can be detected at its best in a good *dolmades*. The leaves need to be cooked briefly before using, so that they are pliable and don't crack or break as you wrap the food. Bring to the boil and simmer for about 1 minute. The leaves should then be drained and separated until you are ready to use them for wrapping.

DANDELION

Any child who has picked dandelions for his or her rabbits or guinea pigs and has watched them gobble them up greedily will know that this weed, though hated by the gardener in the family, must have something going for it. Some gardeners, however, are very partial to dandelion and raise the plant carefully so that the leaves are fresh and tender for salad dishes and in France dandelions can often be seen for sale at market.

Look in any book of herbal remedies,

and dandelions will feature prominently. They are a well-known diuretic, their French name - *pissenlits* (piss-a-bed) – attesting to this in no uncertain terms.

Although it's gratifying to pick your own vegetables for free, it is recommended, if you like dandelions, that you buy the domestic seeds and grow your own. These are likely to be the juiciest and

least bitter plants. If you do pick your own, do so well away from the road-side and wash the leaves carefully.

Dandelion leaves can be added to salads or used in *pissenlits au lard*, where whole young dandelion plants are dressed in vinaigrette and then covered in finely chopped pieces of salt pork or bacon and bacon fat.

SORREL

Sorrel is not always available to be bought, although it is in France and is greatly prized. However, it grows wild in cool soils or you could grow it in your own garden. Young leaves are delicious in salads, or, later in the year, use it in soups or sauces to accompany fish. It has a sharp, distinct, lemon flavour and is commonly teamed with eggs and cream.

ORACHE

Although not related to spinach, this beautiful red- or golden-leaved plant is called mountain spinach and its large leaves can be treated like spinach.

GOOD KING HENRY AND FAT HEN

These greens are both members of the goosefoot family and were very popular vegetables in Tudor times. Today, Good King Henry has all but disappeared, and Fat Hen only grows wild as a weed. Both were superseded by spinach, which they are said to resemble in taste, although Fat Hen is milder.

NETTLES

Wild food enthusiasts get very excited about nettles as food, perhaps because they are plentiful and free and maybe because they take pleasure in eating something that everyone else avoids. Of course, once cooked the nettle's sting completely disappears. They should be picked when they are very young and are good used in soups.

Opposite above left: Fresh vine leaves.
Opposite above right: Dandelion.
Opposite below: Sorrel.
Right: Good King Henry.
Below: Nettles.

CHINESE GREENS

CHINESE CABBAGE/LEAVES (PE-TSAI)

The Chinese cabbage, also called Napa cabbage, has pale green, crinkly leaves with long, wide, white ribs. Its shape is a little like a very fat head of celery, which gives rise to one of its alternative names, celery cabbage. It is pleasantly crunchy with a faint cabbage flavour and since it is available all year round, it makes a useful winter salad component. Chinese cabbage is also very good stir-fried with a tasty sauce. It is an essential ingredient of many oriental recipes.

Buying and Storing

For some reason, Chinese leaves almost always look fresh and perky when on sale in the supermarket, which probably indicates that they travel well and are transported quickly. Avoid any with discoloured or damaged stems. The leaves should be pale green and straight without blemishes or bruises. They will keep for up to six days in the salad drawer of the fridge.

Preparing

Remove the outside leaves and slice as much as you need.

Many Chinese greens are members of the brassica family. If you go into a popular and reasonably large Chinese supermarket, you'll be astonished at the varieties of green vegetables for sale. Discovering their names, on the other hand, can be a bit of a hit-and-miss undertaking, because the shop keepers, although always well intentioned, rarely know the English name, if indeed there is one.

CHINESE MUSTARD GREENS

Mustard greens are worth buying if you can, as they are very good to eat. The plant is a member of the cabbage family, but is grown in Europe solely for its mustard seed. In India and Asia it has long been grown for its oil seed, but the Chinese developed the plant for its leaves as well. These are deep green and slightly puckered-looking and have a definite mustard flavour, which can be quite fiery.

If you grow your own, then you'll be able to enjoy the young leaves which can be added to lettuce to spice up salads. Older leaves are best stir-fried and then dressed with a light Chinese sauce. They are also good when cooked with onion and garlic and served as a side dish to accompany pork or bacon.

Preparing and Cooking

Break apart the stalks, rinse, then cut both stalks and leaves into thick or thin slices. These can then be stir-fried with garlic and onions, or cooked and served as you would Swiss chard. Pak choi has a pleasant flavour, milder than mustard greens, yet with more bite than the bland Chinese cabbage.

CHINESE BROCCOLI

This is another leafy vegetable, but with slender heads of flowers that look a little like our own broccoli, except that the flowers are usually white or yellow. Once the thicker stalks are trimmed, the greens can be sliced and cooked and served in the same way as Chinese mustard greens.

Opposite left: Chinese mustard greens
Opposite right: Chinese leaves
Left: Chinese broccoli
Below: Pak choi

Cooking and Serving

If adding to salads, combine Chinese cabbage with something fairly forceful, like endive or rocket, and add a well-flavoured dressing. If adding to a stir-fry, cook with garlic, ginger and other fairly strong flavours. While the faint cabbage flavour will be lost, you will still get the pleasant crunchy "bite" of the stalk, and the leaves will carry the sauce.

PAK CHOI

If you frequent your local Chinese super-market, you will almost certainly have come across pak choi. In English it should correctly be called Chinese cel-ery cabbage and its thick stalks, joined at the end in a smallish root, are vaguely celery-like. Its leaves, on the other hand, are generally large and spoon-shaped. There are many different species of this vegetable, and smaller specimens look more like the tops of radish having small slim stalks. Consequently the vegetable can be known by all sorts of picturesque names, like "horse's ear" and "horse's tail". There is no rule for discovering exactly what you are buying, but the important thing is to choose a fresh plant whatever its size: look for fresh green leaves and crisp stalks.

KOHLRABI

Kohlrabi looks something like a cross between a cabbage and a turnip and is often classified as a root vegetable even though it grows above ground. It is a member of the brassica family, but, unlike cabbages, it is the bulbous stalk that is edible, as opposed to the flowering heads.

There are two varieties of kohlrabi: one purple, the other pale green. They have the same mild and fresh-tasting flavour, not unlike water chestnuts. It is neither as peppery as turnip nor as distinctive as cabbage, but it is easy to see why people think it a little like both. It can be served as an alternative to carrots or turnips.

History

Although kohlrabi is not a very popular vegetable in Britain, it is commonly eaten in other parts of Europe, as well as in China, India and Asia. In Kashmir, where it is grown extensively, there are many recipes – the bulbs are often finely sliced and eaten in salads and the greens are cooked in mustard oil with garlic and chillies.

Buying and Storing

Kohlrabi is best when small and young, since larger specimens tend to be coarse and fibrous. It keeps well for 7–10 days if stored in a cool place.

Preparing

Peel the skin with a knife and then cook whole or slice.

Cooking

Very small kohlrabi are tender and can be braised or boiled whole. However, if they are any bigger than 5cm/2in in diameter, they can be stuffed. To do this, hollow out a little before braising and then stuff with fried onions and tomatoes, for instance. For sliced kohlrabi, fry until just tender and serve with butter or a creamy sauce. Kohlrabi can also be baked long and slow in gratin dishes, with, for instance, potatoes as a variation of *Gratin Dauphinois*. Alternatively, par-boil them and bake in the oven covered with a cheese sauce.

SWISS CHARD

Swiss chard is one of those vegetables that needs plenty of water when growing, which explains why it is a popular garden vegetable in many places which have a high rainfall. Gardeners are very fond of Swiss chard, not only because it is delicious to eat but also because it is so very striking.

Swiss chard is often likened to spinach. Although the leaves have similarities they are not related and chard is on an altogether larger scale. Swiss chard leaves are large and fleshy and have distinctive white ribs. The flavour is stronger and more robust than spinach. It is popular in France where it is baked with rice, eggs and milk in *tians*, and cooked in a celebrated pastry from Nice – *tourte de blettes*. This is a sweet tart filled with raisins, pine nuts, apples and Swiss chard bound together with eggs. It is also often combined with eggs in frittatas and tortillas.

Swiss chard is a member of the beet family and is called by several names on this theme, including seakale beet and spinach beet.

Ruby or rhubarb chard has striking red ribs and leaf beet is often cultivated as a decorative plant, but they both have the same flavour, and unlike sugar beet and beetroot, they are cultivated only for their leaves.

Buying and Storing

Heads of chard should be fresh and bright green; avoid those with withered leaves or flabby stems. It keeps better than spinach but should be eaten within a couple of days.

Preparing

Some people buy or grow chard for the white stems alone and discard the leaves (or give them to pet guinea pigs), but this is a waste of a delicious vegetable. The leaf needs to be separated from the ribs, and this can be done roughly with a sharp knife (see right) or more precisely using scissors. The ribs can then be sliced. Either shred the leaves, or blanch them and use them to wrap little parcels of fragrant rice or other food. If the chard is young and small, the ribs do not need to be removed.

Cooking

For pies, frittatas and gratins, chard leaves and ribs can be cooked together. Gently sauté the ribs in butter and oil and then add the leaves a minute or so later. Alternatively, the ribs can be simmered in a little water until tender and the leaves added a few minutes later or steamed over the top.

Opposite above: Kohlrabi
Opposite below: Purple kohlrabi
Above: Swiss Chard

GREENS RECIPES

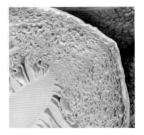

Greens are so good for you we really should eat lots
more. They're also versatile and quite delicious, so
there's no excuse either! Broccoli Crumble and
Balti-style Cauliflower with Tomatoes are quick
and easy dishes, or try Broccoli and Chicken
Lasagne or Spinach in Filo with Three Cheeses for
great family eating. Stir-fried Brussels Sprouts
presents sprouts in whole new and delicious light,
while the traditional Greek dish, Dolmades, is
surprisingly simple to prepare.

BROCCOLI AND CHICKEN LASAGNE

DEFINITELY DIFFERENT FROM TRADITIONAL LASAGNE, THIS DISH IS TOPPED WITH MOUTHWATERING MELTING MOZZARELLA.

SERVES SIX

INGREDIENTS
450g/1lb broccoli, broken into florets
450g/1lb chicken breasts, skinned
   and boned
15ml/1 tbsp sunflower oil
25g/1oz/2 tbsp butter
1 onion, finely chopped
1 garlic clove, chopped
600ml/1 pint/2½ cups passata or
   creamed sieved tomatoes
2.5ml/½ tsp thyme
2.5ml/½ tsp oregano
about 12 sheets pre-cooked lasagne
275g/10oz/1¼ cups fromage frais
75g/3oz Parmesan cheese, grated
225g/8oz mozzarella cheese,
   thinly sliced
salt and freshly ground black pepper

1 Preheat the oven to 180°C/350°F/ Gas 4 and then butter a large shallow ovenproof dish. Steam the broccoli until nearly tender. Strain and set aside.

2 Cut the chicken into thin strips. Heat the oil and butter in a frying pan and fry the chicken for a few minutes until lightly browned. Then transfer to a plate using a slotted spoon and set aside.

3 Add the onion and garlic to the pan and fry for 3–4 minutes until the onion has softened and is lightly golden brown. Stir in the passata or creamed tomatoes, thyme, oregano and seasoning, and cook for about 3–4 minutes over a moderate heat until the sauce is slightly thickened, stirring regularly.

4 Spoon half the tomato sauce into the prepared dish. Add a layer of lasagne and then half the chicken and half the broccoli. Dot with half the fromage frais and sprinkle with half the Parmesan cheese. Put another layer of lasagne on top and spoon over the remaining tomato sauce, chicken, broccoli and fromage frais. End with a layer of lasagne.

5 Arrange the mozzarella cheese slices on top and sprinkle with the remaining Parmesan cheese. Bake in the oven for 30–35 minutes until the top is golden.

BROCCOLI CRUMBLE

SERVES FOUR

INGREDIENTS
25g/1oz/2 tbsp butter or margarine
2 leeks, thinly sliced
25g/1oz/¼ cup plain flour
150ml/¼ pint/⅔ cup milk
120ml/4fl oz/½ cup water
225g/8oz broccoli, broken into florets
25g/1oz Parmesan cheese
salt and freshly ground black pepper
For the topping
115g/4oz/1 cup plain flour
5ml/1 tsp dried basil
75g/3oz/6 tbsp butter or margarine
50g/2oz/1 cup fresh brown or
   white breadcrumbs
a pinch of salt

1 Preheat the oven to 190°C/375°F/ Gas 5. Melt the butter in a flameproof casserole or saucepan and fry the leeks for 2–3 minutes until softened. Stir in the flour and then gradually add the milk and water. Bring to the boil, add the broccoli, season and simmer, partly covered, for 5 minutes.

2 Stir in the Parmesan cheese, season with salt and pepper and pour into a medium-size ovenproof dish.

3 To make the topping, mix the flour with the basil and salt. Rub in the butter or margarine stir in the breadcrumbs. Sprinkle over the broccoli and then bake in the oven for 20–25 minutes, or until the topping is golden.

SPINACH AND CANNELLINI BEANS

THIS HEARTY DISH CAN BE MADE WITH ALMOST ANY DRIED BEAN, SUCH AS BLACK-EYED BEANS,
HARICOTS OR CHICK-PEAS. IT IS A GOOD DISH TO SERVE ON A COLD EVENING. IF USING CANNED BEANS,
DRAIN, THEN RINSE UNDER RUNNING COLD WATER.

SERVES FOUR

INGREDIENTS
    225g/8oz cannellini beans,
      soaked overnight
    60ml/4 tbsp olive oil
    1 slice white bread
    1 onion, chopped
    3–4 tomatoes, peeled and chopped
    a good pinch of paprika
    450g/1lb spinach
    1 garlic clove, halved
    salt and freshly ground black pepper

5 Add the onion and tomato mixture to the spinach, mix well and stir in the cannellini beans. Place the garlic and fried bread in a food processor and process until smooth. Stir into the spinach and bean mixture. Add 150ml/¼ pint/⅔ cup cold water and then cover and simmer gently for 20–30 minutes, adding more water if necessary.

1 Drain the beans, place in a saucepan and cover with water. Bring to the boil and boil rapidly for 10 minutes. Cover and simmer for about 1 hour until the beans are tender. Drain.

2 Heat 30ml/2 tbsp of the oil in a frying pan and fry the bread until it is golden brown. Transfer to a plate.

3 Fry the onion in 15ml/1 tbsp of the oil over a gentle heat until soft but not brown, then add the tomatoes and continue cooking over a gentle heat.

4 Heat the remaining oil in a large pan, stir in the paprika and then add the spinach. Cover and cook for a few minutes until the spinach has wilted.

SPINACH IN FILO WITH THREE CHEESES

THIS IS A GOOD CHOICE TO SERVE WHEN VEGETARIANS AND MEAT EATERS ARE GATHERED TOGETHER FOR A MEAL AS, WHATEVER THEIR PREFERENCE, EVERYONE SEEMS PARTIAL TO THIS TASTY DISH.

SERVES FOUR

INGREDIENTS
    450g/1lb spinach
    15ml/1 tbsp sunflower oil
    15g/½oz/1 tbsp butter
    1 small onion, finely chopped
    175g/6oz ricotta cheese
    115g/4oz/¾ cup feta cheese, cut into
      small cubes
    75g/3oz Gruyère or Emmenthal
      cheese, grated
    15ml/1 tbsp fresh chopped chervil
    5ml/1 tsp fresh chopped marjoram
    5 large or 10 small sheets filo pastry
    40–50g/1½–2oz butter, melted
    salt and freshly ground black pepper

1 Preheat the oven to 190°C/375°F/ Gas 5. Cook the spinach in a large saucepan over a moderate heat for 3–4 minutes until the leaves have wilted, shaking the saucepan occasionally. Strain and press out the excess liquid.

2 Heat the oil and butter in a saucepan and fry the onion for 3–4 minutes until softened. Remove from the heat and add half of the spinach. Combine, using a metal spoon to break up the spinach.

3 Add the ricotta cheese and stir until evenly combined. Stir in the remaining spinach, again chopping it into the mixture with a metal spoon. Fold in the feta and Gruyère or Emmenthal cheese, the chervil, marjoram and seasoning.

4 Lay a sheet of filo pastry measuring 30cm/12 in square on a work surface. (If you have small filo sheets, lay them side by side, and overlapping by about 2.5cm/1in in the middle.) Brush with melted butter and cover with a second sheet; brush this with butter and build up five layers of pastry in this way.

5 Spread the filling over the pastry, leaving a 2.5cm/1in border. Fold the sides inwards and then roll up.

6 Place the roll, seam side down, on a greased baking sheet and brush with the remaining butter. Bake in the oven for about 30 minutes until golden brown.

CAULIFLOWER AND MUSHROOM GOUGÈRE

This is an all-round favourite vegetarian dish. When cooking it for meat lovers, chopped roast ham or fried bacon can be added.

SERVES FOUR TO SIX

INGREDIENTS
  300ml/½ pint/1¼ cups water
  115g/4oz/½ cup butter or margarine
  150g/5oz/1¼ cups plain flour
  4 eggs
  115g/4oz Gruyère or Cheddar cheese,
    finely diced
  5ml/1 tsp Dijon mustard
  salt and freshly ground black pepper
For the filling
  ½ x 400g/14oz can tomatoes
  15ml/1 tbsp sunflower oil
  15g/½oz/1 tbsp butter or margarine
  1 onion, chopped
  115g/4oz button mushrooms, halved
    if large
  1 small cauliflower, broken into
    small florets
  a sprig of thyme
  salt and freshly ground black pepper

1 Preheat the oven to 200°C/400°F/
Gas 6 and butter a large ovenproof dish.
Place the water and butter together in a
large saucepan and heat until the butter
has melted. Remove from the heat and
add all the flour at once. Beat well with a
wooden spoon for about 30 seconds until
smooth. Allow to cool slightly.

2 Beat in the eggs, one at a time, and
continue beating until the mixture is
thick and glossy. Stir in the cheese and
mustard and season with salt and
pepper. Spread the mixture around the
sides of the ovenproof dish, leaving a
hollow in the centre for the filling.

3 To make the filling, purée the
tomatoes in a blender or food processor
and then pour into a measuring jug. Add
enough water to make up to 300ml/
½ pint/1¼ cups of liquid.

4 Heat the oil and butter in a flameproof
casserole and fry the onion for about
3–4 minutes until softened but not
browned. Add the mushrooms and cook
for 2–3 minutes until they begin to be
flecked with brown. Add the cauliflower
florets and stir-fry for 1 minute.

5 Add the tomato liquid, thyme and
seasoning. Cook, uncovered, over a
gentle heat for about 5 minutes until the
cauliflower is only just tender.

6 Spoon the mixture into the hollow in
the ovenproof dish, adding all the liquid
with it. Bake in the oven for about
35–40 minutes, until the outer pastry is
well risen and golden brown.

COOK'S TIP
For a variation, ham or bacon can be
added. Use about 115–150g/4–5oz
thickly sliced roast ham and add to the
sauce at the end of step 5.

BALTI-STYLE CAULIFLOWER <u>WITH</u> TOMATOES

BALTI IS A TYPE OF MEAT AND VEGETABLE COOKING FROM PAKISTAN AND NORTHERN INDIA. IT CAN REFER BOTH TO THE PAN USED FOR COOKING, WHICH IS LIKE A LITTLE WOK, AND THE SPICES USED. IN THE ABSENCE OF A GENUINE BALTI PAN, USE EITHER A WOK OR A HEAVY-BASED FRYING PAN.

SERVES FOUR

INGREDIENTS
30ml/2 tbsp vegetable oil
1 onion, chopped
2 garlic cloves, crushed
1 cauliflower, broken into florets
5ml/1 tsp ground coriander
5ml/1 tsp ground cumin
5ml/1 tsp ground fennel seeds
2.5ml/½ tsp garam masala
a pinch of ground ginger
2.5ml/½ tsp chilli powder
4 plum tomatoes, peeled, seeded
 and quartered
175ml/6fl oz/¾ cup water
175g/6oz fresh spinach, roughly
 chopped
15–30ml/1–2 tbsp lemon juice
salt and freshly ground
 black pepper

1 Heat the oil in a balti pan, wok or large frying pan. Add the onion and garlic and stir-fry for 2–3 minutes over a high heat until the onion begins to brown. Add the cauliflower florets and stir-fry for a further 2–3 minutes until the cauliflower is flecked with brown.

2 Add the coriander, cumin, fennel seeds, garam masala, ginger and chilli powder and cook over a high heat for 1 minute, stirring all the time. Then add the tomatoes, water and salt and pepper. Bring to the boil then reduce the heat, cover and simmer for 5–6 minutes until the cauliflower is just tender.

3 Stir in the chopped spinach, cover and cook for 1 minute until the spinach is tender. Add enough lemon juice to sharpen the flavour and adjust the seasoning to taste.

4 Serve straight from the pan, with an Indian meal or with chicken or meat.

HOT BROCCOLI TARTLETS

IN FRANCE, HOME OF THE CLASSIC QUICHE LORRAINE, YOU CAN FIND A WHOLE VARIETY OF SAVOURY TARTLETS, FILLED WITH ONIONS, LEEKS, MUSHROOMS AND BROCCOLI. THIS VERSION IS SIMPLE TO PREPARE AND WOULD MAKE AN ELEGANT START TO A MEAL.

MAKES EIGHT TO TEN

INGREDIENTS
    15ml/1 tbsp oil
    1 leek, finely sliced
    175g/6oz broccoli, broken into florets
    15g/½oz/1 tbsp butter
    15g/½oz/2 tbsp plain flour
    150ml/¼ pint/⅔ cup milk
    50g/2oz goat's Cheddar or farmhouse
      Cheddar, grated
    salt and freshly ground black pepper
    fresh chervil, to garnish
For the pastry
    175g/6oz/1½ cups plain flour
    75g/3oz/6 tbsp butter
    1 egg

1 To make the pastry, place the flour and a pinch of salt in a bowl. Rub in the butter. Add the egg to make a dough, using a little cold water if necessary, Knead lightly, then wrap in clear film and leave to rest in the fridge for 1 hour.

2 Preheat the oven to 190°C/375°F/Gas 5. Let the dough return to room temperature for 10 minutes and then roll out on a lightly floured surface and line 8–10 deep patty tins. Prick the bases with a fork and bake in the oven for about 10–15 minutes until the pastry is firm and lightly golden. Increase the oven temperature to 200°C/400°F/Gas 6.

3 Heat the oil in a small saucepan and sauté the leek for 4–5 minutes until soft. Add the broccoli, and stir-fry for about 1 minute, then add a little water. Cover and steam for 3–4 minutes until the broccoli is just tender.

4 Melt the butter in a separate saucepan, stir in the flour and cook for a minute, stirring all the time. Slowly add the milk and stir to make a smooth sauce. Add half of the cheese and season with salt and pepper.

5 Spoon a little broccoli and leek into each tartlet case and then spoon over the sauce. Sprinkle each tartlet with the remaining cheese and then bake in the oven for about 10 minutes until golden.

6 Serve the tartlets as part of a buffet or as a starter, garnished with chervil.

CHARD PASTIES

CHARD, LIKE SPINACH, GOES PARTICULARLY WELL IN PASTIES. UNLIKE SOME GREEN VEGETABLES, IT CAN SURVIVE A LITTLE EXTRA COOKING AND IS SUBSTANTIAL ENOUGH TO BE THE PRINCIPAL INGREDIENT IN A DISH. FOR A MORE FLAVOURSOME PASTRY, REPLACE A LITTLE OF THE BUTTER WITH GRATED CHEESE.

SERVES FOUR

INGREDIENTS
675g/1½lb Swiss chard
25g/1oz/2 tbsp butter or margarine
1 onion, finely chopped
75g/3oz streaky bacon, chopped
50g/2oz Gruyère cheese, grated
25g/1oz/½ cup fresh brown or white breadcrumbs
90ml/6 tbsp single cream
salt and freshly ground black pepper
For the pastry
275g/10oz/2½ cups plain flour
150g/5oz/generous ½ cup butter or margarine
beaten egg, for glazing

1 To make the pastry, place the flour and salt in a mixing bowl and rub in the butter or margarine. Add a little cold water and mix to a soft dough. Knead lightly on a floured surface. Wrap in clear film and chill for 30 minutes.

2 Trim the stalks of the chard and then chop both the leaves and stalks. Place in a heavy-based pan, cover and cook over a low heat for 6–8 minutes until the stalks are tender and the leaves wilted, shaking the pan occasionally. Strain, then press out the excess liquid, place in a mixing bowl and leave to cool.

3 Melt the butter in a small frying pan and fry the onion and bacon for about 4–5 minutes until the onion is lightly golden and the bacon browned.

4 Add the onion and bacon to the chard and stir in the cheese, breadcrumbs, cream and seasoning to taste. Preheat the oven to 200°C/400°F/Gas 6.

5 Divide the pastry into four and roll out into rounds. Spoon the filling on to the centre of each and dampen the edges with water. Bring the sides together over the filling and press together to seal. Brush with beaten egg and then put on an oiled baking sheet. Bake for about 15–20 minutes until the pastry is golden.

TURNIP TOPS <u>WITH</u> PARMESAN <u>AND</u> GARLIC

TURNIP TOPS HAVE A PRONOUNCED FLAVOUR AND ARE GOOD WHEN COOKED TOGETHER WITH OTHER STRONG-FLAVOURED INGREDIENTS SUCH AS ONIONS, GARLIC AND PARMESAN CHEESE. THEY DO NOT NEED TO BE COOKED LONG AS THE LEAVES ARE QUITE TENDER.

<u>SERVES FOUR</u>

INGREDIENTS

   45ml/3 tbsp olive oil
   2 garlic cloves, crushed
   4 spring onions, sliced
   350g/12oz turnip tops, thinly sliced,
     tough stalk removed
   50g/2oz Parmesan cheese, grated
   salt and freshly ground black pepper
   shavings of Parmesan cheese,
     to garnish

1 Heat the olive oil in a large saucepan and fry the garlic for a few seconds. Add the spring onions, stir-fry for 2 minutes and then add the turnip tops.

2 Stir-fry for a few minutes so that the greens are coated in oil, then add about 50ml/2fl oz/¼ cup water. Bring to the boil, cover and simmer until the greens are tender.

3 Once the excess liquid has evaporated, stir in the Parmesan cheese. Serve at once with extra shavings of cheese, if liked, to garnish.

PASTA WITH SAVOY CABBAGE AND GRUYÈRE

THIS IS AN INEXPENSIVE AND SIMPLE DISH WITH A SURPRISING TEXTURE AND FLAVOUR. THE CABBAGE IS COOKED SO THAT IT HAS "BITE", CONTRASTING WITH THE SOFT CONSISTENCY OF THE PASTA.

SERVES FOUR

INGREDIENTS
1 small Savoy or green cabbage,
    thinly sliced
25g/1oz/2 tbsp butter
1 small onion, chopped
350g/12oz pasta, e.g. tagliatelle,
    fettucine or penne
15ml/1 tbsp chopped fresh parsley
150ml/¼ pint/⅔ cup single cream
50g/2oz Gruyère or Cheddar cheese,
    grated
about 300ml/½ pint/1¼ cups hot
    vegetable or chicken stock
salt and freshly ground black
    pepper

1 Preheat the oven to 180°C/350°F/
Gas 4 and butter a large casserole. Place
the cabbage in a mixing bowl.

2 Melt the butter in a small frying pan
and fry the onion until softened. Stir into
the cabbage in the bowl.

3 Cook the pasta according to the
instructions, until *al dente*.

4 Drain well and stir into the bowl with
the cabbage and onion. Add the parsley
and mix well and then pour into the
prepared casserole.

5 Beat together the cream and Gruyère
or Cheddar cheese and then stir in the
hot stock. Season well and pour over the
cabbage and pasta, so that it comes
about halfway up the casserole. If
necessary, add a little more stock.

6 Cover tightly with foil or a lid and cook
in the oven for 30–35 minutes, until the
cabbage is tender and the stock is
bubbling. Remove the lid of the
casserole for the last 5 minutes of the
cooking time to brown the top.

STIR-FRIED BRUSSELS SPROUTS

SERVES FOUR

INGREDIENTS
    450g/1lb Brussels sprouts
    15ml/1 tbsp sunflower oil
    6–8 spring onions, cut into 2.5cm/
        1in lengths
    2 slices fresh root ginger
    40g/1½oz/¼ cup flaked almonds
    150–175ml/5–6fl oz/⅔–¾ cup
        vegetable or chicken stock
    salt

1 Trim the bases of the Brussels sprouts and remove any large outer leaves. Cut into slices about 7mm/⅓in thick.

2 Heat the oil in a wok or heavy-based frying pan and fry the spring onions and the ginger for about 2–3 minutes, stirring frequently. Add the almonds and stir-fry over a moderate heat until both the onions and almonds begin to brown.

3 Remove and discard the ginger, reduce the heat and stir in the Brussels sprouts. Stir-fry for a few minutes and then pour in the stock and cook over a gentle heat for 5–6 minutes or until the sprouts are nearly tender.

4 Add a little salt, if necessary, and then increase the heat to boil off the excess liquid. Spoon into a warmed serving dish and serve immediately.

BRUSSELS SPROUTS GRATIN

SERVES FOUR

INGREDIENTS
    15g/½oz/1 tbsp butter
    150ml/¼ pint/⅔ cup whipping cream
    150ml/¼ pint/⅔ cup milk
    25g/1oz Parmesan cheese, grated
    675g/1½lb Brussels sprouts,
        thinly sliced
    2 garlic cloves, finely chopped
    salt and freshly ground black pepper

1 Preheat the oven to 150°C/300°F/ Gas 2 and butter a shallow ovenproof dish. Blend together the cream, milk, Parmesan cheese and seasoning.

2 Put a layer of Brussels sprouts in the base of the prepared dish, sprinkle with a little garlic and pour over about a quarter of the cream mixture. Add another layer of sprouts and continue building layers in this way, ending with the remaining cream and milk.

3 Cover loosely with greaseproof paper and then bake for 1–1¼ hours. Halfway through cooking, remove the paper and press the sprouts under the liquid in the dish. Return to the oven to brown.

PAK CHOI WITH LIME DRESSING

FOR THIS THAI RECIPE, THE COCONUT DRESSING IS TRADITIONALLY MADE USING FISH SAUCE, BUT VEGETARIANS COULD USE MUSHROOM KETCHUP INSTEAD. BEWARE, THIS IS A FIERY DISH!

SERVES FOUR

INGREDIENTS
6 spring onions
2 pak-choi
30ml/2 tbsp oil
3 fresh red chillies, cut into
 thin strips
4 garlic cloves, thinly sliced
15ml/1 tbsp crushed peanuts
For the dressing
15–30ml/1–2 tbsp fish sauce
30ml/2 tbsp lime juice
250ml/8fl oz/1 cup coconut milk

1 To make the dressing, blend together the fish sauce and lime juice, and then stir in the coconut milk.

2 Cut the spring onions diagonally into slices, including all but the very tips of the green parts.

3 Using a large sharp knife, cut the pak-choi into very fine shreds.

4 Heat the oil in a wok and stir-fry the chillies for 2–3 minutes until crisp. Transfer to a plate using a slotted spoon.

5 Stir-fry the garlic for 30–60 seconds until golden brown and transfer to the plate with the chillies.

6 Stir-fry the white parts of the spring onions for about 2–3 minutes and then add the green parts and stir-fry for a further 1 minute. Add to the plate with the chillies and garlic.

7 Bring a large pan of salted water to the boil and add the pak-choi; stir twice and then drain immediately.

8 Place the warmed pak-choi in a large bowl, add the coconut dressing and stir well. Spoon into a large serving bowl and sprinkle with the crushed peanuts and the stir-fried chilli mixture. Serve either warm or cold.

COOK'S TIP
Coconut milk is available in cans from large supermarkets and Chinese stores. Alternatively, creamed coconut is available in packets. To use creamed coconut, place 115g/4oz/½ cup in a jug and pour over 250ml/8fl oz/1 cup boiling water. Stir well until dissolved.

DOLMADES

DOLMADES ARE STUFFED VINE LEAVES, A TRADITIONAL GREEK DISH. IF YOU CAN'T OBTAIN FRESH VINE LEAVES, USE A PACKET OF BRINED VINE LEAVES. SOAK THE LEAVES IN HOT WATER FOR 10 MINUTES THEN RINSE AND DRY WELL ON KITCHEN PAPER BEFORE USE.

MAKES 20–24

INGREDIENTS

20–30 fresh young vine leaves
30ml/2 tbsp olive oil
1 large onion, finely chopped
1 garlic clove, crushed
225g/8oz/3 cups cooked long grain rice, or mixed white and wild rice
about 45ml/3 tbsp pine nuts
15ml/1 tbsp flaked almonds
40g/1½oz/generous ¼ cup sultanas
15ml/1 tbsp snipped chives
15ml/1 tbsp finely chopped fresh mint
juice of ½ lemon
150ml/¼ pint/⅔ cup white wine
hot vegetable stock
salt and freshly ground black pepper
sprig of mint, to garnish
Greek yogurt, to serve

1 Bring a large pan of water to the boil then cook the vine leaves for about 2–3 minutes. They will darken and go limp after about 1 minute and simmering for a further minute or so ensures they are pliable. If using leaves from a packet, place them in a large bowl, cover with boiling water and leave for a few minutes until the leaves can be easily separated. Rinse them under cold water and drain on kitchen paper.

2 Heat the oil in a small frying pan and fry the onion and garlic for 3–4 minutes over a gentle heat until soft.

3 Spoon the onion and garlic mixture into a bowl and add the cooked rice.

4 Stir in 30ml/2 tbsp of the pine nuts, the almonds, sultanas, chives, mint, lemon juice and seasoning and mix well.

5 Lay a vine leaf on a clean surface, with veined side uppermost. Place a spoonful of filling near the stem, fold the lower part of the leaf over it and roll up, folding in the sides as you go. Continue stuffing the vine leaves in this way.

6 Line the base of a deep frying pan with four large vine leaves. Place the stuffed vine leaves close together in the pan, seam side down, in a single layer.

7 Add the wine and enough stock just to cover the vine leaves. Now place a plate directly over the leaves, then cover and simmer gently for 30 minutes, checking to make sure the pan does not boil dry.

8 Chill the vine leaves, then serve garnished with the remaining pine nuts a sprig of mint and a little yogurt.

BEANS, PEAS AND SEEDS

Sweet and succulent, beans and peas are the vegetables we first

turn to when we need a tasty accompaniment. Okra, like

mangetouts and most fresh beans come complete with pods.

Podded peas are best when absolutely fresh, dried beans

give us another huge dimension of vegetable dishes, while

sweetcorn is a delight, whether kept on the cob or

served as kernels on the side.

BROAD BEANS

One of the delights of having a garden is discovering how truly delicious some vegetables are when garden fresh. This seems particularly true of broad beans, which have a superb sweet flavour that sadly can never be reproduced in the frozen product. If you're lucky enough to grow or be given fresh broad beans, don't worry about recipes; just cook them until tender and serve with butter. It will be a revelation! However, if you're not one of those lucky few, don't dismiss broad beans, as they are still a really versatile vegetable. They can be used in soups or casseroles, and, since they have a mealy texture, they also purée very well.

History

People have been eating broad beans almost since time began. A variety of wild broad bean grew all over southern Europe, north Africa and Asia, and they would have been a useful food for early man. There is archaeological evidence that by Neolithic times broad beans were being farmed, making them one of the first foods to be cultivated.

Broad beans will grow in most climates and most soils. They were a staple food for people throughout the Dark Ages and the Middle Ages, and were grown for feeding people and livestock until the potato replaced them in the seventeenth and eighteenth centuries. Broad beans were an important source of protein for the poor, and dried they would have provided nourishing meals for families until the next growing season.

Nutrition

Beans are high in both protein and carbohydrates and are also a good source of vitamins A, B1 and B2. They also provide potassium and iron as well as several other minerals.

Buying and Storing

Buy the beans as fresh as possible. The pods should preferably be small and tender. Use as soon as possible.

Preparing

Very young beans in tender pods, no more than 7.5cm/3in in length, can be eaten pod and all; top and tail, and then slice roughly. Usually, however, you will need to shell the beans. Elderly beans are often better skinned after they are cooked to rid them of the strong, bitter flavour that puts many people off this vegetable.

Cooking

Plunge shelled beans (or in their pods if very young) into rapidly boiling water and cook until just tender. They can also be par-boiled and then finished off braised in butter. For a simple purée, blend the cooked beans with garlic cooked in butter, cream and a pinch of fresh herbs, such as savory or thyme.

LIMA BEANS

These are popular in the US, named after the capital of Peru, and are sold mainly shelled. They are an essential ingredient in the Native-American dish *succotash*. Lima beans should be cooked in a little boiling water until tender. Elderly beans need skinning after they are cooked. The dried bean, also known as the butter bean, can be large or small. These large beans tend to become mushy when cooked so are best used in soups or purées.

Above: Broad beans
Below: Lima beans
Opposite: Runner beans

RUNNER BEANS

The runner bean is native to South America, where it has been cultivated for more than 2,000 years, and there is archaeological evidence of its existence much earlier than that.

It is a popular vegetable to grow. Most home vegetable gardeners have a patch of runner beans – they are easy to grow and, like all legumes, their roots contain bacteria that help renew the nitrogen supplies in the soil.

They have a more robust flavour and texture than French beans and also are distinct from green beans in several ways: They are generally much larger with long, flattened pods; their skin is rough textured, although in young beans this softens during cooking; and they

have purple beans within the pods, unlike green beans whose beans are mostly white or pale green. Nevertheless, the runner bean belongs to the same family as all the green beans.

Buying and Storing

Always buy young beans as the pods of larger beans are likely to be tough. The pods should feel firm and fresh; if you can see the outline of the bean inside the pod it is likely to be fibrous – although you could leave the beans to dry out and use the dried beans later in the season. Ideally, the beans inside should be no larger than your small fingernail.

Use as soon as possible after buying; they do not store well.

Preparing

Runner beans need to be topped and tailed and they may also need stringing. Carefully put your knife through the top of the bean without cutting right through it, and then pull downwards; if a thick thread comes away, the beans need stringing, so do the same on the other side. The beans can then be sliced using either a sharp knife or a slicer. Slice through the beans lengthways, not diagonally, so that you will be able to serve them with just a little skin and lots of flesh.

Cooking

Plunge the beans into boiling salted water and cook until *al dente*.

PEAS

Fresh peas are wonderful – try tasting them raw, straight from their pod. Unfortunately, the season for garden peas is short, and frozen peas, which are the next best thing, never quite come up to the mark. If you grow your own peas, for three or four weeks in early summer, you can eat like kings; otherwise you can buy them from a good greengrocer, who may be able to keep you supplied all through the early summer.

History

Peas have an even longer history than broad beans, with the archaeological evidence showing they were cultivated as long ago as 5700 BC. High in protein and carbohydrate, they would have been another important staple food and were eaten fresh, or dried in soups or potage.

Pease porridge is mentioned in a Greek play written in 5 BC. Pease pudding, probably something similar, made with split peas with onion and herbs, is an old-fashioned but still very popular dish, especially in the north of England, and is traditionally eaten with pork.

But one of the first recipes for peas, comes from *Le Cuisinier Français*, which was translated into English in the middle of the seventeenth century. It gives a recipe for *petits pois à la française* (peas cooked with small hearted lettuces) – still a popular recipe today.

Varieties

Mangetouts: These are eaten whole and have a delicate flavour, providing they are not overcooked. Unfortunately, they are easy to overcook and the texture then becomes rather slippery. Alternatively, blanch or stir-fry them. They are also good served raw in salads.

Petits pois: These are not, as you might expect, immature peas but are a dwarf variety. Gardeners grow their own, but they are not available fresh in the shops as they are mainly grown commercially for canning or freezing.

Snow peas, Sugar peas, Sugar snaps: These have the distinct fresh flavour of raw peas and are more plump and have more snap than mangetouts.

Buying and Storing

Only buy fresh peas, and use them as soon as possible. It is wiser to buy frozen peas rather than old peas, which can be tough and dry. In top condition, the pods are bright green and lively looking; the more withered the pod, the longer they have been hanging around. It is possible to surreptitiously sample peas on occasions, to check if they are fresh (greengrocers don't seem to mind so long as you buy something).

Preparing

Shelling peas can be very relaxing. Press open the pods and use your thumb to push out the peas *(below)*. Mangetouts and sugar snaps just need to be topped and tailed *(below right)*.

Opposite: peas.
Above right: Sugar snap peas.

Cooking

Cook peas with a sprig of mint in a pan of rapidly boiling water or in a covered steamer until tender. Alternatively, melt butter in a flameproof casserole, add the peas and then cover and sweat over a gentle heat for 4–5 minutes. Cook mangetouts and snow peas in any of these ways but for a shorter time.

GREEN BEANS

Whether you call beans French beans, wax beans, haricots or green beans, they all belong to a large and varied family.

History

The bean is a New World vegetable that had been cultivated for thousands of years by native people in both the north and south of the continent, which accounts for its wide diversity.

Varieties

One variety or another is available all year round and so they are one of the most convenient fresh green vegetables.
French beans: This name encompasses a range of green beans, including the snap bean and bobby bean. They are mostly fat and fleshy and when fresh, should be firm so that they break in half with a satisfying snapping sound.

Haricots verts: These are considered the best French beans and are delicate and

slim in shape. They should be eaten when very young and no more than 6–7.5cm/2½–3in in length.
Thai beans: These long beans are similar to French beans and they can be prepared and cooked in the same way.
Yellow wax beans: This is also a French bean and has a mild, slightly buttery taste.

Buying and Storing

Whatever variety, beans should be bright and crisp. Avoid wilted ones, or those with overly mature pods which feel spongy when lightly squeezed. They do not keep well, so use as soon as possible after buying or picking.

Preparing

To top and tail the beans: gather them together in one hand and then slice away the top 5mm/¼in (see below), then do the same at the other end. If necessary, pull off any stringy bits.

Cooking

Plunge the beans into rapidly boiling salted water and cook until *al dente*. If overcooked, beans have a flabby texture and also lose much of their flavour. Drain and toss them in butter or serve in a sauce with shallots and bacon. For salad dishes, cook until just tender and then refresh under cold water. They are excellent with a vinaigrette. Serve with carrots or other root vegetables and savour the contrast in flavours.

Opposite above: Bobby beans
Opposite below: Yellow wax beans
Right: Haricots verts
Below: Thai beans

SWEETCORN

Fresh sweetcorn, eaten on the cob with salt and a little butter is deliciously sweet. Some gardeners who grow it have a pan ready on the boil, so that when they cut the corn it goes into the pan in only the time it takes to race up from the garden to the kitchen. Buying it from the supermarket is inevitably a bit risky, although if it is purchased in season, sweetcorn can be very good indeed.

History

In 1492, as Christopher Columbus disembarked on the island now called Cuba, he was met by Native Americans offering two gifts of hospitality – one was tobacco and the other something the Indians called *maïs*. The English word for staple food was then corn, so that when Columbus and his crew saw that maize was the staple food for the Indians, it was dubbed "Indian corn".

Corn originated in South America and had enormous significance to the Native Americans of the whole continent, who were said to have lived and died by corn. They referred to it as their "first mother and father, the source of life". By far their most important food, the corn plant was used for their shelters and for fences, and they also wore corn and decorated their bodies with it.

The Aztecs conducted corn planting ceremonies that including human sacrifices, and other tribes had similar customs to appease the god "corn". Countless myths and legends have been woven around corn, each tribe telling a slightly different story, but each on the same theme of planting and harvesting corn. For anthropologists and historians, they make compelling study.

Nutrition

Corn is a good carbohydrate food and is rich in vitamins A, B and C. It contains protein, but not as much as most other cereals. It's also a good source of potassium, magnesium, phosphorus and iron.

Varieties

There are five main varieties of corn – popcorn, sweetcorn, dent corn, flint corn and flour corn. Dent corn is the most commonly grown worldwide, for animal

feeds and oil, and the corn we eat on the cobs is sweetcorn. Baby sweet cobs of corn are picked when immature and are cooked and eaten whole.

Buying and Storing

As soon as corn is picked, its sugar begins to turn to starch and therefore the sooner it goes into the pot, the better. Wherever possible, buy locally grown sweetcorn.

Look for husks that are clean and green and tassels which are golden, with no sign of matting. The corn itself should look plump and yellow. Avoid cobs with pale or white kernels or those with older shrivelled kernels which will undoubtedly be disappointing.

Preparing

Strip away the husks. To use the kernels for recipes, cut downwards using a sharp knife from top to bottom *(left)*.

Cooking

Cook corn-on-the-cob in plenty of boiling salted water until tender. Timing depends on the size of the cobs but 10–15 minutes will normally be enough. Serve them with sea salt and butter, but if the cobs are really sweet, leave out the butter. Stir-fry baby sweetcorn cobs briefly and serve in oriental dishes.

Opposite: Sweetcorn cobs
Below: Baby sweetcorn cobs

OKRA

History

Okra originated in Africa. In the sixteenth century, when African people were enslaved by the Spanish and shipped to the New World, they took with them the few things they could, including the plants and seeds from home: dried peas, yams, ackee – and okra. This lantern-shaped pod containing rows of seeds oozes a sticky mucilaginous liquid when cooked, and it was popular not only for its subtle flavour but also for thickening soups and stews.

The plant thrived in the tropical climate and by the nineteenth century, when the slave trade was finally abolished, okra was important in the cuisine of the Caribbean and southern United States. In and around New Orleans, the Creoles, the American-born descendants of European-born settlers, adopted a popular native American-Indian dish called gumbo. An essential quality of this famous dish was its thick gluey consistency. The Indians used filé powder (the dry pounded leaves of the sassafras tree), but okra was welcomed as a more satisfactory alternative.

Gumbos are now the hallmark of Creole cooking, and in some parts of America, the word "gumbo" is an alternative word for okra itself.

Buying and Storing

Choose young, small pods as older ones are likely to be fibrous. They should be bright green, firm and slightly springy when squeezed. Avoid any that are shrivelled or bruised. They will keep for a few days in the salad drawer of the fridge.

Preparing

When cooking whole, trim the top but don't expose the seeds inside or the viscous liquid will ooze into the rest of the dish. If, however, this is what you want, slice thickly or thinly according to the recipe (right). If you want to eliminate some of this liquid, first soak the whole pods in acidulated water (water to which lemon juice has been added) for about an hour.

Cooking

The pods can be steamed, boiled or lightly fried, and then added to or used

with other ingredients. If cooked whole, okra is not mucilaginous but is pleasantly tender. Whether cooked whole or sliced, use garlic, ginger or chilli to perk up the flavour, or cook Indian-style, with onions, tomatoes and spices.

Above: Okra

DRIED BEANS AND PEAS

Dried beans feature in many traditional cuisines all over the world, from Mexican re-fried beans to Italy's *pasta e fagioli*. They are nutritious, providing a good source of protein when combined with rice, and they are a marvellous store cupboard standby.

Black-eyed Beans: Sometimes called black-eyed peas, these small cream-coloured beans have a black spot or eye. When cooked, they have a tender, creamy texture and a mildly smoky flavour. Black-eyed beans are widely used in Indian cooking.

Chana Dhal: Chana dhal is very similar to yellow split peas but smaller in size and with a slightly sweeter taste. It is used in a variety of vegetable dishes.

Chick-peas: These round beige-coloured pulses have a strong, nutty flavour when cooked. As well as being used for some curries, they are also ground into a flour which is widely used in many Indian dishes such as *pakoras* and *bhajees*.

Flageolet Beans: Small oval beans which are either white or pale green in colour. They have a very mild, refreshing flavour and feature in classic French dishes.

Green Lentils: Also known as continental lentils, these have quite a strong flavour and retain their shape during cooking. They are very versatile and are used in a number of dishes.

Haricot Beans: Small, white oval beans, haricot beans are ideal for Indian cooking because not only do they retain their shape but they also absorb the flavours of the spices.

Kidney Beans: Kidney beans are one of the most popular pulses. They are dark red/brown, kidney-shaped beans with a strong flavour.

Mung Beans: These are small, round green beans with a slightly sweet flavour and creamy texture. When sprouted they produce the familiar beansprouts.

Red split lentils: A readily available lentil that can be used for making dhal. Use instead of toovar dhal.

Toovar dhal: A dull orange-coloured split pea with a very distinctive earthy flavour. Toovar dhal is available plain and in an oily variety.

Soaking and Cooking Tips

Most dried pulses, except lentils, need to be soaked overnight before cooking. Wash the beans thoroughly and remove any small stones and damaged beans. Put into a large bowl and cover with plenty of cold water. When cooking, allow double the volume of water to beans and boil for 10 minutes. This initial boiling period is essential to remove any harmful toxins. Drain, rinse and cook in fresh water. The cooking time for all pulses varies depending on the type and their freshness. Pulses can be cooked in a pressure cooker to save time. Lentils, on the whole, do not need soaking. They should be washed in several changes of cold water before being cooked.

Above (clockwise from top): Red split lentils, green lentils, toovar dhal, chana dhal
Left (clockwise from bottom right): Mung beans, flageolet beans, chick-peas, haricot beans, black-eyed beans, kidney beans

BEAN, PEA AND SEED RECIPES

Whether you're looking for classic side dishes, or for something more unusual, peas and beans are a great choice. Broad Beans à la Paysanne or Peas with Baby Onions and Cream are favourites everywhere; India-style Okra or Runner Beans with Garlic will please the more adventurous. Sweetcorn is particularly versatile; use it for snacks such as Sweetcorn and Cheese Pasties, or for a delicious main course soup, Sweetcorn and Scallop Chowder.

LAMB AND BROAD BEAN COUSCOUS

THIS SIMPLE-TO-MAKE STEW INCLUDES BOTH LAMB AND CHICKEN. IT IS SERVED ON A BED OF COUSCOUS WITH A SPICY SAUCE FOR POURING OVER.

SERVES FOUR

INGREDIENTS
30–45ml/2–3 tbsp vegetable oil
350g/12oz lean lamb, cut into cubes
3 skinless chicken pieces, cut into
   large chunks
1 large onion, chopped
2 garlic cloves, crushed
3 carrots, cut into 4cm/1½in lengths
1 small parsnip, cut into chunks
4 tomatoes, skinned and chopped
400ml/14fl oz/1⅔ cups chicken stock
1 cinnamon stick
2.5ml/½ tsp ground ginger
a sprig of thyme
1 small red or green pepper, seeded
   and sliced
225g/8oz shelled broad beans
5–10ml/1–2 tsp Tabasco or
   chilli sauce
salt and freshly ground black pepper
For the couscous
400g/14oz/2⅓ cups couscous
15ml/1 tbsp olive oil
a pinch of salt

1 Heat 30ml/2 tbsp oil in a flameproof casserole and fry the cubes of lamb until browned. Drain and transfer to a plate. Add the chicken pieces and cook until brown. Drain and add to the plate.

2 Heat a further 15ml/1 tbsp oil and fry the onion and garlic over a gentle heat for 4–5 minutes until softened. Add the carrots and parsnip, stir-fry for a few minutes and then add the tomatoes, stock, cinnamon stick, ginger, thyme and seasoning, together with the meat. Bring to the boil, stirring occasionally, and then reduce the heat, cover and simmer gently for about 45–60 minutes until the meat is cooked and very tender.

3 Meanwhile, in a large bowl rub the olive oil and salt into the couscous. Sprinkle with about 120ml/4fl oz/½ cup warm water and mix so that it swells slightly. Leave for 5–10 minutes. Place the soaked couscous in a colander. Set over the lamb stew, then cover and steam for about 15 minutes.

4 Add the pepper and broad beans to the stew and simmer for 10 minutes until the vegetables are cooked.

5 Just before serving, ladle about 150ml/¼ pint/⅔ cup of the cooking liquid into a small pan. Add a little Tabasco sauce and heat gently. Taste and add more Tabasco sauce, if liked, for a hotter and spicier sauce, and then pour into a warmed serving jug.

6 Spoon the couscous on to a large warmed serving plate and pour the stew over. Serve with the hot sauce.

BROAD BEANS À LA PAYSANNE

SERVES FOUR

INGREDIENTS
15ml/1 tbsp olive oil
1 onion, finely chopped
75g/3oz lean ham in a thick slice,
   finely diced
350g/12oz shelled broad beans
2 Little Gem lettuces, chopped
75ml/3fl oz/⅓ cup chicken or
   vegetable stock
50ml/2fl oz/¼ cup single cream
salt and freshly ground black pepper
sprigs of mint or chervil, to garnish

1 Heat the oil in a saucepan. Fry the onion and ham until soft. Add the beans and lettuce. Cover and cook gently for 6–8 minutes, stirring occasionally.

2 Stir in the stock, cream and seasoning and cook over a very low heat for about 20–30 minutes. Stir occasionally, taking care not to break up the beans.

3 Turn into a warmed serving dish and garnish with a sprig of mint or chervil. Serve with grilled meat or an omelette.

COOK'S TIP
Larger broad beans sometimes have a tough outer skin. It is a good idea to cook them briefly, peel off the outer skin and just use the tender green centres.

PEAS WITH BABY ONIONS AND CREAM

IDEALLY, USE FRESH PEAS AND FRESH BABY ONIONS. FROZEN PEAS ARE AN ACCEPTABLE SUBSTITUTE IF FRESH ONES AREN'T AVAILABLE, BUT FROZEN ONIONS TEND TO BE INSIPID AND ARE NOT WORTH USING. ALTERNATIVELY, USE THE WHITE PARTS OF SPRING ONIONS.

SERVES FOUR

INGREDIENTS
175g/6oz baby onions
15g/½ oz/1 tbsp butter
900g/2lb fresh peas (about
   350g/12oz shelled or frozen)
150ml/¼ pint/⅔ cup double cream
15g/½oz/2 tbsp plain flour
10ml/2 tsp chopped fresh parsley
15–30ml/1–2 tbsp lemon juice
   (optional)
salt and freshly ground black pepper

1 Peel the onions and halve them if necessary. Then melt the butter in a flameproof casserole. Fry the onions for 5–6 minutes over a moderate heat, until they begin to be flecked with brown.

3 Using a small whisk, blend the cream with the flour. Remove the pan from the heat and stir in the combined cream and flour, parsley and seasoning to taste.

4 Cook over a gentle heat for about 3–4 minutes, until the sauce is thick. Taste and adjust the seasoning; add a little lemon juice to sharpen, if liked.

2 Add the peas and stir-fry for a few minutes. Add 120ml/4fl oz/¾ cup water and bring to the boil. Partially cover and simmer for about 10 minutes until both the peas and onions are tender. There should be a thin layer of water on the base of the pan – add a little more water if necessary or, if there is too much liquid, remove the lid and increase the heat until the liquid is reduced.

MANGETOUTS WITH CHICKEN AND CORIANDER

MANGETOUTS ARE SO DELICATE AND FRESH-TASTING THAT IT SEEMS A CRIME TO DO ANYTHING AT ALL WITH THEM, BARRING FLASH COOKING AND SERVING THEM HOT OR COLD WITH A LITTLE BUTTER OR A VINAIGRETTE DRESSING. THEY ARE EXCELLENT IN STIR-FRIES, ADDING COLOUR AND TEXTURE.

SERVES FOUR

INGREDIENTS
  4 boned and skinned chicken breasts
  225g/8oz mangetouts
  45ml/3 tbsp vegetable oil, plus
    oil, for deep frying
  3 garlic cloves, finely chopped
  2.5cm/1in piece fresh root ginger,
    freshly grated
  5–6 spring onions, cut into
    4cm/1½in lengths
  10ml/2 tsp sesame oil
For the marinade
  5ml/1 tsp cornflour
  15ml/1 tbsp light soy sauce
  15ml/1 tbsp medium dry sherry
  15ml/1 tbsp vegetable oil
For the sauce
  5ml/1 tsp cornflour
  10–15ml/2–3 tsp dark soy sauce
  120ml/4fl oz/½ cup chicken stock
  30ml/2 tbsp oyster sauce
  boiled rice, to serve

1 Cut the chicken into strips about 1 x 4cm/½ x 1½in. For the marinade, blend together the cornflour and soy sauce. Stir in the sherry and oil. Pour over the chicken, turning the pieces over to coat evenly, and leave for 30 minutes.

2 Trim the mangetouts and plunge into a pan of boiling salted water. Bring back to the boil and then drain and refresh them under cold running water.

3 To make the sauce, mix together the cornflour, soy sauce, stock and oyster sauce and set aside.

4 Heat the oil in a deep fryer. Drain the chicken strips and fry, in batches if necessary, for about 30 seconds to brown. Drain and transfer to a plate using a slotted spoon.

5 Heat 15ml/1 tbsp of the vegetable oil in a wok and add the garlic and ginger. Stir-fry for about 30 seconds. Add the mangetouts and stir-fry for 1–2 minutes. Transfer to a plate and keep warm.

6 Heat the remaining vegetable oil in the wok, add the spring onions and stir-fry for 1–2 minutes. Add the chicken and stir-fry for 2 minutes. Pour in the sauce, reduce the heat and cook until it thickens and the chicken is cooked through.

7 Stir in the sesame oil, and pour over the mangetouts. Serve with boiled rice.

FRENCH BEAN SALAD

ALTHOUGH BEAN SALADS ARE DELICIOUS SERVED WITH A SIMPLE VINAIGRETTE DRESSING, THIS DISH IS A LITTLE MORE ELABORATE. IT DOES, HOWEVER, ENHANCE THE FRESH FLAVOUR OF THE BEANS.

SERVES FOUR

INGREDIENTS
    450g/1lb French beans
    15ml/1 tbsp olive oil
    25g/1oz/2 tbsp butter
    ½ garlic clove, crushed
    50g/2oz/1 cup white breadcrumbs
    15ml/1 tbsp chopped fresh
      parsley
    1 egg, hard-boiled and finely chopped
For the dressing
    30ml/2 tbsp olive oil
    30ml/2 tbsp sunflower oil
    10ml/2 tsp white wine vinegar
    ½ garlic clove, crushed
    1.5ml/¼ tsp French mustard
    a pinch of sugar
    a pinch of salt

3 Heat the oil and butter in a frying pan and fry the garlic for 1 minute. Stir in the breadcrumbs and fry over a moderate heat for about 3–4 minutes until golden brown, stirring frequently.

4 Remove the pan from the heat and stir in the parsley and then the egg. Sprinkle the breadcrumb mixture over the French beans. Serve warm or at room temperature.

1 Trim the French beans and cook in boiling salted water for 5–6 minutes until tender. Drain the beans and refresh them under cold running water and place in a serving bowl.

2 Make the salad dressing by blending the oils, vinegar, garlic, mustard, sugar and salt thoroughly together. Pour over the beans and toss to mix.

COOK'S TIP
For a more substantial salad, boil about 450g/1lb scrubbed new potatoes until tender, cool and then cut them into bite-size chunks. Stir into the French beans and then add the dressing.

FRENCH BEANS WITH BACON AND CREAM

SERVES FOUR

INGREDIENTS

   350g/12oz French beans
   50–75g/2–3oz bacon, chopped
   25g/1oz/2 tbsp butter or margarine
   15ml/1 tbsp plain flour
   350ml/12fl oz/1½ cups milk
    and single cream, mixed
   salt and freshly ground black pepper

1 Preheat the oven to 190°C/375°F/ Gas 5. Trim the beans and cook in lightly salted boiling water for about 5 minutes until just tender. Drain and place them in an ovenproof dish.

2 Dry-fry the bacon until crisp, crumble into very small pieces and stir into the beans in the dish.

3 Melt the butter or margarine in a saucepan, stir in the flour and then add the milk and cream mixture to make a smooth sauce. Season well with salt and ground black pepper.

4 Pour the sauce over the beans and carefully mix it in. Cover lightly with a piece of foil and bake in the oven for 15–20 minutes until hot.

RUNNER BEANS <u>WITH</u> GARLIC

*DELICATE AND FRESH-TASTING FLAGEOLET BEANS AND GARLIC ADD A DISTINCT FRENCH FLAVOUR TO
THIS SIMPLE SIDE DISH. SERVE TO ACCOMPANY ROAST LAMB OR VEAL.*

SERVES FOUR

INGREDIENTS
  225g/8oz flageolet beans
  15ml/1 tbsp olive oil
  25g/1oz/2 tbsp butter
  1 onion, finely chopped
  1–2 garlic cloves, crushed
  3–4 tomatoes, peeled and chopped
  350g/12oz runner beans, prepared
    and sliced
  150ml/¼ pint/⅔ cup white wine
  150ml/¼ pint/⅔ cup vegetable stock
  30ml/2 tbsp chopped fresh parsley
  salt and freshly ground black pepper

1 Place the flageolet beans in a large
saucepan of water, bring to the boil and
simmer for ¾–1 hour until tender. Drain.

2 Heat the oil and butter in a large
frying pan and sauté the onion and garlic
for 3–4 minutes until soft. Then add the
chopped tomatoes and continue cooking
over a gentle heat until they are soft.

3 Stir the flageolet beans into the onion
and tomato mixture, then add the runner
beans, wine, stock and a little salt. Stir
well. Cover and simmer for 5–10 minutes
until the runner beans are tender.

4 Increase the heat to reduce the liquid,
then stir in the parsley and season with a
little more salt, if necessary, and pepper.

INDIAN–STYLE OKRA

WHEN OKRA IS SERVED IN INDIAN RESTAURANTS IT IS OFTEN FLAT AND SOGGY BECAUSE IT HAS BEEN OVERCOOKED OR LEFT STANDING. HOWEVER, WHEN YOU MAKE THIS DISH YOURSELF, YOU WILL REALIZE JUST HOW DELICIOUS OKRA CAN BE.

SERVES FOUR

INGREDIENTS
350g/12oz okra
2 small onions
2 garlic cloves, crushed
1cm/½in piece fresh root ginger
1 green chilli, seeded
10ml/2 tsp ground cumin
10ml/2 tsp ground coriander
30ml/2 tbsp vegetable oil
juice of 1 lemon

3 Reduce the heat and add the garlic and ginger mixture. Cook for about 2–3 minutes, stirring frequently, and then add the okra, lemon juice and 105ml/7 tbsp water. Stir well, cover tightly and simmer over a low heat for about 10 minutes until tender. Transfer to a serving dish, sprinkle with the fried onion rings and serve at once.

1 Trim the okra and cut into 1cm/½in lengths. Roughly chop one of the onions and place in a food processor or blender with the garlic, ginger, chilli and 90ml/ 6 tbsp water. Process to a paste. Add the cumin and coriander and blend again.

2 Thinly slice the remaining onion into half rings; fry in the oil for 6–8 minutes until golden brown. Transfer to a plate using a slotted spoon.

SWEETCORN AND CHEESE PASTIES

THESE TASTY PASTIES ARE REALLY SIMPLE TO MAKE AND EXTREMELY MOREISH. WHY NOT MAKE DOUBLE THE AMOUNT — THEY'LL GO LIKE HOT CAKES?

MAKES 18 TO 20

INGREDIENTS
  250g/9oz sweetcorn
  115g/4oz feta cheese
  1 egg, beaten
  30ml/2 tbsp whipping cream
  15g/½oz Parmesan cheese, grated
  3 spring onions, chopped
  8–10 small sheets filo pastry
  115g/4oz/ ½ cup butter, melted
  freshly ground black pepper

1 Preheat the oven to 190°C/375°F/ Gas 5 and butter two patty tins.

2 If using fresh sweetcorn, strip the kernels from the cob using a sharp knife and simmer in a little salted water for 3–5 minutes until tender. For canned sweetcorn, drain and rinse well under cold running water.

3 Crumble the feta cheese into a bowl and stir in the sweetcorn. Add the egg, cream, Parmesan cheese, spring onions and ground black pepper, and stir well.

4 Take one sheet of pastry and cut it in half to make a square. (Keep the unused pastry covered with a damp cloth to prevent it drying out.) Brush with melted butter and then fold into four, to make a smaller square (about 7.5cm/3in).

5 Place a heaped teaspoon of mixture in the centre of each pastry square and then squeeze the pastry around the filling to make a "money bag" casing.

6 Continue making pasties until all the mixture is used up. Brush the outside of each "bag" with any remaining butter and then bake in the oven for about 15 minutes until golden. Serve hot.

SWEETCORN AND SCALLOP CHOWDER

FRESH HOME-GROWN SWEETCORN IS IDEAL FOR THIS CHOWDER, ALTHOUGH CANNED OR FROZEN ALSO WORK WELL. THIS SOUP IS ALMOST A MEAL IN ITSELF AND MAKES A PERFECT LUNCH DISH.

SERVES FOUR TO SIX

INGREDIENTS

  2 ears of corn or 200g/7oz frozen
    or canned sweetcorn
  600ml/1 pint/2½ cups milk
  15g/½oz/ 1 tbsp butter or margarine
  1 small leek or onion, chopped
  40g/1½oz smoked streaky bacon,
    finely chopped
  1 small garlic clove, crushed
  1 small green pepper, seeded
    and diced
  1 celery stalk, chopped
  1 medium potato, diced
  15ml/1 tbsp plain flour
  300ml/½ pint/1¼ cups chicken
    or vegetable stock
  4 scallops
  115g/4oz cooked fresh mussels
  a pinch of paprika
  150ml/¼ pint/⅔ cup single cream
    (optional)
  salt and freshly ground black pepper

1 Slice down the ears of fresh corn to remove the kernels; thaw frozen corn and drain and rinse canned corn. Place half of the kernels in a food processor and process with a little of the milk.

2 Melt the butter or margarine in a large saucepan and gently fry the leek or onion, bacon and garlic for 4–5 minutes until the leek or onion is soft but not browned. Add the green pepper, celery and potato; sweat over a gentle heat for a further 3–4 minutes, stirring frequently.

3 Stir in the flour and cook for about 1–2 minutes until the mixture is golden and frothy. Gradually stir in the milk and corn mixture, stock, the remaining milk and corn kernels and seasoning.

4 Bring to the boil and then reduce the heat to a gentle simmer, and cook, partially covered, for 15–20 minutes until the vegetables are tender.

5 Pull the corals away from the scallops and slice the white flesh into 5mm/¼in slices. Stir the scallops into the soup, cook for 4 minutes and then stir in the corals, mussels and paprika. Allow to heat through for a few minutes and then stir in the cream, if using. Adjust the seasoning to taste and serve.

SQUASHES

In their bright and beautiful colours, these are the vegetables that say autumn. Locally grown courgettes are available from mid to late summer, as are the pretty pattypans. Marrows follow in late summer and then come the winter squashes — acorn squash, kabocha, onion squash and pumpkins — just in time for Hallowe'en and pumpkin pie.

COURGETTES

Courgettes are the best loved of all the squashes as they are so versatile. They are quick and easy to cook and are succulent and tender with a delicate, unassuming flavour. Unlike other squashes, they are available all year.

   Vegetables taste best when eaten immediately after they have been picked; this particularly applies to courgettes. They have a long season and are good to grow since the more you cut, the more the plants produce. Left unchecked, they turn into marrows.

Varieties

The courgette is classified as a summer squash, *Cucurbita pepo*, along with the marrow and the pattypan squash.

Courgettes: Sometimes called zucchini, courgettes are basically immature marrows. The word is a diminutive of the French *courge*, meaning marrow, and similarly zucchini means miniature *zucca*, Italian for gourd. Courgettes have a deep green skin, with firm pale flesh. The seeds and pith found in marrows have yet to form but are visible in more mature courgettes. Conversely, the prized baby courgettes have no suggestion of seeds or pith and the flesh is completely firm.

Yellow courgettes: These are bright yellow and somewhat straighter than green courgettes. They have a slightly firmer flesh than green courgettes but are otherwise similar.

Pattypan squashes: These little squashes look like tiny custard squashes. They can be pale green, yellow or white and have a slightly firmer texture than courgettes, but a similar flavour. They can be sliced and grilled in the same way as courgettes but, to make the most of their size and shape, steam them whole until tender.

Summer crooknecks: Pale yellow with curves at the neck and a bumpy skin, crooknecks are prepared and cooked in the same way as courgettes.

Italian courgettes: These very long, thin courgettes are grown in Italy. They are treated liked ordinary courgettes but are strictly a bottle gourd.

Buying and Storing

Courgettes should be firm with a glossy, healthy-looking skin. Avoid any that feel squashy or generally look limp, as they will be dry and not worth using. Choose small courgettes whenever possible and buy in small quantities as needed.

Preparing

The tiny young courgettes need no preparation at all, and if they still have their flowers, so much the better. Other courgettes should be topped and tailed and then prepared according to the recipe, either sliced or slit for stuffing.

Cooking

Baby courgettes require little or no cooking. Steam them whole or blanch them. Sliced larger courgettes can be steamed or boiled but take care that they do not overcook as they go soggy very quickly. Alternatively, grill, roast or fry them. Try dipping slices in a light batter and then shallow frying in a blend of olive and sunflower oil. To roast, place them in an ovenproof dish, scatter with crushed garlic and a few torn basil leaves and sprinkle with olive oil; then bake in a very hot oven until just tender, turning the slices occasionally.

Opposite above: Pattypan squashes
Opposite below left: Baby courgettes
Opposite below right Yellow courgettes
Right: Italian courgettes beside white and green courgettes

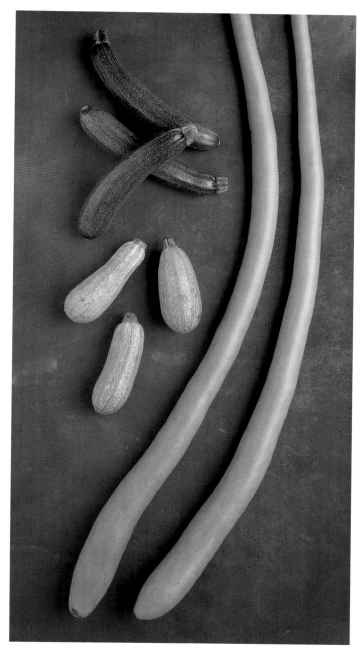

MARROWS AND SUMMER SQUASHES

Vegetable marrow is classified as a summer squash yet it is rather the poor relation of squashes. Most of the edible flesh is water and at best it is a rather bland vegetable, with a slightly sweet flavour. At worst, it is insipid and if cooked to a mush (which isn't unheard of), it is completely tasteless.

Marrows can be stuffed, although it involves a lot of energy expended for very little reward; but marrow cooked over a low heat in butter with no added water (so that it steams in its own juice) brings out the best in it.

History

Marrows, like all the summer and winter squashes, are native to America. Squashes were eaten by Native Americans, traditionally with corn and beans, and in an Iroquois myth the three vegetables are represented as three inseparable sisters. Although the early explorers would almost certainly have come into contact with them, they were not brought back home, and the vegetable marrow was not known in England until the nineteenth century. Once introduced, however, it quickly became very popular. Mrs Beeton gives eight recipes for vegetable marrow and observes that "it is now extensively used". No mention at all is made of courgettes, which of course are simply immature marrows, as any gardener will know.

Varieties

The word "marrow" as a general term tends to refer to the summer squashes. At the end of summer and in the early autumn a good variety of the large summer squashes is available.

Vegetable marrows: This is the proper name for the large prize marrows, beloved of harvest festivals and country fairs. Buy small specimens whenever possible.

Spaghetti squashes/marrows: Long and pale yellow, like all marrows these squashes can grow to enormous sizes, but try to buy small specimens for convenience as well as flavour. They got their name from the resemblance of the cooked flesh to spaghetti.

To boil a spaghetti squash, first pierce the end, so that the heat can reach the middle, then cook for about 25 minutes or until the skin feels tender. Cut the squash in half lengthways, remove the seeds, and then fork the strands of flesh out on to a plate. It has a fragrant, almost honey and lemon flavour and tastes good with garlic butter or pesto.

Custard marrows: These are pretty, pale green squashes with scalloped edges and a similar flavour to courgettes. If possible, buy small specimens, about 10cm/4in across. Boil these whole until tender, then cut a slice off the tops, scoop out the seeds and serve with a knob of butter.

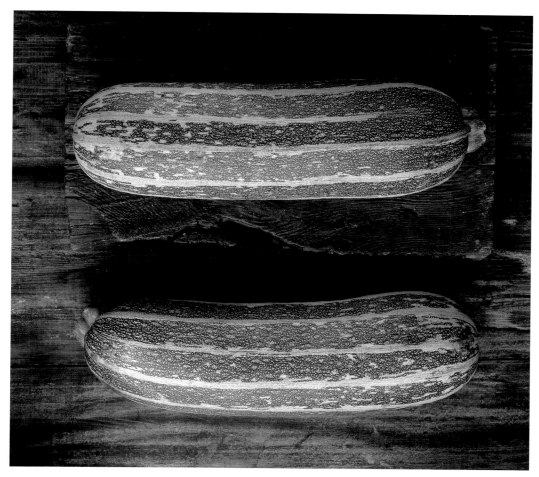

Buying and Storing

Buy vegetables that have clear, and unblemished flesh, and avoid any with soft or brown patches. Vegetable marrows and spaghetti squashes will keep for several months provided they are kept in a cool, dark place. Custard marrows will keep up to a week.

Preparing

Wash the skin. For sautéing or steaming, or if the skin is tough, peel it away. For braised marrow, cut into chunks and discard the seeds and pith (see right). For

stuffing, cut into slices or lengthways and discard the seeds and pith.

Cooking

Place chunks of marrow in a heavy-based pan with a little butter, cover and cook until tender. It can then be livened up with garlic, herbs or tomatoes. For stuffed marrow, blanch first, stuff, then cover or wrap it in foil to cook.

Opposite left: Spaghetti squashes
Opposite right: Custard marrows
Above: Vegetable marrows

PUMPKINS <u>AND</u> WINTER SQUASHES

Pumpkins are the most famous of the winter squashes; aesthetically they are one of nature's most pleasing vegetables for their huge size, their colour and the smoothness of their skin. They originally came from America and, from a culinary point of view, they have their home there.

The very name squash comes from America and as well as pumpkins, the family includes acorn, butternut and turban squashes to name but a few. There are simply hundreds of different squashes, including Sweet Dumpling, Queensland Blue (from Australia), Calabaza, Cushaw and Golden Nugget.

History

The tradition of eating pumpkin at Thanksgiving came from when the Pilgrim Fathers, who had settled in New England, proclaimed a day of prayer and thanksgiving for the harvest. In early times the pumpkin was served with its head and seeds removed, the cavity filled with milk, honey and spices, and baked until tender. The custom of eating pumpkin at Thanksgiving has remained but it is now served differently: puréed pumpkin, either fresh or tinned, is used to make golden tarts.

Varieties

There are a huge number of varieties of winter squashes and, confusingly, many are known by several different names. However, from a cooking point of view, most are interchangeable although it is best to taste dishes as you cook them, as seasoning may differ from one to the other. In general, they all have a floury and slightly fibrous flesh and a mild, almost bland flavour tinged with sweetness. Because of this blandness, they harmonize well with other ingredients.
Acorn squashes: These are small and heart-shaped with a beautiful deep green or orange skin, or a mixture of the two. Peel, then use as for pumpkins or bake whole, then split and serve with butter.
Butternut squashes: Pear-shaped, these are a buttery colour. Use in soups or in any pumpkin recipe.
Delicata squashes: This pretty pale yellow squash has a succulent yellow flesh,

tasting like a cross between sweet potato and butternut squash.
English pumpkins: These have a softer flesh than the American variety and are good for soups or, if puréed, combined with potatoes or other root vegetables.
Hubbard squashes: These large winter squashes have a thick, bumpy, hard shell which can range in colour from bright orange to dark green. If they are exceptionally large, they are sometimes sold in halves or large wedges. They have a grainy texture and are best mashed with butter and seasoning.
Kabocha squashes: Attractive bright green squashes with a pale orange flesh.

They are similar in flavour and texture to acorn squashes and can be prepared and cooked in the same way.
Onion squashes: Round, yellow or pale orange, onion squashes have a mild flavour, less sweet than pumpkin but still with a slightly fruity or honey taste. They are good in risottos or in most pumpkin recipes.

Above (clockwise from right): A pumpkin hybrid, kabocha squash, Acorn squash.
Right: clockwise from top right: Hybrid squash, two golden acorn squashes, two small and one large pumpkin.

Buying and Storing

All winter squashes may be stored for long periods. Buy firm, unblemished vegetables with clear smooth skins.

Preparing

For larger squashes, or for those being used for soups or purées, peel and cut into pieces then remove the seeds (left).

Cooking

Boil in a little water for 20 minutes or until tender, then mash and serve with butter and plenty of salt and pepper. Smaller squashes can be baked whole in their skins, then halved, seeded and served with butter and maple syrup. Pumpkin and other squashes can also be lightly sautéed in butter before adding stock, cream or chopped tomatoes.

Pumpkins: Large, bright yellow or orange squashes, with a deep orange flesh. They have a sweet, slightly honeyed, flavour and are very much a taste North Americans and Australians grow up with. However, they are not to everyone's liking and some people find them rather cloying. Pumpkin soup, pumpkin bread and pumpkin pie are part of the American tradition, as are faces carved from the shell at Hallowe'en.

EXOTIC GOURDS

While the squashes are native to America, most gourds originated in the Old World – from Africa, India and the Far East. However, over the millennia, the seeds crossed water and, over the centuries, people crossed continents so that now squashes and gourds are common all over the world. Both belong to the family *Cucurbitacea*, and both are characterised by their rapid-growing vines.

Bottle gourds: Bottle gourds are still a familiar sight in Africa, where they are principally grown not for their fruit, but for their dried shells. The gourds can grow to enormous sizes and the shells are used for water bottles, cups and musical instruments. The young fruit can be eaten, but it is extremely bitter and is normally only added to highly flavoured stews, like curries.

Chayotes: The chayote (pronounced chow-chow) is a popular gourd in all sorts of regions of the world and can be found in any ethnic supermarket, be it Chinese, African, Indian or Caribbean. In each it is known by a different name, christophine being the Caribbean term, but choko, shu-shu and chinchayote are among its many other names used else-where. Unlike most gourds, it originated in

Mexico but was widely grown throughout the tropics after the invasions of the Spanish.

It is a pear-shaped fruit with a large central stone and has a cream-coloured or green skin. It has a bland flavour, similar to marrow, and a slightly firmer texture something like pumpkin. It is commonly used in Caribbean cooking, primarily as a side dish or in soufflés. Alternatively it can be used raw in salads.

Chinese bitter melons: These are a common vegetable in all parts of Asia and go by a myriad of names – bitter gourd and bitter cucumber to name two. They are popular throughout Asia, eaten when very young, but are extremely bitter and rarely eaten in the West. They are easily recognized as they have warty, spiny skins, looking like a toy dinosaur. The skins are white when young but will probably have ripened to a dark green by the time they appear in the shops.

Most recipes from China suggest you halve the gourd, remove the pulp, and then slice before boiling for several minutes to remove their bitterness. They can then be added to stir-fries or other oriental dishes.

Opposite left: Sweet dumpling
Opposite right: Pumpkin
Top right: Chinese bitter melon
Right: Loofah
Below: Chayote

Smooth and angled loofahs: The smooth loofah must be one of the strangest plants. When young it can be eaten, although it is not much valued. However, the plant is grown almost exclusively for sponges, used everywhere as a back rub in the bath. The ripe loofahs are picked and, once the skin has been stripped off and the seeds shaken out, allowed to dry. The plant then gradually dries to a fibrous skeleton and thence moves to bathrooms everywhere. Angled or ribbed loofahs are more commonly eaten but are only edible when young as they become very bitter when mature. They taste a bit like courgettes and are best cooked in a similar way, either fried in butter or cooked with tomatoes, garlic and oil.

CUCUMBERS

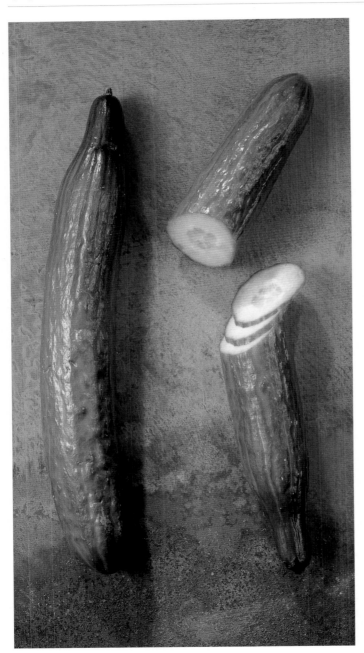

The Chinese say food should be enjoyed for its texture as well as for its flavour. Cucumbers have a unique texture and refreshing cool taste. An afternoon tea with cucumber sandwiches, thinly sliced cucumber between wafer-thin white buttered bread, is a delight of contrasts – the soft bread, the smooth butter and the cool crisp cucumber.

Varieties

English cucumbers: These are the cucumbers the English are most familiar with. They have fewer seeds and thinner skin than the ridged cucumber.
Gherkins: These are tiny cucumbers with bumpy, almost warty skins and are mostly pickled in vinegar and eaten with cold meats or chopped into mayonnaise.
Kirbys: Small cucumbers, available in the United States and used for pickling.
Ridged cucumbers: These are smaller than most cucumbers with more seeds and a thick, bumpy skin. You can buy them all over France but otherwise they tend to be available only in specialist greengrocers. The waxed ones need to be peeled before eating but most ridged cucumbers on the Continent are unwaxed and good without peeling.

Buying and Storing

Cucumbers should be firm from top to bottom. They are often sold pre-wrapped in plastic and can be stored in the salad drawer of the fridge for up to a week. Remove the plastic packaging once you've begun to use a cucumber. Discard once it begins to go soggy.

Preparing

Whether you peel a cucumber or not is a matter of personal preference, but wash it if you don't intend to peel it. Some producers use wax coatings to give a glossy finish; these cucumbers must be peeled. If you are in doubt, buy organic cucumbers. Special citrus peelers can remove strips of peel to give an attractive striped effect when sliced.

Serving

Thinly sliced cucumber is most frequently served with a light dressing or soured cream. In Greece cucumber

is an essential part of a Greek country salad, *horiatiki salata,* cut into thick chunks and served with tomatoes, peppers and feta and dressed simply with olive oil and a little wine vinegar. Iced cucumber soup is delicious, and cucumber can also be puréed with yogurt, garlic and herbs and served with soured cream stirred in.

Cooking

Cucumbers are normally served raw, but are surprisingly good cooked. Cut the cucumber into wedges, remove the seeds and then simmer for a few minutes until tender. Once drained, return the cucumber to the pan and stir in a little cream and seasoning.

Left: Cucumbers
Above left: Ridged cucumbers
Above right: Baby cucumbers
Right: Kirbys

SQUASH RECIPES

Pumpkins and squashes need long slow cooking, which is why these are the vegetables you need for warming dishes such as Pumpkin Soup, Onion Squash Risotto and Baked Marrow in Cream and Parsley. Courgettes on the other hand are best cooked quickly. Baked Courgettes, stuffed with goat's cheese, and Courgettes Italian-style, are cooked so that maximum flavour is retained, and the result is perfection.

ONION SQUASH RISOTTO

THIS RISOTTO PROVIDES A WARM AND COMFORTING MEAL AFTER A TIRING DAY. FOR A VEGETARIAN ALTERNATIVE SIMPLY OMIT THE BACON AND USE VEGETABLE STOCK.

SERVES FOUR

INGREDIENTS
    1 onion squash or pumpkin, about
        900g/1kg/2–2¼lb
    30ml/2 tbsp olive oil
    1 onion, chopped
    1–2 garlic cloves, crushed
    115g/4oz streaky bacon, chopped
    115g/4oz/generous ½ cup arborio rice
    600–750ml/1–1¼ pints/2½–3 cups
        chicken stock
    40g/1½oz Parmesan cheese, grated
    15ml/1 tbsp chopped fresh parsley
    salt and freshly ground black pepper

1 Halve or quarter the onion squash or pumpkin, remove the seeds and skin, and then cut into chunks about 1–2cm/½–¾in in size.

2 Heat the oil in a flameproof casserole and fry the onion and garlic for about 3–4 minutes, stirring frequently. Add the bacon and continue frying until both the onion and bacon are lightly golden.

3 Add the squash or pumpkin, stir-fry for a few minutes. Add the rice and cook for about 2 minutes, stirring all the time.

4 Pour in about half of the stock and season. Stir well and then half cover and simmer gently for about 20 minutes, stirring occasionally. As the liquid is absorbed, add more stock and stir to prevent the mixture sticking to the base.

5 When the squash and rice are nearly tender, add a little more stock. Cook, uncovered for 5–10 minutes. Stir in the Parmesan cheese and parsley and serve.

PUMPKIN SOUP

THE SWEET FLAVOUR OF PUMPKIN IS GOOD IN SOUPS, TEAMING WELL WITH OTHER MORE SAVOURY INGREDIENTS SUCH AS ONIONS AND POTATOES TO MAKE A MILD AND SOOTHING DISH.

SERVES FOUR TO SIX

INGREDIENTS
    15ml/1 tbsp sunflower oil
    25g/1oz/2 tbsp butter
    1 large onion, sliced
    675g/1½lb pumpkin, cut into
        large chunks
    450g/1lb potatoes, sliced
    600ml/1 pint/2½ cups vegetable stock
    a good pinch of nutmeg
    5ml/1 tsp chopped fresh tarragon
    600ml/1 pint/2½ cups milk
    about 5–10ml/1–2 tsp lemon juice
    salt and freshly ground black pepper

1 Heat the oil and butter in a heavy-based saucepan and fry the onion for 4–5 minutes over a gentle heat until soft but not browned, stirring frequently.

2 Add the pumpkin and potato, stir well and then cover and sweat over a low heat for about 10 minutes until the vegetables are almost tender, stirring occasionally to prevent them from sticking to the pan.

3 Stir in the stock, nutmeg, tarragon and seasoning. Bring to the boil and then simmer for about 10 minutes until the vegetables are completely tender.

4 Allow to cool slightly, then pour into a food processor or blender and purée until smooth. Pour back into a clean saucepan and add the milk. Heat gently and then taste, adding the lemon juice and extra seasoning if necessary. Serve piping hot with crusty brown bread.

BAKED COURGETTES

THIS RECIPE IT IS PARTICULARLY DELICIOUS WHEN VERY SMALL AND VERY FRESH COURGETTES ARE USED. THE CREAMY YET TANGY GOAT'S CHEESE PROVIDES AN EXCELLENT CONTRAST WITH THE DELICATE FLAVOUR OF THE YOUNG COURGETTES.

SERVES FOUR

INGREDIENTS
    8 small courgettes, about 450g/1lb
      total weight
    15ml/1 tbsp olive oil, plus extra
      for greasing
    75–115g/3–4oz goat's cheese, cut
      into thin strips
    a small bunch fresh mint, finely
      chopped
    freshly ground black pepper

1 Preheat the oven to 180°C/350°F/ Gas 4. Cut out eight rectangles of foil large enough to encase each courgette and brush each with a little oil.

2 Trim the courgettes and cut a thin slit along the length of each.

3 Insert pieces of goat's cheese in the slits. Add a little mint and sprinkle with the olive oil and black pepper.

4 Wrap each courgette in the foil rectangles, place on a baking sheet and bake for about 25 minutes until tender.

COOK'S TIP
Almost any cheese could be used in this recipe. Mild cheeses, however, such as a mild Cheddar or mozzarella, will best allow the flavour of the courgettes to be appreciated to their full.

COURGETTES ITALIAN-STYLE

USE GOOD QUALITY OLIVE OIL AND SUNFLOWER OIL. THE OLIVE OIL GIVES A DELICIOUS FRAGRANCY BUT IS NOT ALLOWED TO OVERPOWER THE COURGETTES.

SERVES FOUR

INGREDIENTS
15ml/1 tbsp olive oil
15ml/1 tbsp sunflower oil
1 large onion, chopped
1 garlic clove, crushed
4–5 courgettes, cut into 1cm/½in
   slices
150ml/¼ pint/⅔ cup chicken
   or vegetable stock
2.5ml/½ tsp fresh chopped oregano
salt and freshly ground black pepper
chopped fresh parsley, to garnish

3 Stir in the stock, oregano and season to taste. Simmer gently for 8–10 minutes, until the liquid has almost evaporated. Spoon the courgettes into a serving dish, sprinkle with parsley and serve.

1 Heat the oils in a large frying pan and fry the onion and garlic over a moderate heat for 5–6 minutes until the onion has softened and is beginning to brown.

2 Add the courgettes and fry for about 4 minutes until they just begin to be flecked with brown. Stir frequently.

MARROWS WITH GNOCCHI

A SIMPLE WAY WITH MARROW, THIS DISH MAKES AN EXCELLENT ACCOMPANIMENT TO GRILLED MEAT BUT IT IS ALSO GOOD WITH A VEGETARIAN DISH, OR SIMPLY SERVED WITH GRILLED TOMATOES. GNOCCHI ARE AVAILABLE FROM MOST SUPERMARKETS; ITALIAN DELICATESSENS MAY ALSO SELL FRESH GNOCCHI.

SERVES FOUR

INGREDIENTS
1 small marrow, cut into
   bite-size chunks
50g/2oz/ ¼ cup butter
400g/14oz packet gnocchi
½ garlic clove, crushed
salt and freshly ground black pepper
chopped fresh basil, to garnish

1 Preheat the oven to 180°C/350°F/ Gas 4 and use some of the butter to grease a large ovenproof dish. Place the marrow in a single layer in the dish. Dot all over with the remaining butter.

2 Place a double piece of buttered greaseproof paper over the top. Cover with an ovenproof plate or lid so that it presses the marrow down, and then place a heavy, ovenproof weight on top of that. (Use a couple of old-fashioned scale weights.)

3 Put in the oven to bake for about 15 minutes, by which time the marrow should just be tender.

4 Meanwhile, cook the gnocchi in a large saucepan of boiling salted water for 2–3 minutes, or according to the instructions on the packet. Drain well.

5 Stir the garlic and gnocchi into the marrow. Season and then place the greaseproof paper over the marrow and return to the oven for 5 minutes (the weights are not necessary).

6 Just before serving, sprinkle the top with a little chopped fresh basil.

BAKED MARROW WITH CREAM AND PARSLEY

THIS IS A REALLY GLORIOUS WAY WITH A SIMPLE AND MODEST VEGETABLE. TRY TO FIND A SMALL, FIRM AND UNBLEMISHED MARROW FOR THIS RECIPE, AS THE FLAVOUR WILL BE SWEET, FRESH AND DELICATE. YOUNG MARROWS DO NOT NEED PEELING; MORE MATURE ONES DO.

SERVES FOUR

INGREDIENTS

1 small young marrow, about 900g/2lb
30ml/2 tbsp olive oil
15g/½oz/1 tbsp butter
1 onion, chopped
15ml/1 tbsp plain flour
300ml/½ pint/1¼ cups milk and
    single cream mixed
30ml/2 tbsp chopped fresh parsley
salt and freshly ground black pepper

1 Preheat the oven to 180°C/350°F/ Gas 4 and cut the marrow into pieces measuring about 5 x 2.5cm/2 x 1in.

2 Heat the oil and butter in a flameproof casserole and fry the onion over a gentle heat until very soft.

3 Add the marrow and sauté for 1–2 minutes and then stir in the flour. Cook for a few minutes, then stir in the milk and cream mixture.

4 Add the parsley and seasoning, stir well and then cover and cook in the oven for 30–35 minutes. If liked, remove the lid for the final 5 minutes of cooking to brown the top. Alternatively, serve the marrow in its rich pale sauce.

COOK'S TIP
Chopped fresh basil or a mixture of basil and chervil also tastes good in this dish.

CUCUMBER AND TROUT MOUSSE

THIS IS A VERY LIGHT, REFRESHING MOUSSE, MAKING THE MOST OF THE CLEAN TASTE OF CUCUMBER. SERVE IT AS A STARTER OR FOR A LIGHT LUNCH WITH A GREEN SALAD. YOU COULD ALSO ARRANGE A CHERVIL LEAF OR A VERY THIN LEMON SLICE ON THE TOPPING.

SERVES SIX

INGREDIENTS

1 small cucumber
2-3 smoked trout fillets, about
   175g/6oz total weight
115g/4oz/½ cup fromage frais
15ml/1 tbsp powdered gelatine
150ml/¼ pint/⅔ cup vegetable stock
12–14 pimiento-stuffed olives, sliced
30ml/2 tbsp lemon juice
5ml/1 tsp finely chopped
   fresh tarragon
150ml/¼ pint/⅔ cup whipping cream
2 egg whites
salt and freshly ground black pepper
   lettuce leaves and peeled prawns,
   to garnish
For the topping
   15ml/1 tbsp powdered gelatine
   90ml/6 tbsp vegetable stock

1 Lightly oil six ramekin dishes. To prepare the topping, take one-quarter of the cucumber and slice thinly. Sprinkle the gelatine over the stock, leave to soak for a few minutes and then place over a saucepan of simmering water and stir until completely dissolved.

2 Spoon a little of the gelatine mixture into each dish and arrange two or three cucumber slices on top. Put in the fridge to set. Pour over the remaining gelatine mixture and return to the fridge to set.

3 To make the mousse, peel and very finely dice the remaining cucumber and put in a bowl. Flake the fish, discarding the skin and any bones and add to the cucumber. Beat in the fromage frais.

4 Sprinkle the gelatine over 30ml/2 tbsp of water in a bowl and leave to soak for a few minutes. Place over a saucepan of simmering water and stir until dissolved.

5 Heat the stock. Stir in the gelatine and leave until cool but not set. Pour over the trout mixture and stir in the olives, lemon juice, tarragon and seasoning.

6 Lightly whip the cream and whisk the egg whites until stiff. Fold the cream into the trout mixture, followed by the egg whites. Spoon the mousse into the ramekin dishes, levelling the surface. Cover and chill for 1–2 hours and then unmould on to serving plates.

7 Garnish with lettuce leaves with a few peeled prawns scattered over, and any remaining tarragon.

LOOFAH AND AUBERGINE RATATOUILLE

LOOFAHS HAVE A SIMILAR FLAVOUR TO COURGETTES AND CONSEQUENTLY TASTE EXCELLENT WITH AUBERGINES AND TOMATOES. UNLESS USING VERY YOUNG LOOFAHS, WHICH ARE BEST, ENSURE THAT YOU PEEL AWAY THE ROUGH SKIN, AS IT CAN BE SHARP.

SERVES FOUR

INGREDIENTS

   1 large or 2 medium aubergines
   450g/1lb young loofahs or
     sponge gourds
   1 large red pepper, cut into
     large chunks
   225g/8oz cherry tomatoes
   225g/8oz shallots, peeled
   10ml/2 tsp ground coriander
   60ml/4 tbsp olive oil
   2 garlic cloves, finely chopped
   a few coriander leaves
   salt and freshly ground black pepper

1 Cut the aubergine into thick chunks and sprinkle the pieces with salt. Set aside in a colander for about 45 minutes and then rinse well under cold running water and pat dry.

2 Preheat the oven to 220°C/425°F/ Gas 7. Slice the loofahs into 2cm/¾in pieces. Place the aubergine, loofah and pepper pieces, together with the tomatoes and shallots in a roasting tin which is large enough to take all the vegetables in a single layer.

3 Sprinkle with the ground coriander and olive oil and then scatter over the chopped garlic and coriander leaves. Season to taste.

4 Roast for about 25 minutes, stirring the vegetables occasionally, until the loofah is golden brown and the peppers are beginning to char at the edges. Stir, then place in a warmed serving dish.

CHOCOLATE COURGETTE CAKE

THE RECIPE FOR THIS MOIST CHOCOLATE CAKE FLAVOURED WITH COURGETTES OR ZUCCHINI, COMES FROM AMERICA. ALTHOUGH AN UNLIKELY COMBINATION, IT IS A DELICIOUS VARIATION WELL WORTH TRYING.

SERVES FOUR TO SIX

INGREDIENTS
   115g/4oz/½ cup margarine
   130ml/4½fl oz/½ cup sunflower oil
   115g/4oz/generous ½ cup caster sugar
   225g/8oz/1⅓ cups soft brown sugar
   3 eggs, beaten
   130ml/4½fl oz/½ cup milk
   350g/12oz/3 cups plain flour
   10ml/2 tsp baking powder
   60ml/4 tbsp cocoa powder
   2.5ml/½ tsp ground allspice
   450g/1lb courgettes, peeled
     and grated
   5ml/1 tsp vanilla essence
   225g/8oz plain chocolate dots

1 Preheat the oven to 190°C/375°F/ Gas 5 and line a 23 x 33cm/9 x13in baking tin with non-stick baking paper.

2 Cream the margarine, oil and sugars together until light and fluffy, then gradually beat in the eggs and milk.

3 Sift the flour, baking powder, cocoa powder and ground allspice together and fold gently into the mixture.

4 Stir in the grated courgettes and vanilla essence and spoon the mixture into the prepared tin. Smooth the top using a palette knife and sprinkle the chocolate dots over the top.

5 Bake in the oven for 35–45 minutes until the cake is firm and a knife comes out clean. Cut into squares while still warm and then leave to cool.

PUMPKIN AND HAM FRITTATA

A FRITTATA IS AN ITALIAN VERSION OF THE SPANISH TORTILLA, A SUBSTANTIAL OMELETTE MADE OF EGGS AND VEGETABLES. ALTHOUGH FRITTATAS ARE SOMETIMES EATEN COLD, THIS ONE TASTES BETTER WARM OR HOT, SERVED WITH CRUSTY BREAD.

SERVES FOUR

INGREDIENTS
30ml/2 tbsp sunflower oil
1 large onion, chopped
450g/1lb pumpkin, chopped into
 bite-size pieces
200ml/7fl oz/scant 1 cup
 chicken stock
115g/4oz smoked ham, chopped
6 eggs
10ml/2 tsp chopped fresh marjoram
salt and freshly ground black pepper

1 Preheat the oven to 190°C/375°F/Gas 5 and oil a large shallow ovenproof dish. Heat the oil in a large frying pan and fry the onion for 3–4 minutes until softened.

2 Add the pumpkin and fry over a brisk heat for 3–4 minutes, stirring frequently. Stir in the stock, cover and simmer over a gentle heat for 5–6 minutes until the pumpkin is slightly tender. Add the ham.

3 Pour the mixture into the prepared dish. Beat the eggs with the marjoram and a little seasoning. Pour into the dish and then bake for 20–25 minutes until the frittata is firm and lightly golden.

VEGETABLE FRUITS

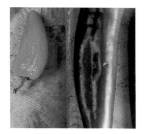

What would we do without our fabulous range of vegetable fruits? Here are the most colourful, and probably most versatile of all our vegetables. Tomatoes and peppers are the basis of countless dishes, with chillies adding their particular personality to any dish where a little extra something is required. Aubergines too are wonderfully versatile and for a Caribbean flavour, there are plantains and green bananas.

TOMATOES

Next to onions, tomatoes are one of the most important fresh ingredients in the kitchen. In Mediterranean cooking, they are fundamental. Along with garlic and olive oil, they form the basis of so many Italian, Spanish and Provençal recipes that it is hard to find many dishes in which they are not included.

History

Tomatoes are related to potatoes, aubergines and sweet and chilli peppers, and all are members of the nightshade family. Some very poisonous members of this family may well have deterred our ancestors from taking to tomatoes. Indeed, the leaves of tomatoes are toxic and ingestion can result in very bad stomach aches.

Tomatoes are native to western South America. By the time of the Spanish invasions in the sixteenth century, they were widely cultivated throughout the whole of South America and Mexico. Hernán Cortés, conqueror of the Aztecs, sent the first tomato plants, a yellow variety, to Spain.

However, people did not instinctively take to this "golden apple". English horticulturists mostly grew them as ornamental plants for their gardens and had little positive to say about them as food. Spain is recorded as the first country to use tomatoes in cooking, stewing them with oil and seasoning. Italy followed suit, but elsewhere they were treated with suspicion.

The first red tomatoes arrived in Europe in the eighteenth century, brought to Italy by two Jesuit priests. They were gradually accepted in northern Europe where, by the mid-nineteenth century, they were grown extensively, eaten raw, cooked or used for pickles.

Above right: Red and yellow cherry tomatoes
Rght: Yellow pear tomatoes
Opposite above: Round or salad tomatoes on the vine
Opposite below: Beefsteak tomatoes

Varieties

There are countless varieties of tomatoes, ranging from the huge beef tomatoes that measure 10cm/4in across, to tiny cherry tomatoes, not much bigger than a thumb nail. They come in all shapes too – elongated, plum-shaped or slightly squarish and even pear-shaped.

Beefsteak tomatoes: Large, ridged and deep red or orange in colour, these have a good flavour so are good in salads.

Canned tomatoes: Keep a store of canned tomatoes, especially in the winter when fresh ones tend to taste insipid. Tomatoes are one of the few vegetables that take well to canning, but steer clear of any that are flavoured with garlic or herbs. It is far better to add flavouring yourself.

Cherry tomatoes: These small, dainty tomatoes were once the prized treasures of keen gardeners but are now widely available. Although more expensive than round tomatoes, they have a sweet flavour and are worth paying the extra

money for serving in salads or for cooking whole.

Plum tomatoes: Richly flavoured with fewer seeds than regular tomatoes, these Italian-grown tomatoes are usually used for cooking, although they can be used in salads.

Round or salad tomatoes: These are the common tomatoes found in greengrocers and supermarkets. They vary in size according to the exact type and season. Sun-ripened tomatoes have the best flavour, but for year-round availability the fruit is often picked and ripened off the plant. These tomatoes are very versatile in everyday cooking. Adding a pinch of sugar and taking care to season the dish well helps to overcome any weakness in flavour.

Sun-dried tomatoes: This is one of the fashionable foods of the late eighties and early nineties. They add an evocative flavour to many Mediterranean dishes but don't use them too indiscriminately.

Tomato purée: This is good for adding an intense tomato flavour, but use carefully or the flavour will be overpowering. Tubes have screw tops and are better than cans as, once they are opened, they can be kept for up to 4-6 weeks in the fridge.

Yellow tomatoes: These are exactly like red tomatoes – they may be round, plum or cherry-size – except they are yellow.

Buying and Storing

Ideally, tomatoes should be allowed to ripen slowly on the plant so that their flavour can develop. Consequently, home-grown tomatoes are best, followed by those grown and sold locally. When buying from a supermarket or your greengrocer, look at the leafy green tops; the fresher they look the better. Buy locally grown beefsteak or cherry tomatoes for salads; plum tomatoes for rich sauces. Paler tomatoes or those tinged with green will redden if kept in a brown paper bag or the salad drawer of the fridge, but if you intend to use tomatoes straight away, buy bright red specimens. Overripe tomatoes, where the skin has split and they seem to be bursting with juice, are excellent in soups. However, check for any sign of mould or decay, as this will spoil all your good efforts.

Preparing

Slice tomatoes across rather than downwards for salads and pizza toppings. For wedges, cut downwards into halves, quarters or eighths depending on the size of the tomato.

Cooking

Among the many classic tomato dishes is tomato soup, cooked to a delicate orange colour with stock or milk, or simmered with vegetables, garlic and basil. *À la provençale* indicates that tomatoes are in the dish; in Provençal and Italian cooking, tomatoes are used with fish, meat and vegetables, in sauces and stuffings, with pasta and in superb salads. The Italian *tri colore salata* is a combination of large tomatoes, mozzarella and basil (the three colours of the Italian flag). The natural astringency of tomatoes means that, in salads, they need only be sprinkled with a fruity olive oil.

Chopped Tomatoes

Chopped tomatoes add a depth of flavour to all sorts of meat and vegetable dishes. Ideally, even in fairly rustic meals, the tomatoes should be peeled, since the skin can be irritating to eat once cooked. Some sauce recipes also recommend seeding tomatoes: cut the tomato into halves and scoop out the seeds before chopping (see above).

Skinning Tomatoes

Cut a cross in the tops of the tomatoes, then place in a bowl and pour over boiling water. Leave for a minute (see above), Use a sharp knife to peel away the skin, which should come away easily. Do a few at a time (five at most) otherwise they will begin to cook while soaking. Boil water for the next batch when you have finished peeling.

AUBERGINES

Many varieties of aubergines are grown and cooked all over the world. In Europe, Asia and America, they feature in a multitude of different dishes.

History

Although aubergines are a member of the nightshade family and thus related to potatoes, tomatoes and peppers, they were not discovered in the New World. The first mention of their cultivation is in China in 5 BC, and they are thought to have been eaten in India long before that. It was the Moors who introduced the aubergine to Spain some 1,200 years ago and it was grown in Andalucia. It is likely that they also introduced it to Italy, and possibly from there to other southern and eastern parts of Europe.

In spite of their popularity in Europe, aubergines did not become popular in Britain or the United States until very recently. Although previous generations of food writers knew about them, they gave only the occasional recipe for cooking with them.

Opposite: Plum tomatoes
Top: Aubergines
Above: Baby aubergines
Left: Japanese aubergines

Meanwhile, in the southern and eastern parts of Europe, aubergines had become extremely well liked, and today they are one of the most popular vegetables in the Mediterranean. Indeed, Italy, Greece and Turkey claim to have 100 methods of cooking them. In the Middle East, they are also a central part of their cuisine.

Varieties

There are many different varieties of aubergines, varying in colour, size and shape according to their country of origin. Small ivory-white and plump aubergines look like large eggs (hence their name in the States: eggplant). Pretty striped aubergines may be either purple or pink and flecked with white irregular stripes. The Japanese or Asian aubergine is straight and very narrow, ranging in colour from a variegated purple and white to a solid purple. It has a tender, slightly sweet flesh. Most aubergines, however, are either glossy purple or almost black and can be long and slim or fat like zeppelins. All aubergines have a similar flavour and

texture; they taste bland yet slightly smoky when cooked, and the flesh is spongy to touch when raw, but soft after cooking.

Buying and Storing

Aubergines should feel heavy and firm to the touch, with glossy, unblemished skins. They will keep well in the salad drawer of the fridge for up to two weeks.

Preparing

When frying aubergines for any dish where they need slicing (e.g. ratatouille), it is a good idea to salt the slices first in order to draw out some of their moisture, otherwise, they absorb enormous quantities of oil during cooking (they absorb copious amounts anyway, but

salting reduces this slightly). Salting also used to be advised to reduce their bitterness but today's varieties are rarely bitter. To salt aubergines, cut into slices, about 1cm/¹/₂ in thick for fried slices, (see top right) or segments (see above right) and sprinkle generously with salt. Leave to drain in a colander for one hour, then rinse and gently squeeze out the moisture from each slice or carefully pat dry with a piece of muslin.

Cooking

Aubergine slices can be fried in olive oil, as they are or first coated in batter – both popular Italian and Greek starters.

For moussaka, *parmigiana* and other dishes where aubergines are layered with other ingredients, fry the slices

briefly in olive oil. This gives them a tasty crust, while the inside stays soft.

To make a purée, such as for Poor Man's Caviar, first prick the aubergine all over with a fork and then roast in a medium oven for about 30 minutes until tender. Scoop out the flesh and mix with spring onions, lemon juice and olive oil. One of the most famous aubergine dishes is *Imam Bayaldi* – "the Iman fainted" – fried aubergines stuffed with onions, garlic, tomato, spices and lots of olive oil.

Opposite above: White aubergines
Opposite below: Striped aubergines
Above: Thai aubergines, including white, yellow and pea aubergines

PEPPERS

In spite of their name, peppers have nothing to do with the spice pepper used as a seasoning, although early explorers may have been mistaken in thinking the fruit of the shrubby plant looked like the spice they were seeking. It is thanks to this 400-year-old mistake that the name "pepper" has stuck.

History

The journeys Christopher Columbus and the conquistadors made were partly to find the spices Marco Polo had found a hundred years earlier in the Far East. Instead of the Orient, however, Columbus "discovered" the Americas, and instead of spices, he found maize, potatoes and tomatoes. He would have noted, though, that the Native Americans flavoured their food with ground peppers, and since it was hot, like pepper, perhaps wishful thinking coloured his objectivity. In any case, he returned with these new vegetables, calling them peppers and advertising them as more pungent than those from Caucasia.

Varieties

Peppers and chillies are both members of the capsicum family. To distinguish between them, peppers are called sweet peppers, bell peppers and even bullnose peppers and come in a variety of colours – red, green, yellow, white, orange and a dark purple-black.

The colour of the pepper tells you something about its flavour. Green are the least mature and have a fresh "raw" flavour. Red peppers are ripened green peppers and are distinctly sweeter. Yellow/orange peppers taste more or less like red peppers, although perhaps slightly less sweet and if you have a fine palate you may be able to detect a difference. Black peppers have a similar flavour to green peppers but when cooked are a bit disappointing as they turn green; so if you buy them for their dramatic colour, they are best used raw in salads.

In Greece and other parts of southern Europe, longer, slimmer peppers are often available which have a much more pronounced sweet and pungent flavour than the bell-shaped peppers – although this may be because they are locally picked and are therefore absolutely fresh when they reach the market. Whichever is the case, they are quite delicious.

Buying and Storing

Peppers should look glossy and sprightly and feel hard and crisp; avoid any that look wrinkled or have damp soft patches. They will keep for a few days at the bottom of the fridge.

Preparing

To prepare stuffed peppers, cut off the top and then cut away the inner core and pith, and shake out the seeds. The seeds and core are easily removed when you are halving, quartering or slicing.

Cooking

There are countless ways of cooking peppers. Sliced, they can be fried with onions and garlic in olive oil and then braised with tomatoes and herbs. This is the basic ratatouille; other vegetables, such as courgettes and aubergines, can of course be added.

Peppers can be roasted, either with ratatouille ingredients or with only onions and garlic. Cut into large pieces, place in a roasting pan and sprinkle with olive oil, torn basil and seasoning. Roast in a very hot oven (220°C/425°F/Gas 7) for about 30 minutes, turning occasionally. Grilled peppers are another superb dish. Once grilled they can be skinned to reveal a soft, luxurious texture and added to salads.

Opposite above: Red, green and orange peppers
Opposite below: Yellow peppers
Above left: White peppers
Above right: Purple peppers

Skinning Peppers

Cut the pepper into quarters lengthways and grill, skin side up (see above), until the skin is charred and evenly blistered. Place the pieces immediately into a polythene bag (use tongs or a fork as they will be hot) and close the top of the bag with a tie or knot. Leave for a few minutes and then remove from the bag and the skin will peel off easily.

CHILLIES

Some people apparently become so addicted to the taste of hot food that they carry little jars of chopped dried chillies around with them and scatter them over every meal. Although this is a bit extreme, it is chillies more than any other ingredient that spice up our mealtimes.

Varieties

Chillies really are the most important seasoning in the world after salt. Unlike peppers, to which they are closely related, the different varieties of chilli can have widely different heat values – from the "just about bearable" to the "knock your head off" variety.

Anaheim Chilli: A long, thin chilli with a blunt end, named after the Californian city. It can be red or green and has a mild, sweet taste.

Ancho Chilli/Pepper: These look like tiny peppers. They are mild enough to taste their underlying sweetness.

Bird's-eye or bird chilli: These small red chillies are fiery hot. Also known as pequin chillies.

Cayenne pepper: This is made from the dried, ground seeds and pods of chillies. The name comes from the capital of French Guiana, north of Brazil, although the cayenne chilli does not grow there any longer and the pepper is made from chillies grown all over the world.

Early jalapeño: A popular American chilli, which starts dark green and gradually turns to red.

Habañero: Often called Scotch Bonnet, this is the hottest of all chillies and is small and can be green, red or yellow. Colour is not a real guide to its heat, so don't be fooled into thinking that green ones are mild. They are all *very* hot. The habañero comes from Mexico and is frequently used in Mexican and Caribbean dishes.

Hot gold spike: A large, pale, yellow-green fruit grown in the south-western United States. It is very hot.

Above: Bird's-eye chillies
Left: Habañero chillies (in and below bowl) and yellow wax peppers

Preparing

The capsaicin in all chillies is most concentrated in the pith inside the pod and this, together with the seeds, should be cut away (see below) unless you want maximum heat. Capsaicin irritates the skin and especially the eyes, so take care when preparing chillies. Either wear gloves or wash your hands well after handling chillies.If you rub your eyes, even if you have washed your hands carefully, it will be painful.

Poblano: A small, dark green chilli, served whole in Spain either roasted or grilled. They are mostly mild but you can get the rogue fiery one, so beware if you are eating them whole.

Red chilli: These are long and rather wrinkled chillies which are green at first and then gradually ripen to red. They are of variable hotness and, because they are so long and thin, are rather fiddly to prepare.

Serrano chilli: A long, red and extremely hot chilli.

Tabasco: A sauce made with chillies, salt and vinegar; first produced in New Orleans. It is a fiery sauce, popular in Creole, Caribbean and Mexican cookery – or indeed in any dish requiring a bit of last minute heat.

Yellow wax pepper: Pale yellow to green, these can vary from mild to hot.

Buying and Storing

Some fresh chillies look wrinkled even in their prime and therefore this is not a good guide to their freshness. They should, however, be unblemished, and avoid any which are soft or bruised.

The substance which makes the chilli hot is a volatile oil called capsaicin. This differs not only from one type to another but also from plant to plant, depending on growing conditions; the more the plant has to struggle to survive in terms of light, water and soil, etc, the more capsaicin will be produced. It is thus impossible to tell how hot a chilli will be before tasting, although some types are naturally hotter than others. The belief that green chillies are milder than red ones does not necessarily follow; but generally red chillies will have ripened for longer in the sun so they will only be sweeter for all that sunshine.

Chillies can be stored in a polythene bag in the fridge for a few days.

Cooking

In Mexican cooking chillies play a vital, and almost central role. It is hard to think of any savoury Mexican dish that does not contain either fresh chillies or some form of processed chilli, whether canned, dried or ground. Other cuisines, however, are equally enthusiastic about chillies. They are essential in curries and similar dishes from India and the Far East, and in Caribbean and Creole food they are also used extensively.

If you have developed a tolerance for really hot food, then there is no reason why you shouldn't add as many as you wish. In general, however, use chillies discreetly, if for no better reason than you can't take the heat away if you make a mistake.

Above left: Ancho chillies (left) and Anaheim chillies (on board)

PLANTAINS AND GREEN BANANAS

While bananas are well and truly fruit, eaten almost exclusively as a dessert or by themselves as fruit, plantains can reasonably be considered among the vegetable fraternity because they have a definite savoury flavour, are normally eaten as a first or main course and can only be eaten once cooked.

Varieties

Plantains: Also known as cooking bananas, these have a coarser flesh and more savoury flavour than sweet bananas. While superficially they look exactly like our own bananas, they are, on closer inspection, altogether larger and heavier looking. They can vary in colour from the unripe fruit, which is green, through yellow to a mottled black colour, which is when the fruit is completely ripe.

Green bananas: Only certain types of green bananas are used in African and Caribbean cooking, and the "greenish" bananas you will find in most Western supermarkets are normally unripe eating bananas. If you need green bananas for a recipe, look out for them in West Indian or African shops.

Preparing

Plantains: These are inedible raw and must be cooked before eating. Unless very ripe, the skin can be tricky to remove. With yellow and green plantains, cut the fruit into short lengths, then slit the skin along the natural ridge of each piece of plantain. Gently ease the skin away from the flesh and pull until it peels off completely (see below).

Once peeled, plantains can be sliced horizontally or into lengths and roasted or fried. As with bananas, plantains will discolour if exposed to the air so, if not using immediately, sprinkle with lemon juice or place in a bowl of salted water.

Green bananas: Prepare these in a similar way. As with plantains, green bananas should not be eaten raw and are usually boiled, either in their skins or not, according to the recipe.

If making green banana crisps, use a potato peeler to produce the thinnest slices (see left).

If cooking plantains or green bananas in their skins, slit the skin lengthways along the sides and place in a saucepan of salted water. Bring to the boil, simmer gently for about 20 minutes until tender and then cool. The peel can then easily be removed before slicing.

Cooking and Serving

Plantains and green bananas have an excellent flavour. In many African and Caribbean recipes they are roasted or fried and then served simply with salt. However, if boiled, they can be sliced and served in a simple salad with a few sliced onions, or added to something far more elaborate like a gado gado salad, with mango, avocado, lettuce and prawns.

Plantains also make a delicious soup, often teamed with sweetcorn. After frying an onion and a little garlic, add two sliced and peeled plantains with tomatoes, if liked. Fry gently for a few minutes and then add vegetable stock to cover and one or two sliced chillies, together with about 175g/6oz sweetcorn. Simmer gently together until the plantain is tender.

Opposite above: Plantains
Opposite below: Green bananas
Below: Canned ackee

ACKEE

Ackee is a tropical fruit which is used in a variety of savoury dishes, mainly of Caribbean origin, where the fruit is very popular. The fruit itself is bright red and, when ripe, bursts open to reveal three large black seeds and a soft, creamy flesh resembling scrambled eggs. It has a slightly lemony flavour and is served with saltfish to make one of Jamaica's national dishes. Only buy ripe fruit as, when underripe, certain parts of the fruit are toxic.

However, unless you are visiting the Caribbean you are probably only likely to find ackee in cans, and indeed most recipes call for canned ackee which is a good substitute for the fresh fruit.

Jamaican cooks also use ackee to add a subtle flavour to a variety of vegetable and bean dishes. The canned ackee needs very little cooking, and should be added to dishes in the last few minutes of cooking. Take care when stirring into a dish as it breaks up very easily.

AVOCADOS

The avocado has been known by many names – butter pear and alligator pear to name but two. It earned the title butter pear clearly because of its consistency, but alligator pear was the original Spanish name. Although you would be forgiven for thinking this was due to its knobbly skin (among some varieties), the name in fact derives from the Spanish which was based on the Aztec word, the basically unpronounceable *ahuacatl*. From this to the easily-said alligator and thence to avocado was but two short steps.

History

The avocado is a New World fruit, native to Mexico, but while it would have been "discovered" by the Old World explorers, it didn't actually become popular food in Europe until the middle of the twentieth century, when modern transport meant that growers in California, who started farming avocados in the mid-nineteenth century, could market the fruit world-wide. Avocados are now also exported by South Africa and Australia.

Nutrition

The avocado is high in protein and carbohydrate. It is one of the few fruits that contains fat, and it is also rich in potassium, vitamin C, some B vitamins and vitamin E. Its rich oils, particularly its vitamin E content, mean that it is not only useful as food, but for skin and hair care too, something the Aztecs and Incas were aware of a thousand years ago. The cosmetics industry may have been in its infancy, but it still knew a good thing when it saw it.

Because of their valuable protein and vitamin content, avocados are a popular food for babies. They are easily blended, and small children generally enjoy their creamy texture and pleasant flavour.

Varieties

There are four varieties: Hass, the purple-black small knobbly avocado, the Ettinger and Fuerte, which are pear-shaped and have smooth green skin, and the Nabal, which is rounder in shape. The black-coloured Hass has golden-yellow flesh; green avocados have pale green to yellow flesh.

Buying and Storing

The big problem in buying avocados is that they're never ripe when you want them to be . How often do you see shoppers standing by the avocados, searching for that rare creature, the perfectly ripe avocado? Most times they all feel as hard as rocks; that or else they're hopelessly soft and squashy and clearly past their best. The proper and sensible thing to do is buy a few days before you need it. An unripe avocado will ripen in 4 –7 days at room temperature. Once it is ripe, it will keep well in the fridge for a few days, but you still need to plan ahead if you want to be sure of the perfect avocado.

The alternative is to hope for the best and keep feeling around until you find a ripe fruit. A perfect avocado should have a clean, unblemished skin without any brown or black patches. If ripe, it should "give" slightly if squeezed gently in the hand, but not so much that it actually feels soft. Overripe avocados are really not worth bothering with, however persuasive and generous the offer from the man on the market. The flesh will be unattractively brown and stringy and the bits of good flesh you do manage to salvage will be soft and pulpy – good for a dip, but nothing much else.

Preparing

Although they are simple fruits, avocados can be the devil to prepare. Once peeled, you are left with a slippery object which is then almost impossible to remove from the stone.

If you intend to eat the avocados in halves, it's fairly simple just to prise out the stone once halved. If you want to slice the fruit, use this tip I learnt from my chef friend. The only thing you need is a very sharp knife. Cut the avocado in half, remove the stone and then, with the skin still on, cut through the flesh and the skin to make slices. It is then relatively simple to strip off the peel.

Remember to sprinkle the slices with lemon juice as the flesh discolours once exposed to the air.

Cooking

Most popular raw, avocados can also be baked, grilled or used in sautéed and sauced dishes.

Serving Ideas

As well as prawns or vinaigrette, a half avocado can hold a mixture of chopped tomatoes and cucumber, a mild garlic cheese dip or a soured cream potato salad. Slices of avocado are delicious served with sliced fresh tomatoes and mozzarella, sprinkled simply with olive oil, lemon juice and black pepper. Avocados can be chopped and added to a salad, or puréed for a rich dressing.

In Mexico, where avocados grow in abundance, there are countless avocado recipes. Guacamole is perhaps the best known, but they are also eaten in soups and stews and commonly used to garnish tacos and enchiladas.

BREADFRUIT

Breadfruit is the name for a tropical tree that grows on the islands of the South Pacific ocean. The fruit of the tree is about the size of a small melon with a rough rind and a pale, mealy flesh.

Preparing

The fruit should be peeled and the core removed.

Cooking

Breadfruit can be treated like potatoes: the flesh may be boiled, baked or fried. It is a staple food for the people of the Pacific islands who bake the flesh, or dry and grind it for biscuits, breads and puddings. It has a sweet flavour and soft texture when ripe.

*Opposite (clockwise from the right):
Fuerte, Hass and Nabal avocados
Right: Breadfruit*

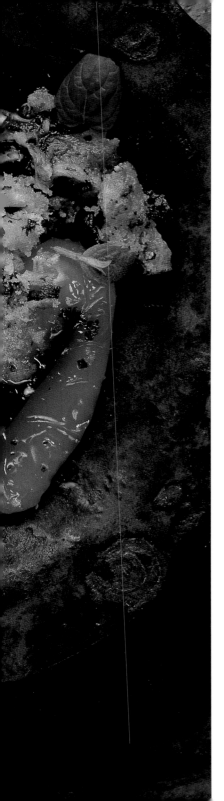

VEGETABLE
FRUIT
RECIPES

Vegetable fruits are the perfect excuse for letting your cook's imagination run riot. Tomatoes, peppers, chillies and aubergines have a wonderful affinity, and by simply putting two or three of these ingredients together, almost by magic you have a superb summer supper. Whether it's Aubergine and Courgette Bake, Gazpacho, Spinach and Pepper Pizza or Eggs Flamenco, our favourite vegetable fruits play a starring role. And if you fancy sampling Caribbean cuisine, try Plantain Appetizer, served with piquant Guacamole.

AUBERGINE <u>AND</u> COURGETTE BAKE

*THIS IS A WONDERFULLY WARMING DISH FOR A WINTER'S DAY. USE
FRESH BASIL, IF AVAILABLE AS THE TASTE IS FAR SUPERIOR.*

SERVES FOUR TO SIX

INGREDIENTS
1 large aubergine
30ml/2 tbsp olive oil
1 large onion, chopped
1–2 garlic cloves, crushed
900g/2lb tomatoes, peeled
 and chopped
a handful of basil leaves, shredded
 or 5ml/1tsp dried basil
15ml/1 tbsp chopped fresh parsley
2 courgettes, sliced lengthways
plain flour, for coating
75–90ml/5–6 tbsp sunflower oil
350g/12oz mozzarella, sliced
25g/1oz Parmesan cheese, grated
salt and freshly ground black pepper

1 Slice the aubergine, sprinkle with salt
and set aside for 45–60 minutes. Heat
the olive oil in a large frying pan. Fry the
onion and garlic for 3–4 minutes until
softened. Stir in the tomatoes, half the
basil and parsley, and seasoning. Bring
to the boil. Reduce the heat and cook,
stirring, for 25–35 minutes, or until
thickened to a pulp.

2 Rinse and dry the aubergines. Dust
the aubergines and courgettes with flour.

3 Heat the sunflower oil in another
frying pan and fry the aubergine and
courgettes until golden brown. Set aside.

4 Preheat the oven to 180°C/350°F/
Gas 4. Butter an ovenproof dish. Put a
layer of aubergines and then courgettes
in the dish, pour over half the sauce and
scatter with half the mozzarella. Sprinkle
over most of the remaining basil and a
little parsley. Repeat the layers, ending
with mozzarella. Sprinkle the Parmesan
cheese and remaining herbs on top and
bake for 30–35 minutes. Serve at once.

AUBERGINES <u>WITH</u> TZATZIKI

SERVES FOUR

INGREDIENTS
2 aubergines
oil, for deep frying
salt
For the batter
75g/3oz/⅔ cup plain flour
a pinch of salt
1 egg
120–150ml/4–5fl oz/½–⅔ cup milk,
 or half milk, half water
pinch of salt
For the tzatziki
½ cucumber, peeled and diced
150ml/¼ pint/⅔ cup natural yogurt
1 garlic clove, crushed
15ml/1 tbsp chopped fresh mint

1 To make the tzatziki, place the
cucumber in a colander, sprinkle with
salt and leave for 30 minutes. Rinse,
drain well and pat dry on kitchen paper.
Mix the yogurt, garlic, fresh mint and
cucumber in a bowl. Cover and chill.
Slice the aubergine lengthways. Sprinkle
with salt. Leave for 1 hour.

2 To make the batter, sift the flour and
salt into a large bowl, add the egg and
liquid and beat until smooth.

3 Rinse the aubergines and then pat
dry. Heat 1cm/½in of oil in a large frying
pan. Dip the aubergine slices in the
batter and fry them for 3–4 minutes until
golden, turning once. Drain on kitchen
paper and serve with the tzatziki.

GAZPACHO

GAZPACHO IS A CLASSIC SPANISH SOUP. IT IS POPULAR ALL OVER SPAIN BUT NOWHERE MORE SO THAN IN ANDALUCIA, WHERE THERE ARE HUNDREDS OF VARIATIONS. IT IS A COLD SOUP OF TOMATOES, TOMATO JUICE, GREEN PEPPER AND GARLIC, WHICH IS SERVED WITH A SELECTION OF GARNISHES.

SERVES FOUR

INGREDIENTS
  1.5kg/3–3½lb ripe tomatoes
  1 green pepper, seeded and
    roughly chopped
  2 garlic cloves, crushed
  2 slices white bread, crusts removed
  60ml/4 tbsp olive oil
  60ml/4 tbsp tarragon wine vinegar
  150ml/¼ pint/⅔ cup tomato juice
  a good pinch of sugar
  salt and freshly ground black pepper
  ice cubes, to serve
For the garnishes
  30ml/2 tbsp sunflower oil
  2–3 slices white bread, diced
  1 small cucumber, peeled and
    finely diced
  1 small onion, finely chopped
  1 red pepper, seeded and finely diced
  1 green pepper, seeded and finely
    diced
  2 hard-boiled eggs, chopped

1 Skin the tomatoes, then quarter them and remove the cores.

2 Place the pepper in a food processor and process for a few seconds. Add the tomatoes, garlic, bread, olive oil and vinegar and process again. Finally, add the tomato juice, sugar, seasoning and a little extra tomato juice or cold water and process. The consistency should be thick but not too stodgy.

3 Pour into a bowl and chill for at least 2 hours but no more than 12 hours, otherwise the textures deteriorate.

4 To prepare the bread cubes to use as a garnish, heat the oil in a frying pan and fry them over a moderate heat for about 4–5 minutes until golden brown. Drain well on kitchen paper.

5 Place each garnish in a separate small dish, or alternatively arrange them in rows on a large plate.

6 Just before serving, stir a few ice cubes into the soup and then spoon into serving bowls. Serve with the garnishes.

TOMATO AND BASIL TART

In France, pâtisseries display mouth-watering savoury tarts in their windows. This is a very simple yet extremely tasty tart made with rich shortcrust pastry, topped with slices of mozzarella cheese and tomatoes, and enriched with olive oil and basil leaves.

SERVES FOUR

INGREDIENTS
 150g/5oz mozzarella,
  thinly sliced
 4 large tomatoes, thickly sliced
 about 10 basil leaves
 30ml/2 tbsp olive oil
 2 garlic cloves, thinly sliced
 sea salt and freshly ground
  black pepper
For the pastry
 115g/4oz/1 cup plain flour
 a pinch of salt
 50g/2oz/¼ cup butter or margarine
 1 egg yolk

1 To prepare the pastry, mix together the flour and salt, then rub in the butter and the egg yolk. Use cold water to make a smooth dough; knead lightly on a floured surface. Place in a polythene bag and chill for about 1 hour.

2 Preheat the oven to 190°C/375°F/ Gas 5. Remove the pastry from the fridge and allow about 10 minutes for it to return to room temperature. Roll out into a 20cm/8in round. Press into the base of a 20cm/8in flan dish or tin. Prick all over with a fork and then bake in the oven for about 10 minutes until firm but not brown. Allow to cool slightly on a wire rack. Reduce the oven temperature to 180°C/350°F/Gas 4.

3 Arrange the mozzarella slices over the pastry base. On top, arrange a single layer of the sliced tomatoes, overlapping them slightly. Dip the basil leaves in olive oil and arrange them on the tomatoes.

4 Scatter the garlic on top, drizzle with the remaining olive oil and season with a little salt and a good sprinkling of black pepper. Bake for 40–45 minutes, until the tomatoes are well cooked. Serve hot.

ITALIAN ROAST PEPPERS

SIMPLE AND EFFECTIVE, THIS DISH WILL DELIGHT ANYONE WHO LIKES PEPPERS. IT CAN BE EATEN EITHER AS A STARTER SERVED WITH CIABATTA, OR AS A LIGHT LUNCH WITH COUSCOUS OR RICE.

SERVES FOUR

INGREDIENTS
  4 small red peppers, halved, cored
    and seeded
  30–45ml/2–3 tbsp capers, chopped
  10–12 black olives, stoned
    and chopped
  2 garlic cloves, finely chopped
  50–75g/2–3 oz mozzarella, grated
  25–40g/1–1½oz/½–¾ cup fresh white
    breadcrumbs
  120ml/4fl oz/½ cup white wine
  45ml/3 tbsp olive oil
  5ml/1 tsp finely chopped fresh mint
  5ml/1 tsp chopped fresh parsley
  freshly ground black pepper

1 Preheat the oven to 180°C/350°F/ Gas 4 and butter a shallow ovenproof dish. Place the peppers tightly together in the dish and sprinkle over the chopped capers, black olives, garlic, mozzarella and breadcrumbs.

2 Pour over the wine and olive oil and then sprinkle with the mint, parsley and freshly ground black pepper.

3 Bake for 30–40 minutes until the topping is crisp and golden brown.

SWEET PEPPER CHOUX WITH ANCHOVIES

THE RATATOUILLE VEGETABLES IN THIS DISH ARE ROASTED INSTEAD OF STEWED, AND HAVE A WONDERFUL AROMATIC FLAVOUR. ANY COMBINATION OF RED, GREEN OR YELLOW PEPPERS CAN BE USED. FOR VEGETARIANS, OMIT THE ANCHOVIES.

SERVES SIX

INGREDIENTS
300ml/½ pint/1¼ cups water
115g/4oz/½ cup butter or margarine
150g/5oz/1¼ cups plain flour
4 eggs
115g/4oz Gruyère or Cheddar cheese, finely diced
5ml/1 tsp Dijon mustard

For the filling
3 peppers; red, yellow and green
1 large onion, cut into eighths or sixteenths
3 tomatoes, peeled and quartered
1 courgette, sliced
6 basil leaves, torn in strips
1 garlic clove, crushed
30ml/2 tbsp olive oil
about 18 black olives, stoned
45ml/3 tbsp red wine
175ml/6fl oz/¾ cup passata or puréed canned tomatoes
50g/2oz can anchovy fillets, drained
salt and freshly ground black pepper

1 Preheat the oven to 240°C/475°F/Gas 9 and then grease six individual ovenproof dishes. For the filling, halve the peppers, discard the seeds and core and cut into 2.5cm/1in chunks.

2 Place the peppers, onion, tomatoes and courgette in a roasting tin. Add the basil, garlic and olive oil, stirring so the vegetables are well coated. Sprinkle with salt and pepper and then roast for about 25–30 minutes until the vegetables are just beginning to blacken at the edges.

3 Reduce the oven temperature to 200°C/400°F/Gas 6. To make the choux pastry, put the water and butter or margerine together in a large saucepan, and heat until the butter melts. Remove from the heat and add all the flour at once. Beat well with a wooden spoon for about 30 seconds until smooth. Allow to cool slightly.

4 Beat in the eggs, one at a time, and then continue beating until the mixture is thick and glossy. Stir in the diced cheese and the mustard, then season to taste with salt and ground black pepper. Spoon the mixture around the sides of the prepared dishes.

5 Spoon the vegetables into a large mixing bowl, together with any juices or scrapings from the base of the pan. Add the olives and stir in the wine and the passata or puréed tomatoes. (Alternatively, you can stir these into the roasting tin, but allow the tin to cool slightly first otherwise the liquid will boil and evaporate.)

6 Divide the pepper mixture among the six dishes and arrange the drained anchovy fillets on top. Bake in the oven for about 25–35 minutes until the choux pastry is puffy and golden. Serve hot with a fresh green salad.

EGGS FLAMENCO

A VARIATION OF THE POPULAR BASQUE DISH PIPERADE, THE EGGS ARE COOKED WHOLE INSTEAD OF BEING BEATEN BEFORE THEY ARE ADDED TO THE PEPPER MIXTURE. THE RECIPE IS KNOWN AS CHAKCHOUKA IN NORTH AFRICA AND MAKES A GOOD LUNCH OR SUPPER DISH.

SERVES FOUR

INGREDIENTS
2 red peppers
1 green pepper
30ml/2 tbsp olive oil
1 large onion, finely sliced
2 garlic cloves, crushed
5–6 tomatoes, peeled and chopped
120ml/4fl oz/½ cup puréed canned
   tomatoes or tomato juice
a good pinch of dried basil
4 eggs
40ml/8 tsp single cream
a pinch of cayenne pepper (optional)
salt and freshly ground black pepper

1 Preheat the oven to 180°C/350°F/ Gas 4. Seed and thinly slice the peppers. Heat the olive oil in a large frying pan. Fry the onion and garlic gently for about 5 minutes, stirring, until softened.

2 Add the peppers to the onion and fry for 10 minutes. Stir in the tomatoes and puréed tomatoes or juice, the basil and seasoning. Cook gently for a further 10 minutes until the peppers are soft.

3 Spoon the mixture into four ovenproof dishes, preferably earthenware. Make a hole in the centre and break an egg into each. Spoon 10ml/2 tsp cream over the yolk of each egg and sprinkle with a little black pepper or cayenne, as preferred.

4 Bake in the oven for 12–15 minutes until the white of the egg is lightly set. Serve at once with chunks of crusty warm Spanish or French bread.

SPINACH AND PEPPER PIZZA

MAKES TWO 30cm/12in PIZZAS

INGREDIENTS
   450g/1lb fresh spinach
   60ml/4 tbsp single cream
   25g/1oz Parmesan cheese, grated
   15ml/1 tbsp olive oil
   1 large onion, chopped
   1 garlic clove, crushed
   ½ green pepper, seeded and
      thinly sliced
   ½ red pepper, seeded and thinly sliced
   175–250ml/6–8fl oz/¾–1 cup passata
      or puréed tomatoes
   50g/2oz black olives, stoned
      and chopped
   15ml/1 tbsp chopped fresh basil
   175g/6oz mozzarella, grated
   175g/6oz Cheddar cheese, grated
   salt
For the dough
   25g/1oz fresh yeast or 15ml/1 tbsp
      dried yeast and 5ml/1 tsp sugar
   about 225ml/7fl oz/⅞ cup warm water
   350g/12oz/3 cups strong white flour
   30ml/2 tbsp olive oil
   5ml/1 tsp salt

1 To make the dough, cream together the fresh yeast and 150ml/¼ pint/⅔ cup of the water and set aside until frothy. If using dried yeast, stir the sugar into 225ml/7fl oz/⅞ cup water, sprinkle over the yeast and leave until frothy.

2 Place the flour and salt in a large bowl, make a well in the centre and pour in the oil and yeast mixture. Add the remaining water, if using fresh yeast, mix to make a stiff but pliable dough. Knead on a lightly floured surface for about 10 minutes until smooth and elastic.

3 Shape the dough into a ball and place in a lightly oiled bowl, cover with oiled clear film and leave in a warm place for about 1 hour until it has doubled in size.

4 To prepare the topping, cook the spinach over a moderate heat for 4–5 minutes until the leaves have wilted. Strain and press out the excess liquid. Place in a bowl and mix with the cream, Parmesan cheese and salt to taste.

5 Heat the oil in a frying pan and fry the onion and garlic over a moderate heat for 3–4 minutes until the onion has slightly softened. Add the peppers and continue cooking until the onion is lightly golden, stirring regularly.

6 Preheat the oven to 220°C/425°F/ Gas 7. Knead the dough briefly on a lightly floured surface. Divide the dough and roll out into two 30cm/12in rounds.

7 Spread each base with the passata sauce or puréed tomatoes. Add the onions and peppers and then spread over the spinach mixture. Scatter the olives and basil leaves and sprinkle with the mozzarella and Cheddar cheese.

8 Bake in the oven for 15–20 minutes, or until the crust is lightly browned and the top is beginning to turn golden. Allow to cool slightly before serving.

ENCHILADAS <u>WITH</u> HOT CHILLI SAUCE

IN MEXICO, CHILLIES APPEAR IN ALMOST EVERY SAVOURY DISH, EITHER IN THE FORM OF CHILLI POWDER OR CHOPPED, SLICED OR WHOLE. BY MEXICAN STANDARDS, THIS IS A LOW-HEAT VERSION OF THE POPULAR CHICKEN ENCHILADAS. IF YOU LIKE YOUR FOOD HOT, ADD EXTRA CHILLIES TO THE SAUCE.

SERVES FOUR

INGREDIENTS
　8 wheat tortillas
　175g/6oz Cheddar cheese, grated
　1 onion, finely chopped
　350g/12oz cooked chicken, cut into
　　small chunks
　300ml/½ pint/1¼ cups soured cream
　1 avocado, sliced and tossed in lemon
　　juice, to garnish
For the *salsa picante*
　1–2 green chillies
　15ml/1 tbsp vegetable oil
　1 onion, chopped
　1 garlic clove, crushed
　400g/14oz can chopped tomatoes
　30ml/2 tbsp tomato purée
　salt and freshly ground black pepper

3 Preheat the oven to 180°C/350°F/ Gas 4 and butter a shallow ovenproof dish. Take one tortilla and sprinkle with a good pinch of cheese and chopped onion, about 40g/1½oz of chicken and 15ml/1 tbsp of *salsa picante*. Pour over 15ml/1 tbsp of soured cream, roll up and place, seam side down, in the dish. Make seven more enchiladas.

4 Pour the remaining *salsa* over the top and sprinkle with the remaining cheese and onion. Bake in the oven for about 25–30 minutes until the top is golden. Serve with the remaining soured cream, either spooned over or in a separate jug, and garnish with the sliced avocado.

1 To make the *salsa picante*, cut the chillies in half lengthways and carefully remove the cores and seeds. Slice the chillies very finely. Heat the oil in a frying pan and fry the onion and garlic for about 3–4 minutes until softened. Add the tomatoes, tomato purée and chillies. Simmer gently, uncovered, for about 12–15 minutes, stirring frequently.

2 Pour the sauce into a food processor or blender, and process until smooth. Return to the heat and cook very gently, uncovered, for a further 15 minutes. Season to taste then set aside.

HOT-SOUR CHICK-PEAS

THIS DISH, KHATTE CHOLE, IS EATEN AS A SNACK ALL OVER INDIA, SOLD BY ITINERANT STREET VENDORS. THE HEAT OF THE CHILLIES IS TEMPERED PARTLY BY THE CORIANDER AND CUMIN, WHILE THE LEMON JUICE ADDS A WONDERFUL SOURNESS.

SERVES FOUR

INGREDIENTS

    350g/12oz/1⅞ cups chick-peas,
      soaked overnight
    60ml/4 tbsp vegetable oil
    2 onions, very finely chopped
    225g/8oz tomatoes, peeled and
      finely chopped
    15ml/1 tbsp ground coriander
    15ml/1 tbsp ground cumin
    5ml/1 tsp ground fenugreek
    5ml/1 tsp ground cinnamon
    1–2 hot green chillies, seeded and
      finely sliced
    about 2.5cm/1in fresh root
      ginger, grated
    60ml/4 tbsp lemon juice
    15ml/1 tbsp chopped fresh coriander
    salt

1 Drain the chick-peas and place them in a large saucepan, cover with water and bring to the boil. Cover and simmer for 1–1¼ hours until tender, making sure the chick-peas do not boil dry. Drain, reserving the cooking liquid.

2 Heat the oil in a large flameproof casserole. Reserve about 30ml/2 tbsp of the finely chopped onions and fry the rest in a heatproof casserole over a moderate heat for 4–5 minutes, stirring often, until tinged brown.

3 Add the tomatoes and continue cooking over a moderately low heat for 5–6 minutes until soft. Stir frequently, mashing the tomatoes to a pulp.

4 Stir in the coriander, cumin, fenugreek and cinnamon. Cook for 30 seconds and then add the chick-peas and 350ml/12fl oz/1½ cups of the reserved cooking liquid. Season with salt, cover and simmer gently for about 15–20 minutes, stirring occasionally and adding more cooking liquid if the mixture becomes too dry.

5 Meanwhile, mix the reserved onion with the chilli, ginger and lemon juice.

6 Just before serving, stir the onion and chilli mixture and the coriander into the chick-peas, and adjust the seasoning.

GUACAMOLE

THIS IS QUITE A FIERY VERSION OF A POPULAR MEXICAN DISH, ALTHOUGH PROBABLY NOWHERE NEAR AS
HOT AS YOU WOULD BE SERVED IN MEXICO, WHERE IT SEEMS HEAT KNOWS NO BOUNDS!

SERVES FOUR

INGREDIENTS
  2 ripe avocados, peeled and stoned
  2 tomatoes, peeled, seeded and
    finely chopped
  6 spring onions, finely chopped
  1–2 chillies, seeded and
    finely chopped
  30ml/2 tbsp fresh lime or lemon juice
  15ml/1 tbsp chopped fresh coriander
  salt and freshly ground black pepper
  coriander sprigs, to garnish

1 Put the avocado halves into a large
bowl and mash them roughly with a
large fork.

2 Add the remaining ingredients. Mix
well and season according to taste. Serve
garnished with fresh coriander.

PLANTAIN APPETIZER

PLANTAINS ARE A TYPE OF COOKING BANANA WITH A LOWER SUGAR CONTENT THAN DESSERT BANANAS. THEY ARE UNSUITABLE FOR EATING RAW BUT CAN BE USED IN A WIDE RANGE OF DISHES. THIS DELICIOUS ASSORTMENT OF SWEET AND SAVOURY PLANTAINS IS A POPULAR DISH IN AFRICA.

SERVES FOUR

INGREDIENTS
2 green plantains
45ml/3 tbsp vegetable oil
1 small onion, very thinly sliced
1 yellow plantain
½ garlic clove, crushed
salt and cayenne pepper

1 Peel one of the green plantains and cut into wafer-thin rounds, preferably using a potato peeler.

2 Heat about 15ml/1 tbsp of the oil in a large frying pan and fry the plantain slices for 2–3 minutes until golden, turning occasionally. Transfer to a plate lined with kitchen paper and keep warm.

3 Peel and coarsely grate the other green plantain and then mix with the sliced onion.

4 Heat 15ml/1 tbsp of the remaining oil in the pan and fry the plantain and onion mixture for 2–3 minutes until golden, turning occasionally. Transfer to the plate with the plantain slices.

5 Peel the yellow plantain, cut into small chunks. Sprinkle with cayenne pepper. Heat the remaining oil and fry the yellow plantain and garlic for 4–5 minutes until brown. Drain and sprinkle with salt.

SALAD VEGETABLES

Colour is the name of the game these days when it comes to salads. No longer do we have to suffer the limp green salads of old. The choice of radicchio, lamb's lettuce, rocket and endive, not to mention the many varieties of lettuce, means that today's salads are bursting with different flavours and textures — a treat for the eye and the palette.

LETTUCE

One aspect of lettuce that sets it apart from any other vegetable is that you can only buy it in one form – fresh.

History

Lettuce has been cultivated for thousands of years. In Egyptian times it was sacred to the god Min, and tubs of lettuce were ceremoniously carried before this fertility god. It was then considered a powerful aphrodisiac, yet for Greeks and Romans lettuce was thought to have quite the opposite effect, making you sleepy and generally soporific. Chemists today do confirm that lettuce contains a hypnotic similar to opium, and in herbal remedies lettuce is recommended for insomniacs.

Varieties

There are hundreds of different varieties of lettuce. Today, an increasing variety is available in the shops so that the salad bowl can be wealth of colour and texture.

Round Lettuces

Sometimes called head or cabbage lettuces, round lettuces have cabbage-like heads and include:
Butterheads: These are the classic lettuces seen in kitchen gardens. They have a pale heart and floppy, loosely packed leaves. They have a pleasant flavour as long as they are fresh.
Crispheads: Crisp lettuces, such as Iceberg, have an excellent crunchy texture and will keep their vitality long after butterheads have faded and died.
Looseheads: These are non-hearting lettuce with loose leaves and include lollo rosso and lollo biondo, oakleaf lettuce and Red Salad Bowl. Although they are not particularly remarkable for their flavour, they look superb.

Cos Lettuces

The cos is the only lettuce that would have been grown in antiquity. It is known

Above right: Butterhead lettuce
Right: Lollo rosso lettuce
Opposite above: Cos lettuce
Opposite below left: Lamb's lettuce
Opposite below right: Little Gem

by two names: cos, derived from the Greek island where it was found by the Romans; and romaine, the name used by the French after it was introduced to France from Rome. There are two cos lettuces, both with long, erect heads.

Cos: Considered the most delicious lettuce, this has a firm texture and a faintly nutty texture. It is the correct lettuce for Caesar Salad, one of the classic salads.

Little Gems: In appearance Little Gems look like something between a baby cos and a tightly furled butterhead. They have firm hearts and are enjoyed for their distinct flavour. Like other lettuce hearts, they cope well with being cooked.

LAMB'S LETTUCE OR CORN SALAD

This popular winter leaf does not actually belong to the lettuce family (it is related to Fuller's teasel), but as it makes a lovely addition to salads, this seems a good place to include it. Called mâche in France, it has spoon-shaped leaves and an excellent nutty flavour.

Nutrition

As well as containing vitamins A, C and E, lettuce provides potassium, iron and calcium, as well as traces of other minerals.

Buying and Storing

The best lettuce is the one fresh from the garden. The next best thing to do is to buy lettuce from a farm shop or pick-your-own (although if fertilizers and pesticides are used, their flavour will be disappointing compared to the organic product).

Today, lettuce is frequently sold ready shredded and packed with herbs and any other ingredients. Whether you buy lettuce pre-packed or from the shelf, it must be fresh. Soil and bugs can be washed off but those with limp or yellow leaves are of no use. Eat lettuce as soon as possible after purchasing; in the meantime keep it in a cool dark place, such as the bottom of the fridge.

Making Salads

Salads can be made by using only one lettuce or a mixture of many. There are no rules but choose leaves that give contrast in texture and colour as well as flavour. Fresh herbs, such as parsley, coriander and basil also add another interesting dimension.

Tear rather than cut the leaves of loose-leafed lettuce; icebergs and other large lettuces are commonly sliced or shredded. Eat salad as soon as possible after preparing.

Dressings should be well-flavoured with a hint of sharpness but must never be too astringent. Make them in a blender, a screw-top jar or in a large bowl so that the ingredients can be thoroughly blended. Always use the best possible oils and vinegars, in roughly the proportion of five oil to one vinegar or lemon juice. Use half good olive oil and half sunflower oil, or for a more fragrant dressing, a combination of walnut and sunflower oil. A pinch of salt and pepper is essential, English or French mustard is optional and the addition of a little sugar will blunt the flavour.

Add the dressing to the salad when ready to serve – never earlier.

ROCKET

Rocket has a wonderful peppery flavour and is excellent in a mixed green salad. It has small, bright green dandelion-shaped leaves. The Greeks and Romans commonly ate rocket (arugula) in mixed salads, apparently because it helped counterbalance the dampening effect lettuce had on the libido – rocket's aphrodisiac properties in antiquity are well catalogued. Seeds used to be sown around the statues of Priapus, the mythological Greek god of fertility and protector of gardens and herbs and son of Aphrodite and Dionysus.

Buying and Storing

Rocket is to be found either among the salads or fresh herbs in supermarkets. Buy fresh green leaves and use soon after purchasing. The leaves can be kept immersed in cold water.

Preparing and Serving

Discard any discoloured leaves. Add rocket to plain green salads, or grind with garlic, pine nuts and olive oil for a dressing for pasta.

Since it has such a striking flavour, a little rocket goes a long way, making it an excellent leaf for garnishing. It tastes superb contrasted with grilled goat's cheese, or one or two leaves can be added to sandwiches, or loosely packed into pitta bread pockets together with tomatoes, avocado, peanuts and bean sprouts, for example.

Opposite above: Oak leaf lettuce
Opposite below: curly endive
Below: Rocket

CHICORY AND RADICCHIO

Chicory, radicchio, endive and escarole are all related to each other and when they are tasted together you can easily detect their family resemblance. Their names are occasionally interchanged: chicory is often referred to as Belgian or French endive and French and Belgian *chicorée* is the English curly endive.

CHICORY

During the late eighteenth century, chicory was grown in Europe for its root, which was added to coffee. A Belgian, M. Brezier, discovered that the white leaves could be eaten, a fact he kept secret during his lifetime; but after his death chicory became a very popular vegetable, first in Belgium and later elsewhere in Europe. Its Flemish name is *witloof*, meaning "white leaf", and its characteristic pale leaf is due to its being grown in darkness; the paler it is, the less bitter its flavour.

Chicory can be eaten raw but is commonly cooked, either baked, stir-fried or poached. To eat raw, separate the leaves and serve with fruit, such as oranges or grapefruit, which counteract chicory's slight bitterness.

RADICCHIO

This is one of many varieties developed from wild chicory. It looks like a small lettuce with deep wine-red leaves and striking cream ribs and owes its splendid foliage to careful shading. If it is grown completely in the dark the leaves are marbled pink, and those that have been exposed to some light can be patched with a green or copper colour. Its flavour tends to be bitter but contrasts well with green salads. Radicchio can be stir-fried or poached, although the leaves turn an unexciting dark green when cooked.

CURLY ENDIVE AND ESCAROLE

These are robust salad ingredients in both flavour and texture. The curly-leaved endive looks like a green frizzy mop and the escarole is broad-leaved, but both have a distinct bitter flavour. Serve mixed with each other and a well-flavoured dressing. This dampens down the bitter flavour but leaves the salad a with a pleasant "bite".

Preparing

To prepare chicory, take out the core at the base with a sharp knife (see left) and discard any wilted or damaged leaves. Rinse thoroughly, then dry the leaves.

Above: Chicory
Opposite above: Radicchio
Opposite below: Lollo biondo

Preparing Salad Leaves

1 Pull the leaves from the stalk and discard any wilted or damaged leaves.

2 Wash the leaves in plenty of cold water, swirling gently to make sure all the dirt and any insects are washed away.

3 Place the washed leaves in a soft dish towel and then gently pat dry.

4 Place in a dish towel in a polythene bag. Chill in the fridge for about 1 hour.

RADISHES

Radishes have a peppery flavour that can almost be felt in the nostrils as you bite into one. Their pungency depends not only on the variety but also on the soil in which they are grown. Freshly harvested radishes have the most pronounced flavour and crisp texture.

Varieties

Radishes were well loved throughout antiquity and consequently there are many varieties worldwide. Both the small red types and the large white radishes are internationally popular.

Red radishes: These small red orbs have many pretty names, such as Cherry Belle and Scarlet Globe, but are mostly sold simply as radish. They are available all year round, have a deep pink skin, sometimes paler or white at the roots and a firm white flesh. Their peppery flavour is milder in the spring and they are almost always eaten raw. Finely sliced and sandwiched in bread and butter, they make an interesting *hors d'oeuvre*.

French breakfast radishes: These are red and white and slightly more elongated than the red radish. They tend to be

milder than English radishes and are popular in France either eaten on their own or served with other raw vegetables as *crudités*.

Mooli or daikon radishes: Sometimes known as the oriental radish, the mooli is a smooth-skinned, long, white radish. Those bought in the shops have a mild flavour, less peppery than the red radish – perhaps because they lose their flavour after long storage. However moolis eaten straight from the garden are hot and peppery. They can be eaten raw or pickled, or added to stir-fries.

Buying and Storing

Buy red radishes that are firm with crisp leaves. If at all possible, buy moolis or daikons which still have their leaves; this is a good indication of their freshness as they wilt quickly. The leaves should be green and lively and the skins clear with no bruises or blemishes. They can be stored in the fridge for a few days.

Preparing and Serving

Red radishes need only to be washed. They can then be sliced or eaten whole by themselves or in salads. You can make a feature of them by slicing into a salad of, say, oranges and walnuts, perhaps with a scattering of rocket and dressed with a walnut oil vinaigrette. To use moolis in a stir-fry, cut into slices and add to the dish for the last few minutes of cooking. They add not only flavour but also a wonderfully juicy and crunchy texture to a dish.

Opposite: Red radishes
Above: French breakfast radishes
Right: Mooli or daikon radishes

WATERCRESS

Watercress is perhaps the most robustly flavoured of all the salad ingredients and a handful of these leaves is all you need to perk up a rather dull green salad. It has a distinctive "raw" flavour, both peppery and slightly pungent and this, together with its bright green leaves, make it a popular garnish.

Watercress, as the name suggests, grows in water. It requires fast-flowing clean water to thrive and is really only successful around freshwater springs on chalk hills. The first watercress beds were cultivated in Europe, but now the vegetable is grown worldwide.

Nutrition

Watercress is extremely rich in vitamins A, B2, C, D and E. The plant is also rich in calcium, potassium and iron and provides significant quantities of sulphur and chloride.

Buying and Storing

Only buy fresh-looking watercress – the darker and larger the leaves the better. Avoid any with wilted or yellow leaves. It will keep for several days in the fridge or, better still, submerged in a bowl of water, or arranged in a jar of cold water, and kept in a cool place.

Preparing

Discard any yellow leaves and remove thick stalks which will be too coarse for salads or soups. Small sprigs can be added to salads.

Cooking

For soups and purées, either blend watercress raw or cook briefly in stock, milk or water. Cooking inevitably destroys some of the nutrients, however cooked watercress has a milder flavour, while still keeping its unique peppery taste.

WINTER CRESS

Winter cress or land cress is often grown as an alternative to watercress, when flowing water is not available. It looks like a robust form of watercress and indeed has a similar if even more assertive flavour, with a distinct peppery taste. Use as you would use watercress, either in salads or in soups.

MUSTARD AND CRESS

Mustard and cress are often grown together, to provide spicy greenery as a garnish or for salads. They are available all year round.

Mustard seedlings germinate 3–4 days sooner than the cress, so if you buy this mixture from the supermarket, or grow your own on the windowsill, in the first instance the punnets will only show mustard seedlings.

History

Cress, grown for thousands of years, was known first to the Persians. There is a story that the Persians would always eat cress before they baked bread, and there are other references in antiquity to people eating cress with bread.

Serving

Nowadays mustard and cress are often enjoyed in sandwiches, either served simply with butter, or with avocado, cucumber or egg mayonnaise added. Cress probably wouldn't be substantial enough as a salad in itself, but, with its faint spicy flavour, it can perk up a plain green salad, and it is also excellent in a tomato salad, dressed simply with olive oil and tarragon vinegar.

Opposite above: Watercress
Opposite below: Winter cress
Above right: Mustard seedlings
Right: Cress seedlings

SALAD VEGETABLE RECIPES

Salads can be as simple or complicated as you like. Main meal salads such as Chicken Livers and Green Salad or Warm Duck Salad with Orange would make an excellent lunch or supper dish. But, if you're looking for a something less elaborate, choose a Caesar Salad or the Rocket and Grilled Chèvre Salad, and serve as a starter or side salad. Salad leaves can even be cooked. Baked Chicory with Palma Ham is a famous classic, while Radicchio Pizza gives a modern twist to an old favourite.

CHICKEN LIVERS AND GREEN SALAD

CHICKEN LIVERS HAVE A WONDERFULLY ROBUST FLAVOUR THAT COMPLEMENTS A SALAD WITH A PIQUANT DRESSING. IF YOU ARE SHORT OF TIME YOU CAN BUY READY PREPARED SALADS WHICH ARE AVAILABLE FROM MOST SUPERMARKETS.

SERVES FOUR

INGREDIENTS
a selection of fresh salad leaves
4 spring onions, finely sliced
15ml/1 tbsp roughly chopped
   flat leaf parsley
115g/4oz unsmoked streaky bacon,
   chopped
450g/1lb chicken livers
seasoned plain flour, for dusting
15ml/1 tbsp sunflower oil
25g/1oz/2 tbsp butter or margarine
salt and freshly ground black pepper
For the dressing
100ml/3½fl oz/⅓ cup sunflower oil
30–45ml/2–3 tbsp lemon juice
5ml/1 tsp French mustard
1 small garlic clove, crushed

1 To make the dressing, place the oil, lemon juice, French mustard, garlic and seasoning in a screw-top jar and shake vigorously to mix.

2 Place the salad leaves in a large bowl with the spring onions and parsley. Pour over the dressing, toss briefly and then arrange on four individual serving plates.

3 Dry-fry the bacon in a frying pan until golden brown. Transfer to a plate using a slotted spoon and keep warm.

4 Trim the chicken livers, pat dry on kitchen paper and then dust them thoroughly with the seasoned flour.

5 Heat the oil and butter or margarine in a frying pan; fry the livers over a fairly high heat for about 8 minutes, turning occasionally until cooked as preferred; either cooked through or slightly pink inside.

6 Arrange the chicken livers on the salad leaves and scatter the crisp bacon pieces over the top.

CAESAR SALAD

A CLASSIC SALAD WITH AN EGG YOLK DRESSING, THIS MUST BE MADE USING COS LETTUCE. THE ORIGINS OF ITS NAME ARE A MYSTERY. SOME PEOPLE SAY IT WAS INVENTED BY AN ITALIAN, CAESAR CARDINI, IN MEXICO, AND OTHERS CLAIM THAT IT COMES FROM CALIFORNIA.

SERVES FOUR

INGREDIENTS
1 cos lettuce
8 anchovies, chopped
40g/1½oz shavings of Parmesan
   cheese
For the dressing
2 egg yolks
2.5ml/½ tsp French mustard
50ml/2fl oz/¼ cup olive oil
50ml/2fl oz/¼ cup sunflower oil
15ml/1 tbsp white wine vinegar
a pinch of salt
For the croûtons
1 garlic clove, crushed
60–75ml/4–5 tbsp olive oil
75g/3oz stale white bread,
   cut into cubes

1 Place the garlic in the oil and set aside for about 30 minutes for the garlic flavour to infuse into the oil.

2 To make the dressing, place the egg yolks, mustard, olive oil, sunflower oil, vinegar and salt in a screw-top jar and shake well to emulsify.

3 To make the croûtons, strain the garlic oil into a frying pan and discard the garlic. When hot, fry the bread until golden and then drain on kitchen paper.

4 Arrange the lettuce leaves in a salad bowl. Pour over the dressing and gently fold in the anchovies and croûtons. Scatter with Parmesan shavings.

RADICCHIO PIZZA

This unusual pizza topping consists of chopped radicchio with leeks, tomatoes and Parmesan and mozzarella cheeses. The base is a scone dough, making this a quick and easy supper dish to prepare. Serve with a crisp green salad.

SERVES TWO

INGREDIENTS
½ x 400g/14oz can chopped tomatoes
2 garlic cloves, crushed
a pinch of dried basil
25ml/1½ tbsp olive oil, plus extra
   for dipping
2 leeks, sliced
100g/3½oz radicchio, roughly
   chopped
20g/¾oz Parmesan, grated
115g/4oz mozzarella cheese, sliced
10–12 black olives, stoned
basil leaves, to garnish
salt and freshly ground black pepper
For the dough
225g/8oz/2 cups self-raising flour
2.5ml/½ tsp salt
50g/2oz/¼ cup butter or margarine
about 120ml/4fl oz/½ cup milk

1 Preheat the oven to 220°C/425°F/
Gas 7 and grease a baking sheet. Mix the
flour and salt in a bowl, rub in the butter
or margarine and gradually stir in the
milk and mix to a soft dough.

2 Roll the dough out on a lightly floured
surface to make a 25–28cm/10–11in
round. Place on the baking sheet.

3 Purée the tomatoes and then pour
into a small saucepan. Stir in one of the
crushed garlic cloves, together with the
dried basil and seasoning, and simmer
over a moderate heat until the mixture is
thick and reduced by about half.

4 Heat the olive oil in a large frying pan
and fry the leeks and remaining garlic for
4–5 minutes until slightly softened. Add
the chopped radicchio and cook, stirring
continuously for a few minutes, and then
cover and simmer gently for about
5–10 minutes. Stir in the Parmesan
cheese and season with salt and pepper.

5 Cover the dough base with the tomato
mixture and then spoon the leek and
radicchio mixture on top. Arrange the
mozzarella slices on top and scatter over
the black olives. Dip a few basil leaves in
olive oil, arrange on top and then bake
the pizza for 15–20 minutes until the
scone base and top are golden brown.

WARM DUCK SALAD WITH ORANGE

THE DISTINCT, SHARP FLAVOUR OF RADICCHIO, CURLY ENDIVE AND FRESH ORANGES COMPLEMENTS THE RICH TASTE OF THE DUCK TO MAKE THIS A SUPERB DISH. IT IS GOOD SERVED WITH STEAMED BABY NEW POTATOES FOR AN ELEGANT MAIN COURSE.

SERVES FOUR

INGREDIENTS
    2 boneless duck breasts
    salt
    2 oranges
    curly endive, radicchio and lamb's
        lettuce
    30ml/2 tbsp medium dry sherry
    10–15ml/2–3 tsp dark soy sauce

1 Rub the skin of the duck breasts with salt and then slash the skin several times with a sharp knife.

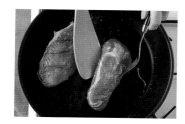

2 Heat a heavy cast-iron frying pan and fry the duck breasts, skin side down at first, for 20–25 minutes, turning once, until the skin is well browned and the flesh is cooked to your preference. Transfer to a plate to cool slightly and pour off the excess fat from the pan.

3 Peel the oranges then separate into segments and use a knife to remove all the pith, catching the juice in a small bowl. Arrange the salad leaves in a shallow serving bowl.

4 Heat the duck juices in the pan and stir in 45ml/3 tbsp of the reserved orange juice. Bring to the boil, add the sherry and then just enough soy sauce to give a piquant, spicy flavour.

5 Cut the duck into thick slices and arrange over the salad. Pour over the warm dressing and serve.

BAKED CHICORY <u>WITH</u> PARMA HAM

ALTHOUGH CHICORY IS SOMETIMES TOO HARSHLY FLAVOURED FOR SOME PEOPLE'S TASTES, SIMMERING IT
BEFORE BRAISING ELIMINATES ANY BITTERNESS SO THAT THE FLAVOUR IS PLEASANTLY MILD.

SERVES FOUR

INGREDIENTS
    4 heads of chicory
    25g/1oz/2 tbsp butter
    250ml/8fl oz/1 cup vegetable
      or chicken stock
    4 slices Parma ham
    75g/3oz mascarpone cheese
    50g/2oz Emmenthal or Cheddar
      cheese, sliced
    salt and freshly ground black pepper

4 Remove the chicory using a slotted
spoon. Lay out the Parma ham slices and
place one piece of chicory on each of the
slices. Roll up and place, side by side, in
a single layer in the prepared dish.

5 Simmer the stock until it is reduced
by about half and then remove from the
heat. Stir in the mascarpone cheese and
pour the sauce over the chicory. Lay the
slices of Emmenthal or Cheddar cheese
over the top and bake in the oven for
about 15 minutes until the top is golden
and the sauce is bubbling.

1 Preheat the oven to 180°C/350°F/
Gas 4. Grease an ovenproof dish. Trim
the chicory and remove the central core.

2 Melt the butter in a large saucepan
and gently sauté the chicory over a
moderate heat for 4–5 minutes, turning
occasionally, until the outer leaves begin
to turn transparent.

3 Add the stock and a little seasoning,
bring to the boil and then cover and
simmer gently for 5–6 minutes until the
chicory is almost tender.

ROCKET AND GRILLED CHÈVRE SALAD

FOR THIS RECIPE, LOOK OUT FOR CYLINDER-SHAPED GOAT'S CHEESE FROM A DELICATESSEN OR FOR SMALL ROLLS THAT CAN BE CUT INTO HALVES, WEIGHING ABOUT 50G/2OZ. SERVE ONE PER PERSON AS A STARTER OR DOUBLE THE RECIPE AND SERVE TWO EACH FOR A LIGHT LUNCH.

SERVES FOUR

INGREDIENTS
    about 15ml/1 tbsp olive oil
    about 15ml/1 tbsp vegetable oil
    4 slices French bread
    45ml/3 tbsp walnut oil
    15ml/1 tbsp lemon juice
    225g/8oz cylinder-shaped goat's
      cheese
    a generous handful of rocket leaves
    about 115g/4oz curly endive
    salt and freshly ground black pepper
For the sauce
    45ml/3 tbsp apricot jam
    60ml/4 tbsp white wine
    5ml/2 tsp Dijon mustard

1 Heat the two oils in a frying pan and fry the slices of French bread on one side only, until lightly golden. Transfer to a plate lined with kitchen paper.

4 Preheat the grill a few minutes before serving the salad. Cut the goat's cheese into 50g/2oz rounds and place each piece on a croûton, untoasted side up. Place under the grill and cook for 3–4 minutes until the cheese melts.

5 Toss the rocket and curly endive in the walnut oil dressing and arrange attractively on four individual serving plates. When the cheese croûtons are ready, arrange on each plate and pour over a little of the apricot sauce.

2 To make the sauce, heat the jam in a small saucepan until warm but not boiling. Push through a sieve, into a clean pan, to remove the pieces of fruit, and then stir in the white wine and mustard. Heat gently and keep warm until ready to serve.

3 Blend the walnut oil and lemon juice and season with a little salt and pepper.

CHINESE LEAVES AND MOOLI WITH SCALLOPS

HERE'S A SPEEDY STIR-FRY MADE USING CHINESE CABBAGE, MOOLI AND SCALLOPS. BOTH THE MOOLI AND CHINESE LEAVES HAVE A PLEASANT CRUNCHY "BITE". YOU NEED TO WORK QUICKLY, SO HAVE EVERYTHING PREPARED BEFORE YOU START COOKING.

SERVES FOUR

INGREDIENTS
10 prepared scallops
75ml/5 tbsp vegetable oil
3 garlic cloves, finely chopped
1cm/½in piece fresh root ginger,
   finely sliced
4–5 spring onions, cut lengthways
   into 2.5cm/1in pieces
30ml/2 tbsp medium dry sherry
½ mooli (daikon), cut into
   1cm/½in slices
1 Chinese cabbage, chopped
   lengthways into thin strips
For the marinade
5ml/1 tsp cornflour
1 egg white, lightly beaten
a pinch of white pepper
For the sauce
5ml/1 tsp cornflour
45ml/3 tbsp oyster sauce

1 Rinse the scallops and separate the corals from the white meat. Cut each scallop into 2–3 pieces and slice the corals. Place them on two dishes.

2 For the marinade, blend together the cornflour, egg white and white pepper. Pour half over the scallops and the rest over the corals. Leave for 10 minutes.

3 To make the sauce, blend the cornflour with 60ml/4 tbsp water and the oyster sauce and set aside.

4 Heat about 30ml/2 tbsp of the oil in a wok, add half of the garlic and let it sizzle, and then add half the ginger and half of the spring onions. Stir-fry for about 30 seconds and then stir in the scallops (not the corals).

5 Stir-fry for 30–60 seconds until the scallops start to become opaque, then reduce the heat and add 15ml/1 tbsp of the sherry. Cook briefly and then spoon the scallops and the cooking liquid into a bowl and set aside.

6 Heat another 30ml/2 tbsp of oil in the wok, add the remaining garlic, ginger and spring onions and then stir-fry for 1 minute. Add the corals, stir-fry briefly and transfer to a dish.

7 Heat the remaining oil and add the mooli. Stir-fry for about 30 seconds and then stir in the cabbage. Stir-fry for about 30 seconds more then add the oyster sauce mixture and about 60ml/4 tbsp water. Allow the cabbage to simmer briefly and then stir in the scallops and corals, together with all their liquid, and cook briefly to heat through.

RADISH, MANGO AND APPLE SALAD

RADISH IS A YEAR-ROUND VEGETABLE AND THIS SALAD CAN BE SERVED AT ANY TIME OF YEAR, WITH ITS CLEAN, CRISP TASTES AND MELLOW FLAVOURS. SERVE WITH SMOKED FISH, SUCH AS ROLLS OF SMOKED SALMON, OR WITH CONTINENTAL HAM OR SALAMI.

<u>SERVES FOUR</u>

INGREDIENTS
    10–15 radishes
    1 apple, peeled cored and
        thinly sliced
    2 celery stalks, thinly sliced
    1 small ripe mango
    salt and freshly ground black pepper
    sprigs of dill, to garnish
For the dressing
    120ml/4fl oz/½ cup soured cream
    10ml/2 tsp creamed horseradish
    15ml/1 tbsp chopped fresh dill

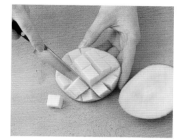

3 Cut through the mango lengthways either side of the stone and make even criss-cross cuts through each side section. Bend each section back to separate the cubes, remove them with a small knife and add to the bowl. Pour the dressing over the vegetables and fruit and stir gently so that all the ingredients are coated in the dressing. When ready to serve, spoon the salad into an attractive salad bowl and garnish with sprigs of dill.

1 To prepare the dressing, blend together the soured cream, horseradish and dill in a small jug or bowl and season with a little salt and pepper.

2 Top and tail the radishes and then slice them thinly. Add to a bowl together with the thinly sliced apple and celery.

WATERCRESS SOUP

SERVES FOUR

INGREDIENTS
15ml/1 tbsp sunflower oil
15g/½oz/1 tbsp butter
1 onion, finely chopped
1 potato, diced
about 175g/6oz watercress
400ml/14fl oz/1⅔ cups chicken
  or vegetable stock
400ml/14fl oz/1⅔ cups milk
lemon juice
salt and freshly ground black pepper
soured cream, to serve (optional)

1 Heat the oil and butter in a large saucepan and fry the onion over a gentle heat until soft but not browned. Add the potato, fry gently for 2–3 minutes and then cover and sweat for 5 minutes over a gentle heat, stirring occasionally.

2 Strip the watercress leaves from the stalks and roughly chop the stalks.

3 Add the stock and milk to the pan, stir in the chopped stalks and season with salt and pepper. Bring to the boil and then simmer gently, partially covered, for 10–12 minutes until the potatoes are tender. Add all but a few of the watercress leaves and simmer for 2 minutes.

4 Process the soup in a food processor or blender, and then pour into a clean saucepan and heat gently with the reserved watercress leaves. Taste when hot and add a little lemon juice and adjust the seasoning.

5 Pour the soup into warmed soup dishes and swirl in a little soured cream, if using, just before serving.

COOK'S TIP
Provided you leave out the cream, this is a low calorie but nutritious soup, which, served with crusty bread, makes a very satisfying meal.

WATERCRESS AND TWO-FISH TERRINE

THIS IS A PRETTY, DELICATE DISH, IDEAL FOR A SUMMER BUFFET PARTY OR PICNIC. SERVE WITH LEMON MAYONNAISE OR SOURED CREAM, AND A WATERCRESS AND GREEN SALAD.

SERVES SIX TO EIGHT

INGREDIENTS
350g/12oz monkfish, filleted
175g/6oz lemon sole, filleted
1 egg and 1 egg white
45–60ml/3–4 tbsp lemon juice
40–50g/1½–2o/1 cup fresh white
  breadcrumbs
300ml/½ pint/1¼ cups whipping
  cream
75g/3oz smoked salmon
175g/6oz watercress, roughly chopped
salt and freshly ground black pepper

1 Preheat the oven to 180°C/350°F/ Gas 4 and line a 1.5 litre/2½ pint/6¼ cup loaf tin with non-stick baking paper.

2 Cut the fish into rough chunks, discarding the skin and bones. Put the fish into a food processor with a little salt and pepper.

3 Process briefly and add the egg and egg white, lemon juice, breadcrumbs and cream. Process to a paste. Put the mixture into a bowl. Take 75ml/5 tbsp of the mixture and process with the smoked salmon. Transfer to a separate bowl. Take 75ml/5 tbsp of the white fish mixture and process with the watercress.

4 Spoon half of the white fish mixture into the base of the prepared loaf tin and smooth the surface with a palette knife.

5 Spread over the watercress mixture, then the smoked salmon mixture and finally spread over the remaining white fish mixture and smooth the top.

6 Lay a piece of buttered non-stick baking paper on top of the mixture and then cover with foil. Place the loaf tin in a roasting tin, half-filled with boiling water and cook in the oven for 1¼–1½ hours. Towards the end of the cooking time the terrine will begin to rise, which indicates that it is ready.

7 Allow to cool in the tin and then turn on to a serving plate and peel away the baking paper. Chill for 1–2 hours.

MUSHROOMS

Delicious, succulent, soft, chewy — all sorts of adjectives can be used when describing mushrooms. There are now so many to choose from and each has its own particular flavour and character. From firm favourites such as button and field mushrooms, to ceps, morels and oyster mushrooms that grow in woodlands, these delicacies deserve a starring role in a multitude of dishes.

BUTTON MUSHROOMS

There is nothing like fried mushrooms on toast for breakfast, served sizzling hot straight from the pan. Once cooked, mushrooms, especially fried ones, go soft and flabby quite quickly; they still taste OK but the pleasure is not so great.

History

In the past, mushrooms have had a firm association with the supernatural and even today their connection with the mysterious side of life hasn't completely disappeared. Fairy rings – circles of mushrooms – inexplicably appear overnight in woods and fields, and thunder is still thought to bring forth fresh crops of mushrooms.

Many types of mushrooms and fungi are either poisonous or hallucinogenic, and in the past their poisons have been distilled for various murderous reasons.

The use of the term mushroom to mean edible species, and toadstool to mean those considered poisonous, has no scientific basis, and there is no simple rule for distinguishing between the two. Picking wild mushrooms is not safe unless you are really confident about identifying edible types. In France, people go to their local pharmacy to have the wild mushrooms they have gathered identified.

Varieties

Button/white mushrooms: Cultivated mushrooms are widely available in shops and are sold when very young and tiny as button mushrooms. The slightly larger ones are known as closed cap, while larger ones still are open capped or open cup mushrooms. They have ivory or white caps with pinky/beige gills which darken as they mature. All have a pleasant unassuming flavour.

Chestnut mushrooms: These have a thicker stem and a darker, pale brown cap. They have a more pronounced "mushroomy" flavour and a meatier texture than white mushrooms.

Buying and Storing

It is easy to see whether or not button mushrooms are fresh – their caps will be clean and white, without bruises. The longer they stay on the shelves, the darker and more discoloured the caps become, while the gills beneath turn from pink to brown.

If possible, use the paper bags that are provided in supermarkets nowadays when buying mushrooms. Mushrooms in plastic bags sweat in their own heat, and eventually turn slippery and unappetizing. If you have no choice or you buy mushrooms in wrapped

cartons, transfer loose to the bottom of the fridge as soon as possible. Even so they will keep only for a day or two.

Preparing and Cooking

Mushrooms should not be washed but wiped with a damp cloth or a piece of kitchen paper (see below). This is partly because you don't want to increase their water content, and also because they should be fried as dry as possible.

Unless the skins are very discoloured, it should not be necessary to peel them, although you probably will need to trim the very base of the stem.

Mushrooms are largely composed of water and shrink noticeably during the cooking process. They also take up a lot of fat as they cook so it is best to use butter or a good olive oil for frying. Fry mushrooms briskly over a moderately high heat so that as they shrink the water evaporates and they don't stew in their own juice. For the same reason do not fry too many mushrooms at once in the same pan.

Most of the recipes in this book use fried mushrooms as their base and are completely interchangeable – so if you can't get wild mushrooms or chestnut mushrooms, for instance, button mushrooms can be used instead.

Above left: Button mushrooms
Opposite above: Flat mushrooms
Opposite below left: Chestnut mushrooms (top) and open capped or cup mushrooms
Opposite below right: Field mushrooms

FIELD MUSHROOMS

Field mushrooms are the wild relatives of the cultivated mushroom and when cooked have a wonderful aroma. Flat mushrooms, although indistinguishable from field mushrooms in appearance, have probably been cultivated and are also excellent. Connoisseurs say that only wild mushrooms have any flavour but many would argue against this. However, if you know where to find field mushrooms, keep the secret to yourself (most mushroom devotees seem to know this) and count yourself lucky!

Buying and Storing

Field mushrooms are sometimes available in the autumn in farm shops. Since they are likely to have been picked recently, they should be fresh unless obviously wilting. Unless you intend to stuff them, don't worry if they are broken in places because you will be slicing them anyway. Use as soon as possible after purchase.

Preparing

Trim the stalk bottoms if necessary and wipe the caps with a damp cloth. Slice or chop according to the instructions in the recipe.

Cooking

For true field mushrooms, you need do nothing more complicated than simply fry them in butter or olive oil with a suggestion of garlic if liked. However, like flat mushrooms, field mushrooms can be used for stuffing, in soups or any mushroom recipe. They are darker than button mushrooms and will colour soups and sauces brown, but the flavour will be extremely good.

When stuffing mushrooms, gently fry the caps on both sides for a few minutes. The stalks can be chopped and added to the stuffing or they can be used for soups or stocks.

WOODLAND MUSHROOMS

Varieties

Ceps: Popular in France, where they are known as *cèpes* and in Italy where they are called *porcini*, these meaty, bun-shaped mushrooms have a fine almost suede-like texture and a good flavour. Instead of gills they have a spongy texture beneath the cap and unless they are very young it is best to scrape this away as it goes soggy when cooked. Ceps are excellent fried in oil or butter over a brisk heat to evaporate the liquid and then added to omelettes.

Alternatively, an Italian way of cooking is to remove the stalk and the spongy tubes, and brush the tops with olive oil. Grill for about 10 minutes under a moderate grill and then turn them over

and pour olive oil and a sprinkling of garlic into the centre. Grill for a further 5 minutes and then serve sprinkled with seasoning and parsley.

Chanterelles: Frilly, trumpet-shaped chanterelles are delicate mushrooms which range in colour from cream to a vivid yellow. Later, winter chanterelles, have greyish-lilac gills on the underside of their dark caps. Chanterelles have a delicate, slightly fruity flavour and a firm, almost rubbery texture. They are difficult to clean as their tiny gills tend to trap grit and earth. Rinse them gently under cold running water and then shake dry. Fry in butter over a gentle heat to start with so they exude their liquid and then increase the heat to boil it off. They are delicious

with scrambled eggs, or served alone with finely cut toast on the side.

Horns of Plenty/Black Trumpets: Named after its shape, this mushroom ranges in colour from mid-brown to black. As it is hollow, it will need to be brushed well to clean or, if a large specimen, sliced in half. This is a very versatile mushroom, and goes particularly well with fish.

Hedgehog Fungus: This mushroom is difficult to find either on sale or on the woodland floor, but it has great culinary value and is much sought after. Small, young specimens can be cooked whole or sliced, or even used raw in salads. More mature mushrooms may be bitter and are best cooked with butter and herbs. It goes well with both meat and fish.

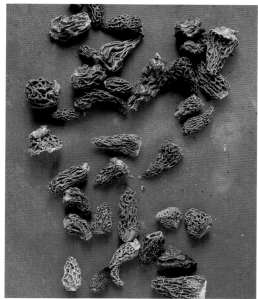

Morels: These are the first mushroom of the year, appearing not in autumn but in spring. In Scandinavia they are called the "truffles of the north" and are considered among the great edible fungi. They are cone-shaped with a crinkled spongy cap but are hollow inside. You will need to wash them well under running water as insects tend to creep into their dark crevices. Morels need longer cooking than most fungi: sauté them in butter, add a squeeze of lemon and then cover and simmer for an hour until tender. The juices can then be thickened with cream or egg yolks.

Dried mushrooms: Most wild mushrooms are available dried. To reconstitute, soak in warm water for about 20–30 minutes; in the case of morels when they are to be added to stews, soak them for about 10 minutes. Dried mushrooms, particularly ceps, have an intense flavour.

Left (clockwise from the top): Hedgehog fungus, Horn of Plenty, chanterelles
Above left: Morels
Above right: Dried mushrooms
Right: Winter chanterelles

WILD MUSHROOMS <u>AND</u> OTHER FUNGI

Mushroom gathering, a seasonal event throughout Eastern Europe, Italy and France, is increasingly popular in Britain. The French are particularly enthusiastic: in autumn whole families drive to secret locations to comb the ground for prizes like shaggy ink caps or ceps. Wild mushrooms are sold in supermarkets.

OYSTER MUSHROOMS

These ear-shaped fungi grow on rotting wood. Cap, gills and stem are all the same colour, which can be greyish brown, pink or yellow. They are now widely cultivated, although they are generally thought of as wild. Delicious both in flavour and texture, they are softer than the button mushroom when cooked but seem more substantial, having more "bite" to them.

Buying and Storing

Fresh specimens are erect and lively looking with clear gills and smooth caps. They are often sold packed in plastic

boxes under clear film wrappings and will wilt and go soggy if left on the shelf for too long. Once purchased, remove them from the packaging and use as soon as possible.

Preparing

Oyster mushrooms rarely need trimming at all but if they are large, tear rather than cut them into pieces. In very large specimens the stems can be tough and should be discarded.

Cooking

Fry in butter until tender – they take less time than white mushrooms. Do not overcook oyster mushrooms as the flavour will be lost and the soft texture will turn more rubbery.

Above: Grey oyster mushrooms
Left: Pink and yellow oyster mushrooms

ENOKITAKI MUSHROOMS

This is another Japanese mushroom. The wild variety is orangey-brown with shiny caps but outside Japan, you will probably only be able to locate the cultivated variety, which are similarly fine, with pin-sized heads, but are pale coloured with snowy white caps. They have a delicate, sweet and almost fruity flavour. In Japanese cookery they are added to salads or used to garnish soups or hot dishes. Since they become tough if overcooked, add enokitaki mushrooms at the very last minute of cooking.

SHIITAKE MUSHROOMS

Shiitake mushrooms were once only available in oriental stores, but these Japanese fungi are now commonly found in supermarkets. They are among a variety of tree mushrooms (called *take* in Japan, the *shii* being the hardwood tree from which they are harvested). They have a meaty, slightly acid flavour and a distinct slippery texture. Unlike button mushrooms that can be flash-fried, shi-itake need to be cooked through, although even this only takes 3–5 minutes. Add them to stir-fries for a delicious flavour and texture. Alternatively, fry them in oil until tender, sprinkle with sesame oil and then serve with a little soy sauce.

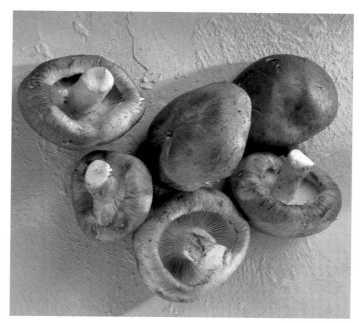

Above: Enokitaki mushrooms
Right: Shiitake mushrooms

MUSHROOM RECIPES

Nearly everyone has a favourite mushroom dish. Mushrooms

have the ability to go with almost anything, which is why there

is always such a range of dishes when it comes to these fungi.

Cream of Mushroom Soup, Soufflé Omelette with Mushroom

Sauce, Stuffed Mushrooms and Boeuf en Croûte with

Mushroom Filling will appeal to traditional tastes but for those

who fancy something different, try Gnocchi with Oyster

Mushrooms or Tagliatelle Fungi.

CREAM OF MUSHROOM SOUP

A GOOD MUSHROOM SOUP MAKES THE MOST OF THE SUBTLE AND SOMETIMES RATHER ELUSIVE FLAVOUR OF MUSHROOMS. BUTTON MUSHROOMS ARE USED HERE FOR THEIR PALE COLOUR; CHESTNUT OR, BETTER STILL, FIELD MUSHROOMS GIVE A FULLER FLAVOUR BUT TURN THE SOUP BROWN.

SERVES FOUR

INGREDIENTS
275g/10oz/3¾ cups
   button mushrooms
15ml/1 tbsp sunflower oil
40g/1½oz/3 tbsp butter
1 small onion, finely chopped
15ml/1 tbsp plain flour
450ml/¾ pint/1¾ cups vegetable stock
450ml/¾ pint/1¾ cups milk
pinch of dried basil
30–45ml/2–3 tbsp single cream
salt and freshly ground black pepper
fresh basil leaves, to garnish

1 Separate the mushroom caps from the stalks. Finely slice the caps and finely chop the stalks.

2 Heat the oil and half the butter in a heavy-based saucepan and add the onion, mushroom stalks and half of the sliced mushroom caps. Fry for about 1–2 minutes, stirring frequently, and then cover and sweat over a gentle heat for 6–7 minutes, stirring occasionally.

3 Stir in the flour and cook for about 1 minute. Gradually add the stock and milk, to make a smooth thin sauce. Add the basil, and season with salt and pepper. Bring to the boil and then simmer, partly covered, for 15 minutes.

4 Cool slightly and then pour the soup into a food processor or blender and process until smooth. Melt the rest of the butter in a frying pan and fry the remaining mushrooms caps gently for 3–4 minutes until they are just tender.

5 Pour the soup into a clean saucepan and stir in the sliced mushrooms. Heat until very hot and adjust the seasoning. Add a little cream and serve sprinkled with fresh basil leaves.

SOUFFLÉ OMELETTE WITH MUSHROOM SAUCE

A SOUFFLÉ OMELETTE INVOLVES A LITTLE MORE PREPARATION THAN AN ORDINARY OMELETTE BUT THE RESULT IS LIGHT YET SATISFYINGLY FILLING.

SERVES ONE

INGREDIENTS
2 eggs, separated
15g/½oz/1 tbsp butter
sprig of parsley or coriander
For the mushroom sauce
15g/½oz/1 tbsp butter
75g/3oz/generous 1 cup button
   mushrooms, thinly sliced
15ml/1 tbsp plain flour
85–120ml/3–4fl oz/½ cup milk
5ml/1 tsp chopped fresh parsley
   (optional)
salt and freshly ground black pepper

1 To make the mushroom sauce, melt the butter in a saucepan or frying pan and fry the thinly sliced mushrooms for 4–5 minutes until tender.

2 Stir in the flour and then gradually add the milk, stirring all the time, to make a smooth sauce. Add the parsley, if using, and season with salt and pepper. Keep warm to one side.

3 Beat the egg yolks with 15ml/1 tbsp water and season with a little salt and pepper. Whisk the egg whites until stiff and then fold into the egg yolks using a metal spoon. Preheat the grill.

4 Melt the butter in a large frying pan and pour the egg mixture into the pan. Cook over a gentle heat for 2–4 minutes. Place the frying pan under the grill and cook for a further 3–4 minutes until the top is golden brown.

5 Slide the omelette on to a warmed serving plate, pour over the mushroom sauce and fold the omelette in half. Serve garnished with a sprig of parsley or coriander.

STUFFED MUSHROOMS

THIS IS A CLASSIC MUSHROOM DISH, STRONGLY FLAVOURED WITH GARLIC. USE FLAT MUSHROOMS OR FIELD MUSHROOMS THAT ARE SOMETIMES AVAILABLE FROM FARM SHOPS.

SERVES FOUR

INGREDIENTS

450g/1lb large flat mushrooms
butter, for greasing
about 75ml/5 tbsp olive oil
2 garlic cloves, minced or very
   finely chopped
45ml/3 tbsp/¾-1 cup finely chopped
   fresh parsley
40–50g/1½–2oz fresh white
   breadcrumbs
salt and freshly ground black pepper
sprig of flat leaf parsley, to garnish

1 Preheat the oven to 180°C/350°F/ Gas 4. Cut off the mushroom stalks and reserve on one side.

2 Arrange the mushroom caps in a buttered shallow dish, gill side upwards.

3 Heat 15ml/1 tbsp of oil in a frying pan and fry the garlic briefly. Finely chop the mushroom stalks; mix with the parsley and breadcrumbs. Add the garlic, salt and pepper and 15ml/1tbsp of the oil. Pile a little mixture on each mushroom.

4 Add the remaining oil to the dish and cover the mushrooms with buttered greaseproof paper. Bake for about 15–20 minutes, removing the paper for the last 5 minutes to brown the tops. Garnish with a sprig of flat leaf parsley.

COOK'S TIP
The cooking time for the mushrooms depends on their size and thickness. If they are fairly thin, cook for slightly less time. They should be tender but not too soft when they are cooked. If a stronger garlic flavour is preferred, do not cook the garlic before combining it with the breadcrumb mixture.

BOEUF EN CROÛTE WITH MUSHROOM FILLING

A DUXELLES FILLING OF FINELY-CHOPPED MUSHROOMS, SHALLOTS, GARLIC AND PARSLEY IS THE CLASSIC FILLING FOR BOEUF EN CROÛTE. THESE INDIVIDUAL VERSIONS ARE GOOD SERVED WITH BOILED OR STEAMED NEW POTATOES AND A GREEN VEGETABLE.

SERVES FOUR

INGREDIENTS
    4 fillet steaks, about
        115–150g/4–5oz each
    a little Dijon mustard
    25g/1oz/2 tbsp butter
    275g/10oz puff pastry
    25g/1oz/½ cup white breadcrumbs
    beaten egg, for glazing
    salt and freshly ground black pepper
    sprigs of parsley or chervil, to garnish
For the duxelles filling
    25g/1oz/2 tbsp butter
    4 shallots, finely chopped
    1–2 garlic cloves, crushed
    225–275g/8–10oz flat mushrooms,
        finely chopped
    15ml/1 tbsp finely chopped parsley

1 Preheat the oven to 220°C/425°F/ Gas 7. Rub a little mustard over each of the steaks and season with pepper. Melt the butter in a heavy-based frying pan and fry the steaks for about 1–2 minutes each side, so that they are browned on the outside but still red in the centre. Transfer to a plate to cool.

4 Cut the pastry into four and roll out each piece very thinly to a 18cm/7in square. Cut the corners from each square and spread a spoonful of the mushroom mixture in the centre. Top with a steak and sprinkle with a spoonful of fresh breadcrumbs.

5 Bring the sides of the pastry up to the centre and seal with water. Place seam side down on a baking sheet. Decorate with pastry trimmings and brush each with the beaten egg. Bake for about 20 minutes, until golden brown. Serve garnished with parsley or chervil.

2 To make the filling, melt the butter and fry the shallots and garlic briefly. Stir in the finely chopped mushrooms.

3 Fry over a fairly high heat for about 3–4 minutes, stirring, until the juices run. Lower the heat and cook gently for 4–5 minutes until the mixture is dry. Add the parsley and seasoning and cool.

GNOCCHI WITH OYSTER MUSHROOMS

GNOCCHI MAKE AN UNUSUAL AND PLEASANT ALTERNATIVE TO PASTA. THEY ARE BLAND ON THEIR OWN BUT BRING OUT THE FLAVOUR OF THE OYSTER MUSHROOMS IN THIS DISH WHILE THEIR SOFT TEXTURE CONTRASTS WITH THE FIRMNESS OF THE FUNGI.

SERVES FOUR

INGREDIENTS
225g/8oz oyster mushrooms
15ml/1 tbsp olive oil
1 onion, finely chopped
1 garlic clove, crushed
4 plum tomatoes, peeled and chopped
45–60ml/3–4 tbsp vegetable stock
  or water
salt and freshly ground black pepper
2 x 300g/11oz packet plain
  potato gnocchi
a large knob of butter
10ml/2 tsp chopped fresh parsley
Parmesan cheese shavings,
  to garnish

1 Trim the mushrooms and tear into smaller pieces, if large. Heat the oil in a large frying pan; fry the onion and garlic over a low heat for about 4–5 minutes until softened but not browned.

2 Increase the heat, add the mushrooms to the pan and sauté for about 3–4 minutes, stirring constantly.

3 Stir in the chopped tomatoes, stock or water and seasoning. Cover and simmer for about 8 minutes until the tomatoes are very soft and reduced to a pulp. Stir occasionally.

4 Cook the gnocchi in a large pan of salted boiling water for 2–3 minutes (or according to the instructions on the packet) then drain well and toss with the butter. Place in a large warmed serving bowl and stir in the chopped parsley.

5 Pour the mushroom and tomato mixture over the top, stir briefly and sprinkle with the Parmesan cheese.

COOK'S TIP
If the mushrooms are very large, the stalks are likely to be tough, therefore they should be discarded. Always tear rather than cut oyster mushrooms.

SEAFOOD AND OYSTER MUSHROOM STARTER

THIS DISH IS REMARKABLY QUICK TO PREPARE. IT CAN BE MADE INTO A MORE SUBSTANTIAL DISH BY STIRRING 275-350G/10-12OZ COOKED PASTA SHELLS INTO THE SAUCE AT THE END.

SERVES FOUR

INGREDIENTS
15ml/1 tbsp olive oil
15g/½oz/1 tbsp butter
1 garlic clove, crushed
175g/6oz oyster mushrooms,
  halved or quartered
115–175g/4–6oz peeled prawns
115g/4oz cooked mussels, optional
juice of ½ lemon
15ml/1 tbsp medium dry sherry
150ml/¼ pint/⅔ cup double cream
salt and freshly ground black pepper

1 Heat the oil and butter in a frying pan and sauté the garlic for a few minutes, then add the mushrooms. Cook over a moderate heat for 4–5 minutes until soft, stirring from time to time.

2 Reduce the heat and stir in the prawns, mussels, if using, and lemon juice. Cook for 1 minute, stirring all the time. Stir in the sherry and cook for 1 minute.

3 Add the cream and cook gently until heated through but not boiling. Taste and adjust the seasoning and then spoon into warmed serving dishes. Serve at once with chunks of Italian bread.

TAGLIATELLE FUNGI

THE MUSHROOM SAUCE IS QUICK TO MAKE AND THE PASTA COOKS VERY QUICKLY; BOTH NEED TO BE COOKED AS NEAR TO SERVING AS POSSIBLE SO CAREFUL COORDINATION IS REQUIRED. PUT THE PASTA IN TO COOK WHEN THE CRÈME FRAÎCHE IS ADDED TO THE SAUCE.

SERVES FOUR

INGREDIENTS

about 50g/2oz/4 tbsp butter
225–350g/8–12oz chanterelles
  or other wild mushrooms
15ml/1 tbsp plain flour
150ml/¼ pint/⅔ cup milk
90ml/6 tbsp crème fraîche
15ml/1 tbsp chopped fresh parsley
275g/10oz fresh tagliatelle
olive oil
salt and freshly ground black pepper

3 Add the crème fraîche, parsley, mushrooms and seasoning, and stir well. Cook very gently to heat through and then keep warm while cooking the pasta.

4 Cook the pasta in a large saucepan of boiling water for about 4–5 minutes (or according to the instructions on the packet). Drain well, toss in a little olive oil then turn on to a warmed serving plate. Pour the mushroom sauce over and serve immediately.

COOK'S TIP
Chanterelles are a little tricky to wash, as they are so delicate. However, since these are woodland mushrooms, it's important to clean them thoroughly. Hold each one by the stalk and let cold water run under the gills to dislodge hidden dirt. Shake gently to dry.

1 Melt 40g/1½oz/3 tbsp of the butter in a frying pan and fry the mushrooms for about 2–3 minutes over a gentle heat until the juices begin to run. Increase the heat and cook until the liquid has almost evaporated. Transfer the mushrooms to a bowl using a slotted spoon.

2 Stir in the flour, adding a little more butter if necessary, and cook for about 1 minute, and then gradually stir in the milk to make a smooth sauce.

SHIITAKE FRIED RICE

SHIITAKE MUSHROOMS HAVE A STRONG, MEATY MUSHROOMY AROMA AND FLAVOUR. THIS IS A VERY EASY RECIPE TO MAKE, AND ALTHOUGH IT IS A SIDE DISH IT COULD ALMOST BE A MEAL IN ITSELF.

SERVES FOUR

INGREDIENTS
2 eggs
45ml/3 tbsp vegetable oil
350g/12oz shiitake mushrooms
8 spring onions, sliced diagonally
1 garlic clove, crushed
½ green pepper, chopped
25g/1oz/2 tbsp butter
175–225g/6–8oz/about 1 cup long
   grain rice, cooked
15ml/1 tbsp medium dry sherry
30ml/2 tbsp dark soy sauce
15ml/1 tbsp chopped fresh coriander
salt

1 Beat the eggs with 15ml/1 tbsp cold water and season with a little salt.

2 Heat 15ml/1 tbsp of the oil in a wok or large frying pan, pour in the eggs and cook to make a large omelette. Lift the sides of the omelette and tilt the wok so that the uncooked egg can run under the cooked egg. When done, roll up the omelette and slice thinly.

3 Remove and discard the mushroom stalks if tough and slice the caps thinly, halving them if they are large.

4 Heat 15ml/1 tbsp of the remaining oil in the wok and stir-fry the spring onions and garlic for 3–4 minutes until softened but not brown. Transfer them to a plate using a slotted spoon.

5 Add the pepper, stir-fry for about 2–3 minutes, then add the butter and the remaining 15ml/1 tbsp of oil. As the butter begins to sizzle, add the sliced mushrooms and stir-fry over a moderate heat for 3–4 minutes until soft.

6 Loosen the rice grains as much as possible. Pour the sherry over the mushrooms and then stir in the rice.

7 Heat the rice over a moderate heat, stirring all the time to prevent it sticking. If the rice seems very dry, add a little more oil. Stir in the reserved onions and omelette slices, the soy sauce and coriander. Cook for a few minutes until heated through, then serve.

COOK'S TIP
Unlike risotto, for which rice is cooked along with the other ingredients, Chinese fried rice is always made using cooked rice. If you use 175–225g/6–8oz uncooked long grain, you will get about 450–500g/16–20oz cooked rice, enough for four people.

WILD MUSHROOMS IN BRIOCHE

SERVES FOUR

INGREDIENTS
4 small brioches
olive oil, for glazing
20ml/4 tsp lemon juice
sprigs of parsley, to garnish
For the mushroom filling
25g/1oz/2 tbsp butter
2 shallots
1 garlic clove, crushed
175–225g/6–8oz assorted wild
  mushrooms, halved if large
45ml/3 tbsp white wine
45ml/3 tbsp double cream
5ml/1 tsp chopped fresh basil
5ml/1 tsp chopped fresh parsley
salt and freshly ground black pepper

1 Preheat the oven to 180°C/350°F/
Gas 4. Using a serrated or grapefruit
knife, cut a circle out of the top of each
brioche and reserve. Scoop out the
bread inside to make a small cavity.

2 Place the brioches and the tops on a
baking sheet and brush inside and out
with olive oil. Bake for 7–10 minutes
until golden and crisp. Squeeze 5ml/
1 tsp of lemon juice inside each brioche.

3 To make the filling, melt the butter in
a frying pan and fry the shallots and
garlic for 2–3 minutes until softened.

4 Add the mushrooms and cook gently
for about 4–5 minutes, stirring.

5 When the juices begin to run, reduce
the heat and continue cooking for about
3–4 minutes, stirring occasionally, until
the pan is fairly dry.

6 Stir in the wine. Cook for a few more
minutes and then stir in the cream, basil,
parsley and seasoning to taste.

7 Pile the mushroom mixture into the
brioche shells and replace the tops.
Return to the oven and reheat for about
5–6 minutes. Serve as a starter,
garnished sprigs of parsley.

WILD MUSHROOMS WITH PANCAKES

SERVES SIX

INGREDIENTS
225–275g/8–10oz assorted
  wild mushrooms
50g/2oz/¼ cup butter
1–2 garlic cloves
a splash of brandy (optional)
freshly ground black pepper
soured cream, to serve
For the pancakes
115g/4oz/1 cup self-raising flour
20g/¾oz/3 tbsp buckwheat flour
2.5ml/½ tsp baking powder
2 eggs
about 250ml/8fl oz/1 cup milk
a pinch of salt
oil, for frying

1 To make the pancakes, mix together
the flours, baking powder and salt in a
large bowl or food processor. Add the
eggs and milk and beat or process to
make a smooth batter, with about the
consistency of single cream.

2 Grease a large griddle or frying pan
with a little oil and when hot, pour small
amounts of batter (about 15–30ml/
1–2 tbsp per pancake) on to the griddle
or frying pan, spaced well apart.

3 Fry for a few minutes until bubbles
begin to appear on the surface and the
underside is golden, and then flip over.
Cook for about 1 minute until golden.
Keep warm, wrapped in a clean dish
towel. (Makes about 18–20 pancakes.)

4 If the mushrooms are large, cut them
in half. Melt the butter in a frying pan
and add the garlic and mushrooms. Fry
over a moderate heat for a few minutes
until the juices begin to run and then
increase the heat and cook, stirring
frequently, until nearly all the juices have
evaporated. Stir in the brandy, if using,
and season with a little black pepper.

5 Arrange the warm pancakes on a
serving plate and spoon over a little
soured cream. Top with the hot
mushrooms and serve immediately.

COOK'S TIP
This makes a delicious and elegant
starter for a dinner party. Alternatively,
make cocktail-size pancakes and serve
as part of a buffet supper.

INDEX

A
ackee, 443
acorn squashes, 412
alcohol, preserving fruit in, 17
almonds
  almond biscuits, 41
  cold lemon soufflé with
    caramelized almond
    topping, 159
  crunchy-topped fresh apricot
    cake, 89
  fresh lemon tart, 163
  moist orange and almond
    cake, 166
  yellow plum tart, 86
Alphonse Lavalle grapes, 232
Alphonsine mangoes, 186
Alphonso mangoes, 186
Alpine strawberries, 95
Amarelle cherries, 71
Anaheim chillies, 440
Ancho chillies, 440
anchovies
  Caesar salad, 474
  sweet pepper choux with
    anchovies, 453
Anjou pears, 30
apple bananas, 172
apple corers, 12
apple processors, 12
apple segmenters, 12
apples, 20-9
  apple and cider sauce, 56
  apple and red onion
    marmalade, 56
  apple charlottes, 47
  apple crêpes with butterscotch
    sauce, 44
  baked stuffed apples, 42
  carrot, apple and orange
    coleslaw, 340
  cider apples, 29
  crab apples, 29
  Dutch apple cake, 54
  filo-topped apple pie, 51
  French apple tart, 53
  hot blackberry and apple
    soufflés, 115
  radish, mango and apple
    salad, 481
  spiced apple crumble, 42
  tarte Tatin, 50
apricots, 63
  apricot parcels, 88
  caramelized apricots with pain
    perdu, 80
  crunchy-topped fresh apricot
    cake, 89

arbutus, 96
artichokes see globe artichokes;
    Jerusalem artichokes
argula, 465
Ashmead's Kernel apples, 21
Asian pears, 35
asparagus, 288-9
  asparagus soup, 302
  asparagus tart with ricotta, 300
  asparagus with tarragon
    hollandaise, 300
  roast asparagus crêpes, 303
aubergines, 435-7
  aubergine and courgette
    bake, 448
  aubergines with tzatziki, 448
  loofah and aubergine
    ratatouille, 427
  parsnip, aubergine and cashew
    biryani, 337
avocados, 444-5
  celery, avocado and walnut
    salad, 306
  guacamole, 458

B
babacos, 175
bacon
  French beans with bacon and
    cream, 401
  onion squash risotto, 420
  pan-fried sweet potatoes with
    bacon, 343
baking
  fruit, 16
  potatoes, 318, 319
balti-style cauliflower with
    tomatoes, 373
bamboo shoots, 294
bananas, 172-4
  banana and mascarpone
    creams, 212
  banana and pecan bread, 222
  bananas with lime and
    cardamom sauce, 212
  rum and banana waffles, 216
  toffee bananas, 214
Barbillone figs, 236
basil
  tomato and basil tart, 451

Beach plums, 65
bean sprouts, 294-5
beans
  dried, 393
  see also individual types
    of bean
Beauty of Bath apples, 21
beef
  boeuf en croûte with mushroom
    filling, 497
beefsteak tomatoes, 433
beet greens, 326
beetroot, 326
bergamots, 141
Bermuda onions, 266
berries, 93-133
  berry brûlée tarts, 130
  recipes, 113-33
  summer berry crêpes, 116
  summer pudding, 114
Beth pears, 30
Beurré Bosc pears, 30
Beurré Hardi pears, 30
Beurré Superfin pears, 30
Bigarade oranges, 145
Bigarreau cherries, 70
bilberries, 103
Bing cherries, 70
bird's-eye chillies, 440
biryani
  parsnip, aubergine and cashew
    biryani, 337
biscuits
  almond biscuits, 41
  ginger biscuits, 242
bitter oranges, 145
black cherry clafoutis, 78
black-eyed beans, 393
black grapes, 232
black mulberries, 102
Black Tartarian cherries, 70
black trumpets, 488
blackberries, 99-100
  blackberry Kir Royale, 100
  bramble jelly, 132
  coconut jelly with star anise
    fruits, 204

  hot blackberry and apple
    soufflés, 115
blackcurrants, 110-11
  blackcurrant sorbet, 123
  fresh currant bread-and-butter
    pudding, 126
blaeberries, 103
blanching vegetables, 261
blenders, 257
Blenheim Orange apples, 21
Blonde oranges, 144
blood oranges, 144-5
blueberries, 103
  blueberry pie, 129
  cranberry and blueberry
    streusel cake, 127
  fresh berry pavlova, 118
  fresh blueberry muffins, 128
  fruits of the forest, 120
boeuf en croûte with mushroom
    filling, 497
boiling
  potatoes, 319
  vegetables, 260
Bombay mangoes, 186
bottle gourds, 414
bottled figs, 237
box graters, 12
boysenberries, 101
Braeburn apples, 21
bramble jelly, 132
Bramley's Seedling apples, 27
bread
  croûtons, 278
  fresh currant bread-and-butter
    pudding, 126
  summer pudding, 114
breadfruit, 176, 445
brioche
  caramelized apricots with pain
    perdu, 80
  wild mushrooms in
    brioche, 502
broad beans, 384
  broad beans à la paysanne,
    396
  lamb and broad bean
    couscous, 396
broccoflower, 352
broccoli, 354-5
  broccoli and chicken
    lasagne, 368
  broccoli crumble, 368
  hot broccoli tartlets, 374
broccoli, Chinese, 363
brownies, date and walnut, 222
Brussels sprouts, 351
  Brussels sprouts gratin, 378

stir-fried Brussels sprouts, 378
Buissone figs, 236
bullaces, 69
Burbank plums, 64
butterhead lettuces, 462
butternut squashes, 412
butterscotch sauce, apple crêpes
    with, 44
button mushrooms, 486

C
cabbage, 356-8
    pasta with Savoy cabbage and
        Gruyère, 377
Caesar salad, 474
cakes
    chocolate courgette cake, 428
    cranberry and blueberry
        streusel cake, 127
    crunchy-topped fresh apricot
        cake, 89
    Dutch apple cake, 54
    Greek yogurt and fig cake, 249
    lemon and lime syrup
        cake, 167
    moist orange and almond
        cake, 166
    pear and polenta cake, 54
calabrese, 354-5
callaloo, 330
Cambridge Favourite
    strawberries, 95
candied orange peel, 147
candying fruit, 17
canelle knives, 12
canned fruit and vegetables
    apricots, 63
    bananas, 173
    figs, 237
    mandarin oranges, 143
    mangoes, 186
    peaches, 61
    pears, 34
    pineapple, 193
    tomatoes, 433
cannellini beans, spinach and, 370
cantaloupe melons, 228
Cape gooseberries, 191
Cara potatoes, 316
carambolas, 176
caramel
    baked lattice peaches, 82
    berry brûlée tarts, 130
    caramelized apricots with pain
        perdu, 80
    caramelizing fruit, 17
    caramelizing grapes, 235
    citrus fruit flambé with pistachio

    praline, 158
    cold lemon soufflé with
        caramelized almond
        topping, 159
    passion fruit crème caramels
        with dipped physalis, 201
    toffee bananas, 214
Cardinal grapes, 232
cardoons, 291
Carlingford potatoes, 314
carrots, 324-5
    carrot and coriander soup, 342
    carrot, apple and orange
        coleslaw, 340
    eddo, carrot and parsnip
        medley, 346
    glazed carrots with cider, 340
    julienne, 260
Casaba melons, 229
cashew nuts
    parsnip, aubergine and cashew
        biryani, 337
cassava, 331
casseroles, cast-iron/
    flameproof, 257
cauliflower, 352-3
    balti-style cauliflower with
        tomatoes, 373
    cauliflower and mushroom
        gougère, 372
cayenne pepper, 440
celeriac, 293
    celeriac and blue cheese
        roulade, 305
    celeriac gratin, 304
celery, 292-3
    braised celery with goat's
        cheese, 306
    celery, avocado and walnut
        salad, 306
ceps, 488
Champagne
    blackberry Kir Royale, 100
chana dhal, 393
chanterelles, 488
    tagliatelle fungi, 500

chard *see* Swiss chard
Charentais melons, 228
Chasselas grapes, 233
chayotes, 414-15
cheese, savoury recipes
    asparagus tart with ricotta, 300
    aubergine and courgette
        bake, 448
    baked chicory with Parma
        ham, 478
    baked courgettes, 422
    baked leeks with cheese and
        yogurt topping, 283
    baked onions stuffed with
        feta, 276
    braised celery with goat's
        cheese, 306
    broccoli and chicken
        lasagne, 368
    celeriac and blue cheese
        roulade, 305
    enchiladas with hot chilli
        sauce, 456
    leek soufflé, 281
    onion tarts with goat's
        cheese, 276
    pasta with Savoy cabbage and
        Gruyère, 377
    radicchio pizza, 476
    roast asparagus crêpes, 303
    rocket and grilled chèvre
        salad, 479
    spinach and pepper pizza, 455
    spinach in filo with three
        cheeses, 371
    stuffed artichokes, 308
    sweetcorn and cheese
        pasties, 404
    tomato and basil tart, 451
    turnip tops with Parmesan and
        garlic, 376
cheese, sweet recipes
    banana and mascarpone
        creams, 212
    exotic fruit tranche, 219
    lemon coeur à la crème with
        Cointreau oranges, 150
    lemon grass skewers with lime
        cheese, 204
    red grape and cheese
        tartlets, 246
cheesecakes
    lemon and lime cheesecake,
        155
    pomegranate jewelled
        cheesecake, 211
cherimoyas, 177
cherries, 70-1

black cherry clafoutis, 78
fresh cherry and hazelnut
    strudel, 81
spiced fruits jubilee, 75
cherry guavas, 182
cherry plums, 65
cherry stoners, 13
cherry tomatoes, 433
chestnut mushrooms, 486
chestnuts
    cranberry and chestnut
        stuffing, 109
    parsnip and chestnut
        croquettes, 336
chick-peas, 393
    hot-sour chick-peas, 457
chicken
    broccoli and chicken
        lasagne, 368
    chicken with shallots, 284
    enchiladas with hot chilli
        sauce, 456
    mangetouts with chicken and
        coriander, 399
    Mediterranean chicken with
        turnips, 338
chicken livers and green
    salad, 474
chicory, 466
    baked chicory with Parma
        ham, 478
chillies, 440-1
    enchiladas with hot chilli
        sauce, 456
    hot-sour chick-peas, 457
    pickled peach and chilli
        chutney, 90
Chinese bitter melons, 415
Chinese broccoli, 363
Chinese cabbage, 362-3
Chinese chives, 269
    Thai noodles with Chinese
        chives, 280
Chinese greens, 362-3
Chinese leaves and mooli with
    scallops, 480

Chinese mustard greens, 362
chips, 318, 319
chives, 269
chocolate
    chocolate and mandarin truffle
        slice, 154
    chocolate courgette cake, 428
    chocolate, pear and pecan
        pie, 52
    date and walnut brownies, 222
    fruits of the forest with white
        chocolate creams, 120
chopping vegetables, 260
choux pastry
    sweet pepper choux with
        anchovies, 453
chowder, sweetcorn and
    scallop, 405
chutney
    apple and red onion
        marmalade, 56
    fig and date chutney, 251
    mango chutney, 224
    pickled peach and chilli
        chutney, 90
cider
    apple and cider sauce, 56
    glazed carrots with cider, 340
cider apples, 29
citron, 139
citrus fruits, 135-69

citrus fruit flambé with pistachio
    praline, 158
    preparation, 15
    recipes, 149-69
citrus presses, 13
citrus zesters, 12
civet fruit, 180
clafoutis, black cherry, 78
clementines, 142
    clementine jelly, 151
cloudberries, 98
coconut milk
    coconut jelly with star anise
        fruits, 204
    exotic fruit sushi, 203

pak choi with lime dressing, 380
coeur à la crème, lemon, 150
Cointreau
    crêpes Suzette, 156
    lemon coeur à la crème with
        Cointreau oranges, 150
colanders, 257
coleslaw
    carrot, apple and orange
        coleslaw, 340
collards, 359
Comice pears, 31
Conference pears, 31
cooking apples, 27-8
cooking methods
    fruit, 16
    vegetables, 260-1
coriander
    carrot and coriander soup, 342
coring fruit, 12, 14
corn *see* sweetcorn
corn salad, 463
cos lettuces, 462-3
coulis, raspberry, 98
courgettes, 408-9
    aubergine and courgette
        bake, 448
    baked courgettes, 422
    chocolate courgette cake, 428
    courgettes Italian-style, 423
couscous, lamb and broad
    bean, 396
cowberries, 108
Cox's Orange Pippin apples, 22
crab apples, 29
cranberries, 108-9
    cranberry and blueberry
        streusel cake, 127
    cranberry and chestnut
        stuffing, 109
    cranberry sauce, 109
crème caramels, passion fruit, 201
Crenshaw melons, 229
crêpes
    apple crêpes with butterscotch
        sauce, 44
    crêpes Suzette, 156
    roast asparagus crêpes, 303
    summer berry crêpes, 116
    see also pancakes
cress, 471
crisphead lettuces, 462
Crispin apples, 22
crisps, swede, 338
croquettes, parsnip and
    chestnut, 336
croûtons, roast garlic with, 278
crumbles

broccoli crumble, 368
    spiced apple crumble, 42
crystallized fruits, 17
crystallized pineapple, 193
cucumbers, 416-17
    aubergines with tzatziki, 448
    cucumber and trout
        mousse, 426
curly endive, 466
curly kale, 359
currants (dried), 235
curry, samphire with chilled
    fish, 309
curuba, 177
custard
    gooseberry and elderflower
        fool, 119
    plum and custard creams, 74
custard apples, 177
custard marrows, 410
Czar plums, 65

D
daikon radishes, 468
damsons, 68
    damson cheese, 68
    iced gin and damson soufflés, 79
dandelion, 360
Danish pastries
    plum and marzipan pastries, 85
dasheen, 329-30
date plums, 190
dates, 178-9
    date and walnut brownies, 222
    fig and date chutney, 251
    hot date puddings with toffee
        sauce, 215
    pickled peach and chilli
        chutney, 90
    stuffed dates, 179
Dauphine Violette figs, 236
deep-frying
    fruit, 16
    vegetables, 261
Delicata squashes, 412
Denniston's Superb plums, 64

Desirée potatoes, 315
dewberries, 99-100
discoloration, preventing, 14
Discovery apples, 22
dolmades, 381
Doyenné du Comice pears, 31
dragon fruit, 180
dried fruit and vegetables, 17
    apples, 27-8
    apricots, 63
    bananas, 173
    beans, 393
    dates, 178
    figs, 237
    grapes, 235
    mangoes, 187
    mushrooms, 489
    peaches, 61
    pears, 34
    peas, 393
    persimmons, 190
    pineapple, 193
drinks, apple, 29
duck
    duck in bitter orange sauce, 147
    warm duck salad with
        orange, 477
durians, 180
Dutch apple cake, 54

E
Early Rivers cherries, 70
Early Sulphur gooseberries, 106
eddo, 329-30
    eddo, carrot and parsnip
        medley, 346
eggplant *see* aubergines
eggs
    eggs flamenco, 454
    pumpkin and ham frittata, 429
    soufflé omelette with mushroom
        sauce, 494
Egremont Russet apples, 22
Ein d'Or melons, 229
elderberries, 104
elderflowers, 104
    gooseberry and elderflower
        fool, 119
    lychee and elderflower
        sorbet, 202
electric juice extractors, 13

elephant garlic, 271
Elsanta strawberries, 95
Elstar apples, 22
Elvira strawberries, 95
Empire apples, 22
enchiladas with hot chilli
    sauce, 456
endive, curly, 466
    rocket and grilled chèvre
        salad, 479
English cherries, 71
English cucumbers, 416
English pumpkins, 412
enokitaki mushrooms, 491
equipment
    fruit preparation, 12-13
    vegetables, 256-7
escarole, 466
Estima potatoes, 315
exotic fruits, 171-225
    exotic fruit salad with passion
        fruit dressing, 207
    exotic fruit sushi, 203
    exotic fruit tranche, 219
    recipes, 199-225
    tropical fruit gratin, 208
exotic gourds, 414-15
exotic root vegetables, 328-31

F
fat hen, 361
feijoas, 181
fennel, 296
    braised fennel with
        tomatoes, 310
    fennel and mussel
        Provençal, 310
fiddlehead ferns, 294
field mushrooms, 487
figs, 236-8
    fig and date chutney, 251
    fig and walnut torte, 244
    fresh fig filo tart, 248
    Greek yogurt and fig cake, 249
filo-topped apple pie, 51
finger potatoes, 316
flageolet beans, 393
    runner beans with garlic, 402
Flame Seedless grapes, 232
Florence fennel, 296
fondant icing, physalis in, 191
food processors, 257
fool, gooseberry and
    elderflower, 119
Forelle pears, 31
fraises des bois, 95
freezing blackberries, 99
French apple tart, 53

French beans, 388
    French bean salad, 400
    French beans with bacon and
        cream, 401
French breakfast radishes, 468
frittata, pumpkin and ham, 429
fritters, 261
    pear and cinnamon fritters, 45
    yam fritters, 346
frosting fruit, 17
fruit
    buying, 14
    cooking methods, 16-17
    equipment, 12-13
    preparation, 14
fruit salads
    exotic fruit salad with passion
        fruit dressing, 207
    fruits of the forest with white
        chocolate creams, 120
frying pans, 257
frying vegetables, 261
Fuji apples, 23
funnels, 13

G
Gala apples, 23
galangal, 331
Galia melons, 228
garden leaves, 360
garlic, 270-1
    garlic mushrooms, 278
    roast garlic with croûtons, 278
    turnip tops with Parmesan and
        garlic, 376
garlic chives, 269
garlic presses, 256
garnishes
    citrus fruit, 15
    fig flowers, 238
Gaviota plums, 64
gazpacho, 450
geans, cherries, 70
gherkins, 416
gin and damson soufflés, iced, 79
ginger, 331
    ginger baskets, 152
    ginger biscuits, 242
    papaya baked with ginger, 206

ginup, 181
glacé cherries, 71
glacé fruits, 17
glacé peaches, 61
globe artichokes, 290-1
    stuffed artichokes, 308
gnocchi
    gnocchi with oyster
        mushrooms, 498
    marrows with gnocchi, 424
goat's cheese
    baked courgettes, 422
    baked leeks with cheese and
        yogurt topping, 283
    braised celery with goat's
        cheese, 306
    onion tarts with goat's
        cheese, 276
    rocket and grilled chèvre
        salad, 479
Golden Delicious apples, 23
golden raspberries, 97
golden watermelons, 231
Golden Wonder potatoes, 315
Goldendrop gooseberries, 106
good King Henry, 361
gooseberries, 106-7
    gooseberry and elderflower
        fool, 119
Gorella strawberries, 95
gougère, cauliflower and
    mushroom, 372
gourds, 414-15
granadillas, 181
Granny Smith apples, 23
grape juice, 234
grapefruit, 136-7
    citrus fruit flambé with pistachio
        praline, 158
    three-fruit marmalade, 168
grapefruit knives, 13
grapefruit segmenters, 13
grapes, 232-5
    caramelizing grapes, 235
    red grape and cheese
        tartlets, 246
grapeseed oil, 234
graters, 256
grating
    citrus zest, 15
    graters, 12
    lemons, 138
gratins
    Brussels sprouts gratin, 378
    celeriac gratin, 304
Greek yogurt and fig cake, 249
green bananas, 173, 174, 442-3
green beans, 388

green cabbage, 358
greengages, 68
greens, 349-81
    recipes, 367-81
Greensleeves apples, 23
Grenadier apples, 27
grilling fruit, 16
guacamole, 458
guavas, 182
guines, cherries, 70

H
habañero chillies, 440
hairy lychees, 196
ham
    broad beans à la
        paysanne, 396
    pumpkin and ham
        frittata, 429
    see also Parma ham
haricot beans, 393
haricots verts, 388
Hautbois strawberries, 95
haws, 105
hazelnuts
    fresh cherry and hazelnut
        strudel, 81
    nectarine and hazelnut
        meringues, 76
Heritage raspberries, 97
hips, rose, 105
hollandaise sauce
    asparagus with tarragon
        hollandaise, 300
honeydew melons, 229
horned cucumbers, 183
horned melons, 183
horns of plenty, 488
horseradish, 325
Hosui pears, 35
hot gold spike chillies, 440
hot-sour chick-peas, 457
Howgate Wonder apples, 27
Hubbard squashes, 412
huckleberries, 102
hybrid berries, 101

I
ice cream, fresh strawberry, 122
iced gin and damson soufflés, 79
Ida Red apples, 23
Indian figs, 195
Indian-style okra, 403
Italia grapes, 232
Italian courgettes, 409
Italian fennel, 296
Italian roast peppers, 452

J
jackfruit, 182
Jaffa oranges, 144
jalapeño chillies, 440
Jamaican fruit trifle, 210
Jamaican plums, 183
James Grieve apples, 23
jams
    melon and star anise jam, 250
    strawberry jam, 133
Japonica quinces, 37
jelly
    bramble jelly, 132
    clementine jelly, 151
    coconut jelly with star anise
        fruits, 204
    quince jelly, 36
    redcurrant jelly, 111
jelly bags, 13
jelly melons, 183
Jersey Royal potatoes, 314
Jersey White potatoes, 314
Jerusalem artichokes, 321
    artichoke rösti, 344
    artichoke timbales with spinach
        sauce, 344
jicama, 330
Jonagold apples, 23-4
Jonathan apples, 24
Josephine de Malines pears, 31
juca, 331
juice
    grape, 234
    lemon, 139

pomegranate, 195
jujubes, 183
Julie mangoes, 186
julienne strips
    carrots, 260
    citrus rind, 140
    zest, 15

K
Kabocha squashes, 412
Kadota figs, 236
kaffir limes, 140
kaki plums, 190
kale, 359
Katy apples, 24
Kent mangoes, 186
Kerr's Pink potatoes, 315
Key lime pie, 164
Key limes, 140
Khoob melons, 228
Kidd's Orange Red apples, 24
kidney beans, 393
King Edward potatoes, 315
Kir Royale, blackberry, 100
Kirbys, 416
kiwanos, 183
kiwi fruit, 184
knives, 256
kohlrabi, 364
kubos, 184
kumquats, 141
    spiced poached kumquats, 168

L
La Ratte potatoes, 316
lady finger bananas, 172
lamb and broad bean
    couscous, 396
lamb's lettuce, 463
land cress, 470
Langley's Industry
    gooseberries, 106
lasagne, broccoli and chicken, 368
Laxton's Fortune apples, 24
Laxton's Superb apples, 24
leeks, 272-3
    baked leeks with cheese and
        yogurt topping, 283
    leek soufflé, 281
    preparing, 258
    radicchio pizza, 476
    stuffed artichokes, 308
    tagliatelle with leeks and Parma
        ham, 282
lemon, 138-9
    cold lemon soufflé with
        caramelized almond
        topping, 159

fresh lemon tart, 163
lemon and lime
    cheesecake, 155
lemon and lime syrup
    cake, 167
lemon coeur à la crème with
    Cointreau oranges, 150
lemon meringue pie, 162
lemon roulade with lemon curd
    cream, 160
lemon surprise pudding, 156
papaya and lemon relish, 225
three-fruit marmalade, 168
lemon grass skewers with lime
    cheese, 204
lemon sole
    samphire with chilled fish
        curry, 309
    watercress and two-fish
        terrine, 482
lemon squeezers, 12
lemon taps, 13
lentils, 393
lettuce, 462-4
    broad beans à la
        paysanne, 396
    Caesar salad, 474
Leveller gooseberries, 106
lima beans, 384
limequats, 141
limes, 140
    bananas with lime and
        cardamom sauce, 212
    Key lime pie, 164
    lemon and lime
        cheesecake, 155
    lemon and lime syrup
        cake, 167
    lemon grass skewers with lime
        cheese, 204
    pak choi with lime
        dressing, 380
lingonberries, 108
Linzer Delikatess potatoes, 317
liquidizers, 257
Little Gem lettuces, 463
liver
    chicken livers and green
        salad, 474
loganberries, 101
London gooseberries, 106
longans, 184
loofahs, 415
    loofah and aubergine
        ratatouille, 427
loosehead lettuces, 462
loquats, 185
lychees, 185

coconut jelly with star anise
    fruits, 204
lychee and elderflower
    sorbet, 202

M
mâche, 463
McIntosh apples, 24
Malling Jewel raspberries, 97
mandarins, 142, 143
    chocolate and mandarin truffle
        slice, 154
mandolines, 256
mangetouts, 387
    mangetouts with chicken and
        coriander, 399
mangoes, 186-7
    cold mango soufflés topped
        with toasted coconut, 200
    Jamaican fruit trifle, 210
    lemon grass skewers with lime
        cheese, 204
    mango and tamarillo
        pastries, 218
    mango chutney, 224
    mango pie, 220
    radish, mango and apple
        salad, 481
mangosteens, 188
manioc, 331
maracoyas, 188
Maraschino cherries, 71
Marian swedes, 323
Maris Bard potatoes, 314
Maris Peer potatoes, 314
Maris Piper potatoes, 314-315
Marjorie's Seedling plums, 64
marmalade, three-fruit, 168
marrows, 410-11
    baked marrow with cream and
        parsley, 425
    marrows with gnocchi, 424
marsh samphire, 297
marzipan
    baked lattice peaches, 82
    plum and marzipan pastries, 85

mashers, 256
mashing potatoes, 318-319
Mediterranean chicken with
turnips, 338
medlars, 37
melon ballers, 13
melons, 228-30
melon and star anise jam, 250
melon trio with ginger
biscuits, 242
meringues
fresh berry pavlova, 118
lemon meringue pie, 162
nectarine and hazelnut
meringues, 76
Merrick swedes, 323
Merton Pride pears, 31
Mexican limes, 140
Mexican potatoes, 330
microwave cooking, fruit, 16
mincemeat
apricot parcels, 88
minneolas, 143
Mirabelles, 65
monkfish
watercress and two-fish
terrine, 482
Montmorency cherries, 71
mooli, 468
Chinese leaves and mooli with
scallops, 480
Morello cherries, 71
morels, 489
mousses
cucumber and trout mousse, 426
quince and ginger mousse, 41
white chocolate creams, 120
muffins, fresh blueberry, 128
mulberries, 102
mung beans, 393
Muscat grapes, 232, 233
mushrooms, 485-502
boeuf en croûte with mushroom
filling, 497
cauliflower and mushroom
gougère, 372
cream of mushroom soup, 494
garlic mushrooms, 278
gnocchi with oyster
mushrooms, 498
preparing, 258
seafood and oyster mushroom
starter, 498
soufflé omelette with mushroom
sauce, 494
stuffed mushrooms, 496
tagliatelle fungi, 500
wild mushrooms in brioche, 502

wild mushrooms with
pancakes, 502
musk melons, 228
mussels
fennel and mussel
Provençal, 310
seafood and oyster mushroom
starter, 498
mustard and cress, 471
mustard greens, 362

N
Napa cabbage, 362
Napoleon cherries, 70
Napoleon grapes, 232
Nashi pears, 35
Navel oranges, 144
Navelina oranges, 144
navets, 323
nectarines, 62
nectarine and hazelnut
meringues, 76
nectarine relish, 90
spiced fruits jubilee, 75
nettles, 361
new potatoes, 314
noodles
Thai noodles with Chinese
chives, 280

O
Ogen melons, 228
okra, 392
Indian-style okra, 403
omelettes
soufflé omelette with mushroom
sauce, 494
one-crust rhubarb pie, 247
onion squashes, 412
onion squash risotto, 420
onions, 264-7
apple and red onion
marmalade, 56
baked onions stuffed with
feta, 276
onion tarts with goat's
cheese, 276
peas with baby onions and
cream, 398

Onward pears, 31
orache, 360
oranges, 144-7
candied orange peel, 147
citrus fruit flambé with pistachio
praline, 158
cranberry sauce, 109
crêpes Suzette, 156
duck in bitter orange sauce, 147
lemon coeur à la crème with
Cointreau oranges, 150
moist orange and almond
cake, 166
ruby orange sherbet in ginger
baskets, 152
three-fruit marmalade, 168
warm duck salad with
orange, 477
oriental shoots, 294-5
Orleans Reinette apples, 24
ortaniques, 143
ostrich ferns, 294
oyster mushrooms, 490
gnocchi with oyster
mushrooms, 498
seafood and oyster mushroom
starter, 498

P
Packham's Triumph pears, 31
pain perdu, caramelized apricots
with, 80
pak choi, 363
pak choi with lime dressing, 380
palm hearts, 295
pancakes
wild mushrooms with
pancakes, 502
see also crêpes
papayas, 189-90
grilled pineapple with papaya
sauce, 208
Jamaican fruit trifle, 210
lemon grass skewers with lime
cheese, 204
papaya and lemon relish, 225

papaya baked with ginger, 206
paring knives, 12
Parma ham
baked chicory with Parma
ham, 478
tagliatelle with leeks and Parma
ham, 282
parsnips, 320
eddo, carrot and parsnip
medley, 346
parsnip and chestnut
croquettes, 336
parsnip, aubergine and cashew
biryani, 337
Parvin mangoes, 186
Passacrena pears, 31
passion fruit, 189
exotic fruit salad with passion
fruit dressing, 207
passion fruit crème caramels
with dipped physalis, 201
pasta with Savoy cabbage and
Gruyère, 377
pasties
chard pasties, 375
sweetcorn and cheese
pasties, 404
pastries
apricot parcels, 88
baked lattice peaches, 82
fig and walnut torte, 244
mango and tamarillo
pastries, 218
plum and marzipan pastries, 85
see also pies; tarts
patatas bravas, 334
pattypan squashes, 409
pavlova, fresh berry, 118
paw-paws see papayas
pe-tsai, 362-3
peaches, 60-2
baked lattice peaches, 82
peach and redcurrant
tartlets, 84
peach Melba syllabub, 76
pickled peach and chilli
chutney, 90
pears, 30-5
chocolate, pear and pecan
pie, 52
iced pear terrine with Calvados
and chocolate sauce, 40
pear and cinnamon fritters, 45
pear and polenta cake, 54
poached pears in port syrup, 46
peas, 386-7
peas with baby onions and
cream, 398

peas, dried, 393
pecan nuts
    banana and pecan bread, 222
    chocolate, pear and pecan
        pie, 52
peel
    candied orange peel, 147
    julienne strips, 140
    lemon, 139
peelers, 256
peeling
    fruit, 12, 14, 15
    vegetables, 259
Pentland Dell potatoes, 316
pepinos, 191
peppers, 438-9
    eggs flamenco, 454
    gazpacho, 450
    Italian roast peppers, 452
    skinning, 260, 439
    spinach and pepper pizza, 455
    sweet pepper choux with
        anchovies, 453
Perlette grapes, 232
perpetual strawberries, 95
Perry pears, 35
persimmons, 190
petits pois, 387
physalis, 191
    passion fruit crème caramels
        with dipped physalis, 201
pickled peach and chilli chutney,
    90
Piel de Sapo melons, 229
pies
    blueberry pie, 129
    boeuf en croûte with mushroom
        filling, 497
    chard pasties, 375
    filo-topped apple pie, 51
    lemon meringue pie, 162
    mango pie, 220
    one-crust rhubarb pie, 247
    spinach in filo with three
        cheeses, 371
    sweetcorn and cheese
        pasties, 404
pineapple easy slicers, 12
pineapple melons, 228

pineapples, 192-3
    grilled pineapple with papaya
        sauce, 208
    Jamaican fruit trifle, 210
pink currants, 111
Pink Fir Apple potatoes, 317
Pink Lady apples, 24
pistachio nuts
    citrus fruit flambé with pistachio
        praline, 158
pitihayas, 180
pizzas
    radicchio pizza, 476
    spinach and pepper pizza, 455
plantains, 173, 174, 442-3
    plantain appetizer, 459
plum tomatoes, 433
plums, 64-7
    plum and custard creams, 74
    plum and marzipan
        pastries, 85
    spiced fruits jubilee, 75
    yellow plum tart, 86
poaching fruit, 16
poblano chillies, 441
polenta
    pear and polenta cake, 54
pomegranates, 194-5
    pomegranate jewelled
        cheesecake, 211
pomelos, 136, 137
Pomme d'Api apples, 24
port
    poached pears in port syrup, 46
    port-stewed rhubarb with vanilla
        desserts, 243
potato mashers, 256
potato peelers, 256
potatoes, 314-19
    artichoke rösti, 344
    patatas bravas, 334
    potatoes Dauphinois, 334
praline
    citrus fruit flambé with pistachio
        praline, 158
prawns
    seafood and oyster mushroom
        starter, 498
preserving fruit, 17
preserving pans, 13
prickly pears, 195
prunes, 66, 67
pumpkins, 412, 414
    pumpkin and ham frittata, 429
    pumpkin soup, 420
puréeing
    apples, 28
    fruit, 17

Purple Congo potatoes, 318
purple kale, 359
purple sprouting broccoli, 354-5

Q
Quetsch plums, 65
quinces, 36-7
    hot quince soufflés, 48
    quince and ginger mousse, 41
    quince jelly, 36

R
radicchio, 466
    radicchio pizza, 476
radishes, 468-9
    radish, mango and apple
        salad, 481
raisins, 235
rambutans, 196
ramp, 273
Ranier cherries, 70
raspberries, 97-8
    fresh berry pavlova, 118
    fruits of the forest with white
        chocolate creams, 120
    peach Melba syllabub, 76
    raspberry and rose petal
        shortcakes, 124
    raspberry coulis, 98
    raspberry sauce, 203
ratatouille, loofah and
    aubergine, 427
reamers, 13
red bananas, 173
red cabbage, 358
red chillies, 441
Red Delicious apples, 24-5
red onions, 265
red radishes, 468
Red Williams pears, 32
redcurrants, 110, 111
    fresh currant bread-and-butter
        pudding, 126
    peach and redcurrant tartlets, 84
    redcurrant jelly, 111

relishes
    nectarine relish, 90
    papaya and lemon relish, 225
remontant strawberries, 95
Reverend W. Wilkes apples, 27
rhubarb, 239
    one-crust rhubarb pie, 247
    port-stewed rhubarb with vanilla
        desserts, 243
rhubarb chard, 365
rice
    dolmades, 381
    exotic fruit sushi, 203
    onion squash risotto, 420
    parsnip, aubergine and cashew
        biryani, 337
    shiitake fried rice, 501
ridged cucumbers, 416
risotto, onion squash, 420
roast potatoes, 318-319
Rocha pears, 32
rock samphire, 297
rocket, 465
    rocket and grilled chèvre
        lsalad, 479
romaine lettuces, 463
romanescoes, 352
Romano potatoes, 316
root vegetables, 313-47
    preparing, 258
    recipes, 333-47
rose hips, 105
rösti, artichoke, 344
roulades
    celeriac and blue cheese
        roulade, 305
    lemon roulade with lemon curd
        cream, 160
round lettuces, 462
round tomatoes, 433
rowanberries, 105
Royal Gala apples, 23
ruby chard, 365
ruby mangoes, 186
ruby orange sherbet in ginger
    baskets, 152
rum and banana waffles, 216
runner beans, 385
    runner beans with garlic, 402

S
salad tomatoes, 433
salad vegetables, 461-83
    recipes, 473-83
salads
    Caesar salad, 474
    carrot, apple and orange
        coleslaw, 340

celery, avocado and walnut
    salad, 306
chicken livers and green
    salad, 474
French bean salad, 400
preparing, 259
radish, mango and apple
    salad, 481
rocket and grilled chèvre
    salad, 479
warm duck salad with
    orange, 477
salak, 197
salmon
    samphire with chilled fish
        curry, 309
salsify, 327
Salustianas oranges, 144
samphire, 297
    samphire with chilled fish
        curry, 309
Santa Rosa plums, 64
sapodillas, 196
satsumas, 142

saucepans, 257
sauces
    apple and cider sauce, 56
    cranberry sauce, 109
    raspberry coulis, 98
    raspberry sauce, 203
sautéing
    fruit, 16
    potatoes, 319
    vegetables, 261
Savoy cabbage, 356
    pasta with Savoy cabbage and
        Gruyère, 377
scallions, 267
scallops
    Chinese leaves and mooli with
        scallops, 480
    sweetcorn and scallop
        chowder, 405
scorzonera, 327
seafood and oyster mushroom
    starter, 498

segmenting fruit, 14, 15
    grapefruit, 136
    oranges, 145
Serrano chillies, 441
Seville oranges, 145
shaddock, 136
shallots, 268
    chicken with shallots, 284
    glazed shallots, 284
Shamouti oranges, 144
Sharon fruit, 190
sherbet
    ruby orange sherbet in ginger
        baskets, 152
shiitake mushrooms, 491
    shiitake fried rice, 501
shoots and stems, 287-311
    recipes, 299-311
shortcakes, raspberry and rose
    petal, 124
shredding vegetable leaves, 260
sieves, 257
silver kale, 359
skinning
    peppers, 439
    tomatoes, 434
sloes, 69
smoked trout
    cucumber and trout
        mousse, 426
smooth loofahs, 415
snake fruit, 197
snow peas, 387
soft fruit *see* berries; stone fruits
sole
    samphire with chilled fish
        curry, 309
    watercress and two-fish
        terrine, 482
sorbets
    blackcurrant sorbet, 123
    lychee and elderflower
        sorbet, 202
sorrel, 360
soufflé omelette with mushroom
    sauce, 494
soufflés
    cold lemon soufflé with
        caramelized almond
        topping, 159
    cold mango soufflés topped
        with toasted coconut, 200
    hot blackberry and apple
        soufflés, 115
    hot quince soufflés, 48
    iced gin and damson
        soufflés, 79
    leek soufflé, 281

soups
    asparagus soup, 302
    carrot and coriander soup, 342
    cream of mushroom soup, 494
    gazpacho, 450
    pumpkin soup, 420
    sweetcorn and scallop
        chowder, 405
    watercress soup, 482
sour cherries, 71
soursops, 177
spaghetti squashes, 410
Spanish limes, 181
Spanish onions, 264
Spartan apples, 25
spiced fruits jubilee, 75
spiced poached kumquats, 168
spinach, 350-1
    artichoke timbales with spinach
        sauce, 344
    celeriac and blue cheese
        roulade, 305
    spinach and cannellini
        beans, 370
    spinach and pepper pizza, 455
    spinach in filo with three
        cheeses, 371
spring greens, 356
spring onions, 267
sprouting broccoli, 354-5
squashes, 407-29
    recipes, 419-29
star fruit, 176
steamers, 257
steaming
    potatoes, 319
    vegetables, 261
stems and shoots, 287-311
    recipes, 299-311
stewing fruit, 16
stir-frying vegetables, 261
stone fruits, 59-91
    peeling, 15
    recipes, 73-91
    removing stones, 15, 61
stoning equipment, 13
storing
    fruit, 14
    vegetables, 258
strawberries, 94-6
    fresh strawberry ice cream, 122
    fruits of the forest with white
        chocolate creams, 120
    strawberry jam, 133
strawberry guavas, 182
streusel cake, cranberry and
    blueberry, 127
strudel, fresh cherry and

hazelnut, 81
stuffing, cranberry and
    chestnut, 109
Sugar Baby watermelons, 231
sugar bananas, 172
sugar peas, 387
sugar snaps, 387

sugar thermometers, 13
Sultana grapes, 232
sultanas, 235
summer berry crêpes, 116
summer crookneck
    squashes, 409
summer melons, 228
summer pudding, 114
summer squashes, 410-11
sun-dried tomatoes, 433
sunberries, 101
sweating vegetables, 261
swedes, 322-3
    swede crisps, 338
Sweet Gold pineapples, 192
sweet potatoes, 328
    pan-fried sweet potatoes with
        bacon, 343
sweetcorn, 390-1
    sweetcorn and cheese
        pasties, 404
    sweetcorn and scallop
        chowder, 405
Sweetie grapefruit, 136
Swiss chard, 365
    chard pasties, 375
syllabub, peach Melba, 76

T
Tabasco sauce, 441
tagliatelle
    tagliatelle fungi, 500
    tagliatelle with leeks and Parma
        ham, 282
Tahitian limes, 140
tamarillos, 197
    mango and tamarillo pastries,

218
tangelos, 143
tangerines, 142-3
tangleberries, 102
taro, 329-30
tarragon hollandaise, asparagus with, 300
tarts
  asparagus tart with ricotta, 300
  berry brûlée tarts, 130
  chocolate, pear and pecan pie, 52
  exotic fruit tranche, 219
  French apple tart, 53
  fresh fig filo tart, 248
  fresh lemon tart, 163
  hot broccoli tartlets, 374
  Key lime pie, 164
  onion tarts with goat's cheese, 276
  peach and redcurrant tartlets, 84
  red grape and cheese tartlets, 246
  tarte Tatin, 50
  tomato and basil tart, 451
  yellow plum tart, 86
  see also pastries; pies
tayberries, 101
tea breads
  banana and pecan bread, 222
tempura, 261
terrines
  iced pear terrine, 40
  watercress and two-fish terrine, 482
Thai beans, 388
Thai noodles with Chinese chives, 280
thermometers, 13
Thompson Seedless grapes, 232
three-fruit marmalade, 168
Tientsin pears, 35
Tiger watermelons, 231
toffee bananas, 214
toffee sauce, hot date puddings with, 215
tomato purée, 433-4
tomatoes, 432-4

aubergine and courgette bake, 448
balti-style cauliflower with tomatoes, 373
braised fennel with tomatoes, 310
eggs flamenco, 454
gazpacho, 450
patatas bravas, 334
radicchio pizza, 476
skinning, 260, 434
tomato and basil tart, 451
Tommy Atkins mangoes, 186
toovar dhal, 393
tortillas
  enchiladas with hot chilli sauce, 456
tree melon, 191
tree strawberries, 96
tree tomatoes, 197
trifle, Jamaican fruit, 210
tropical fruit gratin, 208
Truffe de Chine potatoes, 318
tummelberries, 101
turnip tops, 355
  turnip tops with Parmesan and garlic, 376
turnips, 322-3
  Mediterranean chicken with turnips, 338
tzatziki, aubergines with, 448

U
ugli fruit, 137

V
Valencia oranges, 145
vanilla desserts, port-stewed rhubarb with, 243
vegetable fruits, 430-59
  recipes, 447-59
vegetable peelers, 12
vegetables
  buying, 258
  cooking methods, 260-1
  equipment, 256-7
  history, 254
  nutrition, 254-5
  preparing, 258-60
  storing, 258
vertus, 323
Victoria plums, 64
Vidalia onions, 266
vine leaves, 360
  dolmades, 381

W
waffles, rum and banana, 216
walnuts
  date and walnut brownies, 222
  fig and walnut torte, 244
  water chestnuts, 295
watercress, 470
  watercress and two-fish terrine, 482
  watercress soup, 482
watermelons, 231
  melon trio with ginger biscuits, 242
whinberries, 103
white cabbage, 358
white grapes, 232
white mulberries, 102
white mushrooms, 486
white onions, 266
whitecurrants, 110, 111
whortleberries, 103
wild leaves, 360-1
wild mushrooms, 490-1
  wild mushrooms in brioche, 502
  wild mushrooms with pancakes, 502

wild raspberries, 97
wild strawberries, 95
Wilja potatoes, 316
Williams Bon Chrétien pears, 32
wine
  blackberry Kir Royale, 100
wineberries, 101
winter cress, 470
winter melons, 229
Winter Nelis pears, 32
winter squashes, 412-14
woks, 257
woodland mushrooms, 488-9
Worcester Pearmain apples, 25
Worcestershire berries, 107

Y
yams, 329
  yam fritters, 346
yellow courgettes, 408
yellow onions, 264
yellow plum tart, 86
yellow raspberries, 97
yellow tomatoes, 434
yellow wax beans, 388
yellow wax peppers, 441
yogurt
  aubergines with tzatziki, 448
  baked leeks with cheese and yogurt topping, 283
  Greek yogurt and fig cake, 249
youngberries, 101

Z
zest
  grating, 15
  lemons, 138, 139
zesters, 12
zucchini see courgettes

ACKNOWLEDGEMENTS

Photographs are by Don Last William Lingwood, Patrick McLeavey and Thomas Odulate/© Anness Publishing except for: p27 ml Harry Smith

Horticultural Photographic Collection (HSHC); p69 t Clive Simms; p95 tl HSHC; b/tr The Garden Picture Library (GPL); p96 br GPL; p98 br Clive Simms

(CS); p100m HSHC, tr A-Z Botanical/Bjorn Svenson; p101 br GPL, tl Derek St. Romaine (DSR), bl HSHC; p102 b HSHC; p106 t DSR; p107 bl/br DSR;

p139 b CS; p111 b GPL; p172 l Peter McHoy; p177 l HSHC, b CS; p178t HSHC; p180 b GPL; p183 t HSHC; p185 t CS; p190 t CS; and p196 t GPL.